SMALL BUSINESS
Critical perspectives on business and management

Critical perspectives on business and management

Other titles in the series

SMALL BUSINESS
Critical perspectives on business and management

Edited by D.J. Storey

VOLUME I

London and New York

First published 2000
by Routledge
11 New Fetter Lane, London EC4P 4EE

Simultaneously published in the USA and Canada
by Routledge
29 West 35th Street, New York, NY 10001

Routledge is an imprint of the Taylor & Francis Group

Typeset in Times by Bookcraft Ltd, Stroud
Printed and bound in Great Britain by TJ International Ltd,
Padstow, Cornwall

British Library Cataloguing in Publication Data
A catalogue record for this book is available from the British
Library

Library of Congress Cataloging in Publication Data
Small Business: critical perspectives on business and
management
    edited by D.J. Storey.
        p.   cm.
    A collection of 62 book and journal articles, all but one
previously published between 1959–1997, with an
introduction by the editor.
    Includes bibliographical references and index.
    ISBN 0-415-18468-1 (4 vol. set)
    1. Small business.   2. New business enterprises.   3. Self
    employed.   4. Entrepreneurship.   I. Storey, D.J.
HD2341.S5687   2000   99-40303
                                                CIP

ISBN 0-415-18468-1 (set)
ISBN 0-415-18469-X (volume I)

Contents

VOLUME III

Acknowledgements

The Publishers would like to thank the following for permission to reprint their material:

Academy of Management, PO Box 3020, Briar Cliff Manor, NY 10510–8020 for permission to reprint Arne L. Kalleberg and KevinT. Leicht, 'Gender and Organisational Performance: Determinants of Small Business Survival and Success', *Academy of Management Journal*, Vol. 34, 1991, pp. 136–61; Robert H. Brockhaus, 'Risk Taking Propensity of Entrepreneurs', *Academy of Management Journal*, Vol. 23, No. 3, 1980, pp. 509–20; James W. Carland, Frank Hoy, William R. Boulton, and Jo Ann C. Carland, 'Differentiating Entrepreneurs from Small Business Owners: A Conceptualization', *Academy of Management Review*, Vol. 9, 1984, pp. 354–59; Richard B. Robinson, Jr. and John A. Pearce II, 'Research Thrusts in Small Firm Strategic Planning', *Academy of Management Review*. Vol. 9, No. 1, 1984, pp. 128–37. Reproduced by permission of the Publisher via Copyright Clearance Center, Inc.

Administrative Science Quarterly for permission to reprint Javier Gimeno, Timothy B. Folta, Arnold C. Cooper and Carolyn C. Woo, 'Survival of the Fittest? Entrepreneurial Human Capital and the Persistence of Underperforming Firms', *Administrative Science Quarterly*, Vol. 42, 1997, pp. 750–83.

American Economic Association for permission to reprint Joseph E. Stiglitz and Andrew Weiss, 'Credit Rationing in Markets with Imperfect Information', *American Economic Review*, Vol. 71, No. 3, 1981, pp. 393–410 ; Zoltan J. Acs and David B. Audretsch, 'Innovation in Large and Small Firms: An Empirical Analysis', *American Economic Review*, Vol. 78, No. 4, 1988, pp. 678–90.

American Sociological Association for permission to reprint Joseph Brüderl, Peter Preisendörfer and Rolf Ziegler, 'Survival Chances of Newly Founded Business Organizations', *American Sociological Review*, Vol. 57, April 1992, pp. 227–42.

Annual Reviews for permission to reprint Howard E. Aldrich and Roger

D. Waldinger, 'Ethnicity and Entrepreneurship', *Annual Review of Sociology*, Vol. 16, 1990, pp. 111–35. © 1990 by Annual Reviews.

Baylor University for permission to reprint Candida G. Brush, 'Research on Women Business Owners: Past Trends, A New Perspective and Future Directions', *Entrepreneurship, Theory and Practice*, Vol.16, No.4, 1992, pp. 5–30; Paul Westhead, 'Survival and Employment Growth Contrasts Between Types of Owner-managed High-technology Firms', *Entrepreneurship Theory and Practice*, Vol. 20, No. 1, 1995, pp. 5–27.

Blackwell Publishers Ltd. for permission to reprint D.J. Storey and A.M. Jones, 'New Firm Formation – A Labour Market Approach to Industrial Entry', *Scottish Journal of Political Economy*, Vol. 34, No. 1, 1987, pp. 37–51; M.E. Beesley and R.T. Hamilton, 'Small Firms Seedbed Role and the Concept of Turbulence', *Journal of Industrial Economics*, Vol. 33, No. 4, December, 1984, pp. 217–29; José Mata and Pedro Portugal, 'Life Duration of New Firms', *Journal of Industrial Economics*, 42, No. 3, September 1994, pp. 227–45; M.J.K. Stanworth and J. Curran, 'Growth and the Small Firm – An Alternative View', *Journal of Management Studies*, Vol. 13, No. 2, 1976, pp. 95–110; David de Meza and Clive Southey, 'The Borrower's Curse: Optimism, Finance and Entrepreneurship', *Economic Journal*, Vol. 106, No. 435, March 1996, pp. 375–86; Robert Cressy, 'Are Business Start-ups Debt Rationed?', *Economic Journal*, Vol. 106, No. 438, 1996, pp. 1253–70; R. Watson, 'Employment Change, Profits and Directors Remuneration in Small and Closely-held UK Companies', *Scottish Journal of Political Economy*, Vol. 37, No. 3, 1990, pp. 259–74.

Blackwell Publishers, MA for permission to reprint Mitchell A. Petersen and Raghuram G. Rajan, 'The Benefits of Lending Relationships: Evidence from Small Business Data', *The Journal of Finance*, Vol. 49, No.1, March 1994, pp. 3–37.

Brookings Institution for permission to reprint Catherine Armington and Marjorie Odle, 'Small Business – How Many Jobs?', *Brookings Review*, Winter, 1982, pp. 14–17.

Cambridge University Press for permission to reprint D.H. Whittaker, 'Sunrise or Sunset for Japan's Small Firms?, in D.H. Whittaker, *Small Firms in the Japanese Economy*, Chapter 11, pp. 199–214, Cambridge University Press: Cambridge, 1997.

Carfax Publishing Limited for permission to reprint Paul D. Reynolds, David J. Storey and Paul Westhead, 'Cross-national Comparisons of the Variation in New Firm Formation Rates', *Regional Studies*, Vol. 28, No. 4 1994, pp. 443–56; David Keeble, 'Small Firms, Innovation and Regional Development in Britain in the 1990s', *Regional Studies*, Vol. 31, No. 3, 1997, pp. 281–93.

Colin Mason for permission to reprint Colin Mason and Richard Harrison, 'Informal Venture Capital in the UK' in A. Hughes and D.J. Storey, (eds), *Finance and the Small Firm*, pp. 64–111, Routledge: London, 1994 .

David Birch for permission to reprint David L. Birch, 'The Job Generation Process': US Department of Commerce, MIT Programme on Neighborhood and Regional Change, 1979.

C.M. Van Praag, The Boston Consulting Group for permission to reprint C. Mirjam Van Praag and Hans Van Ophem, 'Determinants of Willingness and Opportunity to Start as an Entrepreneur', *Kyklos*, Vol. 48, 1995, pp. 513–40.

Elsevier Science for permission to reprint Richard Highfield and Robert Smiley, 'New Business Starts and Economic Activity: An Empirical Investigation', *International Journal of Industrial Organisation*, Vol. 5, 1987, pp. 51–66; Nancy M. Carter, Mary Williams and Paul D.Reynolds, 'Discontinuance Among New Firms in Retail: The Influence of Initial Resources, Strategy and Gender', *Journal of Business Venturing*, Vol. 12, No. 2, 1997, pp. 125–45; Per Davidsson, 'Continued Entrepreneurship: Ability, Need, and Opportunity as Determinants of Small Firm Growth', *Journal of Business Venturing*, Vol. 6, 1989, pp. 405–29; William E. Wetzel, 'The Informal Venture Capital Market: Aspects of Scale and Market Efficiency', *Journal of Business Venturing*, Vol. 2, 1987, pp. 299–313; Timothy Bates, 'Survival Patterns Among Newcomers to Franchising', *Journal of Business Venturing*, Vol. 13, No. 2, 1998, pp. 113–30; Timothy Bates, 'Self-employment Entry Across Industry Groups', *Journal of Business Venturing*, Vol. 10, 1995, pp. 143–56; Sue Birley, 'The Role of Networks in the Entrepreneurial Process', *Journal of Business Venturing*, Vol. 1, 1985, pp. 107–11.

Frank Coffield and Rob MacDonald for permission to reprint R. MacDonald and F. Coffield, 'Risky Business?' in *Risky Business? Youth and the Enterprise Culture*', Chapter 6, pp. 129–164, The Falmer Press: London, 1991.

Greenwood Publishing Group, Inc., Westport, CT for permission to reprint Paul D. Reynolds, 'Nascent Entrepreneurs and Business Start-ups' in Paul D. Reynolds and Sammis B. White (eds), *The Entrepreneurial Process: Economic Growth, Men, Women and Minorities*, pp. 39–66, Quorom Books: Westport, CT and London, 1997

Harvard Business School of Publishing for permission to reprint Neil C. Churchill and Virginia L. Lewis, 'The Five Stages of Small Business Growth', *Harvard Business Review*, Vol. 61, No. 3, 1983, pp. 30–49. Copyright © 1983 by the President and Fellows of Harvard College; all rights reserved.

Indiana University for permission to reprint Arnold C. Cooper and Albert V. Bruno, 'Success Among High-technology Firms', *Business Horizons*, Vol. 20, No. 2, 1977, pp. 16–22.

JAI Press Inc. for permission to reprint James S. Ang, 'Small Business Uniqueness and the Theory of Financial Management', *Journal of Small Business Finance*, Vol. 1, No. 1, 1991, pp. 1–13; Timothy Bates, 'Commercial Bank Financing of White- and Black-owned Small Business Start-ups', *Quarterly Review of Economics & Business*, Vol. 31, No. 1, Spring 1991, pp. 64–80.

John Wiley & Sons, Ltd for permission to reprint Jeffrey G. Covin and Dennis P. Slevin, 'Strategic Management of Small Firms in Hostile and Benign Environments', *Strategic Management Journal*, Vol. 10, 1989, pp. 75–89; Hedley Rees and Anup Shah, 'An Empirical Analysis of Self Employment in the UK', *Journal of Applied Econometrics*, Vol. 1, No. 1, 1986, pp. 95–108.

Kluwer Academic Publishers for permission to reprint Bruce D. Phillips and Bruce A. Kirchhoff, 'Formation, Growth and Survival: Small Firm Dynamics in the US Economy', *Small Business Economics*, Vol. 1, No. 1, 1989, pp. 65–74; Steven J. Davis, John Haltiwanger and Scott Schuh, 'Small Business and Job Creation: Dissecting the Myth and Reassessing the Facts', *Small Business Economics*, Vol. 8, No. 4, August 1996, pp. 297–315; Bruce A. Kirchhoff and Patricia G. Greene, 'Understanding the Theoretical and Empirical Content of Critiques of US Job Creation Research', *Small Business Economics*, Vol. 10, No. 2, March 1998, pp. 153–69; Alessandro Foti and Marco Vivarelli, 'An Econometric Test of the Self-employment Model: The Case of Italy', *Small Business Economics*, Vol. 6, 1994, pp. 81–93.

Kyohei Irie for permission to reprint Kyohei Irie, 'Japanese Venture Capital and its Investment in Asia', *Osaka City University Business Review*, No. 7, 1996, pp. 17–35.

Mark Casson for permission to reprint Mark Casson, 'Growth and Dynamics of the Firm', in *The Entrepreneur*, Chapter 16, pp. 295–324, Barnes & Noble Books: Totowa, New Jersey, 1982.

MIT Press for permission to reprint Timothy Bates, 'Entrepreneur Human Capital Inputs and Small Business Longevity', *The Review of Economics and Statistics*, Vol. 72, No. 4, November 1990, pp. 551–59. © by the President and Fellows of Harvard College.

Organisation for Economic Co-operation and Development for permission to reprint Alex Grey, 'Recent Directions in Labour Market Research using Establishment Data', in *Job Creation and Loss: Analysis, Policy and Data Development*, OECD, Paris, 1996, pp. 27–46; Sergio E. Rossi, 'Credit Guarantee Schemes: The Case of Italy', Presented at OECD meeting, Paris, 27–28 January 1998.

Oxford University Press for permission to reprint E. Penrose, 'The Firm in Theory', Edith Penrose, *The Theory of the Growth of the Firm*, 1959, pp.9–30. © Edith Penrose 1995; Elizabeth Garnsey, 'A Theory of the Early Growth of the Firm', *Industrial and Corporate Change*, Vol. 7, No. 3, 1998, pp. 523–56.

Oxford University Press, NY for permission to reprint E.B. Roberts, 'Technological Entrepreneurship: Birth, Growth and Success', in *Entrepreneurs in High Technology*, Chapter 12, pp. 339–58, Oxford University Press: New York, 1991.

Paul Chapman Publishing Ltd for permission to reprint Richard Barkham, Mark Hart and Eric Hanvey, 'Growth in Small Manufacturing Firms: An Empirical Analysis' in R. Blackburn and P. Jennings (ed), *Small Firms' Contributions to Economic Regeneration*, pp. 112–25, Paul Chapman Publishing: London, 1996.

Pion Limited for permission to reprint J.N. Marshall, N. Alderman, C. Wong and A. Thwaites, 'The Impact of Government-assisted Management Training and Development on Small and Medium-sized Enterprises in Britain', *Environment and Planning C: Government and Policy*, Vol. 11, 1993, pp. 331–48.

Routledge for permission to reprint D.J. Storey, 'Public Policy', in *Understanding the Small Business Sector*, Chapter 8, pp. 253–306, Routledge: London and New York, 1993.

Taylor & Francis for permission to reprint Olav R. Spilling, 'Regional Variation of New Firm Formation: The Norwegian Case', *Entrepreneurship and Regional Development*, Vol. 8, 1996, pp. 217–43; Bengt Johannisson, 'Paradigms and Entrepreneurial Networks – Some Methodological Challenges', *Entrepreneurship and Regional Development*, Vol. 7, 1995, pp. 215–31; John Bryson, Peter Wood and David Keeble, 'Business Networks, Small Firm Flexibility and Regional Development in UK Business Services', *Entrepreneurship and Regional Development*, Vol. 5, 1993, pp. 265–77.

The University of Chicago Press for permission to reprint Michael T. Hannan and John Freeman, 'The Population Ecology of Organisations', *American Journal of Sociology*, Vol. 82, No. 5, 1977, pp. 924–64.

Trevor Jones and Giles Barrett for permission to reprint Trevor Jones, David McEvoy and Giles Barrett, 'Labour Intensive Practices in the Ethnic Minority Firm' in John Atkinson and David Storey, (eds), *Employment, the Small Firm and the Labour Market*, pp. 172–205, Routledge: London and New York, 1993.

University of Texas El Paso, College of Business Administration for permission to reprint Frank Hoy and Trudy G. Verser, 'Emerging Business, Emerging Field: Entrepreneurship and the Family Firm', *Entrepreneurship Theory and Practice*, Vol. 19, No. 1, 1994, pp. 9–23.

The publishers have made every effort to contact authors/copyright holders of works reprinted in *Small Business: Critical Perspectives*. This has not been possible in every case, however, and we would welcome correspondence from those individuals and companies we have been unable to trace.

Preface

The readings in this volume constitute primarily the editor's personal opinion about good research in this area. Inclusion in the volume means that the writing has an important message in the sense of deriving key findings, providing a framework for further analysis or, in some cases, simply addressing important topics. It certainly does not mean that only material in this book is viewed as good research; there is plenty more. Indeed I have tried to make reference to some of it in my editorial introduction.

Putting this together has been a pleasant, if highly time-consuming, exercise. In a number of instances I have established a relationship with scholars – albeit over the Internet or by the use of fax – whose work I had read, but whom I have never met or spoken to. In other cases it was nice simply to re-establish contact.

For anyone contemplating such an exercise I offer the following 'helpful hints'. The first is to have some concept of where the boundaries of your subject have to be drawn. Whilst this text refers to 'small businesses', this constitutes a definitional minefield. In the United States the types of firms covered by the Small Business Administration have less than 500 employees, whereas in the European Union small (and medium sized) enterprises are those with up to 250 employees. Are we to include those businesses where there are no employees – the self-employed? Are we to focus upon those businesses which are entrepreneurial – defined as those exhibiting growth or innovation?

My view is that I was interested in businesses which were clearly not large, and that if the writing had something interesting to say then, in principle, it was worthy of inclusion.

The first selection of articles was identified on a long train journey in which I noted down those pieces of writing which had yielded me pleasure as a reader over a number of years. In this way I identified perhaps forty articles/chapters from books. I then wrote to all these authors, not only asking for permission to reproduce their work, but also including my 'Top 40' list and asking them for comments, particularly on topics which I had omitted, and for their suggestions on additional readings on my chosen topics. I also – out of politeness – asked if they thought that any of the included readings was not up to the mark! Fortunately, nobody suggested that any of the top forty should be excluded, but I did receive many suggestions for the inclusion of additional material. Here I would particularly like to thank Jim Curran, Steve Davis, David Keeble, amongst others, who provided not only suggestions about articles but also sometimes a critique of the whole exercise. Their, and other, suggestions have led to the substantially increased number of included readings in the current volume.

I also have to thank almost all the contributors for reading, and in some instances substantially modifying, the editorial text which I have provided. Here my particular thanks go to Howard Aldrich, Neill Marshall, Robert Cressy, Elizabeth Garnsey, Timothy Bates, Catherine Armington, David Birch, Richard Robinson and Arne Kalleberg who made important changes and constituted almost two-thirds of all contributors who approved the text.

I therefore thank all the people who have contributed to these volumes but, most of all, the project would not have been possible without the co-ordination skills of Glenda Hall. It was she who, being given an article title, (which was probably incorrect), had to obtain a copy of the article, contact the publishers of the article to obtain their consent for publication, attempt to contact the author – who had probably moved (sometimes several times), make sense of my text, circulate it to the authors and liaise with the publishers. All this in her 'spare time'!

General introduction

The papers included in these volumes comprise a substantial mixture of styles. Some are exclusively verbal, whereas others require a degree of mathematical sophistication to understand. I have also sought to include both theoretical and primarily empirical material from a number of academic disciplines. On balance, the academic paradigm from which this volume stems is economics, closely followed by management studies. Several items, however, are derived from entrepreneurship and small business journals that can claim genuinely to be multi-disciplinary. Finally, a smaller number are clearly anchored within sociology and geography.

I have never believed that it is only academic journals that publish the 'best' research in entrepreneurship; I have therefore sought to include material from books and, in one instance, even material that was never published.

In any English language volume of edited works, there is an inevitable bias towards texts that draw their theoretical and empirical material from countries such as the United States and the United Kingdom. I am aware of this and have made a conscious effort to include readings that refer to other countries. However, the focus of the volume is strongly upon conventional developed economies. It therefore does not seek to cover smaller enterprises in less developed countries or economies in transition.

For the benefit of the reader, I have tried to group the articles into parts. These are not of equal size, and some are significantly more heterogeneous than others. There are also notable instances of overlap, when it was marginal whether a particular article should be placed in one part or another. Nevertheless the grouping of articles is intended to focus the reader's attention upon a specific topic.

My prime contribution has been to provide an editorial overview of the articles and so my text is also separated into parts that correspond with the readings. The overview tries to provide an accurate, but often considerably simplified, statement of the key findings of the articles. In a number of parts it is able to provide a chronological view, whereby the part begins with a 'classic' and moves on to empirical work which seeks to develop the themes identified in the 'classic'. Finally, in some parts, I have allowed myself the liberty of commenting upon both the research conducted and what I see as areas where uncertainty remains despite the excellence of the existing research.

References contained within each chapter refer to the original publication in its entirity.

A bibliography to the general introduction and to the part introductions in all four volumes can be found in Volume IV, starting on page 1531.

Chronological table of reprinted articles

Year	Author	Article	Source	Vol.	Chap.
1959	E. Penrose	The Firm in Theory	E. Penrose, *The Theory of the Growth of the Firm*, Oxford University Press: Oxford, 9–30	II	14
1976	M.J.K. Stanworth and J. Curran	Growth and the Small Firm – An Alternative View	*Journal of Management Studies* 13, 2 , 95–110	II	13
1977	Arnold C. Cooper and Albert V. Bruno	Success Among High-technology Firms	*Business Horizons* 20, 2, 16–22	IV	46
1977	Michael T. Hannan and John Freeman	The Population Ecology of Organisations	*American Journal of Sociology* 82, 5, 924–964	I	1
1979	David L. Birch	The Job Generation Process	US Department of Commerce, MIT Programme on Neighborhood and Regional Change	II	18
1980	Robert H. Brockhaus Sr.	Risk Taking Propensity of Entrepreneurs	*Academy of Management Journal* 23, 3, 509–20	IV	49
1981	Joseph E. Stiglitz and Andrew Weiss	Credit Rationing in Markets with Imperfect Information	*American Economic Review* 71, 3, 393–410	II	25
1982	Catherine Armington and Marjorie Odle	Small Business – How Many Jobs?	*Brookings Review* Winter, 14–17	II	19
1982	Mark Casson	Growth and Dynamics of the Firm	Mark Casson, *The Entrepreneur*, Barnes and Noble Books: Totowa, New Jersey, 295–324	IV	52
1983	Neil C. Churchill and Virginia L. Lewis	The Five Stages of Small Business Growth	*Harvard Business Review* 61, 3, 30–49	II	12
1984	M.E. Beesley and R.T. Hamilton	Small Firms' Seedbed Role and the Concept of Turbulence	*Journal of Industrial Economics* 33, 4, 217–29	I	5

Year	Author	Article	Source	Vol.	Chap.
1984	James Carland, Frank Hoy, William R. Boulton and Jo Ann C. Carland	Differentiating Entrepreneurs from Small Business Owners: A Conceptualization	Academy of Management Review 9, 354–59	IV	50
1984	Richard B. Robinson, Jr. and John A. Pearce II	Research Thrusts in Small Firm Strategic Planning	Academy of Management Review 9, 1, 128–37	IV	55
1985	Sue Birley	The Role of Networks in the Entrepreneurial Process	Journal of Business Venturing 1, 107–11	IV	61
1986	Hedley Rees and Anup Shah	An Empirical Analysis of Self-employment in the UK	Journal of Applied Econometrics 1, 1, 95–108	IV	57
1987	Richard Highfield and Robert Smiley	New Business Starts and Economic Activity: An Empirical Investigation	International Journal of Industrial Organisation 5, 51–66	I	3
1987	D.J. Storey and A.M. Jones	New Firm Formation – A Labour Market Approach to Industrial Entry	Scottish Journal of Political Economy 34, 1, 37–51	I	4
1987	William E. Wetzel, Jr.	The Informal Venture Capital Market: Aspects of Scale and Market Efficiency	Journal of Business Venturing 2, 299–313	II	31
1988	Zoltan J. Acs and David B. Audretsch	Innovation in Large and Small Firms: An Empirical Analysis	American Economic Review 78, 4, 678–90	IV	45
1989	Jeffrey G. Covin and Dennis P. Slevin	Strategic Management of Small Firms in Hostile and Benign Environments	Strategic Management Journal 10, 75–89	IV	56
1989	Per Davidsson	Continued Entrepreneurship: Ability, Need, and Opportunity as Determinants of Small Firm Growth	Journal of Business Venturing 6, 405–29	II	16

Year	Author	Article	Source	Vol.	Chap.
1989	Bruce D. Phillips and Bruce A. Kirchhoff	Formation, Growth and Survival; Small Firm Dynamics in the US Economy	Small Business Economics 1, 1, 65–74	II	20
1990	Howard E. Aldrich and Roger Waldinger	Ethnicity and Entrepreneurship	Annual Review of Sociology 16, 111–35	III	37
1990	Timothy Bates	Entrepreneur Human Capital Inputs and Small Business Longevity	Review of Economics and Statistics 72, 4, 551–59	I	9
1990	Robert Watson	Employment Change, Profits and Directors' Remuneration in Small and Closely-held UK Companies	Scottish Journal of Political Economy 37, 3, 259–74	II	33
1991	James S. Ang	Small Business Uniqueness and the Theory of Financial Management	Journal of Small Business Finance 1, 1, 1–13	II	24
1991	Timothy Bates	Commercial Bank Financing of White- and Black-owned Small Business Start-ups	Quarterly Review of Economics & Business 31, 1, 64–80	III	38
1991	Arne L. Kalleberg and Kevin T. Leicht	Gender and Organisational Performance: Determinants of Small Business Survival and Success	Academy of Management Journal 34, 136–61	III	40
1991	R. MacDonald and F. Coffield	Risky Business?	Risky Business? Youth and the Enterprise Culture, The Falmer Press: London, 129–64	I	6
1991	E.B. Roberts	Technological Entrepreneurship: Birth, Growth and Success	E.B. Roberts, Entrepreneurs in High Technology, Oxford University Press: New York, 339–58	IV	47
1992	Josef Brüderl, Peter Preisendörfer and Rolf Ziegler	Survival Chances of Newly Founded Business Organizations	American Sociological Review, 57, 227–42	I	10

Year	Author	Article	Source	Vol.	Chap.
1992	Candida G. Brush	Research on Women Business Owners: Past Trends, a New Perspective and Future Directions	*Entrepreneurship, Theory and Practice* 16, 4, 5–30	III	41
1993	John Bryson, Peter Wood and David Keeble	Business Networks, Small Firm Flexibility and Regional Development in UK Business Services	*Entrepreneurship and Regional Development* 5, 265–77	IV	62
1993	Trevor Jones, David McEvoy and Giles Barrett	Labour Intensive Practices in the Ethnic Minority Firm	John Atkinson and David Storey, (eds) *Employment, the Small Firm and the Labour Market*, Routledge: London and New York, 172–205	III	39
1993	J.N. Marshall, N. Alderman, C. Wong and A. Thwaites	The Impact of Government-assisted Management Training and Development on Small and Medium-sized Enterprises in Britain	*Environment and Planning C: Government and Policy* 11, 331–48	III	34
1994	José Mata and Pedro Portugal	Life Duration of New Firms	*Journal of Industrial Economics* 42, 3, 227–45	I	7
1994	Alessandro Foti and Marco Vivarelli	An Econometric Test of the Self-employment Model: The Case of Italy	*Small Business Economics* 6, 81–93	IV	59
1994	Frank Hoy and Trudy G. Verser	Emerging Business, Emerging Field: Entrepreneurship and the Family Firm	*Entrepreneurship Theory and Practice* 19, 1, 9–23	IV	53
1994	Colin Mason and Richard Harrison	Informal Venture Capital in the UK	A. Hughes and D.J. Storey, (eds) *Finance and the Small Firm*, Routledge: London, 64–111	II	32
1994	Mitchell A. Petersen and Raghuram G. Rajan	The Benefits of Lending Relationships: Evidence from Small Business Data	*The Journal of Finance* 49, 1, 3–37	II	27

Year	Author	Article	Source	Vol.	Chap.
1994	Paul D. Reynolds, David J. Storey and Paul Westhead	Cross-national Comparisons of the Variation in New Firm Formation Rates	*Regional Studies* 28, 4, 443–56	III	42
1994	D.J. Storey	Public Policy	*Understanding the Small Business Sector* Routledge: London and New York, 253–306	III	35
1995	Timothy Bates	Self-employment Entry Across Industry Groups	*Journal of Business Venturing* 10, 143–56	IV	58
1995	Bengt Johannisson	Paradigms and Entrepreneurial Networks – Some Methodological Challenges	*Entrepreneurship and Regional Development* 7, 215–31	IV	60
1995	C. Mirjam Van Praag and Hans Van Ophem	Determinants of Willingness and Opportunity to Start as an Entrepreneur	*Kyklos* 48, 513–40	I	2
1995	Paul Westhead	Survival and Employment Growth Contrasts Between Types of Owner-managed High-technology Firms	*Entrepreneurship Theory and Practice* 20, 1, 5–27	IV	48
1996	Richard Barkham, Mark Hart and Eric Hanvey	Growth in Small Manufacturing Firms: An Empirical Analysis	R. Blackburn and P. Jennings, (ed) *Small Firms Contributions to Economic Regeneration*, Paul Chapman Publishing: London, 112–25	II	17
1996	Robert Cressy	Are Business Startups Debt-rationed?	*Economic Journal* 106, 438, 1253–70	II	28
1996	Steven J. Davis, John Haltiwanger and Scott Schuh	Small Business and Job Creation: Dissecting the Myth and Reassessing the Facts	*Small Business Economics* 8, 4, 297–315	II	22
1996	David de Meza and Clive Southey	The Borrower's Curse: Optimism, Finance and Entrepreneurship	*Economic Journal* 106, 435, 375–86	II	26

Year	Author	Article	Source	Vol.	Chap.
1996	Alex Grey	Recent Directions in Labour Market Research using Establishment Data	*Job Creation and Loss: Analysis, Policy and Data Development*, OECD: Paris, 27–46	II	21
1996	Kyohei Irie	Japanese Venture Capital and its Investment in Asia	*Osaka City University Business Review* 7, 17–35	II	30
1996	Olav R. Spilling	Regional Variation of New Firm Formation: The Norwegian Case	*Entrepreneurship and Regional Development* 8, 217–43	III	43
1997	Nancy M. Carter, Mary Williams and Paul D. Reynolds	Discontinuance Among New Firms in Retail: The Influence of Initial Resources. Strategy and Gender	*Journal of Business Venturing* 12, 2, 125–45	I	8
1997	Javier Gimeno, Timothy B. Folta, Arnold C. Cooper and Carolyn Y. Woo	Survival of the Fittest? Entrepreneurial Human Capital and the Persistence of Underperforming Firms	*Administrative Science Quarterly* 42, 750–83	I	11
1997	David Keeble	Small Firms, Innovation and Regional Development in Britain in the 1990s	*Regional Studies* 31, 3, 281–93	III	44
1997	Bruce A. Kirchhoff and Patricia G. Greene	Understanding the Theoretical and Empirical Content of Critiques of US Job Creation Research	*Small Business Economics* 10, 2, 153–69	II	23
1997	Paul D. Reynolds	Nascent Entrepreneurs and Business Start-ups	Paul D. Reynolds and Sammis B. White, (eds) *The Entrepreneurial Process: Economic Growth, Men, Women and Minorities*, Quorom Books: Westport, CT and London, 39–66	IV	51
1997	D.H. Whittaker	Sunrise or Sunset for Japan's Small Firms?	D.H. Whittaker, *Small Firms in the Japanese Economy*, Cambridge University Press: Cambridge, 199–214	III	36
1998	Timothy Bates	Survival Patterns Among Newcomers to Franchising	*Journal of Business Venturing* 13, 2, 113–30	IV	54

Year	Author	Article	Source	Vol.	Chap.
1998	Elizabeth Garnsey	A Theory of the Early Growth of the Firm	*Industrial and Corporate Change* 7, 3, 523–56	II	15
1998	Sergio E. Rossi	Credit Guarantee Schemes: The Case Of Italy	Presented at OECD meeting, Paris, 27–28 January	II	29

Part 1

Births

Introduction

This part begins with the article by Hannan and Freeman that can genuinely be regarded as a classic, defined as one providing a theoretical or empirical analysis that is extensively quoted and used as a basis for further work. It develops a biological/ecological analogy to economic organisations. The reason for its inclusion at the beginning is that it addresses the fundamental question of 'Why does the economy have such a range of firms of different sizes and ages at any one point in time?'

In part, but only in part, the answer is that diversity reflects the scale of births in terms of new organisations coming into existence. In most developed economies at least ten per cent of the existing stock of businesses in year t did not exist in year t–1. This raises the key questions about new organisations: who starts them, why, and in what circumstances?

Van Praag and Van Ophem address these questions by arguing that new firms reflect a combination of willingness and opportunity on the part of their founders. Clearly, new businesses exhibit both of these characteristics but, as the authors illustrate, some individuals are willing to become entrepreneurs but lack the opportunity. These individuals do not start in business. The value of the article is not only in making this important distinction, but also in helpfully reviewing a range of literature on attitudes to new business formation.

In the economic literature there has been considerable discussion about the circumstances in which new businesses are formed. At its most simplistic, there is assumed to exist a queue of potential entrepreneurs waiting for price to persistently exceed long run average cost – at which point 'entry' takes place. The inference from this is that business formations are highest in times of prosperity when profits are high. The Highfield and Smiley article, however, casts some doubt upon this simplistic view. It examines business formations, both over time and from a cross-sectional perspective. Whilst the cross-sectional perspective provides some support for the positive role of profitability, the time series suggests that the macro-economic climate in which small business formation rates are highest is when unemployment is increasing and GDP growth is weak.

The Storey and Jones article, taking a cross-sectional perspective, also presents evidence that job shedding is a key stimulant to entrepreneurship/new business formation. It would, however, be mischievous to imply that the evidence consistently suggests that sluggish macro-economic circumstances are associated with high new business formation rates. Instead a 'mixture' of findings on this issue still continues to emerge (Taylor 1999).

Whilst included within the part on 'births', the Beesley and Hamilton article emphasises the interdependence between the births of firms and the deaths of firms. It introduces the concept of turbulence which, at its most basic, can be considered as births plus deaths. The value of the turbulence concept is in providing insights into why certain geographical areas exhibit both high birth-rates and high death-rates. The Beesley and Hamilton article itself shows that, in general, birth-rates and death-rates are positively correlated at a sectoral level. Hence, whilst these two concepts are often considered separately, they are also valuably considered jointly.

1

The Population Ecology of Organizations*

Michael T. Hannan and John Freeman[1]

*Source: *American Journal of Sociology* 82, 5 (1977), 924–64.

A population ecology perspective on organization-environment relations is proposed as an alternative to the dominant adaptation perspective. The strength of inertial pressures on organizational structure suggests the application of models that depend on competition and selection in populations of organizations. Several such models as well as issues that arise in attempts to apply them to the organization-environment problem are discussed.

Introduction

Analysis of the effects of environment on organizational structure has moved to a central place in organizations theory and research in recent years. This shift has opened a number of exciting possibilities. As yet nothing like the full promise of the shift has been realized. We believe that the lack of development is due in part to a failure to bring ecological models to bear on questions that are pre-eminently ecological. We argue for a reformulation of the problem in population ecology terms.

Although there is a wide variety of ecological perspectives, they all focus on selection. That is, they attribute patterns in nature to the action of selection processes. The bulk of the literature on organizations subscribes to a different view, which we call the adaptation perspective.[2] According to the adaptation perspective, sub-units of the organization, usually managers or dominant coalitions, scan the relevant environment for opportunities and threats, formulate strategic responses, and adjust organizational structure appropriately.

The adaptation perspective is seen most clearly in the literature on management. Contributors to it usually assume a hierarchy of authority and control that locates decisions concerning the organization as a whole at the top. It follows, then, that organizations are affected by their environments, according to the ways in which managers or leaders formulate strategies, make decisions, and implement them. Particularly successful managers are able either to buffer their organizations from environmental disturbances or to manage smooth adjustments that require minimal disruption of organizational structure.

A similar perspective, often worded differently, dominates the sociological literature on the subject.

It plays a central role in Parsons's (1956) functional analysis of organization-environment relations and it is found in the more strictly Weberian tradition (see Selznick 1957). It is interesting to note that, while functionalists have been interested in system effects and have based much of the logic of their approach on survival imperatives, they have not dealt with selection phenomena. This is probably a reaction against organization theory which reflects social Darwinism.

Exchange theorists have also embraced the adaptation perspective (Levine and White 1961). And it is natural that theories emphasizing decision making take the adaptation view (March and Simon 1958; Cyert and March 1963). Even Thompson's (1967) celebrated marriage of open-systems and closed-systems thinking embraced the adaptation perspective explicitly (see particularly the second half of Thompson's book).

Clearly, leaders of organizations do formulate strategies and organizations do adapt to environmental contingencies. As a result at least some of the relationship between structure and environment must reflect adaptive behavior or learning. But there is no reason to presume that the great structural variability among organizations reflects only or even primarily adaptation.

There are a number of obvious limitations on the ability of organizations to adapt. The stronger the pressures, the lower the organizations' adaptive flexibility and the more likely that the logic of environmental selection is appropriate. As a consequence, the issue of structural inertia is central to the choice between adaptation and selection models.

The possibility that organization structure contains a large inertial component was suggested by Burns and Stalker (1961) and Stinchcombe (1965). But, on the whole the subject has been ignored. A number of relevant propositions can be found in the organizations literature, however.

Inertial pressures arise from both internal structural arrangements and environmental constraints. A minimal list of the constraints arising from internal considerations follows.

1   An organization's investment in plant, equipment, and specialized personnel constitutes assets that are not easily transferable to other tasks or functions. The ways in which such sunk costs constrain adaptation options are so obvious that they need not be discussed further.

2   Organizational decision makers also face constraints on the information they receive. Much of what we know about the flow of information through organizational structures tells us that leaders do not obtain

anything close to full information on activities within the organization and environmental contingencies facing the subunits.

3   Internal political constraints are even more important. When organizations alter structure, political equilibria are disturbed. As long as the pool of resources is fixed, structural change almost always involves redistribution of resources across subunits. Such redistribution upsets the prevailing system of exchange among subunits (or subunit leaders). So at least some subunits are likely to resist any proposed reorganization. Moreover the benefits of structural reorganization are likely to be both generalized (designed to benefit the organization as a whole) and long-run. Any negative political response will tend to generate short-run costs that are high enough that organizational leaders will forego the planned reorganization. (For a more extensive discussion of the ways in which the internal political economy of organizations impedes change or adaptation, see Downs [1967] and Zald [1970].)

4   Finally, organizations face constraints generated by their own history. Once standards of procedure and the allocation of tasks and authority have become the subject of normative agreement, the costs of change are greatly increased. Normative agreements constrain adaptation in at least two ways. First, they provide a justification and an organizing principle for those elements that wish to resist reorganization (i.e., they can resist in terms of a shared principle). Second, normative agreements preclude the serious consideration of many alternative responses. For example, few research-oriented universities seriously consider adapting to declining enrolments by eliminating the teaching function. To entertain this option would be to challenge central organizational norms.[3]

The external pressures toward inertia seem to be at least as strong. They include at least the following factors.

1   Legal and fiscal barriers to entry and exit from markets (broadly defined) are numerous. Discussions of organizational behavior typically emphasize barriers to entry (state licensed monopoly positions, etc.). Barriers to exit are equally interesting. There are an increasing number of instances in which political decisions prevent firms from abandoning certain activities. All such constraints on entry and exit limit the breadth of adaptation possibilities.

2   Internal constraints upon the availability of information are paralleled by external constraints. The acquisition of information about relevant environments is costly, particularly in turbulent situations where the information is most essential. In addition, the type of specialists employed by the organization constrains both the nature of the

information it is likely to obtain (see Granovetter 1973) and the kind of specialized information it can process and utilize.

3   Legitimacy constraints also emanate from the environment. Any legitimacy an organization has been able to generate constitutes an asset in manipulating the environment. To the extent that adaptation (e.g., eliminating undergraduate instruction in public universities) violates the legitimacy claims, it incurs considerable costs. So external legitimacy considerations also tend to limit adaptation.

4   Finally, there is the collective rationality problem. One of the most difficult issues in contemporary economics concerns general equilibria. If one can find an optimal strategy for some individual buyer or seller in a competitive market, it does not necessarily follow that there is a general equilibrium once all players start trading. More generally, it is difficult to establish that a strategy that is rational for a single decision maker will be rational if adopted by a large number of decision makers. A number of solutions to this problem have been proposed in competitive market theory, but we know of no treatment of the problem for organizations generally. Until such a treatment is established we should not presume that a course of action that is adaptive for a single organization facing some changing environment will be adaptive for many competing organizations adopting a similar strategy.

A number of these inertial pressures can be accommodated within the adaptation framework. That is, one can modify and limit the perspective in order to consider choices within the constrained set of alternatives. But to do so greatly limits the scope of one's investigation. We argue that in order to deal with the various inertial pressures the adaptation perspective must be supplemented with a selection orientation.

We consider first two broad issues that are preliminary to ecological modelling. The first concerns appropriate units of analysis. Typical analyses of the relation of organizations to environments take the point of view of a single organization facing an environment. We argue for an explicit focus on populations of organizations. The second broad issue concerns the applicability of population ecology models to the study of human social organization. Our substantive proposal begins with Hawley's (1950, 1968) classic statement on human ecology. We seek to extend Hawley's work in two ways: by using explicit competition models to specify the process producing isomorphism between organizational structure and environmental demands, and by using niche theory to extend the problem to dynamic environments. We argue that Hawley's perspective, modified and extended in these ways, serves as a useful starting point for population ecology theories of organizations.

Population thinking in the study of organization environment relations

Little attention is paid in the organizations literature to issues concerning proper units of analysis (Freeman 1975). In fact, choice of unit is treated so casually as to suggest that it is not an issue. We suspect that the opposite is true – that the choice of unit involves subtle issues and has far reaching consequences for research activity. For instance, in the case at hand, it determines which of several ecological literatures can be brought to bear on the study of organization-environment relations.

The comparison of unit choice facing the organizational analyst with that. facing the bioecologist is instructive. To oversimplify somewhat, ecological analysis is conducted at three levels: individual, population, and community. Events at one level almost always have consequences at other levels. Despite this interdependence, population events cannot be reduced to individual events (since individuals do not reflect the full genetic variability of the population) and community events cannot be simply reduced to population events. Both the latter employ a population perspective which is not appropriate at the individual level.

The situation faced by the organizations analyst is more complex. Instead of three levels of analysis, he faces at least five: (1) members, (2) subunits, (3) individual organizations, (4) populations of organizations, and (5) communities of (populations of) organizations. Levels 3–5 can be seen as corresponding to the three levels discussed for general ecology, with the individual organization taking the place of the individual organism. The added complexity arises because organizations are more near decomposable into constituent parts than are organisms. Individual members and subunits may move from organization to organization in a manner which has no parallel in nonhuman organization.

Instances of theory and research dealing with the effects of environments on organizations are found at all five levels. For example, Crozier's well-known analysis of the effects of culture on bureaucracy focuses on the cultural materials members bring to organizations (1964). At the other end of the continuum we find analyses of "organizational fields" (Turk 1970; Aldrich and Reiss 1976). But, the most common focus is on *the* organization and *its* environment. In fact, this choice is so widespread that there appears to be a tacit understanding that individual organizations are the appropriate units for the study of organization-environment relations.

We argue for a parallel development of theory and research at the population (and, ultimately, the community) level. Because of the differing opinions about levels of analysis, "population" has at least two referents. Conventional treatments of human ecology suggest that the populations relevant to the study of organization-environment relations are those aggregates of members attached to the organization or, perhaps, served by the organization. In this sense, the organization is viewed as analogue to a community: it has collective means of adapting to environmental situations. The unit character of a population so defined depends on shared fate. All members share to some extent in the consequences of organizational success or failure.

We use the term population in a second sense: to refer to aggregates of organizations rather than members. Populations of organizations must be alike in some respect, that is, they must have some unit character. Unfortunately, identifying a population of organizations is no simple matter. The ecological approach suggests that one focus on common fate with respect to environmental variations. Since all organizations are distinctive, no two are affected identically by any given exogenous shock. Nevertheless, we can identify classes of organizations which are relatively homogeneous in terms of environmental vulnerability. Notice that the populations of interest may change somewhat from investigation to investigation depending on the analyst's concern. Populations of organization referred to are not immutable objects in nature but are abstractions useful for theoretical purposes.

If we are to follow the lead of population biologists, we must identify an analogue to the biologist's notion of species. Various species are defined ultimately in terms of genetic structure. As Monod (1971) indicates, it is useful to think of the genetic content of any species as a blueprint. The blueprint contains the rules for transforming energy into structure. Consequently all of the adaptive capacity of a species is summarized in the blueprint. If we are to identify a species analogue for organizations we must search for such blueprints. These will consist of rules or procedures for obtaining and acting upon inputs in order to produce an organizational product or response.

The type of blueprint one identifies depends on substantive concerns. For example, Marschak and Radner (1972) employ the term "organizational form"[4] to characterize the key elements of the blueprint as seen within a decision-making framework. For them the blueprint or form has two functions: an information function that describes the rules used in obtaining, processing, and transmitting information about the states of external environments, and an activity function that states the rules used in acting on received information so as to produce an organizational response. To the extent that one can identify classes of organizations that differ with regard to these two functions, one can establish classes or forms of organization.

Since our concerns extend beyond decision making, however, we find Marschak and Radner's definition of forms too limiting. In fact, there is no reason to limit a priori the variety of rules or functions that may define relevant blueprints. So for us, an organizational form is a blueprint for organizational action, for transforming inputs into outputs. The blueprint can usually be inferred, albeit in somewhat different ways, by examining any of the following: (1) the formal structure of the organization in the narrow sense – tables of organization, written rules of operation, etc.; (2) the patterns of activity within the organization – what actually gets done by whom; or (3) the normative order – the ways of organising that are defined as right and proper by both members and relevant sectors of the environment.

To complete the species analogue, we must search for qualitative differences among forms. It seems most likely that we will find such differences in the first and third areas listed above, formal structure and normative order. The latter offers particularly intriguing possibilities. Whenever the history of an organization, its politics, and its social structure are encoded in a normative claim (e.g., professionalization and collegial authority), one can use these claims to identify forms and define populations for research.

Having defined the organizational form, we can provide a more precise definition of a population of organizations. Just as the organizational analyst must choose a unit of analysis, so must he choose a system for study. Systems relevant to the study of organization-environment relations are usually defined by geography, by political boundaries, by market or product considerations, etc. Given a systems definition, a population of organizations consists of all the organizations within a particular boundary that have a common form. That is, the population is the form as it exists or is realized within a specified system.

Both uses of the term population (and the ecological theories implied thereby) are likely to prove beneficial to the study of organizational structure. The first, more common, view suggests that organizational structure ought to be viewed as an outcome of a collective adaptive process. According to this view, structure and change ought to depend on the adaptiveness of subunits and on the differential access of subunits to environmental resources. The second view ignores the adaptive activities of elements within the organization except as they constitute organizational structure. It focuses on the organization as an adapting unit. Certainly both perspectives are needed. We are concerned here only with the latter, however.

Finally, we would like to identify the properties of populations most interesting to population ecologists. The main concern in this regard was expressed clearly by Elton (1927): "In solving ecological problems we are concerned with *what animals do* in their capacity as whole, living animals, not as dead animals or as a series of parts of animals. We have next to study the circumstances under which they do those things, and most important of all, the limiting factors which prevent them from doing certain other things. By solving these questions it is possible to discover the reasons for *the distribution and numbers of animals in nature*." Hutchinson (1959) in the subtitle to his famous essay, "Homage to Santa Rosalia," expressed the main focus even more succinctly: "Why Are There So Many Kinds of Animals?" Taking our lead from these distinguished ecologists, we suggest that a population ecology of organizations must seek to understand the distributions of organizations across environmental conditions and the limitations on organizational structures in different environments, and more generally seek to answer the question, Why are there so many kinds of organizations?

Discontinuities in ecological analysis

Utilization of models from ecology in the study of organizations poses a number of analytic challenges involving differences between human and nonhuman organizations with regard to their essential ingredients. Consider, first, the nongenetic transmission of information. Biological analyses are greatly simplified by the fact that most useful information concerning adaptation to the environment (which information we call structure) is transmitted genetically. Genetic processes are so nearly invariant that extreme continuity in structure is the rule. The small number of imperfections generates structural changes, which, if accepted by the environment, will be transmitted with near invariance. The extreme structural, invariance of species greatly simplifies the problem of delimiting and identifying populations. More important, the adaptiveness of structure can be unambiguously identified with net reproduction rates. When a population with given properties increases its net reproduction rate following an environmental change, it follows that it is being selected for fitness. This is why modern biologists have narrowed the definition of fitness to the net reproductive rate of population.

Human social organization presumably reflects a greater degree of learning or adaptation. As a result it is more difficult to define fitness in a precise way. Under at least some conditions, organizations may undergo such extreme structural change that they shift from one form to another As a result, extreme adaptation may give rise to observed changes that mimic selection. This is particularly problematic when the various organizational forms are similar on many dimensions.

We have argued previously (Hannan and Freeman 1974) for a composite measure of fitness that includes both selection (actual loss of organizations) and mobility among forms (extreme adaptation). Fitness would then be defined as the probability that a given form of organization would persist in a certain environment. We continue to believe that such an approach has value, but we now believe that it is premature to combine adaptation and selection processes. The first order of business is to study selection processes for these situations in which inertial pressures are sufficiently strong that mobility among forms is unlikely.

Furthermore, it is worth noting that the capacity to adapt is itself subject to evolution (i.e., to systematic selection). As we argue below, organizations develop the capacity to adapt at the cost of lowered performance levels in stable environments. Whether or not such adaptable organizational forms will survive (i.e., resist selection) depends on the nature of the environment and the competitive situation. Therefore, a selection point of view treats high levels of adaptability as particular evolutionary outcomes.

There is a second sense in which human ecology appears to differ from bioecology. Blau and Scott (1962) point out that, unlike the usual biological situation, individual organizations (and populations of organizations) have the potential to expand almost without limit. The expandability of primitive elements is a problem because of our focus on the distribution of organizational forms over environments. A given form (e.g., formal bureaucracy) can expand throughout some system, market, or activity, either because one bureaucracy grows or because many bureaucracies are founded. Either process will generate an increase in the prevalence of bureaucratic organizational activity. A literal application of population ecology theory to the problem of organizational change would involve simply counting relative numbers in populations. Such a procedure may miss a phenomenon of central interest to the organizational analyst. Winter (1964), in discussing the analytic problem raised here, suggests distinguishing between survival, which describes the fate of individual organizations, and viability, which describes the "share of market" of a given organizational form.

We find at least as much merit in another perspective on the issue of size. Many theorists have asserted that structural change attends growth; in other words, a single organization cannot grow indefinitely and still maintain in original form. For instance, a mouse could not possibly maintain the same proportion of body weight to skeletal structure while growing as big as a house. It would neither look like a mouse nor operate physiologically like a mouse. Boulding (1953) and Haire (1959) argue that the same is true for organizations. Caplow (1957), building on work by Graicunas (1933) and others, argues that the ability of each member of an organization to carry on face-to-face interactions with each of the others declines with the number of organizational participants. This creates a shift in the nature of interactions such that they assume a more impersonal, formal style. Blau and a number of co-authors have argued for similar causal effects of size on structure (Blau and Scott 1962, pp. 223–42; Blau and Schoenherr 1971; Blau 1972). If it is true that organizational form changes with size, selection mechanisms may indeed operate with regard to the size distribution. When big organizations prevail it may be useful to view this as a special case of selection, in which the movement from "small form" to "large form" is theoretically indistinguishable from the dissolution ("death") of small organizations and their replacement by (the "birth" of) large organizations.

In sum, we have identified a number of challenges. The first concerns the two sources of change, selection and adaptive learning. We feel that the organizations literature has over-emphasized the latter at the expense of the former. Much more is known about decision-making practices, forecasting, and the like than about selection in populations of organizations. The second challenge involves the distinction between selection and viability. Whether such a distinction is necessary depends on the results of research on size which is currently being pursued by many organization researchers.

The principle of isomorphism

In the best developed statement of the principles of human ecology, Hawley (1968) answers the question of why there are so many kinds of organizations. According to Hawley, the diversity of organizational forms is isomorphic to the diversity of environments. In each distinguishable environmental configuration one finds, in equilibrium, only that organizational form optimally adapted to the demands of the environment. Each unit experiences constraints which force it to resemble other units with the same set of constraints. Hawley's explanation places heavy emphasis on communication patterns and structural complements of those patterns: "[organization units] must submit to standard terms of communication and to standard procedures in consequence of which they develop similar internal arrangements within limits imposed by their respective sizes" (1968, p. 334).

While the proposition seems completely sound from an ecological perspective, it does not address a number of interesting considerations. There are at least two respects in which the isomorphism formulation must be modified and extended if it is to provide satisfactory answers to the question posed. The first modification concerns the mechanism or mechanisms responsible for equilibrium. In this respect, the principle of isomorphism must be supplemented by a criterion of selection and a competition theory. The second modification deals with the fact that the principle of isomorphism neither speaks to issues of optimum adaptation to changing environments nor recognizes that populations of organizations often face multiple environments which impose somewhat inconsistent demands. An understanding of the constraints on organizational forms seems to require modelling of multiple dynamic environments. Of course, we cannot fully extend Hawley's principle here. We attempt only to outline the main issues and suggest particular extensions.

Competition theory

The first of the needed extensions is a specification of the optimization process responsible for isomorphism. We have already discussed two mechanisms: selection and adaptive learning. Isomorphism can result either because nonoptimal forms are selected out of a community of organizations or because organizational decision makers learn optimal responses and adjust organizational behavior accordingly. We continue to focus on the first of these processes: selection.

Consideration of optimization raises two issues: Who is optimizing, and what is being optimized? It is quite commonly held, as in the theory of the firm, that organizational decision makers optimize profit over sets of organizational actions. From a population ecology perspective, it is the environment which optimizes.[5] Whether or not individual organizations are consciously adapting, the environment selects out optimal combinations of organizations. So if there is a rationality involved, it is the "rationality" of natural selection. Organizational rationality and environmental rationality may coincide in the instance of firms in competitive markets. In this case, the optimal behavior of each firm is to maximize profit and the rule used by the environment (market, in this case) is to select out profit maximizers. Friedman (1953) makes use of this observation to propose a justification of the theory of the firm in terms of the principles of evolution. However, Winter (1964) has argued convincingly that the actual situation is much more complicated than this and that it is most unusual for individual rationality and environmental or market rationality to lead to the same optima. When the two rationalities do not agree, we are concerned with the optimizing behavior of the environment.

A focus on selection invites an emphasis on competition. Organizational forms presumably fail to flourish in certain environmental circumstances because other forms successfully compete with them for essential resources. As long as the resources which sustain organizations are finite and populations have unlimited capacity to expand, competition must ensue.

Hawley (1950, pp. 201–3) following Durkheim (1947) among others, places a heavy emphasis on competition as a determinant of patterns of social organization. The distinctive feature of his model is the emphasis on the indirect nature of the process: "The action of all on the common supply gives rise to a reciprocal relation between each unit and all the others, if only from the fact that what one gets reduces by that amount what the others can obtain … without this element of indirection, that is, unless units affect one another through affecting a common limited supply, competition does not exist" (Hawley 1950, p. 202). In Hawley's model, competition processes typically involve four stages: (1) demand for resources exceeds supply; (2) competitors become more similar as standard conditions of competition bring forth a uniform response; (3) selection eliminates the weakest competitors; and (4) deposed competitors differentiate either territorially or functionally, yielding a more complex division of labor.

It is surprising that there is almost no reliance on competitive mechanisms in Hawley's later work. In particular, as we noted above, the rationale given for the isomorphism principle uses an adaptation logic. We propose to balance that treatment by adding an explicit focus on competition as a mechanism producing isomorphism.[6] In so doing, we can bring a rich set of formal models to bear on the problem.

The first step in constructing an ecological model of competition is to state the nature of the population growth process. At a minimum we wish the model to incorporate the idea that resources available at any moment for each form of organization are finite and fixed. This corresponds with Hawley's notion of limited supply and Stinchcombe's (1965) argument that human communities have limited "capacities for organizing." We also wish to incorporate the view that the rate at which units are added to populations of organizations depends on how much of the fixed capacity has already been exhausted. The greater the unexhausted capacity in an environment, the faster should be the rate of growth of populations of organizations. But the rate at which populations of organizations can expand into unused capacity varies among forms of organization. So there are two distinctive ecological considerations: the capacity of the environment to support forms of organization and the rate at which the populations grow (or decline) when the environmental support changes.

In order to state the model formally, it is helpful to begin with the control function that Hummon, Doreian, and Teuter (1975) use to add dynamic considerations to Blau's theory of size and differentiation. The control model states that the rate of change in the size of any unit (here a population of organizations) varies proportionately with the difference between existing size, X, and the equilibrium level of size, X^*, permitted in that environment. Then one possible representation would be

$$\frac{dX}{dt} = f(X^* - X) = r(X^* - X) \tag{1}$$

In (1) X^* and r represent the limited supply or environmental capacity and the structural ability of the population of organizations to respond to changes in the environment, respectively.

A particular form of the general growth model in (1) underlies most population ecology work on competition. This is the logistic growth model (for per capita growth):

$$\frac{dX_1}{dt} = r_1 X_1 \left(\frac{k_1 - X_1}{k_1} \right) \tag{2}$$

where X_1 denotes population size, k_1 is the capacity of the environment to support X_1 (this parameter is usually called the carrying capacity), and r_1 is the so-called natural rate of increase of the population or the rate at which the population grows when it is far below the carrying capacity.

As we indicated above, both k and r are ecological parameters of fundamental importance. Our research group has begun to compare various forms of organization by estimating the parameters of models like (2) for each form of organization. We have been successful to date in relating structural features of organizations such as complexity of core activity to variations in r and k (Nielsen and Hannan 1977; Freeman and Brittain 1977). This work, together with that of Hummon et al. (1975), gives us confidence that the model in (1) and/or (2) gives a good approximation of the growth of populations of organizations.

Up to this point we have presumed that the limits on growth reflect the finite nature of the environment (e.g., community wealth and mix of occupational skills). It is now time to reintroduce competition. According to Hawley, competition enters indirectly when the competitors lower the fixed supply. We can model this by following the lead of bioecologists and extending the logistic growth model. For example, consider a second population of organizations whose size is denoted by X_2. The two populations are said to compete if the addition of units of either decreases the rate of growth of the other. This will be the case when both populations are sustained by the same types of resources. Then the appropriate model is represented in the following system of growth equations (known as the Lotka-Volterra equations for competing populations):

$$\frac{dX_1}{dt} = r_1 X_1 \left(\frac{k_1 - X_1 - \alpha_{12} X_2}{k_1} \right)$$

$$\frac{dX_2}{dt} = r_2 X_2 \left(\frac{k_2 - X_2 - \alpha_{21} X_1}{k_2} \right)$$
(3)

The coefficients α_{12} and α_{21}, called competition coefficients, denote the magnitude of the effect of increases in one population on the growth of the other. In this simple formulation, the only consequence of competition is to lower the carrying capacity of the environment for a population of organizations.

Analysis of (3) produces interesting qualitative results. It is not difficult to show that a stable two-population equilibrium exists for the system in (3) only if

$$\frac{1}{\alpha_{21}} < \frac{k_2}{k_1} < \alpha_{12}$$
(4)

Therefore, very similar populations (i.e., populations with competition coefficients near unity) can coexist only under a very precise $k_2 k_1$ ratio. As a result, when $\alpha_{12} = \alpha_{21} = 1$, no two-population equilibrium can be stable: any exogenous shock will result in the elimination of one of the populations. This result supports the generality of the widely cited "principle of competitive exclusion" (Gause 1934).[7] According to this principle, no two populations can continuously occupy the same niche. Populations are said to occupy the same niche to the extent that they depend on identical environmental resources. If they are identical, then the addition of an element to

X_2 has the same consequences for growth in X_1 as does the addition of an element to X_1; in other words, the competition coefficients are unity. The broad conclusion is that the greater the similarity of two resource-limited competitors, the less feasible is it that a single environment can support both of them in equilibrium.

If two populations of organizations sustained by identical environmental resources differ in some organizational characteristic, that population with the characteristic less fit to environmental contingencies will tend to be eliminated. The stable equilibrium will then contain only one population which can be said to be isomorphic to the environment.

In order to see the implications of the model for organizational diversity, we extend the Lotka-Volterra system to include M competitors:

$$\frac{dX_i}{dt} = r_i X_i (k_i - X_i - \Sigma \alpha_{ij} X_j) / k_i \qquad (i = 1, \dots, M).$$ (5)

The general system (5) has a community equilibrium:

$$k_i = X_i + \Sigma \alpha_{ij} X_j \qquad\qquad (i = 1, \dots, M).$$ (6)

These equations can be expressed in matrix form:

$$k = Ax,$$ (7)

where x and k are $(M \times 1)$ column vectors and A is the community matrix:

$$A = \begin{pmatrix} 1 & \alpha_{12} & . & . & . & \alpha_{1m} \\ \alpha_{21} & 1 & . & . & . & . \\ . & . & . & . & . & . \\ . & . & . & . & . & . \\ . & . & . & . & . & . \\ \alpha_{m1} & . & . & . & . & 1 \end{pmatrix}$$

whose elements are the competition coefficients.

The so-called theory of community structure entails the analysis of the equilibrium behavior of the system of equation (7) from the perspective of postulated competition processes.[8] The results, though stated in terms of species diversity, are quite general. In particular, one can show that when growth in population is constrained only by resource availability, the number of distinct resources sets an upper bound on diversity in the system.[9] Even more generally, the upper bound on diversity is equal to the number of distinct resources plus the number of additional constraints on growth (Levin 1970).

It is difficult to apply either result directly in order to calculate the upper bound on diversity even in the non-human context. The chief difficulty is that of identifying distinct constraints. A good deal of empirical work is required if one is to judge how different two constraints must be in order to have distinct consequences for community equilibria. The theorems do, however, imply useful qualitative results. If one can identify environmental changes which add constraints to a system or eliminate them, one can conclude that the upper bound of diversity is increased or decreased.

This broad qualitative result has a number of potential applications to the research problems of interest. For example, the expansion of markets and of state control mechanisms through social systems tends to have the consequence of eliminating or reducing the number of constraints which are idiosyncratic to local environments. Viewed from the perspective of the larger system, the process of expansion of the economic and political center should, then, tend to replace some local constraints with more uniform ones. As long as the local environments were heterogeneous at the outset, expansion of the center ought to reduce the number of constraints on organization in the whole system.

The theory just discussed implies on the one hand that the change in constraint structure ought to lower organizational diversity through the elimination of some population.[10] One can imagine, on the other hand, that in some local environments, the combination of unaltered local constraints and new larger system constraints might increase the total number of constraints in the local system. In that case, organizational diversity in those local environments should increase. Such an increase would result in the creation or adoption of new organizational forms.

The increasingly important role of the state in regulating economic and social action provides numerous opportunities for analyzing the impact of changes in constraint structures on the diversity of organizational forms. Consider the impact of licensing laws, minimum wage, health, and safety legislation, affirmative action, and other regulations on organizational action. When such regulations are applied to the full range of organizations in broad areas of activity they undoubtedly alter the size distributions of organizations. Most often they select out the smallest organizations. But it is not difficult to imagine situations in which medium-sized organizations (more precisely, those with some minimum level of complexity) would be more adversely affected. Besides altering size distributions, such regulations undoubtedly affect the diversity of organizational arrangements in other ways. Here one could analyze the impact of state action on the diversity of accounting systems within industries, curricula within universities, departmental structures within hospitals, etc. In each case it would be essential to determine whether the newly imposed constraint replaced lower level constraints, in which case diversity should decline, or whether the constraint cumulated with the existing constraints, in which case organizational diversity would be likely to increase.

To indicate the richness of the simple competition theory we have proposed we will briefly discuss another sort of empirical test. We noted above that research on regulation might concern itself with impacts on distributions of organizations by size. The classical model of organizational size distributions (Simon and Bonini 1958) proposes the following simple process. A number of organizations begin with the same small size. Some fraction are able to make or borrow some useful technical or organizational innovation that permits them to grow to some larger size. During some specified time period the process repeats itself with the same fraction making the innovation required to attain a larger size. Such a growth process eventually yields the lognormal distribution that characterizes so many size distributions.

Competition theory suggests a refinement of this classical model. If, as we argued earlier, large changes in organizational size are accompanied by structural changes (changes in form), organizations of very different size in the same area of activity will tend to exhibit different forms. As a consequence of these structural differences, they will tend to depend on different sets of environmental resource (and constraints). That is, within any area of activity, patterns of resource use will tend to be specialized to segments of the size distribution. This being the case, organizations will compete most intensely with similar size organizations. Also, competition between pairs of organizations within an activity will be a decreasing function of the distance separating them on the size gradient. For example, small local banks compete most with other small banks, to a lesser extent with medium-scale regional banks, and hardly at all with international banks. Under these conditions, significant alterations in the size distribution indicate selection for and against certain organizational forms closely associated with regard to size.

Now let us return to the classical model. When large-sized organizations emerge they pose a competitive threat to medium-sized but hardly any threat to small organizations. In fact, the rise of large organizations may increase the survival chances of small ones in a manner not anticipated in the classical model. When the large organizations enter, those in the middle of the size distribution are trapped. Whatever strategy they adopt to fight off the challenge of the larger form makes them more vulnerable in competition with small organizations and vice versa. That is, at least in a stable environment the two ends of the size distribution ought to outcompete the middle (see below). So in a longitudinal analysis of organizational size distributions we would expect to see the number of medium-sized organizations decline upon the entry of larger organizations. Also, we would expect the fortunes of small organizations to improve as their competitors are removed from the environment. This reasoning holds generally for competition along a single gradient: those in the middle will be eliminated in stable environments (MacArthur 1972, pp. 43–46).

Niche theory

The principle of isomorphism. implies that social organizations in equilibrium will exhibit structural features that are specialized to salient features of the resource environment. As long as the environment is stable and certain, we see no difficulty with this proposition. But does it hold when the environment shifts either predictably or unpredictably among several alternative configurations? Though the issues raised by attempting to answer this question are complex, doing so is crucial to developing adequate models of organizational-environment relations.

Intuition suggests that isomorphism holds as a good approximation only in stable environments. Faced with unstable environments, organizations ought to develop a generalist structure that is not optimally adapted to any single environmental configuration but is optimal over an entire set of configurations. In other words, we ought to find specialized organizations in stable and certain environments and generalist organizations in unstable and uncertain environments. Whether or not this simple proposition holds for social organizations, only empirical research will tell. However, a variety of population ecology models suggests that it is too simplistic. We cannot hope in one paper to develop fully the arguments involved. Instead we indicate the main lines of development with reference to one rather evocative perspective developed by Levins (1962, 1968): the theory of niche width.

The concept of "niche," initially borrowed by biologists from early social science, plays a central role in ecological theory. This is not the place for an extended discussion of the multiple uses of the concept (see Whittaker and Levin 1976). The model which follows uses Hutchinson's (1957) formulation. From this point of view the (realized) niche of a population is defined as that area in constraint space (the space whose dimensions are levels of resources, etc.) in which the population outcompetes all other local populations. The niche, then, consists of all those combinations of resource levels at which the population can survive and reproduce itself.

Each population occupies a distinct niche. For present purposes it suffices to consider cases where pairs of populations differ with respect to a single environmental dimension, E, and are alike with respect to all others. Then relative competitive positions can be simply summarized as in Figure 1.1. As we have drawn this figure, one population, A, occupies a very broad niche, whereas the other, B, has concentrated its fitness, denoted W, on a very narrow band of environmental variation. This distinction, which is usually referred to as generalism versus specialism, is crucial to biological ecology and to a population ecology of organizations.

In essence, the distinction between specialism and generalism refers to whether a population of organizations flourishes because it maximizes its exploitation of the environment and accepts the risk of having that environment change or because it accepts a lower level of exploitation in return for

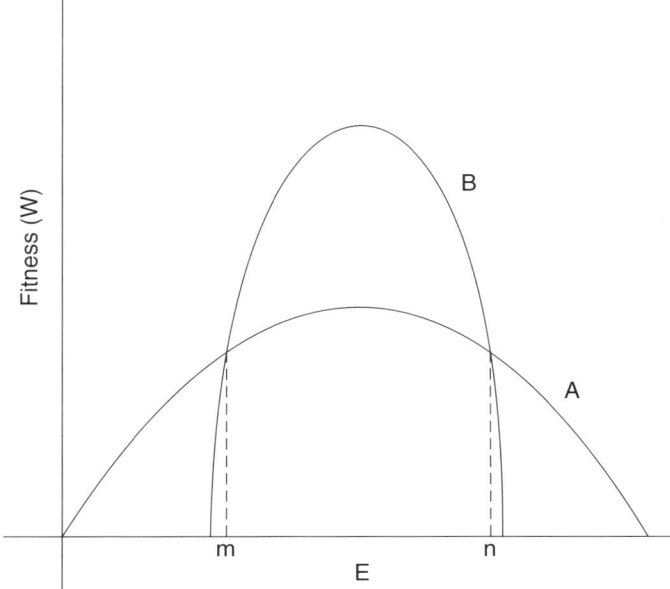

Figure 1.1 Fitness functions (niches) for specialists and generalists.

greater security. Whether or not the equilibrium distribution of organizational forms is dominated by the specialist depends, as we will see, on the shape of the fitness sets and on properties of the environment.

Part of the efficiency resulting from specialism is derived from the lower requirements for excess capacity. Given some uncertainty, most organizations maintain some excess capacity to insure the reliability of performance. In a rapidly changing environment, the definition of excess capacity is likely to change frequently. What is used today may become excess tomorrow, and what is excess today may be crucial tomorrow. Organizations operating in environments where the transition from state to state is less frequent will (in equilibrium) have to maintain excess capacity in a given allocational pattern for longer periods of time. Whereas those charged with assessing performance will be tempted to view such allocations as wasteful, they may be essential for survival. Thompson (1967) has argued that organizations allocate resources to units charged with the function insulating core technology from environmentally induced disruption. So, for example, manufacturing firms may retain or employ legal staffs even when they are not currently facing litigation.

The importance of excess capacity is not completely bound up with the issue of how much excess capacity will be maintained. It also involves the manner in which it is used. Organizations may insure reliable performance by creating specialized units, as Thompson (1967) suggests, or they may allocate excess capacity to organizational roles, by employing personnel with skills and abilities which exceed the routine requirements of their jobs. This is one of the important reasons for using professionals in organizations. Professionals use more resources not only because they tend to be paid more, but also because organizations must allow them more discretion (including the freedom to respond to outside reference groups). Organizations, in turn, become more flexible by employing professionals. They increase their capacity to deal with a variable environment and the contingencies it produces. For example, hospitals and their patients often employ obstetricians and paediatricians in their delivery rooms even though the normal delivery of babies can be performed equally well, and perhaps even better, by midwives. The skills of the medical doctor represent excess capacity to insure reliable performance should delivery not be normal. Usually, the paediatrician examines the infant immediately after birth to see if there is any abnormality requiring immediate action. If the mother is suffering dangerous consequences from giving birth, and the child is also in need of attention, the presence of the paediatrician insures that the obstetrician will not have to choose between them in allocating his attention.

Excess capacity may also be allocated to the development and maintenance of procedural systems. When the certainty of a given environmental state is high, organizational operations should be routine, and co-ordination can be accomplished by formalized rules and the investment of resources in training incumbents to follow those formalized procedures. If in fact the environment were unchanging ($p = 1$), all participants were procedurally skilled, and the procedures were perfectly tuned, there would be no need for any control structure at all, except to monitor behavior. However, when certainty is low, organizational operations are less routine. Under these circumstances, a greater allocation of resources to develop and maintain procedural systems is counterproductive and optimal organizational forms will allocate resources to less formalized systems capable of more innovative responses (e.g., committees and teams). In this case, excess capacity is represented by the increased time it takes such structures to make decisions and by increased co-ordination costs.

The point here is that populations of organizational forms will be selected for or against depending upon the amount of excess capacity they maintain and how they allocate it. It may or may not be rational for any particular organization to adopt one pattern or another. What would seem like waste to anyone assessing performance at one time may be the difference between survival and failure later. Similarly, organizations may survive because high levels of professionalization produce co-ordination by mutual adjustment despite a somewhat chaotic appearance. Others, in which everyone seems to know precisely what he is doing at all times, may fail. Under a given set of environmental circumstances the fundamental ecological question is: which forms thrive and which forms disappear.

Generalism may be observed in a population of organizations, then, either in its reliance upon a wide variety of resources simultaneously or in its maintenance of excess capacity at any given time. This excess capacity allows such organizations to change in order to take advantage of resources which become more readily available. Corporations which maintain an unusually large proportion of their total assets in fluid form ("slack," in terms of theory of the firm; Penrose 1959; Cyert and March 1963) are generalizing. In either case, generalism is costly. Under stable environmental circumstances, generalists will be outcompeted by specialists. And at any given point in time, a static analysis will reveal excess capacity. An implication – shifting our focus to individual generalists – is that outside agents will often mistake excess capacity for waste.

We can investigate the evolution of niche width if we make the assumption that areas under the fitness curve are equal, and that specialists differ from generalists in how they distribute the fixed quantity of fitness over environmental outcomes. Specialists outcompete generalists over the range of outcomes to which they have specialized (because of the fixed level of fitness assumption). As long as the environmental variation remains within that interval (the interval $[m,n]$ in Figure 1.1), generalists have no adaptive advantage and will be selected against. Alternatively, if the environment is only occasionally within the interval, specialists will fare less well than generalists. These brief comments make clear the importance of environmental variation for the evolution of niche width.

To simplify further, consider an environment which can take on only two states and in every period falls in state one with probability p and in state two with probability $q = (1 - p)$. Assume further that variations 5 environmental states are Bernoulli trials (independent from period to period). For this situation Levins (1962, 1968) has shown that optimal niche width depends on p and the "distance" between the two states of the environment.

To see this, we change focus slightly. Since each organization faces two environments, its fitness depends on fitness in the pair. We can summarize the adaptive potential of each organization by plotting these pairs of values (fitness in state 1 and in state 2) in a new space whose axes are fitness in each of the states, as in Figure 1.2. In this representation, each point denotes the fitness of a distinct organizational form. The cloud of points is termed the "fitness set." We presume that all of the naturally possible adaptations are represented in the fitness set.

Our interest is in determining which points in the fitness set will be favored by natural selection. Notice first that all points interior to the set are inferior in terms of fitness to at least some point on the boundary of the set. In this sense the boundary, drawn as a continuous line, represents the optimal possibilities. Since natural selection maximizes fitness, it must choose points on the boundary. This narrows our search to seeking which form(s) on the boundary will be favored.

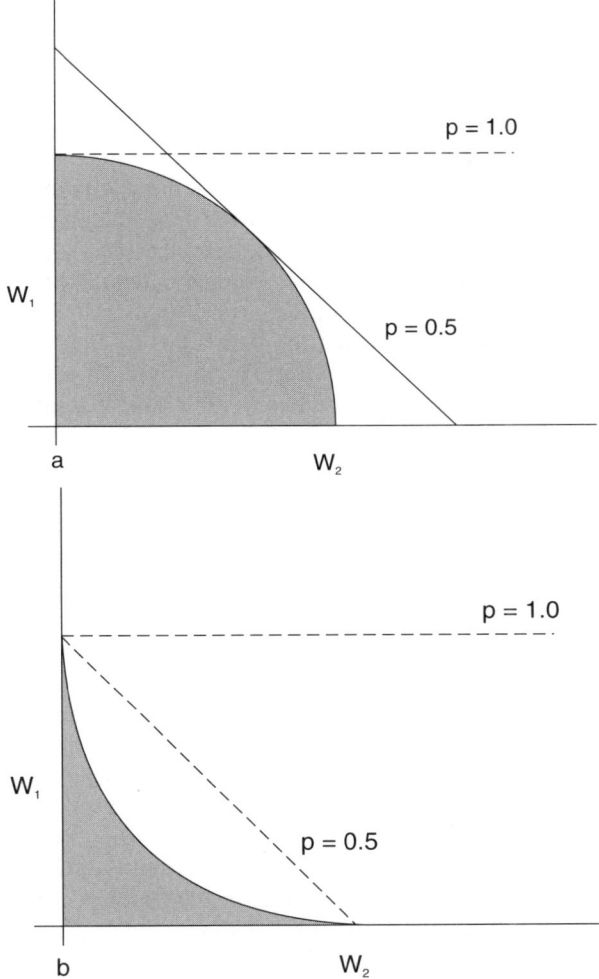

Figure 1.2 Optimal adaptation in fine-grained environment; *a*, convex fitness set; *b*, concave fitness set.

As Figure 1.2b is drawn, no organizational form does particularly well in both states of the environment – no form has high levels of fitness in both. This will be the case when the two states are "far apart" in the sense that they impose very different adaptive contingencies on organizations. In such cases (see Levins 1968), the fitness set will be concave. When the "distance" between states is small, there is no reason why certain organizational forms cannot do well in both environments. In such cases, the fitness set will be convex, as in Figure 1.2a.

The fitness functions in Figures 1.2a and 1.2b describe different adaptive situations. The next step is to model the optimization process. To do so, we introduce a further distinction. Ecologists have found it useful to distinguish both spatial and temporal environmental variation according to grain. Environmental variation is said to be fine-grained when a typical element (organization) encounters many units or replications. From a temporal perspective, variation is fine-grained when typical durations in states are short relative to the lifetime of organizations. Otherwise, the environment is said to be coarse-grained. Demand for products or services is often characterized by fine-grained variation whereas changes in legal structures are more typically coarse-grained.

The essential difference between the two types of environmental variation is the cost of suboptimal strategies. The problem of ecological adaptation can be considered a game of chance in which the population chooses a strategy (specialism or generalism) and then the environment chooses an outcome (by, say, flipping a coin). If the environment "comes up" in a state favorable to the organizational form, it prospers; otherwise, it declines. However, if the variation is fine-grained (durations are short), each population of organizations experiences a great many trials and environment is experienced as an average. When variation is coarse-grained, however, the period of decline stemming from a wrong choice may exceed the organizational capacity to sustain itself under unfavorable conditions.

To capture these differences, Levins introduced an adaptive function to represent how natural selection would weight fitness in each state under the different conditions. In discussing fine-grained variation, we suggest that the environment is experienced as an average.[11] The appropriate adaptive function, then, simply weights fitness in the two states (W_1 and W_2) according to frequency of occurrence: $A(W_1, W_2) = pW_1 + qW_2$. In order to consider optimal adaptation we merely superimpose the adaptive function on the fitness set and find points of tangency of adaptive function and fitness functions. Points of tangency are optimal adaptations. The solutions for various cases are presented in Figure 1.2. If the environment is completely stable (i.e., $p = 1$), then specialism is optimal. If the environment is maximally uncertain (i.e., $p = .5$), generalism is optimal in the convex case (when the demands of the different environments are not too dissimilar) but not in the concave case. In fact, as the model is developed, specialism always wins out in the concave case.

Consider first the case in which the environment is stable (i.e., $p = 1$). Not surprisingly, specialism is optimal. The results for unstable environments diverge. When the fitness set is convex (i.e., the demands of the different environmental states are similar and/or complementary), generalism is optimal. But when the environmental demands differ (and the fitness set is concave), specialism is optimal. This is not as strange a result as it first appears. When the environment changes rapidly among quite different states, the cost of generalism is high. Since the demands in the different states are dissimilar, considerable structural management is required of generalists. But since the environment changes rapidly, these organizations will spend most of their time and energies adjusting structure. It is apparently better under such conditions to adopt a specialized structure and "ride out" the adverse environments.

The case of coarse-grained environments is somewhat more complex. Our intuitive understanding is that since the duration of an environmental state is long, maladaptation ought to be given greater weight. That is, the costs of maladaptation greatly outweigh any advantage incurred by the correct choice. One adaptive function which gives this result is the log-linear model used by Levins: $A(W_1, W_2) = W_1^p W_2^q$. The method of finding optimal adaptations is the same. The results are found in Figure 1.3. Only one case differs from what we found for fine-grained environments: the combination of uncertain and coarse-grained variation with concave fitness sets. We saw above that when such variation is fine-grained, it is better to specialize. When the duration of environmental states is long, however, the costs of this strategy are great. Long periods of nonadaptation will threaten the survival of the organization. In addition, the fact that the environment changes less often means that generalists need not spend most of their time and energies altering structure. Thus generalism is the optimal strategy in this case as we see in Figure 1.3b.

The combination of coarse-grained environmental variation W concave fitness sets raises a further possibility. The optimal adaptation in the face of environmental uncertainty possesses fairly low levels of fitness in either state. It seems clear that there must be a better solution. Levins discusses this case in depth and concludes that for the biological case with genetic transmission of structure "polymorphism" or genetically maintained population heterogeneity will be selected for. The suggestion is that populations combine types (differing, say in color, blood type, etc.) some of which are specialized to state 1 and some to state 2. With such a combination at least a portion of the population will always flourish and maintain the genetic diversity which allows it to continue to flourish when the environment changes state. The set of all such heterogeneous populations (composed of proportions of specialists to each of the two environments) can be represented in the fitness diagrams as a straight line joining the most extreme points with all combinations falling within this line.

Coarse-grained and uncertain variation favors a distinct form of generalism: polymorphism. We do not have to search very far to find an analogous outcome. Organizations may federate in such a way that supra-organizations consisting of heterogeneous collections of specialist organizations pool resources. When the environment is uncertain and coarse-grained and subunits difficult to set up and tear down, the costs of maintaining the unwieldy structure imposed by federation may be more than offset

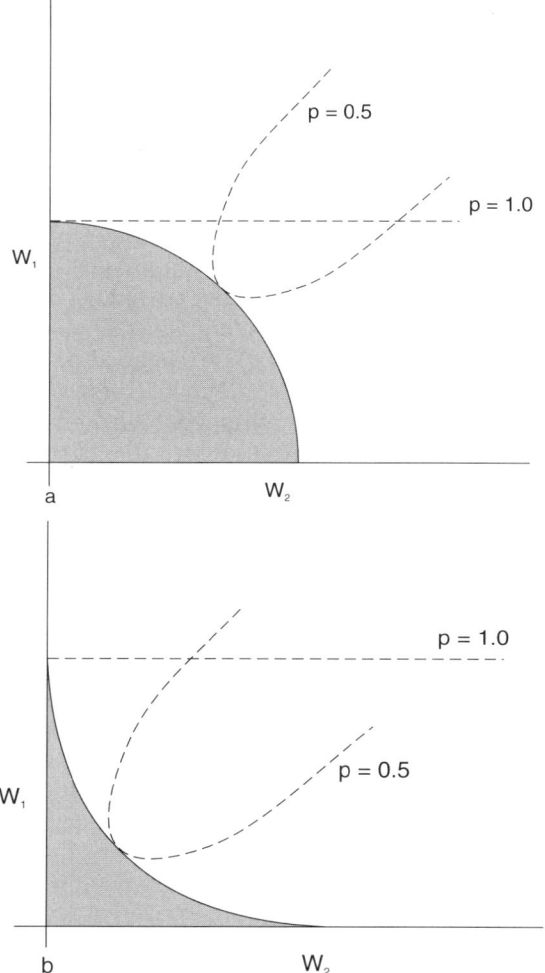

Figure 1.3 Optimal adaptation in coarse-grained environments; *a*, convex fitness
        set; *b*, concave fitness set.

by the fact that at least a portion of the amalgamated organization will do
well no matter what the state of the environment. In terms of the model suggested above there are no other situations in which such federated organizations have a competitive advantage. And even in this case, the only time
during which they have such an advantage is when coarse-grained variation
is uncertain.

Such an amalgamated "holding company" pattern may be observed in
modern universities. Enrolment and research support wax and wane over
time as do the yield on invested endowment securities and the beneficence

of legislatures. Some of these resources follow predictable cycles. Others do not. But it is extremely expensive to build up and dismantle academic units. It is costly not only in money but also in the energies consumed by political conflict. Consequently, universities are constantly "taxing" sub-units with plentiful environments to subsidize less fortunate subunits. It is common, for instance, for universities to allocate faculty positions accord-ing to some fixed master plan, undersupporting the rapidly growing depart-ments and maintaining excess faculty in others. This partial explanation of the unwieldy structures that encompass liberal arts departments, profes-sional schools, research laboratories, etc., is at least as persuasive as expla-nations that emphasize intellectual interdependence among units.

Much more can be said concerning applications of niche theory to orga-nization-environment relations. We have focused on a simple version high-lighting the interplay between competition and environmental variation in the determination of optimal adaptive structure in order to show that the principle of isomorphism needs considerable expansion to deal with multi-ple environmental outcomes and their associated uncertainty. The literature in ecology to which we have made reference is growing exponentially at the moment and new results and models are appearing monthly. The prod-ucts of these developments provide students of organizations with a rich potential for the study of organization-environment relations.

Consider an example. In his analysis of bureaucratic and craft adminis-tration or production, Stinchcombe (1959) argued that construction firms do not rely upon bureaucratically organized administrative staffs because of seasonal fluctuations in demand. Administrative staffs constitute an overhead cost which remains roughly constant over the year. The advan-tage of the otherwise costly (in terms of salaries) craft administration is that co-ordination of work is accomplished through a reliance upon prior socialization of craftsmen and upon organization. Since employment levels can more easily be increased or decreased with demand under a craft system, administrative costs are more easily altered to meet demand.

The fundamental source of this pattern is the seasonal variation in con-struction. In ecological terms, the demand environment is coarse-grained. In addition, the two states defined by season are quite different, resulting in a concave fitness curve. Craft-administered housing construction firms are probably quite inefficient when demand is at its peak and when the kind of housing under construction is standardized. In such situations, we would expect this form of organization to face stiff competition from other firms. For instance, in regions where housing construction is less seasonal, modu-lar housing, mobile homes, and prefabricated housing are more likely to flourish and we would expect the construction business to be more highly bureaucratized.

Another variation in demand is to be found in the business cycle. While seasonal fluctuations are stable (uncertainty is low), interest rates, labor relations, and materials costs are more difficult to predict. Variations of this sort should favor a generalist mode of adaptation. That is, when environments are coarse-grained, characterized by concave fitness curves, and uncertain, populations of organizations will be more likely to survive if they hedge their bets by seeking a wider variety of resource bases. For this reason, we think crafts-administered construction organizations are frequently general contractors who not only build houses but engage in other kinds of construction as well (shopping plazas, office buildings, etc.). In comparison, modular housing is cheaper and the units are installed on rented space. Consequently, interest rates are less important. Since organizations producing this kind of housing do not employ craftsmen but use the cheapest and least skilled labor they can obtain, labor relations are less problematical. It may also be that their reliance on different materials (e.g., sheet aluminum) contributes to a lower level of uncertainty. In consequence, we would expect this form of organization to be more highly specialized in its adaptation (of course there are technical factors which also contribute to this as well).

Craft-administered construction firms are set up in such a way that they can adapt rapidly to changes in demand, and they can adapt to different construction problems by varying the mix of skills represented in their work force. Bureaucratically administered construction firms are more specialized and as a result they are efficient only when demand is high, and very inefficient when it is low. We also believe that they tend to be more specialized with regard to type of construction. Craft-administered organizations sacrifice efficient exploitation of their niche for flexibility. Bureaucratic organizations choose the opposite strategy. This formulation is an extension of Stinchcombe's and serves to show that his argument is essentially ecological.

Discussion

Our aim in this paper has been to move toward an application of modern population ecology theory to the study of organization-environment relations. For us, the central question is, why are there so many kinds of organizations? Phrasing the question in this way opens the possibility of applying a rich variety of formal models to the analysis of the effects of environmental variations on organizational structure.

We begin with Hawley's classic formulation of human ecology. However, we recognize that ecological theory has progressed enormously since sociologists last systematically applied ideas from bioecology to social organization. Nonetheless, Hawley's theoretical perspective remains a very useful point of departure. In particular we concentrate on the principle of isomorphism. This principle asserts that there is a one-to-one correspondence between structural elements of social organization and those units that mediate flows of essential resources into the system. It explains the variations in organizational forms in equilibrium. But any observed isomorphism can arise from purposeful adaptation of organizations to the common constraints they face or because non-isomorphic organizations are selected against. Surely both processes are at work in most social systems. We believe that the organizations literature has emphasized the former to the exclusion of the latter.

We suspect that careful empirical research will reveal that for wide classes of organizations there are very strong inertial pressures on structure arising both from internal arrangements (e.g., internal politics) and the environment (e.g., public legitimation of organizational activity). To claim otherwise is to ignore the most obvious feature of organizational life. Failing churches do not become retail stores; nor do firms transform themselves into churches. Even within broad areas of organizational action, such as higher education and labor union activity, there appear to be substantial obstacles to fundamental structural change. Research is needed on this issue. But until we see evidence to the contrary, we will continue to doubt that the major feature of the world, of organizations arise through learning or adaptation. Given these doubts it is important to explore an evolutionary explanation of the principle of isomorphism. That is, we wish to embed the principle of isomorphism within an explicit selection framework.

In order to add selection processes we propose a competition theory using Lotka-Volterra models. This theory relies on growth models that appear suitable for representing both organizational development and the growth of populations of organizations. Recent work by bioecologists on Lotka-Volterra systems yields propositions that have immediate relevance for the study of organization-environment relations. These results concern the effects of changes in the number and mixture of constraints upon systems with regard to the upper bound of the diversity of forms of organization. We propose that such propositions can be tested by examining the impact of varieties of state regulation both on size distributions and on the diversity of organizational forms within broadly defined areas of activity (e.g., medical care, higher education, and newspaper publishing).

A more important extension of Hawley's work introduces dynamic considerations. The fundamental issue here concerns the meaning of isomorphism in situations in which the environment to which units are adapted is changing and uncertain. Should "rational" organizations attempt to develop specialized isomorphic structural relations with one of the possible environmental states? Or should they adopt a more plastic strategy and institute more generalized structural features? The isomorphism principle does not speak to these issues.

We suggest that the concrete implication of generalism for organizations is the accumulation and retention of varieties of excess capacity. To retain the flexibility of structure required for adaptation to different environmental outcomes requires that some capacities be held in reserve and not committed to action. Generalists will always be outperformed by specialists who, with the same levels of resources, happen to have hit upon optimal environment. Consequently, in any cross-section the generalists, will appear inefficient because excess capacity will often be judged waste. Nonetheless, organizational slack is a pervasive feature of many types of organizations. The question then arises: what types of environments favor generalists? Answering this question comprehensively takes one a long way toward understanding the dynamic of organization environment relations.

We begin addressing this question in be suggestive framework of Levins's (1962, 1968) fitness-set theory. This is one of a class of recent theories that relates the nature of environmental uncertainty to optimal levels of structural specialism. Levins argues that along with uncertainty one must consider the grain of the environment or the lumpiness of environmental outcomes. The theory indicates that specialism is always favored in stable or certain environments. This is no surprise. But contrary to the view widely held in the organizations literature, the theory also indicates that generalism is not always optimal in uncertain environments. When the environment shifts uncertainly among states that place very different demands on the organization, and the duration of environmental states is short relative to the life of the organization (variation is fine-grained), populations of organizations that specialize will be favored over those that generalize. This is because organizations that attempt to adapt to each environmental outcome will spend most of their time adjusting structure and very little time in organizational action directed at other ends.

Stated in these terms, the proposition appears obvious. However, when one reads the literature on organization-environment relations, one finds that it was not so obvious. Most important, the proposition follows from a simple explicit model that has the capacity to unify a wide variety of propositions relating environmental variations to organizational structure.

We have identified some of the leading conceptual and methodological obstacles to applying population ecology models to the study of organization-environment relations. We pointed to differences between human and non-human social organization in terms of mechanisms of structural invariance and structural change, associated problems of delimiting populations of organizations, and difficulties in defining fitness for populations of expandable units. In each case we have merely sketched the issues and proposed short-run simplifications which would facilitate the application of existing models. Clearly, each issue deserves careful scrutiny.

At the moment we are frustrated at least as much by the lack of empirical information on rates of selection in populations of organizations as by the unresolved issues just mentioned. Census data are presented in a manner that renders the calculation of failure rates impossible; and little longitudinal research on populations of organizations has been reported. We do, however, have some information on rates of selection. We know, for example, that failure rates for small businesses are high. By recent estimates upwards of 8 per cent of small business firms in the United States fail each year (Hollander 1967; Bolton 1971; see also Churchill 1955).

In part this high failure rate reflects: what Stinchcombe (1965) called the liability of newness. Many new organizations attempt to enter niches that have already been filled by organizations that have amassed social, economic, and political resources that make them difficult to dislodge. It is important to determine whether there is any selective disadvantage of smallness not of newness.

We doubt that many readers will dispute the contention that failure rates are high for new and/or small organizations. However, much of the sociological literature and virtually all of the critical literature on large organizations tacitly accepts the view that such organizations are not subject to strong selection pressures. While we do not yet have the empirical data to judge this hypothesis, we can make several comments. First, we do not dispute that the largest organizations individually and collectively exercise strong dominance over most of the organizations that constitute their environments. But it does not follow from the observation that such organizations are strong in any one period that they will be strong in every period. Thus, it is interesting to know how firmly embedded are the largest and most powerful organizations. Consider the so-called Fortune 500, the largest publicly owned industrial firms in the United States. We contrasted the lists for 1955 and 1975 (adjusting for pure name changes). Of those on the list in 1955, only 268 (53.6 per cent) were still listed in 1975. One hundred and twenty-two had disappeared through merger, 109 had slipped off the "500," and one (a firm specializing in Cuban sugar!) had been liquidated. The number whose relative sales growth caused them to be dropped from the list is quite impressive in that the large number of mergers had opened many slots on the list. So we see that, whereas actual liquidation was rare for the largest industrial firms in the United States over a twenty year period, there was a good deal of volatility with regard to position in this pseudodominance structure because of both mergers and slipping sales.[12]

Second, the choice of time perspective is important. (Even the largest and most powerful organizations fail to survive over long periods). For example, of the thousands of firms in business in the United States during the Revolution, only thirteen survive as autonomous firms and seven as recognizable divisions of firms (*Nation's Business* 1976). Presumably one needs a longer time perspective to study the population ecology of the largest and most dominant organizations.

Third, studying small organizations is not such a bad idea. The sociological literature has concentrated on the largest organizations for obvious reasons. But if inertial pressures on certain aspects of structure are strong enough, intense selection amount small organizations may greatly constrain the variety observable among large organizations. At least some elements of structure change with size (as we argued earlier) and the pressure toward inertia should not be overemphasized. Nonetheless we see much value in studies of the organizational life cycle that would inform us as to which aspects of structure get locked in during which phases of the cycle. For example, we conjecture that a critical period is that during which the organization grows beyond the control of a single owner/manager. At this time the manner in which authority is delegated, if at all, seems likely to have a lasting impact on organizational structure.This is the period during which an organization becomes less an extension of one or a few dominant individuals and more an organization per se with a life of its own. If the selection pressures at this point are as intense as anecdotal evidence suggests they are, selection models will prove very useful in accounting for the varieties of forms among the whole range of organizations.

The optimism of the previous paragraph should be tempered by the realization that when one examines the largest and most dominant organizations, one is usually considering only a small number of organizations. The smaller the number, the less useful are models that depend on the type of random mechanisms that underlie population ecology models.

Fourth, we must consider what one anonymous reader, caught up in the spirit of our paper, called the anti-eugenic actions of the state in saving firms such as Lockheed from failure. This is a dramatic instance of the way in which large dominant organizations can create linkages with other large and powerful ones so as to reduce selection pressures. If such moves are effective, they alter the pattern of selection. In our view the selection pressure is bumped up to a higher level. So instead of individual organizations failing, entire networks fail. The general consequence of a large number of linkages of this sort is an increase in the instability of the entire system (Simon 1962, 1973; May 1973), and therefore we should see boom and bust cycles of organizational outcomes. Selection models retain relevance, then, even when the systems of organizations are tightly coupled (see Hannan 1976).

Finally, some readers of earlier drafts have (some approvingly, some disapprovingly) treated our arguments as metaphoric. This is not what we intend. In a fundamental sense all theoretical activity involves metaphoric activity (although admittedly the term "analogue" comes closer than does "metaphor"). The use of metaphors or analogues enters into the formulation of "if … then" statements. For example, certain molecular genetic models draw an analogy between DNA surfaces and crystal structures. The latter have simple well-behaved geometric structures amenable to strong topological (mathematical) analysis. No one argues that DNA proteins are crystals; but to the extent that their surfaces have certain crystal-like properties, the mathematical model used to analyze crystals will shed light on the genetic structure. This is, as we understand it, the general strategy of model building.

We have for example, used results that rely on the application of certain logistic differential equations, the Lotka-Volterra equations. No known population (of animals, or of organization) grows in exactly the manner specified by this mathematical model (and this fact has caused numerous naturalists to argue that the model is biologically meaningless). What the equations do is to model the growth path of populations that exist on finite resources in a closed system (where population growth in the absence of competition is logistic and the presence of competing populations lowers carrying capacities in that system). To the extent that the interactions of populations of *Paramecium aureilia* and *P. caudatum* (Gause's experiment) meet the conditions of the model, the model explains certain key features of population dynamics and the relationship of environmental variations to structure. To the extent that the interactions of populations of rational-legal bureaucracies and populations of patrimonial bureaucracies also meet the conditions of the model, the model explains the same important phenomena. Neither the protozoa nor the bureaucracies behave exactly as the model stipulates. The model is an abstraction that will lead to insight whenever the stated conditions are approximated.

Throughout we make a strong continuity-of-nature hypothesis. We propose that, whenever the stated conditions hold, the models lead to valuable insights regardless of whether the populations under study are composed of protozoans or organizations. We do not argue "metaphorically." That is, we do *not* argue as follows: an empirical regularity is found to hold for certain protozoans; because we hypothesize that populations of organizations are like populations of protozoans in essential ways, we propose that the generalizations derived from the latter will hold for organizations as well. This is the kind of reasoning by which biological propositions have most often entered sociological arguments (e.g., the famous – or infamous – organismic analogy advanced by Spencer).

Instead of applying biological laws to human social organization, we advocate the application of population ecology theories. As we have indicated at a number of points these theories are quite general and must be modified for any concrete application (sociological or biological). Our purpose has been twofold. First, we sketched some of the alterations in perspective required if population ecology theories are to be applied to the study of organizations. Second, we wished to stimulate a reopening of the lines of communication between sociology and ecology. It is ironic that Hawley's (1944, p.399) diagnosis of some thirty years ago remains apt today: "Probably most of the difficulties which beset human ecology may be traced to the isolation of the subject from the mainstream of ecological thought. "

Notes

1 This research was supported in part by grants from the National Science Foundation (GS–32065) and the Spencer Foundation. Helpful comments were provided by Amos Hawley, Françoise Nielsen, John Meyer, Marshall Meyer, Jeffrey Pfeffer, and Howard Aldrich.

2 There is a subtle relationship between selection and adaptation. Adaptive learning for individuals usually consists of selection among behavioral responses. Adaptation for a population involves selection among types of members. More generally, processes involving selection can usually be recast at a higher level of analysis as adaptation processes. However, once the unit of analysis is chosen there is no ambiguity in distinguishing selection from adaptation. Organizations often adapt to environmental conditions in concert and this suggests a systems effect. Though few theorists would deny the existence of such systems effects, most do not make them a subject of central concern. It is important to notice that, from the point of view embraced by sociologists whose interests focus on the broader social system, selection in favor of organizations with one set of properties to the disfavor of those with others is often an adaptive process. Societies and communities which consist in part of formal organizations adapt partly through processes that adjust the mixture of various kinds of organizations found within them. Whereas a complete theory of organization would have to consider both adaptation and selection, recognizing that they are complementary processes, our purpose here is to show what can be learned from studying selection alone (see Aldrich and Pfeffer [1976] for a synthetic review of the literature focusing on these different perspectives).

3 Meyer's (1970) discussion of an organization's charter ads further support to the argument that normative agreements arrived at early in an organization's history constrain greatly the organization's range of adaptation to environmental constraints.

4 The term "organizational form" is used widely in the sociological literature (see Stinchcombe 1965).

5 In biological applications, one assumes that power (in the physical sense) is optimized by natural selection in accordance with the so-called Darwin-Lotka law. For the case of human social organization, one might argue that selection optimizes the utilization of a specific set of resources including but not restricted to the power and the time of members.

6 We include only the first and third of Hawley's stages in our model of competition. We prefer to treat uniformity of response and community diversity as consequences of combinations of certain competitive processes and environmental features.

7 This so-called principle has mostly suggestive value (see MacArthur [1972, pp. 43–46] for a penetrating critique of attempts to derive quantitative implications from Gause's principle; most of these criticisms do not apply to the qualitative inferences we consider).

8 We restrict attention to the case in which all entries of A are nonnegative. Negative entries are appropriate for predator/prey (or more generally, host/parasite) relations. The typical result for this case is cyclical population growth.

9 A more precise statement of the theorem is that no stable equilibrium exists for a system of M ompetitors and $N < M$ resources (MacArthur and Levins 1964).

10 For a more comprehensive statement of this argument with reference to ethnic organization, see Hannan (1975).

11 That selection depends on average outcomes is only one hypothesis. Templeton and Rothman (1974) argue that selection depends not on average outcomes but on some minimum level of fitness. Whether average outcomes or some other criterion guides selection in populations of organizations is open to question. We follow Levins in order to keep the exposition simple.

12 From at least some perspectives, mergers can be viewed as changes in form. This will almost certainly be the case when the organizations merged have very different structures. These data also indicate a strong selective advantage for a conglomerate form of industrial organization.

References

Aldrich, Howard E., and Jeffrey Pfeffer. 1976. "Environments of Organizations." *Annual Review of Sociology 2:79–105.*

Aldrich, Howard E., and Albert J. Reiss. 1976. "Continuities in the Study of Ecological Succession: Changes in the Race Composition of Neighborhoods and Their Businesses." *American Journal of Sociology* 81 (January): *846–66.*

Blau, Peter M. 1972. "Interdependence and Hierarchy in Organizations." *Social Science Research* 1 (April): 1–24.

Blau, Peter M., and Richard A. Schoenherr. 1971. *The Structure of Organizations.* New York: Basic.

Blau, Peter M., and W. Richard Scott. 1962. *Formal Organizations.* San Francisco: Chandler.

Bolton, J. E. 1971. Small Firms. Report of the Committee of Inquiry on Small Firms. London: Her Majesty's Stationery Office.

Boulding, Kenneth. 1953. "Toward a General Theory of Growth." *Canadian Journal of Economics and Political Science* 19:326–40.

Burns, Tom, and G. M. Stalker. 1961. *The Management of Innovation.* London: Tavistock.

Caplow, Theodore. 1957. "Organizational Size." *Administrative Science Quarterly* 1 (March): 484–505.

Churchill, Betty C. 1955. "Age and Life Expectancy of Business Firms."*Survey of Current Business* 35 (December): 15–19.

Crozier, Michel. 1964. The Bureaucratic Phenomenon. Chicago: University of Chicago Press.

Cyert, Richard M., and James G. March. 1963. *A Behavioral Theory of the Firm.* Englewood Cliffs, N.J.: Prentice-Hall.

Downs, Anthony. 1967. *Inside Bureaucracy.* Boston: Little, Brown.

Durkheim, E. 1947. *The Division of Labor in Society.* Translated by G. Simpson. Glencoe, Ill.: Free Press.

Elton, C. 1927. *Animal Ecology.* London: Sidgwick & Jackson.

Freeman, John. 1975. "The Unit Problem in Organizational Research." Presented at the annual meeting of the American Sociological Association, San Francisco.

Freeman, John, and Jack Brittain. 1977. "Union Merger Processes and Industrial Environments." *Industrial Relations*, in press.

Friedman, Milton. 1953. *Essays on Positive Economics.* Chicago: University of Chicago Press.

Gause, G. F. 1934. *The Struggle for Existence.* Baltimore: Williams & Wilkins.

Graicunas, V. A. 1933. "Relationship in Organizations." *Bulletin of the International Management Institute* (March), pp. 183–87.

Granovetter, Mark S. 1973. "The Strength of Weak Ties." *American Journal of Sociology 78* (May): 1360–80.

Haire, Mason. 1959. "Biological Models and Empirical Histories of the Growth of Organizations." Pp. 272–306 in *Modern Organization Theory*, edited by Mason Haire. New York: Wiley.

Hannan, Michael T. 1975. "The Dynamics of Ethnic Boundaries." Unpublished. — 1976 "Modeling Stability and Complexity in Networks of Organizations." Presented at the annual meeting of the American Sociological Association, New York.

Hannan, Michael T., and John Freeman. 1974. "Environment and the Structure of

Organizations." Presented at the annual meeting of the American Sociological Association, Montreal.

Hawley, Amos H. 1944. "Ecology and Human Ecology." *Social Forces* 22 (May): 398–405.

— 1950. *Human Ecology: A Theory of Community Structure.* New York: Ronald.

— 1968. "Human Ecology." Pp. 328–37 in *International Encyclopedia of the Social Sciences,* edited by David L. Sills. New York: Macmillan:

Hollander, Edward O., ed. 1967. *The Future of Small Business.* New York: Praeger.

Hummon, Norman P., Patrick Doreian, and Klaus Teuter. 1975. "A Structural.Control Model of Organizational Change." *American Sociological Review 40.* (December): 812–24.

Hutchinson, G. Evelyn. 1957. "Concluding Remarks." *Cold Spring Harbor Symposium on Quantitative Biology* 22:415–27.

— 1959. "Homage to Santa Rosalia, or Why Are There So Many Kinds of Animals?" American Naturalist 93:145–59.

Levin, Simon A. 1970. "Community Equilibrium and Stability: An Extension of the Competitive Exclusion Principle." American Naturalist 104 (September-October): 413–23.

Levine, Sol, and Paul E. White, 1961. "Exchange as a Framework for the Study of Interorganizational Relationships." *Administrative Science Quarterly 5* (March): 583–601.

Levins, Richard. 1962. "Theory of Fitness in a Heterogeneous Environment. I. The Fitness Set and Adaptive Function." *American Naturalist* 96 (November-December): 361–78.

— 1968. *Evolution in Changing Environments.* Princeton, N.J.: Princeton University Press.

MacArthur, Robert H. 1972. Geographical Ecology: *Patterns in the Distribution of Species.* Princeton, N.J.: Princeton University Press.

MacArthur, Robert H., and Richard Levins. 1964. "Competition, Habitat Selection and Character Displacement in Patchy Environment." *Proceedings of the National Academy of Sciences* 51:1207–10.

March, James G., and Herbert Simon. 1958. *Organizations.* New York: Wiley.

Marschak, Jacob, and Roy Radner. 1972. *Economic Theory of Teams.* New Haven, Conn.: Yale University Press.

May, Robert M. 1973. *Stability and Complexity in Model Ecosystems.* Princeton, N.J.: Princeton University Press.

Meyer, John W. 1970. "The Charter: Conditions of Diffuse Socialization in Schools." Pp. 564–78 in *Social Processes and Social Structures,* edited by W. Richard Scott. New York: Holt, Rinehart & Winston.

Monod, Jacques. 1971. *Chance and Necessity.* New York: Vintage.

Nation's Business. 1976. "America's Oldest Companies." 64 (July): 36–37.

Nielsen, Francois, and Michael T. Hannan. 1977. "The Expansion of National Educational Systems: Tests of a Population Ecology Model." *American Sociological Review,* in press.

Parsons, Talcott. 1956. "Suggestions for a Sociological Approach to the Theory of Organizations, I." *Administrative Science Quarterly* 1 (March): 63–85.

Penrose, Edith T. 1959. *The Theory of the Growth of the Firm.* New York: Wiley.

Selznick, Philip. 1957. *Leadership in Administration.* New York: Row, Peterson.

Simon, Herbert A. 1962. "The Architecture of Complexity." *Proceedings of the American Philosophical Society* 106 (December): 467–82.

— 1973. The Organization of Complex Systems." Pp. 1–28 in *Hierarchy Theory: The Challenge of Complex Systems,* edited by H Patee. New York: Braziller.

Simon, Herbert A., and C. P. Bonini. 1958. "The Size Distribution of Business Firms." *American Economic Review* 48 (September): 607–17.

Stinchcombe, Arthur L, 1959. "Bureaucratic and Craft Administration of Production." *Administrative Science Quarterly* 4 (June): 168–87.

— 1965. "Social Structure and Organizations." Pp. 153–93 in *Handbook of Organizations*, edited by James G. March. Chicago: Rand McNally.

Templeton, Alan R., and Edward A. Rothman. 1974. "Evolution in Heterogenous Environments." *American Naturalist* 108 (July–August): 409–28.

Thompson, James D. 1967. *Organizations in Action*. New York: McGraw-Hill.

Turk, Herman. 1970. "Interorganizational Networks in Urban Society: Initial Perspectives and Comparative Research." *American Sociological Review* 35 (February): 1–19.

Whittaker, Robert N., and Simon Levin, eds. 1976. *Niche: Theory and Application*. Stroudsberg, Pa.: Dowden, Hutchinson & Ross.

Winter, Sidney G., Jr. 1964. "Economic 'Natural Selection' and the Theory of the Firm." *Yale Economic Essays* 4:224–72.

Zald, Mayer. 1970. "Political Economy: A Framework for Analysis." Pp. 221–61 in *Power in Organizations*, edited by M. N. Zald. Nashville, Tenn.: Vanderbilt University Press.

2

Determinants of Willingness and Opportunity to Start as an Entrepreneur*

C. Mirjam Van Praag and Hans Van Ophem[1]

*Source: *Kyklos* 48 (1995), 513–40.

Introduction

Since new firm formation has been recognized for a long time as an important source of economic growth and labor demand, the topic of self-employment or entrepreneurship has gained considerable theoretical as well as political interest. Governments are by and large of the opinion that new firm formation is necessary for a healthy economy and that the 'natural' entrepreneurship supply is insufficient. As a result, governments started to provide encouragement programmes for self-employment and studies to evaluate the programmes' effectiveness became desirable. This calls for insight in the individual decision process. Empirical microeconomic studies have started to supply these insights. The objective of self-employment encouragement programmes is to stimulate potential successful entrepreneurs to switch to this occupational status, or to provide promising and enthusiastic would-be entrepreneurs with an opportunity to become self-employed. In order to recruit programme participants efficiently, these categories of would-be entrepreneurs should be located. Hence, it is of interest to identify individual determinants of both opportunity and willingness to become self-employed.

This paper attempts to empirically separate the effects of opportunity and willingness on becoming an entrepreneur. Observing someone as being self-employed implies that the individual both has been willing and has had the opportunity to switch to this occupational status. If either *willingness* (motivation) or *opportunity* (ability and/or capital) is absent, the individual will not become self-employed. We define the unobserved concepts of opportunity and willingness such that their levels should both surpass a given threshold for somebody to become self-employed: opportunity and willingness are each necessary conditions and together they are sufficient to switch to self-employment. We wish to identify the contribution of these unobservable concepts to the decision of a wage worker to start as an entrepreneur. This is done by estimating the bivariate probit model with partial observability (cf. Poirier, 1980). Do individuals who 'decide' not to become self-employed lack the opportunity or rather the willingness or both? And what are the observable variables that constitute the unobserved underlying concept 'opportunity' and what variables explain the 'willingness' to become self-employed? These are the questions we intend to answer. We do so by means of a dynamic approach. Using the observation of switches to self-employment, we explain the probability of becoming an entrepreneur rather than the probability of being one.

The paper is organized as follows. The next section defines opportunity and willingness to become self-employed and explains why we distinguish between them. We relate our model to a long tradition in economics of entrepreneurship, going back to Say (1803), Marshall (1890), Schumpeter (1911) and Knight (1921).

The following section describes Poirier's (1980) bivariate probit model that is used to distinguish the unobservable phenomena of opportunity and willingness.

The next section describes the data (the U.S. National Longitudinal Survey of Youth) and the variables we used. The model is estimated from a subsample of white men (between 20 and 31 years old) who were (un)employed in any year from 1985 to 1988 and who were either (un)employed or self-employed in the next year (1986–1989). We focus on white male labor force participants for homogeneity reasons and for comparability with related studies. The survey, selected because it contains appropriate information on a large number of observations, imposes the restriction on age. Its panel character makes it possible to focus on the dynamics of starting as an entrepreneur.

Both in theoretical and empirical studies various definitions have been used in order to define the concept of 'entrepreneur'[2]. We do not aim at finding a theoretical concept ourselves; we merely focus on an appropriate empirical counterpart of entrepreneurship. The empirical observed phenomenon, closely related to entrepreneurship, that we use (and has been used in most empirical research) is self-employment. Following DeWit (1993), we include in the group of self-employed both individuals who report being self-employed and those who are sole owners of their incorporated businesses: these persons perform no other function than the self-employed and they often incorporate their businesses for the sake of fiscal advantages only.

The next section discusses the maximum likelihood estimates of the empirical model. The results reveal that for most individuals opportunity is the more constraining factor in the selection process into self-employment. Opportunity in turn is dependent on the availability of capital (assets and real estate). These capital requirements can be compensated for by a low regional unemployment rate and by self-employment experience. The results are in accordance with the historical views of Say and Knight. The final section concludes and summarizes the main findings.

Opportunity and willingness

Opportunity is defined as the possibility to become self-employed if one wants to. Important variables determining opportunity are starting capital, entrepreneurial ability and the (macro)economic environment. Young men who are willing to become self-employed have an opportunity to do so whenever they possess enough capital, or can borrow it. It is likely that loans are dependent on the perceived (entrepreneurial) ability of the would-be entrepreneur, given economic conditions. This implies that ability and own capital are substitutes[3]: the opportunity to start as an entrepreneur increases with a (weighted) sum of both.

Willingness to start as an entrepreneur is defined as the valuation of work in self-employment versus remaining (un)employed, for otherwise identical situations. Willingness is positive whenever self-employment is seen as the best available (career) option. Consequently, willingness is dependent on both individual preferences for the special features of self-employment as well as on the available outside options and their perceived attractiveness.

Our wish to distinguish entrepreneurial willingness from opportunity within a dynamic framework is based on our own intuition and on our reading of the important (classical) literature. Before the more recent revival of entrepreneurship research, several important economists, Say (1803), Marshall (1890), Schumpeter (1911) and Knight (1921) have laid the basis. And in contrast with recent contributions, the distinction between opportunity and willingness is quite prominent in this literature. Say (1981) stresses the importance of the availability of a scarce combination of certain moral qualities (ability) necessary for being an entrepreneur. Capital may be borrowed, but only by people who have some additional qualities.

> 'It is commonly requisite for the entrepreneur himself to provide the necessary funds. Not that he must be already rich, for he may work upon borrowed capital; but he must at least be solvent, and have the reputation of intelligence, prudence, probity and regularity;... These requisites shut out a great many competitors.' (Say 1971, p.330).

Marshall's view (1930) largely agrees with Say's. They both argue that ability (though defined differently) is a restricting factor for the supply of individual entrepreneurship. Marshall's entrepreneur may borrow capital, though surviving as an entrepreneur is easier for those who supply their own capital. Schumpeter (1934) argues that ability does not play a significant role, while capital can be borrowed easily. For Schumpeter, the prime restriction on the supply of entrepreneurs is a scarce combination of motivating forces (willingness) of pursuing indirect instead of direct consumption. Knight (1921) argues that capital, due to moral hazard (see LeRoy and Singell, 1987), and willingness, unlike ability, are necessary to just start as an entrepreneur.

> 'Willingness plus power to give guarantees, not backed up by ability, will evidently lead to a dissipation of resources, while ability without the other two factors will be merely wasted.' (Knight 1921, p.283).

Our empirical estimates will identify the relative importance of opportunity (ability and capital) and willingness and the estimates will thereby show which of the diverging views is sustained by our findings.

Current empirical entrepreneurship research within the economics tradition[4] is not in a position to separate the effects of opportunity and willingness on entrepreneurship dynamics. The majority of studies is based on cross-sectional data and can therefore not capture these dynamics. They do not permit distinguishing factors determining survival in entrepreneurship from those that detemine the start as an entrepreneur.

Empirical (person oriented) analyses that are based on duration data and consequently in a position to capture dynamics, are scarcer and do not decompose the propensity to become self-employed into willingness and opportunity. Evans and Leighton (1989) study the individual determinants of observed switches from wage employment to entrepreneurship and compare these results to their findings concerning selection and earnings. One of their key findings is that the availability of more assets results in a larger probability of switching from wage employment to the occupational status of entrepreneur. Evans' and Jovanovic's (1989) (dynamic) study aims at determining whether liquidity constraints play a role in the decision process to become an entrepreneur (and to start at the most profitable scale). They find empirical support for binding liquidity constraints as capital assets have a positive effect on the wage worker's probability to start a business. Holtz-Eakin *et al.* (1994) study the individual determinants of business formation in order to determine whether an individual's wealth affects the probability of becoming an entrepreneur. They employ a unique sample of people who received inheritances. They find that the probability of becoming an entrepreneur rises with the size of the inheritance.

Blanchflower and Oswald (1994) study the determinants of being an entrepreneur as well as being happy as an entrepreneur. Like Holtz-Eakin *et al.* (1994), they find inheritances to be a major determinant of the occupational status of entrepreneur.

We shall contribute to this empirical research base by means of the following potential innovations: The first is the identification of the contribution of opportunity and willingness aspects in the decision process of a labor force participant to become self-employed. The survey material used by Blanchflower and Oswald (1994) indicates that there are more people who would like to become self-employed than the actual number of self-employed. Their analysis based on satisfaction data also points at serious impediments to entrepreneurship. We supply an additional instrument to verify whether indeed opportunity rather than willingness forms the bottleneck in this process.

The only 'serious impediment' however which Blanchflower and Oswald (1994) isolate is the liquidity constraint. Moreover, Evans and Jovanovic (1989), Evans and Leighton (1989) and Holtz-Eakin *et al.* (1994) all find evidence that capital constraints bind, each using different approaches. With our model, we are in a position to uncover whether there are other impediments to self-employment opportunity, keeping motivation or preferences for switching to self-employment constant. This leads to answering the question: is it possible to compensate a lack of capital by, for instance, entrepreneurial ability?

A third contribution is to evaluate what observable variables affect the probability to switch through opportunity and what variables do so through willingness. For example, if we observe within a univariate framework that married men are more inclined to become self-employed than bachelors, is this due to their superior willingness, due to more perceived opportunities or are they less willing but do they face far more opportunities?

We do not know, unless we differentiate between opportunity and willingness in an estimable model. Differentiating between these two concepts helps also to find out whether the effects of certain observable individual characteristics on willingness and opportunity are adverse.

The model

The concepts of willingness and opportunity are not (separately) observed. We only observe whether an individual becomes self-employed or not. And we know that, by definition, men who choose to become self-employed have more willingness and more opportunity than their threshold levels (arbitrarily set at zero). We also know that men who choose not to become self-employed have either less than zero willingness or less than zero opportunity or both. We need an empirical model that uses the available information (revealed preferences) as an input but is able to identify the unobserved underlying concepts as well. Poirier (1980) discusses a (joint-decision) model which meets these requirements. It is known as the bivariate probit model with partial observability[5].

Define two individual specific latent variables, I_{1i}^* representing the opportunity to switch to self-employment and I_{2i}^* reflecting willingness to become self-employed, where i distinguishes individuals. These constructs can be related to observed regressor variables Z by a linear relation:

$$I_{1i}^* = Z_{1i}\gamma_1 - \varepsilon_{1i} \tag{1}$$

$$I_{2i}^* = Z_{2i}\gamma_2 - \varepsilon_{2i} \tag{2}$$

where $Z_{ji} (j = 1,2)$ is the vector of regressors, γ_j is a vector of unknown parameters and ε_{ji} is an error term with mean 0 and (normalized) variance 1. We assume that the error terms have a bivariate standard normal distribution with correlation ρ and are independent from one observation to another. Define two (still unobserved) dummy variables

$$I_{ji} = \begin{cases} 1 & \text{if and only if } I_{ji}^* > 0 \\ 0 & \text{otherwise.} \end{cases} \tag{3}$$

Hence, I_{1i} equals one for a young man with (sufficient) opportunity to become self-employed and it equals zero for a man without (sufficient) opportunity. I_{2i} equals one if and only if a young man is (sufficiently) willing to become self-employed and is zero otherwise. We observe whether an individual becomes self-employed or not, i.e., the realization of the dichotomous variable $I_i = I_{1i} * I_{2i}$. Consequently, the probability of switching to self-employment equals:

$$\Pr(I_i = 1) = \Pr(\min[I_{1i}^*, I_{2i}^*] > 0) =$$
$$\Pr(\varepsilon_{1i} < Z_{1i}\gamma_1, \varepsilon_{2i} < Z_{2i}\gamma_2) = F(Z_{1i}\gamma_1, Z_{2i}\gamma_2, \rho) \tag{4}$$

where $F(.,.,.)$ is the standard normal cumulative distribution function. Maximum likelihood estimates of γ_1, γ_2 and ρ can be obtained by maximizing the loglikelihood function:

$$\log L = \sum_{i=1}^{N} \{I_i \log[F(Z_{1i}\gamma_1, Z_{2i}\gamma 2, \rho)] + (1 - I_i)\log[1 - F(Z_{1i}\gamma_1 Z_{2i}\gamma_2, \rho)]\}$$

where N is the number of observations.

Poirier (1980) has shown that γ_1, γ_2 and ρ are identified as long as Z_{1i} Z_{2i} do not contain exactly the same variables and the explanatory variables exhibit sufficient variation[6].

Maddala (1983, p.279) discusses an alternative model that deals with multiple decision functions and partial observability; it is nested in Poirier's model (an empirical example of this model can be found in Abowd and Farber (1982)), unlike the univariate probit model. Maddala defines Poirier's model as the joint case and the model estimated by Abowd and Farber as the sequential case. In the sequential case I_{2i}^* is a useful concept only for those observations that meet the condition $I_{1i}^* > 0$. For instance, consider the question whether a certain individual is matched to a particular job or not. Suppose the job vacancy is (exclusively) advertised in a newspaper. In order for the match to be realized the individual should first of all apply for the job and secondly be hired by the employer. Individuals who do not apply will certainly not be hired: $I_{1i}^* \leq 0$ and therefore I_{2i}^* can never take on a positive value. 'Nothing ventured, nothing gained'. This sequential case is obtained from the joint case by the parameter restriction $\rho = 0$. However, this parameter restriction is not a necessary but a sufficient condition for obtaining the sequential case, for ρ captures not only the correlation between the error terms but also between the omitted variables in both equations[7]. A following section will show which one of the two bivariate models with partial observability suits the survey data best.

The data: construction and choice of variables

The empirical model is estimated on a sample drawn from the *National Longitudinal Survey of Youth* (NLSY). The first interview amongst the approximately 12,000 respondents was held in 1979 when they were between 14 and 22 years old. Afterwards these rather extensive interviews have been repeated annually. The last year at our disposal is 1989. For homogeneity reason, we use a subsample of 3790 white males.

The observed dependent variable, which we call 'switch', takes on the value 1 in year t if a white male labor force participant, who was not self-employed in year t, reported to be self-employed[8] in year $t + 1$. It takes on the value 0 for labor force participants (excluding self-employed) in year t who have not become self-employed in year $t + 1$[9]. The observable variable 'switch' summarizes for each young man whether the required amounts of opportunity and willingness are present in a given year. Switch = 1 if and only if both conditions are met: opportunity and willingness surpass their threshold values. Table 2.1 shows that switches are rather scarce[10].

Therefore, we are forced to pool observations from the last five years. We proceeded as follows: The frequency of observation is once a year. We assume that a switch between year t and year $t+1$ (self-employed in year $t+1$ but not in t) by labor force participant i is best explained by the values of the variables applying to this individual i in year t. We sampled all individuals for whom switch = 1 in either 1985, 1986, 1987 or 1988. The year t-values were assigned to the explanatory variables of these switchers, while the observed dependent variable takes on value 1. Of the 24 individuals who switched more than once, we randomly retained one year of observation and deleted the other.[11] This left us with 294, (318–24), observations for whom switch = 1. For the remaining observations (individuals for whom switch = 0 during all periods under study), four sets of regressor values (1985, 1986, 1987 and 1988) are available. We have randomly assigned one

Table 2.1 Self–employment and switches in the NLS

Year	Labor force	Self–employed	Switches
n = 3790			
1985	3488	171	71
1986	3561	196	77
1987	3597	208	96
1988	3630	231	74
1989	3643	246	—
Total			318

of these four sets to each of these individuals. Individuals in the resulting sample, consisting of 3451 labor force participants who are not currently self-employed, are between 20 and 31 years old. We created a 'year dummy' variable that denotes the year of observation to check whether time effects exist. The procedure yields a switch percentage of

$$100\% \times \frac{294}{3451} = 8.5\%.$$

The origins of the pooled data are summarized in Table 2.2.

Apart from the time dependent explaining variables we have time independent information like parental background variables, formal education etc. We also constructed some longitudinal variables like experience in self-employment. The variables that we use in the final analysis are defined in Table 2.A1 in the Appendix. After deleting observations with missing values for at least one variable, 2244 out of 3451 observations remained. Table 2.A2 (Appendix) shows the descriptive statistics for this subsample.

Besides the differences between the groups of switchers and non-switchers, there is another interesting comparison between the switchers before they have switched and afterwards. They are shown in Table 2.3.

Switchers stem from a variety of industrial and occupational origins, though especially from the industries construction and trade (wholesale and retail) and the occupation 'craftsman'. Furthermore, 45% of the switchers remain within their own industry, 45% within their occupation and 28% remain within one industry and one occupation. On average, these (self-selected) individuals gain both in satisfaction and in rate of pay as they switch; but their mortgages increase considerably.

To identify our empirical model, and indeed to identify opportunity and willingness, we have to impose at least one exclusion restriction. We make two assumptions:

Table 2.2 Origins of pooled data

Year	Not self–employed labor force participants including switchers	Switches
1985	842	59
1986	872	75
1987	884	92
1988	853	68
Total	3451	294

Table 2.3 Switchers before and after the switch

Variable	Before	After
Industry		
Agriculture	5.7%	9.4%
Construction	25.9%	34.0%
Manufacturing	13.8%	6.7%
Transportation/communication	2.7%	5.1%
Trade	22.6%	12.5%
Business and Repair	8.8%	15.5%
Professional Services	7.7%	5.7%
Others	12.8%	11.1%
Occupation		
Professional/technical	9.1%	11.1%
Managers	9.4%	14.8%
Craftsmen, foremen	34.7%	40.7%
Operatives	12.5%	9.4%
Farmers	2.6%	2.5%
Sales	6.7%	4.7%
Service workers	7.7%	4.7%
Others	17.3%	12.1%
Job satisfaction (1–4)	3.3	3.6
(Hourly) rate of pay	$8.6	$11.6
Rate of pay's standard deviation	$4.9	$8.6
Mortgage loan	$4,500	$65,100

A   The opportunity equation is dependent on the variable 'self-employment experience measured in years' and the willingness equation on
the dummy variable 'ever been self-employed'. This is a sensible
assumption to make: the ability to borrow money ('opportunity') is

likely to depend upon previous experience as an entrepreneur. The relation between willingness and previous length of self-employment experience is less obvious, although the fact that a person has been self-employed is likely to have an impact on willingness.

B   Following Knight (1921) and more recent empirical research, we expect wealthier people to have a higher propensity to become self-employed. We assume capital to affect this propensity exclusively through opportunity and not through willingness[12].

We want to stress that the identification of 'opportunity' and 'willingness' critically depends upon the exclusion restrictions. In principle it is possible to estimate the model only under restriction A. However, in that case identification becomes very thin. Furthermore, the estimated coefficients pertaining to capital variables were not significant in the willingness equation.

With respect to the explanatory variables we make the following comments. Some of these comments relate a variable directly to 'opportunity' or 'willingness'. But keep in mind that we initially use every variable in both the 'opportunity' and the 'willingness' equation. The explanatory variables mentioned in assumptions A and B above are exceptions.

Psychological variables. Social psychologists strongly believe that a measure of internality of someone's locus-of-control beliefs is a determinant of successful entrepreneurship; of entrepreneurship ability. The Rotterscale (1966) is such a measure. The lower an individual's Rotterscale, the less internal are his locus-of-control beliefs and the more he perceives the outcome of an event as beyond his personal control. The dichotomous Rotterscale measure derived from the NLS is equal to 1 for more internal individuals.

Moreover, social psychologists (see Hornaday and Aboud 1971) have found a low religious value amongst entrepreneurs. We include a dummy for people who adhere to stricter religions (Lutheran and Methodist) to verify whether these are less willing to become self-employed. The descriptive statistics suggest to include a dummy that differentiates men that have been extremely outgoing children from the more shy ones.

Human capital variables. Human capital variables, such as age, education, or experience in self-employment are supposed to explain both opportunity and willingness to switch to self-employment. This kind of variables is included in the opportunity equation because human capital is supposed to affect the (by the lender perceived) entrepreneurial abilities. Inclusion of human capital variables in the willingness equation is justified by its expected effect on the availability and desirability of outside options. Education, self-employment experience, the respondent's age and the frequency of former job changes are included in the (final) willingness equation.

Situational variables. There are other variables which can be believed to directly influence a potential lender's decision (perhaps because they affect entrepreneurship ability) and also one's willingness to start as an entrepreneur: these are whether a person is currently unemployed, whether he works in the public sector (instead of the private sector), whether he has severe health limitations or not and whether he is married or not. An individual's central city citizenship (SMSA) might have an impact on both opportunity and willingness.

More macro-oriented indicator for the regional (and temporal) unemployment rate, included in the NLS, may directly affect the opportunity for an individual to become self-employed.

Table 2.A3 of the Appendix contains the results of the saturated model in which all explanatory variables listed above, except for the ones relating to the assumptions, were part of both equations. On the basis of this model we chose the specification presented in the next section: we imposed 6 restrictions and the likelihood-ratio statistic is 2.688. The restricted model is not rejected in favor of the saturated model.

Estimation results and inferences

Table 2.4 summarizes the final estimation results[13]. We comment on the key results reflected in this table.

Financial variables. The estimated assets coefficient does not diverge from the recent empirical findings by Evans and Jovanovic (1989), Evans and Leighton (1989), Holtz-Eakin *et al.* (1994) and Blanchflower and Oswald (1994): a lack of assets restrains the opportunity to become self-employed. But the effect turns out to be relatively small as soon as we add the dummy for real estate ownership. This variable gives scope to the possibility that the additional security that real estate owners can offer to potential lenders (in case of future bankruptcy) influences individual business formation opportunity. Black, De Meza and Jeffreys (1993) find in their more macro-oriented study that the supply of collateral significantly affects business formation in the UK. Table 2.3 showed that mortgage loans are indeed considerably increased by young men who switch to self-employment. Table 2.4 shows that ownership of collateral affects individual (perceived) business opportunities to a large extent.

Psychological variables. The Rotterscale, measuring respondents' internal-locus-of-control beliefs, has no significant effect: neither on

Table 2.4 Estimation results: bivariate probit

	Opportunity equation			Willingness equation		
Variable	Coefficient	(T value)	Derivative	Coefficient	(T value)	Derivative
Financial variables						
Assets	0.006	(1.72)	0.001			
Real estate	0.825	(2.91)	0.125			
Psychological variables						
Rotter	−0.352	(−1.70)	−0.053	0.467	(1.48)	0.028
Lutheran/				−0.277	(−1.79)	−0.017
Methodist						
Outgoing child	−0.335	(−1.40)	−0.051	1.217	(2.11)	0.073
Human capital variables						
Age	−1.686	(−2.04)	−0.255	1.741	(2.12)	0.105
Age squared/10	0.354	(2.12)	0.054	0.374	(−2.34)	−0.022
Education	−0.014	(−0.40)	−0.002	−0.031	(−0.63)	−0.002
Self–empl. exp.	0.353	(2.18)	0.053			
Dummy self exp.				0.574	(1.17)	0.034
Job changes				0.054	(3.26)	0.003
Situational variables						
Unemployed	0.116	(0.27)	0.017	−0.374	(−0.64)	−0.022
Public sector	−0.503	(−1.79)	0.076	0.632	(1.37)	0.038
Married	0.177	(0.76)	0.027	−0.526	(−1.72)	−0.032
Handicap	0.223	(1.10)	0.034			
Low unemp. rate	0.731	(2.12)	0.110			
SMSA	−0.329	(−1.29)	−0.050	0.998	(2.30)	0.060
Constant	19.653	(1.91)	2.970	−19.664	(−1.88)	−1.181
Rho	−0.757	(−3.33)				
Log–likelihood	−692.18					
Number of cases	2244					

opportunity nor on willingness. Evans and Leighton (1989) found no significant effect either of being an 'internal' individual on the transition probability. We thought of the possibility that this insignificance was due to unidentified opposing forces of internality on opportunity and willingness. However, the related variable 'outgoing as a child', which has not been implemented in this type of studies before, has a highly significant and positive effect on willingness to switch. Men who were outgoing as kids are significantly more willing to become self-employed.

The negative coefficient of the religion dummy variable in the willingness equation (taking on value one for the two strict religions) renders some weak empirical support for a low entrepreneurial interest among believers.

Variables related to self-esteem are omitted because they lacked any significance, unlike Say's predictions (1971, p 241–243).

Human capital variables. The data show that the individuals with age 24 have the worst opportunities to start a business. On the other hand individuals of 23 are the most willing to do so across all ages. The majority of young men in our sample is older than 24. Therefore, opportunity is an increasing function of age and willingness is a decreasing function of age for most individuals in our sample. Our findings with respect to age are consistent with both Evans' and Jovanovic's (1989) presumptions and with Miller's (1984) occupational choice model.

Education does not affect the probability to become self-employed; neither through willingness, nor through opportunity. Self-employment experience is a significant determinant of opportunity[14]. For the average young male in the sample, one additional year of experience in self-employment increases the probability of having the opportunity to enter self-employment again by a significant 5.3%[15]. Say (1971) already pointed at the importance of 'knowledge of business' for successful entrepreneurship. An alternative explanation for this positive effect is unobserved heterogeneity. This alternative explanation is however not sustained by a significant influence of former self-employment experience on willingness. The dummy for self-employment experience included in the willingness equation shows that the fact that one has been self-employed in the past does not affect the motivation to become self-employed again. On the one hand, individuals may have become very enthusiastic, even though they quitted; on the other hand, they may have become disillusioned.

The frequency of former job changes has a positive effect on the willingness to become self-employed. This is both consistent with a positive approach, i.e., entrepreneur types change jobs frequently because they like changes (as in Schumpeter 1934) and with the negative approach that frequent job changers are associated with displaced persons (as in Evans and Jovanovic 1989, Shapero 1975).

Situational variables. Unemployed young white males in the US do not face less opportunities and are not more willing to become self-employed in comparison to their (privately) employed counterparts[16]. Public sector workers have somewhat less opportunity to switch to self-employment than wage workers in the private sector. This result is corroborated by the finding that 71% of the founders of the fastest growing US companies got their entrepreneurial idea, which is part of the opportunity, through previous employment (Bhide 1994). This source of ideas is generally not available for public sector workers. Public sector workers are not significantly less willing to make the transition.

We predicted married men to have more opportunity to become self-employed than bachelors for husbands do have wives who either save personnel cost or supply the family with a fixed income. Moreover, we presumed married men to be less willing to engage in a (risky) entrepreneurial venture due to their family responsibility. The empirical evidence only renders (marginally) significant support for the second presumption.

A low (regional and temporal) unemployment rate, defined as a rate lower than 3%, raises the opportunity to start a business significantly: some 11% for the average sampled individual. The effect of living in SMSA is not significant on opportunity and positive on willingness. Whether an individual is physically disabled or not does not seem to influence his opportunities to start a business.

By means of alternative specifications of the opportunity and willingness equations, we found some additional results: the interview year that corresponds to each individual selected in the sample is not significant in explaining opportunity and willingness. Parental background (measured as father's and mother's education level, father's occupation and language usage at home) does not add anything to the explanation either. Brockhaus' finding (1980) that extremely unsatisfied wage workers are pushed into self-employment is not sustained by our data either: low reported job satisfaction did not affect willingness to become self-employed.

Table 2.4 demonstrates ρ to be negative and significant. Apparently the error terms of the willingness and opportunity equations are correlated. Consequently, our model differs significantly from the nested bivariate probit model with partial observability: the sequential case.

Figure 2.1 shows what kind of distribution within the willingness and opportunity region the estimates generate.

Apparently, there are far more individuals willing to become self-employed than individuals who have an opportunity. The number of entrepreneurial starts would be almost seven times as high if everyone who wishes to start had the opportunity to do so. This finding is consistent with research results by Blanchflower and Oswald (1994): there are more individuals who wish to switch to self-employment than the actual number of switchers. This result is also consistent with the several stories about capital restrictions and higher satisfaction amongst self-employed (Blanchflower and Oswald 1994).

Table 2.5 shows which percentage of individuals, self-employed and employed in reality, belongs to each of the quadrants in Figure 2.1.

In order to compare our study to others, we have also estimated a univariate probit with identical independent variables. This is not nested in the bivariate model. However, we have also estimated which percentage of actual self-employed people is predicted by this model to be self-

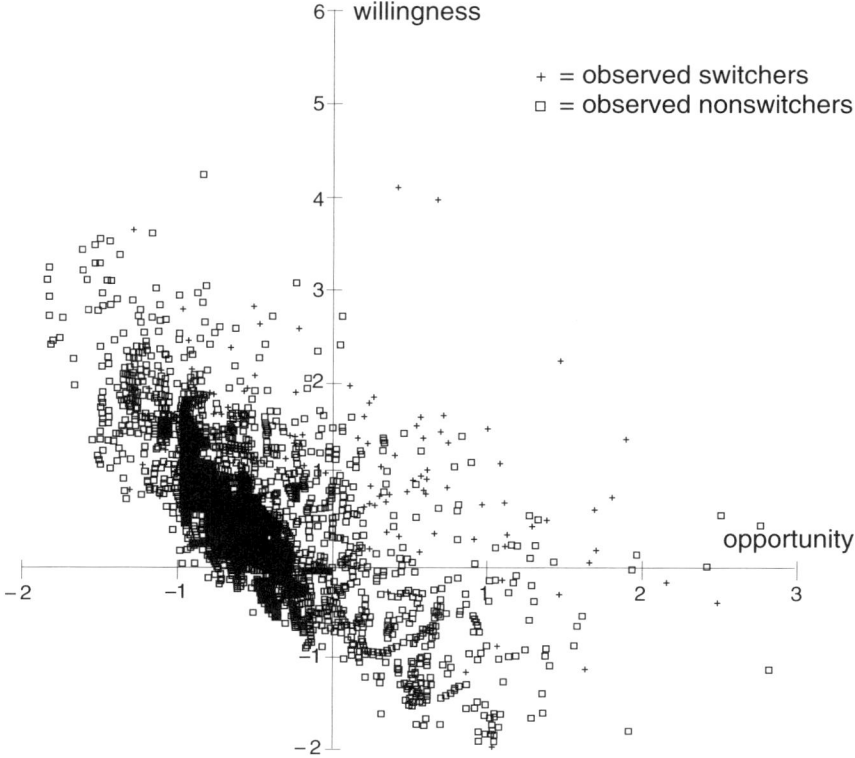

Figure 2.1 Distribution of observations by imputed opportunity and willingness.

employed. The resulting percentage is 10.6%, much lower than the comparable estimate of 28% resulting from the bivariate approach. This is some indicator that the bivariate approach is superior indeed. Univariate probit estimation results are shown in table 2.6.

The parameter estimates themselves differ from the bivariate approach with respect to a number of variables. The effect of the stricter religions is significant here: adhering to one of the stricter religions goes together with a significant lower probability to switch to self-employment. The coefficient of the bivalent variable that indicates whether one has self-employment experience or not has become significant, besides self-employment experience measured in years. Higher educated young men have a significant lower probability to switch to self-employment. The coefficient for the dummy variable that indicates whether a young man is married or not is significantly negative. This is consistent with both the findings by Evans and Jovanovic (1989) and Evans and Leighton (1989).

Our decomposition of effects is not easily derived from this aggregate

Table 2.5 Estimated percentages in each of the quadrants in Figure 2.1

Quadrant	Total	Self–employed	Employed
Willingness > 0, Opportunity > 0	7.7%	28.0%	5.0%
Willingness < = 0, Opportunity > 0	12.3%	6.4%	13.1%
Willingness > 0, Opportunity < = 0	69.0%	61.7%	69.9%
Willingness < = 0, Opportunity < = 0	11.0%	3.8%	12.0%

Table 2.6 Estimation results: unvariate probit

Variable	Coefficient	(T value)	Derivative
Financial variables			
Assets	0.007	(2.22)	0.001
Real estate	0.739	(5.99)	0.128
Psychological variables			
Rotter	−0.075	(−0.86)	−0.012
Lutheran/Methodist	−0.202	(−1.95)	−0.035
Outgoing child	0.302	(2.82)	0.052
Human capital variables			
Age	−0.156	(−0.64)	−0.027
Age squared/10	0.028	(0.58)	0.005
Education	−0.037	(−2.24)	−0.006
Self–empl. exp.	0.218	(2.99)	0.037
Dummy self exp.	0.520	(3.35)	0.089
Job changes	0.038	(4.29)	0.006
Situational variables			
Unemployed	−0.124	(−0.89)	−0.021
Public sector	−0.107	(−0.70)	−0.018
Married	−0.198	(−2.44)	−0.034
Handicap	0.180	(0.90)	0.030
Low unemp. rate	0.755	(2.26)	0.129
SMSA	0.175	(1.62)	0.030
Constant	0.830	(0.27)	0.142
Log–likelihood	−707.53		
Number of cases	2244		

approach by inspection: some surprises remain. This was also the case in the application of Abowd and Farber (1982). Meant as an instrument to decompose regressor effects on the propensity to start as an entrepreneur into effects on opportunity and willingness, the bivariate approach is also a

Table 2.7 Simulated probabilities to become self–employed

Individual	Pr(switch)	Difference with ref. ind.	(T value)
Reference	0.075		
Financial variable			
Real Estate	0.302	0.227	(3.62)
Assets + σ	0.102	0.027	(1.65)
Assets – σ	0.071	–0.004	(–1.83)
Psychological variable			
Outgoing as a kid	0.097	0.022	(0.81)
Human capital variable			
Self–empl. exp. + σ	0.387	0.312	(3.00)
Situational variable			
Low unemp. rate	0.269	0.194	(1.08)

valid instrument to find significant effects that are hidden as insignificant effects in the aggregate.

Inferences. What can we infer from our estimation results? To investigate this, we compare the simulated probability to become self-employed of a reference individual with this probability of an individual who deviates from the reference one with respect to one variable only. The reference individual is defined as having average values for continuous variables and the modal outcome for categorical variables.

The table shows the differences in probability due to changes in one of the independent variables in each category. This difference is large (and significant) if the reference individual suddenly becomes an owner of real estate: this renders a probability difference of almost 23%. A reference individual who faces a capital increase of one standard deviation, experiences a probability increase of 2.7% only (σ = $11,250). Both self-employment experience (measured in years) and a low regional unemployment rate (dummy variable) can compensate for a lack of assets and real estate: they both strongly increase the probability to become self-employed, by 31% and 19% respectively.

Policy implications. What can be learnt from our results by institutions with a mission to increase the US number of young starters in entrepreneurship? As we have obviously revealed opportunity rather than willingness to be the bottleneck, opportunity should be improved by manipulating its instruments.

- The government should take a measure to improve borrowing facilities for starters, as banks and participation companies seem to undersupply this market. The government has a valid incentive to create, for instance, a 'risk fund', since positive external effects of entrepreneurship (economic growth and less unemployment) are obviously present.
- The fact that self-employment experience may serve as a substitute for capital and/or collateral suggests that the United States banks and participation companies believe that entrepreneurship can be learned through experience[17]. Courses that really simulate the entrepreneurial venture should be organized. A qualification from such a course should lead to 'easier borrowing' comparable to the borrowing probabilities of 'experienced starters'. For instance, by having the 'risk fund' come within reach only for 'course graduates'.
- It appears that authorities striving after low unemployment rates serve entrepreneurship opportunities as well. However, authorities want to reduce unemployment by stimulating entrepreneurship and a circle results. Anyhow, starting as an entrepreneur appears to be an upswing activity: entrepreneurship start-ups are stimulated by a low (regional) unemployment rate.

Conclusions

Individuals whom we observe to start as entrepreneurs have not only perceived enough opportunity to do so, they also have perceived this career option as the most attractive one. In our words, they have the opportunity and willingness to become self-employed. Individuals whom we observe not to switch to self-employment are either not willing or do not face the opportunity or both. This paper separates the unobserved concepts of opportunity and willingness for young white male Americans. We assume that opportunity and willingness can be explained by a (partly distinct) set of observed explanatory variables. Opportunity includes variables that are observed equivalents for both capital and entrepreneurial ability, given economic conditions. It is argued that the opportunity to start as an entrepreneur is positively present for men having sufficient assets. If not, capital lenders should be convinced that the potential lender has enough entrepreneurial ability. Whereas opportunity and willingness are both necessary conditions (and together sufficient) to become entrepreneur, capital and ability are assumed to be potential substitutes for meeting the necessary opportunity condition.

A bivariate model with partial observability is estimated on a subsample of the National Longitudinal Survey of Youth. The annual data are pooled in a particular way to obtain a sufficient number of observed switches. The resulting sample includes 264 switches. The key empirical results are:

- By far the majority of young men in the US are willing to become self-employed. Given the opportunity to anyone, the realized amount of switchers would multiply by seven. Opportunity evidently forms the bottleneck in the individual decision process.
- Opportunity is largely determined by capital requirements. These in turn are primarily dependent on real estate ownership. The opportunity for entrepreneurship is also affected by the regional unemployment rate and by entrepreneurial ability, mainly through self-employment experience and age. Willingness is positively affected by outgoingness, by the number of job changes and by one's central citizenship (SMSA). Older people (as of 23) are less and less willing to become self-employed. Religious and or married people have a lower probability to be willing to become self-employed, though not very significantly so. Other variables are insignificant.
- Entrepreneurial ability serves to a certain extent as a substitute for capital requirements. The kind of entrepreneurial ability that increases the opportunity to start largely coincides with entrepreneurship experience.
- As capital seems to be a necessary requirement for becoming self-employed (for starters without experience in entrepreneurship) and since willingness is no constraining factor, we conclude that the US evidence supports Knight's ideas. A first start in entrepreneurship requires assets or collateral. This finding, pointing at binding capital constraints, is in accordance with other empirical estimates by Evans and Jovanovic (1989), Evans and Leighton (1989), Blanchflower and Oswald (1994) and Holtz-Eakin *et al.* (1994). However, the additional finding that experience in entrepreneurship results in a perceived entrepreneurial ability that can serve as a substitute for own capital or real estate is in accordance with the related ideas of Say. Schumpeter's vision is empirically not supported: motivational factors appear not to be the prime constraints in the individual supply of entrepreneurship.

Future research should demonstrate the individual determinants of lasting and successful entrepreneurship for the subsample of individuals that have shown to be willing and in a position to start as an entrepreneur.

Appendix

Table 2.A1 Definition of the variables selected

Variable	Definition
Switch	Dependent variable; =1 if respondent switches from wage employment or unemployment to self–employment
Assets	Total amount of assets (in $1,000)
Real estate	Dummy: =1 if respondent owns some real estate
Rotter	Dummy: =1 if respondent feels: 'direction of life is in control'
Lutheran or Methodist	Dummy: =1 if respondent's religion is Lutheran or Methodist
Outgoing child	Dummy:= 1 if respondent reports to have been an extremely outgoing child
Age	Respondent's age (in years)
Education	Number of years of formal education
Labor exp.	Years of total labor experience
Self–empl. exp.	Years of self–employment experience
Dummy self exp.	Dummy: =1 if resp. has self–employment experience
Job changes	Reported number of different jobs ever had
Unemployed	Dummy: =1 if respondent is unemployed
Public sector	Dummy: =1 if respondent is public sector worker
Married	Dummy: =1 if respondent is married
Handicap	Dummy: =1 if respondent has health limitations
Low unemp. rate	Dummy: =1 if regional unemployment rate is less than 3%
SMSA	Dummy: =1 if respondent lives in SMSA, central city

Table 2.A2 Descriptive statistics

Variable	Mean switchers	(s.d.)	Mean	(s.d.) Non–switchers	Mean all	(s.d.)
Observations	264			1980	2244	
Switch					0.118	(0.32)
Assets	6.24	(25.33)	3.20	(7.60)	3.56	(11.28)
Real estate	0.19	(0.39)	0.051	(0.22)	0.066	(0.25)
Rotter	0.75	(0.44)	0.77	(0.42)	0.76	(0.42)
Lutheran or Methodist	0.14	(0.34)	0.19	(0.39)	0.18	(0.39)
Outgoing child	0.17	(0.38)	0.10	(0.30)	0.11	(0.31)
Age	25.46	(2.65)	25.32	(2.61)	25.34	(2.62)
Education	12.59	(2.46)	12.79	(2.45)	12.77	(2.45)
Self–empl. exp.	0.61	(1.16)	0.12	(0.49)	0.17	(0.63)
Dummy self exp.	0.32	(0.47)	0.079	(0.27)	0.11	(0.31)
Job changes	8.24	(4.87)	6.69	(3.88)	6.87	(4.03)
Unemployed	0.072	(0.26)	0.084	(0.28)	0.082	(0.28)
Public sector	0.053	(0.22)	0.085	(0.28)	0.081	(0.27)
Married	0.37	(0.48)	0.44	(0.50)	0.43	(0.50)
Handicap	0.038	(0.19)	0.029	(0.17)	0.030	(0.17)
Low unemp. rate	0.019	(0.14)	0.006	(0.08)	0.008	(0.09)
SMSA	0.16	(0.37)	0.11	(0.31)	0.12	(0.32)

Table 2.A3 Estimation results of the saturated model. bivariate probit

Variable	Opportunity equation			Willingness equation		
	Coefficient	(T value)	Derivative	Coefficient	(T value)	Derivative
Financial variables						
Assets	0.007	(1.68)	0.000			
Real Estate	0.864	(2.85)	0.123			
Psychological variables						
Rotter	−0.374	(−1.17)	−0.053	0.526	(1.08)	0.029
Lutheran/ Methodist	−0.053	(−0.66)	−0.007	−0.228	(−0.25)	−0.013
Outgoing child	−0.031	(−0.33)	−0.044	1.328	(1.46)	0.073
Human capital variables						
Age	−1.605	(−1.60)	−0.228	1.780	(1.81)	0.098
Age squared/10	0.340	(1.66)	0.048	−0.382	(−1.92)	0.021
Education	−0.023	(−0.36)	−0.003	−0.024	(−0.30)	−0.001
Labor exp.	−0.022	(−0.26)	−0.003	−0.010	(−0.08)	−0.000
Self-empl. exp.	0.362	(1.82)	0.051			
Dummy self exp.				0.635	(0.95)	0.035
Job changes	0.011	(0.02)	0.002	0.045	(1.44)	0.002
Situational variables						
Unemployed	0.178	(0.57)	0.025	−0.056	(−0.65)	−0.031
Public sector	−0.435	(−1.21)	−0.062	0.547	(0.98)	0.030
Married	0.139	(0.45)	0.020	−0.509	(−0.80)	−0.028
Handicap	0.091	(0.12)	0.013	0.200	(0.18)	0.011
Low unemp. rate	0.316	(0.39)	0.045	0.777	(0.40)	0.043
SMSA	−0.302	(−1.08)	−0.043	1.032	(1.72)	0.057
Constant	18.647	(1.49)	2.648	20.116	(−1.54)	−1.108
Rho	−0.679	(−1.88)				
Log–likelihood	−690.84					
Number of cases	2244					

Notes

1   Drs and Dr, Tinbergen Institute and Departments of Economics of the University of Amsterdam, Roetersstraat 11, 1018 WB Amsterdam, The Netherlands. We should like to thank Mars Cramer, Joop Hartog, Hessel Oosterbeek, Andrew Oswald and Gerard Van Den Berg for their helpful comments.

2   Extensive discussions on the various existing theoretical notions can be found in Casson (1991), Barreto (1989) and Hébert and Link (1988).

3   Another explanation for substitutability could be that the 'smarter entrepreneurs' need less capital for a venture. In Evans and Jovanovic (1989) capital and entrepreneurial ability are assumed to be positively correlated; a test reveals a significant negative correlation.

4   An overview is found in Van Praag (1994).

5   Although this model is well known in the econometric literature, we have not encountered an empirical application thus far. Maddala (1983), who describes this model extensively, does not mention an empirical application either.

6   Moreover, the exogenous variables must take on at least as many distinct data configurations as there are unknown parameters in the model, indicating that if a model contains a number of variables taking on many different values, no identification problems will occur (cf Poirier, 1980, p215).

7   We thank Gerard Van den Berg who revealed this point to us.

8   Individuals who start incorporated businesses are included.

9   Switch is probably an underestimate of the real fraction of starters, because self-employment spells that started but ended between interviews are not counted.

10   The reason why the table starts in 1985 will be given in due course.

11   The way we have defined a 'switch' renders a maximum of two switches per individual in the four subsequent observations. The number of men who switched two times is very small. It hardly makes sense to treat double switches as a separate state, consequently we chose to randomly select one of the switches. Due to the correlation of the error terms we can not treat a double switcher as two observations.

12   We disregard the possibility that wealthier people might have lower absolute risk aversion, making them more willing to become self-employed (as in Kihlstrom and Laffont 1979, and Kanbur 1979).

13   The estimates shown are obtained in Gauss. We used Limdep to verify the results. Differences are negligible. The reported t-values are based on White's heteroskedastic consistent estimate of the covariance matrix.

14   Self-employment experience is gathered before 1985 (but as of 1979). The 24 observations that have switched twice may also have gathered this experience afterwards, depending on whether their first or second switch has randomly been selected.

15   The measurement of this variable is not perfect: we increased self-employment experience by the number of weeks between the current and previous interview divided by 52 whenever one reported to be self-employed.

16   We also included 'unemployment experience' in the relationships and found that this does not affect willingness nor opportunity. Surveys on the (ambiguous) relation between unemployment and self-employment can be found in Meager (1992) and Storey (1991).

17   Or that they can screen for superior entrepreneurship qualities by means of this indicator if they believe that its positive effect is due to unobserved heterogeneity.

References

Abowd J.M. and H.S. Farber (1982). Job queues and the union status of workers. *Industrial and Labour Review. 35: 354–367.*

Barreto, H. (1989). *The entrepreneur in economic theory. Disappearance and explanation.* London: Routledge.

Bhide, A. (1994). How Entrepreneurs Craft Strategies That Work, *Harvard Business Review.* 150–161.

Black, J, D. de Meza and D.Jeffreys (1993). House prices, the supply of collateral and the enterprise economy, working paper, University of Exeter.

Blanchflower, D.G. and A.J. Oswald (1994). What makes an entrepreneur? Evidence on Inheritances and Capital Constraints, *Journal of Labor Economics.* forthcoming.

Brockhaus, R.H., Sr. (1980). The effect of job dissatisfaction on the decision to start a business, *Journal of Small Business Management 18.*

Casson, M. (1991). *The entrepreneur. an economic theory.* Worcester: Billing & Sons Ltd.

De Wit, G. (1993). Models of self-employment in a competitive market, *Journal of Economic Surveys.* 7: 367–397.

Evans, D.S. and L.S. Leighton (1989). Some empirical aspects of entrepreneurship, *American Economic Review.* 79: 519–535.

Evans, D.S. and B. Jovanovic (1989). An estimated model of entrepreneurial choice under liquidity constraints, *Journal of Political Economy.* 97: 808–827.

Hébert, R.F. and A.N. Link (1988). *The Entrepreneur, Mainstream Views* and *Radical Critiques.* New York: Praeger.

Holtz-Eakin, D.D. Joulfaian and H.S. Rosen (1994). Entrepreneurial decisions and liquidity constraints, *Rand Journal of Economics.* 25: 334–347.

Hornaday, J.A. and J. Aboud (1971). Characteristics of successful entrepreneurs, *Personnel Psychology 24.*

Kanbur S.M. (1979). Of risktaking and the personal distribution of income, *Journal of Political Economy.* 87: 760–797.

Kihlstrom, R.K and J.J. Laffont (1979). A general equilibrium entrepreneurial theory of new firm formation based on risk aversion, *Journal of Political Economy.* 87: 304–316.

Knight F.H. (1921). *Risk, Uncertainty and Profit.* In: G.I. Stigler (ed.) (1971), Chicago: University Press of Chicago.

Leroy, S.F. and L.D. Singell Jr. (1987). Knight on risk and uncertainty, *Journal of Political Economy.* 95: 394–406.

Maddala, G.S. (1983). *Limited-dependent and qualitative variables in econometrics.* Cambridge University.

Marshall, A. (1930). *Principles of Economics.* London: Macmillan and Co., limited, (first edition 1890).

Meager, N. (1992). Does unemployment lead to self-employment?, *Small Business Economics.* 4: 87–103.

Miller, R.A. (1984). Job matching and occupational choice. *Journal of Political Economy.* 92: 1086–1120.

Poirier, D.J. (1980). Partial observability in bivariate probit models, *Journal of Econometrics.* 12: 209–217.

Rotter, J.B. (1966). Generalized Expectancies for Internal vs. External Control of Reinforcement, in: *Psychological Monographs:* General and Applied, whole 609 80, No 1 (1966).

Say, J-B. (1971). *A treatise on political economy or the production, distribution and consumption of wealth.* New York: Augustus M. Kelley Publishers, (first edition 1803).

Schumpeter, J. (1934). *The theory of economic development.* Cambridge Mass: Harvard University Press.

Shapero, A. (1975). The displaced. uncomfortable entrepreneur, *Psychology Today.* 9: 83 – 88.

Storey D.J. (1991). The birth of new firms – does unemployment matter? A review of the evidence, *Small Business Economics.* 3: 167–178.

Van Praag, C.M. (1994). Determinants of self-employment duration: a competing risks model, Discussion Paper, Tinbergen Institute, Amsterdam, The Netherlands, T1 94–115.

3

New Business Starts and Economic Activity: An Empirical Investigation

Richard Highfield and Robert Smiley[1]

Source: *International Journal of Industrial Organisation* 5 (1987), 51–66.

This paper identifies two types of factors that influence the rate of creation of new firms; macroeconomic and microeconomic. The macroeconomic climate that appears to be most conducive to the formation of small businesses is what might loosely be called sluggish. Lower rates of growth of GNP, lower inflation rates, and greater growth in the unemployment rate were followed by increases in the rate of new incorporations. The cross-sectional or micro-economic factors which lead to higher rates of entry into different industries include higher growth rates in sales, higher research and development intensity, and higher profit rates. We do not find any of the traditional barriers to entry to be related to the rate of new firm creation.

Introduction

What factors influence the rate of the new business starts? This question has been studied in some detail for other economies such as Sweden [Hause and DuRietz (1984)], and for sectors of the U.S. economy such as food [MacDonald (1986)], but never for the U.S. economy as a whole and never for a long period of time. This study presents the analysis of factors influencing the rate of new business starts in a large number of industries, and over a long period of time for the U.S. economy. A number of difficult methodological issues are confronted, and several improvements in empirical estimation techniques are presented.

The importance of understanding the determinants of new business activity should be obvious. An understanding of the dynamics of entry requires an understanding of the determinants of new firm creation as well as entry by existing firms [Caves and Porter (1977)]. Although there are some disputes about the exact numbers, recent empirical work indicates that new small business starts account for a large proportion of new job creation [Birch (1981)]. Furthermore, small business accounts for a disproportionately large amount of technical innovation [Scherer (1980, pp. 407–438)]. Finally, if economic policy makers should want to influence the rate of new business starts, they must first understand the interrelationships between policy variables and this rate.

In the next section we present an analysis of the aggregate rate of new business starts (the new incorporations series) for the period 1947–1984. The next section presents an analysis of the determinants of new business starts across four-digit industries over the time period 1976–1981. A short conclusion follows.

Time series analysis of new firm startups

One of the potentially confounding problems in cross-sectional industry studies of economic phenomena like entry is the existence of economy-wide factors that can affect behavior in all industries. The preferred method of examining such effects would be analysis of a pooled cross-section-time-series data set covering a sufficient number of data periods to allow modelling and testing of both the macro and industry-specific factors determining entry. In the present case our industry data are available for three two-year periods only, making inference regarding macro effects a practical impossibility. As an alternative we will present a basic analysis of economy-wide effects in this section using aggregate macro data, and will turn to the examination of industry-specific effects in the following section.

Our economy-wide entry variable to be explained is the quarterly growth rate (seasonally adjusted at annual rates) of the number of new US incorporations over the period 1948 to 1984.[2] We use the growth rate in preference to the levels for two reasons. The first is that the number of new incorporations displays a strong upward trend that is quite similar to that of most real activity measures, and it is the deviations from this trend that are of interest. The second reason is a statistical one. The growth rate is approximately stationary[3] over the period studied and our techniques rely on the assumption of stationarity.

For potential explanatory variables we have gathered corresponding time series data on several macro variables which might reasonably be related to the rate of entry of new firms. These are the growth rate of real GNP, the growth rate of real expenditures on new plant and equipment,[4] the change in the unemployment rate, the inflation rate[5] and the real interest rate.[6] Again, all of these series are approximately stationary.

What type of business climate leads to a greater increase in the rate of formation of new firms? At least two different macroeconomic scenarios can be constructed that could lead to increases in new business activity. In a 'naive forecasting' scenario, individuals look at present rates of change and levels of important macroeconomic variables and forecast that these trends will continue. Further, individuals would prefer to start new business when the economy is robust. In this case, high rates of growth of new incorporations would accompany (or would lag by several quarters, since the process of incorporation requires some time) high rates of real GNP growth, low real interest rates, high inflation rates, high new plant and equipment expenditure growth and decreases in the unemployment rate.

An alternative scenario, with very different results, might be called an 'opportunistic' scenario. In this case entrepreneurs begin new business ventures when they sense an opportunity or vacuum in current economic activity. For example, a decrease in expenditures on new plant and equipment might present an opportunity or niche into which a new firm, with a newly constructed plant, might move. Similarly an increasing unemployment rate might indicate a lower cost of attracting qualified workers to a new venture, or even a lower opportunity cost of an entrepreneur's own salary foregone. In this scenario we would also expect low growth rates of real GNP, low rates of inflation, and high real interest rates to lead to increases in the rate of formation of new firms. 'Opportunity' and 'necessity' often have similar symptoms.

In our search for causal determinants of entry at the economy-wide level we will propose no structural model. Rather we will employ methods of statistical time series analysis and engage in a simple forecasting experiment. The concept is that models that incorporate data on causal factors should be able to forecast the growth of entry more accurately than models that do not. This is Granger's (1969) notion of causality, and it is based on the simple (albeit restrictive)[7] rule that the future cannot cause the past. It has been implemented extensively in macroeconomic studies on the role of money[8] and by Ashley, Granger and Schmalensee (1980) to examine the relationship between advertising and consumption.

As a first step in our analysis we have tabulated the sample cross-correlations between our new incorporation growth time series and our macro data series. The cross-correlation between two stationary data series is

$$\rho_{xy} = \text{cov}(Y_{t+k}, X_t) / \left[\text{var}(X_t) \, \text{var}(Y_t) \right]^{\frac{1}{2}} \tag{1}$$

i.e., $\rho_{xy}(k)$ is the correlation between Y and X, k periods earlier in time. In general $\rho_{xy}(k) \neq \rho_{yx}(-k)$. If X 'causes' Y but Y does not cause X we expect to find $\rho_{yx}(k) = 0$ for $k \leq -1$ (Y uncorrelated with future X's) but we also expect to find $\rho_{yx}(k) \neq 0$ for some $k \geq 0$ (Y correlated with past X's).

Sample estimates of (1) were calculated according to Box and Jenkins (1976) and are tabulated in Table 3.1 for data for the period 1948:3 through 1977:4. The remaining data were held back for a forecasting test discussed below. The picture painted is an interesting one. The growth rate of new incorporations is negatively correlated with measures of real activity in the prior year (real GNP and new plant expenditure growth) and positively correlated with these measures in the succeeding year.[9] The same picture is apparent in the cross correlations with the change in the unemployment rate

Table 3.1 Sample cross correlations of *DLINC* with various macro variables; period 1948:3 to 1977:4[a]

	k	$SE(\hat{\rho}(k))$	Real GNP growth $\hat{\rho}(k)$	Real P&E exp. growth $\hat{\rho}(k)$	Unemp. rate changes $\hat{\rho}(k)$	Real int. rate $\hat{\rho}(k)$	Inflation $\hat{\rho}(k)$
Macro	−12	0.10	0.04	−0.05	−0.08	−0.08	0.05
variables	−11	0.10	0.04	−0.14	−0.01	−0.06	0.05
lagging	−10	0.10	−0.09	−0.24[b]	0.15	0.00	0.03
incorpora-	−9	0.10	−0.22[b]	−0.19	0.27[b]	0.16	−0.08
tion	−8	0.10	−0.30[b]	−0.09	0.23[b]	0.16	−0.09
growth	−7	0.10	−0.20	−0.03	0.18	0.10	−0.01
	−6	0.09	−0.18	0.09	0.07	0.04	0.05
	−5	0.09	−0.02	0.22[b]	0.01	0.07	0.04
	−4	0.09	−0.05	0.29[b]	−0.07	−0.09	0.15
	−3	0.09	0.13	0.31[b]	−0.21[b]	−0.13	0.16
	−2	0.09	0.23[b]	0.34[b]	−0.44[b]	−0.07	0.09
	−1	0.09	0.34[b]	0.11	−0.43[b]	−0.08	0.07
	0	0.09	0.25[b]	−0.13	−0.16	0.11	−0.14
Macro	1	0.09	0.00	−0.31[b]	0.25[b]	0.19[b]	−0.22[b]
variables	2	0.09	−0.31[b]	0.40[b]	0.45[b]	0.02	−0.09
leading	3	0.09	−0.32[b]	−0.44[b]	0.47[b]	0.09	−0.10
incorpora-	4	0.09	−0.30[b]	−0.10	0.21[b]	−0.02	0.04
tion	5	0.09	−0.07	0.01	−0.06	−0.11	0.15
growth	6	0.09	0.03	0.03	−0.06	−0.14	0.20[b]
	7	0.10	0.04	0.11	−0.07	−0.14	0.22[b]
	8	0.10	−0.03	0.04	−0.04	−0.16	0.23[b]
	9	0.10	−0.03	0.03	−0.01	−0.12	0.19
	10	0.10	−0.10	0.11	−0.07	0.01	0.07
	11	0.10	0.04	0.20	−0.08	−0.02	0.03
	12	0.10	0.06	0.11	−0.06	−0.04	0.05

[a] The large sample standard error of $\hat{\rho}(k)$ is $1/\sqrt{n-k}$, here $n = 118$.
[b] $\hat{\rho}(k)$ is greater than two standard deviations from zero.

and, somewhat weakly, with the real interest rate. Growth in the incorporation rate is positively associated with growing unemployment rates and higher real interest rates in the preceding year and with falling unemployment and lower interest rates in succeeding years. The cross-correlations with the inflation rate also indicate that periods of incorporation growth follow periods of lower inflation. Taken at face value, these results are generally consistent with the 'opportunistic' scenario. Firms may enter to fill the vacuum created by sluggish economic activity, with the result being that activity increases in later periods.[10]

The notion that slowing real activity causes incorporation growth should, however, not be accepted too readily. The fact that incorporation growth is correlated with real variables at both leads and lags suggests that these variables may in fact be jointly determined. This possibility was examined by computing the cross-correlations between the residuals from an ARMA model for each of the macro variables and the variable resulting when the incorporations series is filtered by the same model.[11] This procedure is designed to remove from the incorporation series any systematic movement that might be induced by the macro variable. If the remaining variation is still correlated at leads but uncorrelated at lags of the macro variable then a tentative inference of causality is possible. Only the inflation rate appears to lead (with the same signs as above) but not lag. Knowledge of the inflation rate may help increase the accuracy of forecasts of the incorporation growth rate, but the reverse is not expected to be true.

As was mentioned at the beginning of this section, one test of the notion that the macro variables discussed above play a role in determining incorporation growth is the predictive test. Indeed Ansley (1977) and Ashley, Granger and Schmalensee (1980) have argued quite convincingly that cross-correlation analysis is better viewed as a tool for identifying forecasting models (in the sense that a time series analyst identifies the best forecasting model from within a class of possible models) and that post-sample forecasting tests are more appropriate for investigating causality. Here some simple models for forecasting incorporation growth have been devised. The first, which can be considered a benchmark, is a univariate ARMA model for incorporation growth. Such a model will set a level of predictive accuracy that can be expected from forecasting this variable on the basis of its own past alone. Of course, since an ARMA model is a purely statistical model, the form of the model chosen may depend indirectly on all factors determining incorporation growth.[12] To the extent that the factors we have chosen to focus on here are particularly important in determining entry, we would expect to improve upon the performance of the ARMA model.

The evidence from a simple forecasting competition is presented in Table 3.2. One-step-ahead out-of-sample forecasts of the growth rate of incorporations were made for the 28 quarters 1978:1 through 1984:4 using several simple forecasting models.[13] The results of the ARMA forecasts are given on line 1 of the table. The competing models attempted are a univariate transfer function model involving the inflation rate as an exogenous explanatory variable (an idea supported by the cross-correlation analysis above), three separate bivariate ARMA models relating incorporation growth to real GNP growth, the change in the unemployment rate and new plant and equipment expenditure growth, and a vector autoregression involving all five variables. Only the transfer function model involving the inflation rate reflects a strict causal ordering. All of the other models

Table 3.2 Summary of forecasting results; one-step-ahead out-of-sample forecasts| of incorporation growth for the period 1978:1 through 1984:4.

Forecasting model	Mean absolute forecast error	Root mean squared forecast error
1. Univariate ARMA model	12.05	14.78
2. Transfer function model input variable: inflation rate	11.85	14.64
3. Bivariate ARMA model incorporation growth and real GNP growth	11.37	14.67
4. Bivariate ARMA model incorporation growth and unemployment rate changes	11.03	14.48
5. Bivariate ARMA model incorporation growth and growth in new plant and equipment expenditures	12.41	16.17
6. Vector autoregression involving incorporation growth, inflation, real GNP growth, unemployment rate changes and growth in new plant and equipment expenditures	11.29	14.93

assume joint causation (i.e., they include no exogeneity restrictions).[14] No model relating the real interest rate and incorporation growth was suggested by our analysis.

As seen, none of the models achieves dramatic improvements over the univariate model for incorporation growth. The best model, the bivariate ARMA model with unemployment rate changes, achieves about a 9 per cent reduction in mean absolute forecast error, but a somewhat smaller reduction in root mean squared error, indicating the presence of some large forecasting errors. The second best model, the bivariate ARMA model with real GNP growth, achieves a 6.4 per cent reduction in mean absolute forecast error, and also reduces the root mean squared error by a smaller amount. The coefficients in both models imply the same relationship as indicated by the cross-correlation results. Increases in the unemployment rate and decreases in real GNP growth lead increases in incorporation growth. While a tentative causal relationship appeared in the cross-correlation analysis of the inflation rate, the forecasting improvement achieved by the transfer function model is quite slight.

Although the evidence is by no means overwhelming, the business climate apparently most hospitable to new firm incorporation has not been a robust one: sluggish economic growth seems more likely to spur creation of new firms. The magnitude of the forecasting improvements indicates, however, that most of the variation in growth in incorporations remains unexplained and that none of the macro variables appears to be strongly causal in the sense of Granger. Policy implications are not strong in this setting. Certainly few would suggest the bizarre policy of slowing the economy down in order to create a better climate for new business. What is apparent, however, is an indication that higher incorporation growth goes hand in hand with an economy changing from the worse to the better. This might suggest that further incentives for new business formation could speed recoveries, but we have made no attempt to examine causality in this direction.

Entry determinants at the micro level – cross-sectional relationships

The factors affecting the rate of entry by new firms into different industries are discussed in this section. The section is organized as follows: a model of the entry process is presented first, followed by a discussion of the measurement of the variables. The empirical results are presented last.

A model of entry

The rate of entry E_{it} by new firms into industry i in time period t is modelled as a function of the predicted future profit rate Π_{it} and the entry forestalling profit rate Π_{it}^{N},

$$E_{it} = f\left(\Pi_{it} - \Pi_{it}^{N}\right) + \mu, \tag{2}$$

where

$f(0) = 0$ by the definition of entry forestalling,
$\Pi_{it} = \Pi(\Pi_{it}^{PAST}, GROWTH, RDEXP)$,
$P_{it}^{N} = \Pi^{N} ADS, EXCAPEXP, MESMKT, CAPREQ, RISK, CONC, RDEXP)$,
$\mu = $ all entry orthogonal to excess profits.
Π_{it}^{PAST}: past profit rates in industry i,
GROWTH: past sales growth,
RDEXP: research and development expenditures as a percentage of sales,
ADS: advertising expenditures as a percentage of sales,
MESMKT: the ratio of the plant size necessary to achieve minimum efficient scale, to the size of the market,
CAPREQ: the investment necessary to build a plant of minimum efficient scale,
CAPEXP: new capital expenditures as a percentage of net plant,
EXCAPEXP: CAPEXP – GROWTH,
RISK: a measure of the risk of entry,
CONC: the four firm concentration ratio.

Discussion

Π_{it}: *Predicted post-entry profits are a positive function* (Π) of past profits, growth in sales and research and development expenditures. We will test different functional forms for the relationship between past and predicted future profit rates in the paper, but we would expect the overall relationship to be positive. We would expect future profits to be greater and entry more frequent in industries that are growing more rapidly (*GROWTH*).

A high rate of technical progress in an industry will also indicate a dynamic and evolving situation, and thus might attract new entrants seeking to discover and develop new products and processes. A high ratio of expenditure on research and development to sales (*RDEXP*) would indicate a technologically dynamic industry and signal new entrants.

Π_{it}^{N}: The entry forestalling profit rate is the highest long run profit rate that will not attract entry. Barriers to entry would positively affect the entry forestalling profit rate, and negatively affect the rate of entry, ceteris paribus.[15] The traditional barriers are the ratio of advertising expenditures to sales (*ADS*), the proportion of industry sales required to operate a plant of minimum efficient scale (*MESMKT*), and the amount of capital required to build a plant of minimum efficient scale (*CAPREQ*).

We also attempt to account for the possibility that some incumbent firms may be attempting to pre-empt the market through capacity expansion [Spence (1977)]. *CAPEXP* measures capital expenditures lagged one year divided by net plant. Pre-emption attempts should be indicated when expenditures on plant and equipment exceed industry growth (*EXCAPEXP*).

Risk averse potential entrants will be deterred by high investment risk. We measure risk in two ways. *RISK* is the average variance for industry firms in profits (after taxes as percentage of stockholder's equity) over the five years prior to the period in question. The second risk variable, *BAYRISK*, is a measure of the variability in predicted profits derived from a profit forecasting model discussed below. These are reasonable risk measures for individuals whose investment portfolios are *not* well diversified, which would seem an appropriate description of an individual starting up a new business.[16]

Concentration (CONC) and research intensity (RDEXP) could, in theory, attract or deter entry. Orr (1974) feels that '... when entering highly concentrated industries, the potential entrant must also consider the possibility that established firms may collude to thwart his entry.' Baron's (1973) model predicts that *lower* concentration may deter entry since a symmetric post entry equilibrium would imply smaller size and a higher likelihood that the entrant will be forced to operate below minimum efficient scale.[17] The possibility that high R&D expenditures might be correlated with frequent entry is discussed above. But new entrants into research intensive industries must also raise more risky financial capital, and the difficulty and cost of assembling the necessary human capital may also deter entry.

Measures of the variables

The U.S. Small Business Administration has been compiling entry statistics by four-digit industries only since 1976. The data, which originate from Dun and Bradstreet, are available in two-year increments – 1976–77, 1978–79 and 1980–81.[18] Our entry measures are taken for these three time periods.

The entry rate ($Entry_{it}$) is simply the number of new firms formed in industry i within the time period t, divided by the number of firms in existence in the industry at the beginning of the period. This variable is then transformed as follows:

$$\text{Relative entry rate}_{it} = \text{Entry}_{it} - \overline{\text{Entry}}_t, \qquad (3)$$

where $\overline{\text{Entry}}_t$ is the average entry rate across all industries i for period t. This transformation should control for any economy-wide factors (in the separate time periods) affecting entry rates. Problems of econometric estimation are also avoided since (unlike $Entry_{it}$), the Relative entry rate is unbounded.

The independent variables $PROFIT_{it}$, ADS_{it}, $RDEXP_{it}$, $CAPEXP_{it}$ and $RISK_{it}$ are taken from the Compustat tape. In the case of the first four variables, the observations are lagged one year (i.e., for the 1980–1981 period, ADS_{it} is observed in 1979). $PROFIT_{it}$ is after tax income less extraordinary items and discontinued operations, summed for each firm in industry i, and then divided by the sum of equity capital for industry i firms. $RDEXP_{it}$ and ADS_{it} are the sums of research and development expenditures and advertising expenditures as a proportion of sales. $CAPEXP_{it}$ is the sum of capital expenditures divided by the sum of net plant for firms in the ith industry.

In addition to using a simple lagged profits variable to predict future profits (and thus to signal entry), we have developed a somewhat more sophisticated measure of expected profitability.[19] We have formulated a simple forecasting model for profits which has been applied to each industry.

$$PROFIT_{it} = C + \alpha_1 PROFIT_{it-1} + \alpha_2 PROFIT_{it-2} + e_t.$$

The model is a Bayesian implementation of an autoregressive model in which profits in any period are related in a linear way to profits in the two preceding periods: where e_t is a zero mean, normally distributed error term. Forecasts from this model were generated iteratively[20] beginning in 1974, using annual data, and the forecasts for the years 1976, 1978 and 1980 (called $BAYPROF_{it}$)[21] were used as independent variables.

$BAYRISK_{it}$, is the variance of the predictive distribution of profits (where

$BAYPROF_{it}$ is the mean). Due to its autoregressive nature, the model (3) will account for any time trend in profits. $BAYRISK_{it}$ will then be a risk measure taken after accounting for any underlying time trend.

The sources for the remaining variables are the various censuses.[22] $GROWTH_{it}$ is the annual growth rate in sales or value of shipments from 1972–1977. *MESMKT* is the ratio of the average sales per establishment for establishments in the median size class, to sales for the industry for the year 1977. *CAPREQ* is *MESMKT* multiplied by total assets for the industry, for the year 1977. $CONC_{it}$ is the four firm concentration ratio. We have modified $CONC_{it}$ according to Schwartzman and Bodoff (1971) by first identifying the industries for which a national concentration ratio is not appropriate, since markets are regional or local. For these seven industries, we then added Schwartzman and Bodoff's estimates of the difference between average regional (or local) and national rates to our 1977 national rates. The resulting $CONC_{it}$ should adequately reflect national, regional and local concentration, where appropriate.

Estimation techniques and results

The basic results reported in this section are regressions in which we have pooled observations from the three time periods in our sample. As the independent variable is cross-sectional in nature, there is the possibility that omitted macroeconomic factors can bias the results. To the extent that these economy-wide factors affect entry in a similar way in all industries, we can control for these macro effects by subtracting the mean entry rate $Entry_t$ from the observed, industry specific, entry rate $Entry_{it}$.

The results for the data set that includes measures for all independent variables are presented in Table 3.3. Data are available for one or more time periods for forty industries (four-digit), nearly all of which are manufacturing.[23]

The hypothesis tests are consistent with the finding that high industry growth strongly attracts entry by new firms. This finding is similar to the results of Hause and DuRietz (1984) for Swedish manufacturing industries. Although the F test indicates that the regression equation is clearly significant, the significance of the remaining coefficients is quite limited.

There is marginal support for the hypothesis that industries characterized by high R&D expenditures to sales ratios also experience higher rates of entry. Rather than acting as a barrier to entry, research intensity in an industry seems to attract entry by new firms. RISK, which measures the variance of past profits, also has the hypothesized sign and is marginally significant ($P = 11.9$ per cent, two tailed test). High profit rates in the periods prior to the time period of observation do not appear to signal new entry. None of the other coefficients on the deterrents or barriers to entry are statistically significant.[24]

Table 3.3 115 observations; dependent variable: relative entry rate$_{it}$

Independent variable	Coefficient	Standard error	T statistic
Constant	−0.035987	0.016084	−2.237475
BAYPROF	−0.244044	0.564525	−0.432300
ADS	−0.184650	0.175784	−1.050439
EXCAPEXP	0.029984	0.038803	0.772736
RDEXP	0.374736	0.24009	1.560756
RISK	−0.013461	0.008561	−1.572244
GROWTH	0.360785	0.072860	4.951744[a]
CONC	−0.000262	0.000187	−1.398997
MESMKT	0.311990	0.225176	1.385541
CAPREQ	0.000042	0.000081	0.519121
$\bar{R}^2 = 0.322$, F(10, 105) = 7.0241			

[a] Statistically significant at 1%.

Alternative methods for estimating expected future profits and investment risk were described above. When the equation in Table 3.3 was estimated using $PROFIT_{it}$ (lagged profits) and $BAYRISK_{it}$ (the predicted variance in profits), neither coefficient was significantly different from zero, and the only major result affected was that *RDEXP* was no longer even marginally significant.

The sample size can be substantially enlarged by eliminating independent variables with missing values, In Table 3.4, the variables *ADS*, *CONC* and *CAPREQ* have been dropped and twenty industries (sixty one observations) have been added, mostly in natural resource extraction and services. The findings are much stronger than those in Table 3.3: entry occurs much more frequently in research intensive, rapidly growing industries.

There is also a substantial difference in the explanatory power of the profit variable. The Bayesian profit forecast, *BAYPROF*, is positively and significantly related to the subsequent rate of entry by new firms. The profit forecast using simple lagged profits ($PROFIT_{it}$) and the alternative risk measure were substituted for *BAYPROF* and *RISK* in regressions not reported here. Neither was significantly different from zero at the 10 per cent level. So with this more extensive industry coverage, the Bayesian autoregressive forecasting technique dominates a simple lagged profit forecast.[25] Entrepreneurs do use previously available profit information in deciding whether to risk their capital, but they use it in a sophisticated fashion.

74   *Small Business: Critical Perspectives*

Table 3.4 176 observations; dependent variable: relative entry rate$_{it}$

Independent variable	Coefficient	Standard error	T statistic
Constant	−0.029400	0.007565	−3.886144
BAYPROF	0.257411	0.056791	4.532634[a]
EXCAPEXP	0.003874	0.007649	0.506519
RDEXP	0.219136	0.096291	2.275763[b]
GROWTH	0.295167	0.044189	6.679606[a]
MESMKT	−0.067678	0.112233	−0.603017
RISK	−0.001167	0.006799	−0.171614

$$\bar{R}^2 = 0.316, F(7, 169) = 14.5$$

[a] Statistically significant at 1%.
[b] Statistically significant at 5%

Summary and conclusions

This paper contributes to the industrial organization literature on entry through enabling us to better understand what economic conditions are more hospitable to the creation of new firms, and through application of new methods to better understand these complex relationships. We have identified two types of factors that influence the rate of creation of new firms: macroeconomic and microeconomic factors. Although the evidence is some what weak, the macroeconomic climate that appears to be most conducive to the formation of small businesses is what might loosely be called sluggish. Lower rates of growth of GNP, lower inflation rates, and greater growth in the unemployment rate were followed by increases in the rate of new incorporations. These new incorporations in turn tend to lead periods of more robust economic activity. The cross-sectional or microeconomic factors which affect rates of entry into different industries include higher growth rates in sales, higher research and development intensity, and higher profit rates. We do not find any of the traditional barriers to entry to be related to the rate of new firm creation.

Putting the time series and cross-sectional results together, we have a consistent and interesting picture of entry through the creation of new firms. Individuals decide to form new firms when economic conditions are relatively poor – but they decide to enter industries which are dynamic and robust, as measured by technical progressivity and profitability.

We have utilized some time series techniques which appear to be new to the industrial organization literature. After observing the patterns of leads and lags of new incorporation activity as they are correlated with leads and lags of important macroeconomic variables, we investigate whether knowledge of these macroeconomic variables will allow us to improve on forecasts of the new incorporations growth rate. In the cross-sectional study, we conclude that the lack of relationship in other studies [e.g., McDonald (1986), Orr (1974)] between the profit rate and subsequent new business creation is the result of lack of sophistication in modelling entrepreneurs' expectations about future profit rates.[26] The Bayesian autoregressive model we used to forecast future profit rates seems to indicate quite clearly that present profit rates do influence future entry.

Appendix

Table 3.A1 Industries used in analysis

SIC code	Industry description
Industries used in table 3.3	
2041	Flour and other grain mill products
2046	Wet corn milling
2065	Confectionary products
2082	Malt beverages
2086	Bottled and canned soft drinks
2121	Cigars
2711	Newspapers
2761	Manifold business forms
2834	Pharmaceutical preparations
2841	Soap and other detergents
2844	Toilet preparations
2911	Petroleum refining
3079	Miscellaneous plastic products
3221	Glass containers
3241	Cement, hydraulic
3443	Fabricated plate work, boiler shops
3444	Sheet metal work
3452	Bolts, nuts, rivets, and washers
3494	Valves and pipe fittings
3531	Construction machinery
3533	Oilfield machinery
3622	Industrial controls
3651	Radio and TV receiving sets
3662	Radio and TV communication equipment
3674	Semiconductors and related devices
3693	X–ray apparatus and tubes
3711	Motor vehicle and car bodies
3714	Motor vehicle parts and accessories
3721	Aircraft

continued on next page

Table 3.A1 Industries used in analysis (cont.)

3811	Engineering and scientific instruments
3823	Process control instruments
3825	Instruments to measure electricity
3841	Surgical and medical instruments
3842	Surgical appliances and supplies
3861	Photographic equipment and supplies
3914	Silverware and plated ware
3931	Musical instruments
5012	Automobiles and other motor vehicles
5065	Electronic parts and electronic communication equipment
8911	Engineering and architectural services

Additional industries used in table 4

1021	Copper ores
1211	Bituminous coal and lignite
1311	Crude petroleum and natural gas
1381	Drilling oil and gas wells
1382	Oil and gas exploration services
2111	Cigarettes
3442	Metal doors, sash, and trim
3661	Telephone and telegraph apparatus
5093	Scrap and waste materials –wholesale
5211	Lumber and other building materials –retail
5411	Grocery stores –retail
5712	Furniture stores
5812	Eating places –retail
7011	Hotels, rooming houses, camps, and other lodging places
7372	Computer programming and other software services
7374	Data processing and computer facilities management
7391	Research and development laboratories
7392	Consulting services
7393	Protective services
7395	Photofinishing laboratories

Notes

1 Financial assistance for Robert Smiley was provided by the United States Small Business Administration under contract SBA–9241–OA–85. Robert Frank, Paul Geroski, Robert Hutchens, Bruce Phillips, and especially Robert Masson provided helpful comments on an earlier draft. We would like to thank Margaret Forster for excellent research assistance. The conclusions are the authors' and do not reflect official positions of the Small Business Administration.
2 This data series is compiled monthly by Dun and Bradstreet from State government data. We compute the growth rate from as follows: $[\ln (INC_{at}) - \ln (INC_{t-1})] * 400$, where $INCt$ is the quarterly total.
3 The concept of weak stationarity (or covariance stationarity) is all that is required here. A time series is weakly stationary if it has constant variance and if the covariance between any two points in the series depends only on the amount of time separating them. These properties allow

consistent estimation of the time series mean, variance, autocorrelations and cross-correlations with other stationary time series.

4 From the Bureau of Economic Analysis quarterly P & E survey.

5 The rate of change in the implicit GNP deflator.

6 Calculated as the quarterly average 90-day Treasury Bill rate less inflation.

7 For a comprehensive discussion of causality in econometrics and economic theory, see Zellner (1978).

8 See, for example, Sims (1972,1977), Pierce (1977) and Feige and Pearce (1976).

9 As our incorporation series represents all incorporations, both new firms and some established firms changing ownership structure, we cannot rule out the possibility that some of this relationship is attributable to owners acting to shield assets in bad times.

10 The sample was also split in half and the analog to Table 3.1 computed on both the earlier and later periods. The results for both periods give essentially the same impression as that given in table 1, with the earlier period results being slightly stronger than those above, and the later period slightly weaker. The real interest rate results are the only exception. The weak result above does not appear in the later period.

11 This is called 'prewhitening' the series by Box and Jenkins (1976). Suppose $(B)X_t = (B)e_t$ represents a standard ARMA (p,q) for a model covariance stationary series X_t (one of our macro variables), where $(B) = 1 - \phi_1 B - \cdots - \phi_p B_1^p$, $(B) = 1 - {}_1 B - \cdots - {}_q B_1^q$, B is the backshift (or lag) operator such that $BX_t = X_{t-1}$, and e_t represents a zero mean, constant variance noise process. The prewhitened incorporation growth series a_t is calculated as $a_t = 0^{-1}(B) (B)$(incorporation growth)$_t$. Thus systematic variation in incorporation growth directly induced by systematic variation in X_t is removed. What remains includes systematic variation induced by even random variation in X_t. Of course, if the only channel by which X_t affects or 'causes' incorporation growth is through its systematic (forecastable) variation then we are throwing the baby out with the bath.

12 This fact often goes unrecognized as an explanation of the fact that ARMA forecasts are often competitive with or even superior to forecasts from complex econometric models.

13 I.e., each model was estimated using data from the period 1948:3 to 1977:4. Future incorporation growth was then predicted, the model updated to include data for 1978:1, another prediction was made, the model updated again, and so on.

14 In identifying and estimating the transfer function models and bivariate ARMA models we have followed the suggestions of Box and Jenkins (1976) and Tiao and Box (1981), respectively. To estimate the vector autoregression, which involves eight lags of each of the five variables, we employ the Bayesian techniques of Litterman (1984) and Highfield (1984).

15 See Bain (1956) and Demsetz (1982) for different points of view regarding barriers to entry.

16 If an individual is perfectly well diversified, we would want to use the industry beta.

17 See Masson and Shaanan (1986, pp. 4–5) for a thorough discussion of concentration and entry.

18 The problems of classifying multi-product firms into four-digit industries are well known. Aside from modifying national concentration ratios as discussed below, we have made no modifications to the official SIC classification scheme since we were (ultimately) constrained by Dun and Bradstreet's use of existing codes.

19 Expectations regarding future profitability are also affected by *GROWTH* and *RDEXP*, in addition to past profit rates.

20 By 'iterative' we mean that no future data were used in the generation of the profit forecasts. They are true forecasts, not fitted values from the model.

21 Our profit series for each industry begins in 1971, leaving very few observations with which to estimate the model. A Bayesian method of estimation was employed to overcome this problem. Given the data through 1973 we assume a normal prior distribution on profits in 1974. The mean of this distribution being zero and its standard deviation being 0.5 (i.e., a profit or loss rate of 50 per cent of equity capital is one standard deviation from the mean). Using this very spread out distribution as our starting point we infer a prior distribution for the parameters of eq. (3).

22 Source: U.S. Bureau of the Census (1972, 1977).

23 See table 3A.1 in the appendix for the industries included.

24   These observations are consistent with most of the findings of MacDonald (1986) for food industries.
25   The regression in Table 3.4 was also run with the smaller data set used in Table 3.3. i.e., the Table 3.3 regression was run with *ADS*, *CONC* and *CAPREQ* eliminated. The results for the remaining variables are quite similar to those reported in Table 3.3 indicating that the significance of *BAYPROF* in Table 3.4 is due to the expanded data set, not the elimination of the three variables.
26   But see Masson and Shaanan (1986).

References

Ansley, C.F., 1977, Report on the NBER-NSF seminar on time series, Mimeo. (Graduate School of Business, University of Chicago, IL).

Ashley, R., C.W.J. Granger and R. Schmalensee, 1980, Advertising and aggregate consumption: An analysis of causality, *Econometrica* 48, no. 5, 1149–1167.

Bain, Joe S., 1956, *Barriers to new competition* (Harvard University Press, Cambridge, MA).

Baron, David, 1973, Limit pricing, potential entry and barriers to entry, *American Economic Review*, Sept., 666–674.

Birch, David L., 1981, Who creates jobs?, *The Public Interest*.

Box, G.E.P. and G.M. Jenkins, 1976, *Time series analysis – Forecasting and control* (Holden-Day, San Francisco, CA).

Caves, Richard and Michael Porter, 1977, From entry barriers to mobility barriers: Conjectural decisions and contrived deterrence to new competition, *Quarterly Journal of Economics* 91, 241–261.

Demsetz, Harold, 1982, Barriers to entry, *American Economic Review*, March, 47–57.

Feige, E.L. and D.K. Pearce, 1976, Economically rational expectations: Are innovations in the rate of inflation independent of innovations in measures of monetary and Fiscal policy?, *Journal of Political Economy* 84, June, 449–552.

Granger, C.W.J., 1969, Investigating causal relations by econometric models and cross-spectral methods, *Econometrica* 37, July, 424–438.

Hause, John C. and Gunnar DuRietz, 1984, Entry, industry growth and the microdynamics of industry supply, *Journal of Political Economy* 92, no. 4.

Highfield, R.A., 1984, Forecasting with Bayesian state space models, Technical report (H.G.B. Alexander Research Foundation, Graduate School of Business, University of Chicago, IL).

Litterman, Robert B., 1984, Specifying vector autoregressions for macroeconomic forecasting, *Research Department Staff Report* no. 92 (Federal Reserve Bank of Minneapolis, Minneapolis, MN).

MacDonald, James M., 1986, Entry and exit on the competitive fringe, *Southern Economic Journal* 52, no. 3.

Masson, Robert T. and Joseph Shaanan, 1986, Optimal pricing and the threat of entry: Canadian evidence, Working paper (Cornell University, Ithaca, NY).

Orr, Dale, 1974, The determinants of entry: A study of the Canadian manufacturing industries, *Review of Economics and Statistics*, Feb., 58–66.

Pierce, D.A., 1977, Relationships – and the lack thereof – between economic time series, with special reference to money and interest rates, *Journal of the American Statistical Association* 72, March, 11-21.

Scherer, Frederic M., 1980, *Industrial market structure and economic performance*, 2nd ed. (Rand McNally, Chicago, IL).

Schwartzman, David and Joan Bodoff, 1971, Concentration in regional and local industries, *Southern Economic Journal* 37, Jan., 343–348.

Sims, C.A., 1972, Money, income and causality, *American Economic Review* LXII, Sept., 540–552.

Sims, C.A., 1977, Exogeneity and causal ordering in macroeconomic models, in: C.A. Sims, ed., *New methods in business cycle research: Proceedings from a conference* (Federal Reserve Bank of Minneapolis, Minneapolis, MN) 23–43.

Spence, A. Michael, 1977, Entry, capacity, investment and oligopolistic pricing, *Bell Journal of Economics* 8, Autumn, 534–544.

Standard and Poor's, 1984, Annual industrial compustat tape.

Tiao, G.C. and G.E.P. Box, 1981, Modelling multiple time series with applications, *Journal of the American Statistical Association* 76, 802–816.

U.S. Bureau of the Census, Census of manufacturers – 1972, Census of retail trade – 1972, Census of wholesale trade – 1972, Census of mineral industries – 1972, Census of construction industries – 1972, Census of service industries – 1972 (Washington, DC).

U.S. Bureau of the Census, Census of manufacturers – 1977, Census of retail trade – 1977, Census of wholesale trade – 1977, Census of mineral industries – 1977, Census of construction industries – 1977, Census of service industries – 1977 (Washington, DC).

Zellner, Arnold, 1978, Causality and econometrics, in: K. Brunner and A.H. Meltzer, eds., Three aspects of policy and policymaking, *Carnegie-Rochester Conference Series on Public Policy*, Vol. 10 (North-Holland, Amsterdam) 9–54.

4

New Firm Formation: A Labour Market Approach to Industrial Entry*

D. J. Storey and A. M. Jones[1]

*Source: *Scottish Journal of Political Economy* 34, 1 (1987), 37–51.

Introduction

Although entrants play a central role in the structure/performance para-digm it is apparent that such firms are only indirectly included in the major empirical work on the topic. The central theme of the bulk of these studies is that variations in profitability, at an industry level, can be explained in terms of concentration, and a variety of barriers to entry (Sawyer, 1981). This barrier-orientated approach commonly features the concept of a queue of potential entrants, what Bain (1956) termed the "general condition of entry". However, due to a tendency to concentrate on the diversification of existing enterprises, the socio-economic determinants of new firm found-ers are invariably neglected.

There has been little attempt to directly test for a relationship between the number of entrants and perceived future profits. This is primarily a con-sequence of the difficulty of obtaining suitable data on entrants, whether they are wholly new firms or existing enterprises shifting or diversifying their operations.

This paper uses data for new manufacturing businesses created in North-ern England between 1965 and 1978 and the East Midlands between 1968 and 1975 with a view to testing the validity of the conventional theory of entry. It is recognised that self-employment is an alternative to unemploy-ment (or to paid employment) and an attempt is made to integrate industrial entry and labour search into a single model. This theoretical and empirical development requires that a distinction be made between entrants by trans-fer or diversification and wholly new firms.

Theory

Much of the conventional entry theory has been built upon the concept of the limit price (Waterson 1984, Clarke 1985). This refers to industries in which there are increasing returns to scale up to a level of output which is a significant proportion of the total market. The impact on aggregate supply of an entrant, of at least minimum efficient scale, will be to depress market price and consequently the level of profit. Post-entry profits rather than existing profit levels should therefore be the decision-making criterion for potential entrants. This fact allows existing firms to achieve actual profits at a level (above "normal") such that the level of expected post-entry profits is sufficient to discourage potential entrants.[2] The central thrust of the model is to render outcomes determinate in terms of price.[3]

As noted by Gorecki (1975), a major weakness of the limit pricing hypothesis lies in its inability to distinguish between entrants which are wholly new and existing enterprises which have diversified or transferred from other sectors. The importance of this distinction is that the two categories of firms are likely to respond to different stimuli.[4]

Total entrants into industry i (E_i) are therefore defined to be both wholly new businesses (NF_i) and existing businesses moving into i (TD_i), where wholly new businesses are independent enterprises setting up their first plant;

$$E_i = NF_i + TD_i \tag{1}$$

An existing business, currently operating in industry j, is expected to view a move to i (whether a transfer or a diversification) primarily on the basis of expected post-entry profits in i (π_i) and expected profits in j (π_j), subject to entry barriers (X_i) and any miscellaneous factors (Z_i). An example of the latter could be the reduction in uncertainty gained by vertical integration.

$$TD_i = f\left(\pi_i, \pi_j, X_i^T, Z_i\right) \tag{2}$$

where,

$$\frac{\delta TD_i}{\delta \pi_i} > 0 \quad \frac{\delta TD_i}{\delta \pi_j} < 0 \quad \frac{\delta TD_i}{\delta X_i^T} < 0$$

In equation, (2) X is a vector representing barriers to entry, whether they are economics of scale, product differentiation or absolute cost advantages, and X_i^T refers only to time barriers which apply to this particular group of entrants. Those readers interested in a recent examination of cross entry are referred to Deutsch (1984).

Wholly new firms are formed by individuals all of whom will have the option of obtaining employment in the formal labour market or of being unemployed.[5] Two contrasting views of this process may be offered. The first argues that individuals currently employed in industry *i* are faced by the alternatives of continued employment in *i*, possible employment in *j*, unemployment, or of establishing a new venture. Similarly, in the event of redundancies in industry *i*, the individuals involved may remain unemployed, gain employment in industry *j* or become self-employed.[6] Of those who exercise the latter option it is assumed that the majority will remain in industry *i*, primarily because their "contacts", so important in starting a new firm, will be in that industry. Individuals are more likely to be aware of market gaps, suppliers and the technology of production in the industry in which they were formerly employed.[7]

The majority of new firm founders in the *i*th industry begin their operations with "second-hand" equipment. The price of this equipment depends, in the short-term, primarily upon the extent to which falls in final demand result in reductions in capacity in that industry. A reduction in final demand thus increases spare capacity in the industry leading to plant and machinery being sold off by liquidators and, to a lesser extent, by existing enterprises. In recessionary conditions reductions in capacity by larger enterprises will result in a major increase in the availability of second-hand equipment, dwarfing the increased demand by entrepreneurs starting in business. These characteristics of the second-hand capital market are clearly shown by Binks and Jennings (1986). This reduces the price of second-hand equipment which is the major entry barrier that the entrepreneur faces. The effect, therefore of depressed market conditions in industry *i* may be both to make self-employment relatively more attractive *and* to reduce an important barrier to new firm formation in that industry.

A second view argues that whilst unemployment reduces the opportunity cost of business formation it also depletes the assets of the entrepreneur so making entry more difficult. Indeed the conventional view would be that reduced labour demand reflects poor expected profitability, so discouraging entry. It is therefore an essentially empirical question as to which of these "explanations" is more powerful.

An entry function for wholly new businesses can now be proposed. The independent variables again include expected post-entry profitability in industry $i\left(\pi_i^1\right)$ and a specific set of barriers to entry (X_i^N). But they are now joined by an index of labour shedding (L_i), a specific indicator of employment opportunities in *i*. This variable plays a central role in subsequent analysis,[8] but the two hypotheses outlined above lead to conflicting signs. Two specific characteristics of L_i are possible. The first is net employment change in the *i*th industry i.e. gross job gains minus gross job losses, whilst the second is simply gross employment loss defined as job loss through closures and contractions. Take, now, two industries *i* and *j*, identical in size, in terms of employment and in terms of employment change over time. It is argued that if gross job losses in industry *i* are significantly higher than in *j*, then industry *i* will, *ceteris paribus*, have the higher rates of new firm formation since more individuals will have lost their jobs in that industry and so will be "forced" to consider the entrepreneurial option.[9]

$$NF_i = f\left(\pi_i^1, X_i^N, L_i\right) \quad \frac{\delta NF_i}{\delta\pi_i^1} > 0 \quad \frac{\delta NF_i}{\delta X_i^N} < 0 \tag{3}$$

The net effect of an exogenous reduction in demand for products of industry i on the number of entrants in subsequent periods therefore depends on the magnitude of two conflicting influences. A fall in profitability can be expected to lead to closures and a transfer of existing enterprises out of i but at the same time redundancies may stimulate the formation of wholly new businesses, as former employees find this more attractive than either unemployment or the possibility of obtaining in industry j. The latter will depend upon the extent to which reduced job prospects reduce their assets and the extent to which these new and small firms can be expected to fill "niches" within the existing markets.

The existing work

The main empirical study using number of entrants as the dependent variable was carried out by Mansfield on a multiplicative model of the form:

$$E_{it} = \alpha_0 \pi_{it}^{\alpha 1} X_{it}^{-\alpha 2} Z_{it} \tag{4}$$

where

$$\frac{\delta E_{it}}{\delta\pi_{it}} > 0; \quad \frac{\delta E_{it}}{\delta X_{it}} < 0$$

This model was tested with data for four industries over a variety of periods, yielding ten data points. Mansfield showed that a significant and positive relationship existed between profitability and entry rates. The latter are defined as the number of firms that entered the ith industry during the ith period (and survived until the end of the period) as a proportion of the number in the industry at the beginning of the period. This is only one of the indices of entry since it neglects those entrants which failed to survive the given period. The difference between total entrants and surviving entrants may be considerable since in most of the industries covered by Mansfield the period used is a decade. An examination of data by Dun and Bradstreet for the USA suggests that approximately half of a given year's new manufacturing firms fail to survive for a decade. Mansfield would therefore seem to be underestimating the *total* number of entrants by this amount. Since however he is attempting to explain cross-industry differences this under-enumeration may not be so important, but the absence of a reliable control sample makes even this hypothesis untestable.

The formulation of entry rates used by Mansfield differs in several respects from that used in subsequent attempts to use entries as the dependent variable in regression equations. For example the work by Orr (1974) does not use the gross surviving entry rate favoured by Mansfield, but instead uses the net entry rate. This is defined to be:

$$E_i = 1/4 \sum_{t=1964}^{1967} N_{it} - N_{i(t-1)} \tag{5}$$

where:

$E = E_i \ldots E_{71}$ industries;

N_{it} = number of reporting corporations in the *i*th industry in the *t*th year (Canada);

$N_{it} - N_{i(t-1)}$ is defined as ≥ 0.

Orr therefore selects only those industries where there are more firms in year *t* than in year *t* − 1, consequently his data includes wholly new firms, firms transferring from other industries, and exits. Orr admits that the data may also, in some cases, include firms where the ownership has changed. Finally it has to be recognised that the data source from which Orr draws, only includes firms which have sales exceeding $500,000, at 1967 prices. This means that only firms with at least fifty workers would be included in his sample. If the size distribution of new firms Canada during the period was the same as in the Northern region of England then only 6 per cent of all new firms would be included in Orr's data.

The study by Gorecki (1975) also uses a net entry rate, examining the increased (decreased) number of enterprises in 51 industries in the UK between 1958 and 1963. Gorecki attempts to distinguish between the net change in specialist and in diversifying firms. His sample includes exits, yet there are strong reasons for believing that there is an asymmetry between factors affecting rates of entry and exit. For example, whilst gross entries are postulated to be affected by profitability and entry barriers, empirical studies of gross exits have included profitability and the number of enterprises at risk because of their size (Mansfield 1962, Marcus 1963). Furthermore the study by Henderson (1980) has shown there to be no association between an industry's profitability and the propensity of its establishments to close. More recently Van Herck (1984) has attempted to explain the interrelationships between entry and exit but his empirical work does not make clear the definitions of entry used.

It is clear that a number of formulations of entry rates are theoretically justifiable for testing the relationship between entry and profitability. However, to test for a relationship between the choices open to the individual all new businesses have to be charted, including those which have diversified frorn other industries. Ideally such data should include all sizes of new firms, not simply those which reach a given (usually high) minimum size, and finally it should also include all new firms rather than only those which survive until the end of the period. Such data does not exist for the UK economy as a whole but is available to the authors for Northern England. Valuable data is also available for the East Midlands of England, but on the slightly different basis discussed in the next Section.

Finally it seems likely that the entrepreneur's view of expected post-entry profitability and of the actual height of entry barriers may vary from one location to another. For example, some areas may specialise in the "small" specialist end of a given market whilst other areas may specialise in large scale mass production. Recently two studies have examined the locational differences in *actual* profit rates in broadly comparable firms. Bayldon, Woods and Zafiris (1984) question whether differences exist between inner city and new town location, whilst Fothergill, Gudgin, Kitson and Monk (1984) show that such differences do exist between con-urbations and other areas.

Sources of data

Data on wholly new manufacturing firms in Northern England were derived from records constructed for the County Councils of Cleveland, Durham and Tyne and Wear.[10] Coverage is virtually complete, subject to the limitations of government statistics and the data base contains nearly 5,000 manufacturing establishments which existed at any stage between 1965 and 1978. For each establishment, data on employment are available for most years. In addition further data on, for example, name, address, location, industry (MLH), ownership, date of establishment (if after 1965) and date of closure (where applicable), are available.

The East Midlands data were kindly supplied by Graham Gudgin and Steve Fothergill. The source for this data is the Factory Inspectorate and full details are available in Fothergill and Gudgin (1982). The numbers of wholly new firms existing in 1975 which had been created since 1968 were provided. It must be emphasised that these include only new firms which survived until 1975, and in this important aspect the data differs from that available on the Northern Region.

From this population of manufacturing establishments in the two regions it is possible to identify a group which consists of new independent businesses and to identify the years in which they began operations. In principle it would also be possible to identify existing establishments which switched their industry (cross-entry). However these cases are not included in subsequent analysis because in several cases a change in MLH is a reflection of the industrial classification being initially incorrect, rather than a genuine change of activity.

Finally it would therefore be desirable to have data on profitability and entry barriers specifically for the North and for the East Midlands but unfortunately such data does not exist. It has therefore proved necessary to use national data for both of these measures.

The variables

Entry rates

Four New Firm formation rates are used in this analysis.

a NF_i^N ; takes the total number of wholly new firms in the ith industry (locally-owned sole proprietorships, partnerships, or private limited companies) which traded for the first time between 1965 and 1978 in the counties of Durham, Cleveland or Tyne and Wear. Such firms must be legally independent enterprises, i.e. not subsidiaries of existing enterprises. To identify a formation rate, the number of such wholly new firms is divided by the number of single plant independent firms in the ith industry in Durham, Cleveland and Tyne and Wear in 1965. Hence NF_i^N represents the gross proportionate increase in the number of single plant independent firms in the three counties over the 1965–1978 period.

b NF_i^{NUK} ; if the number of single plant independent firms in the three counties existing in industry i in 1965 were low for some temporary reason then NF_i^N would be an inappropriate index. Instead it may be better to divide the number of wholly new firms in the ith industry by the number of enterprises in the ith industry in the U.K. since this is less likely to be affected by "exceptional" values. Data for numbers of enterprises do not exist for 1965 but the U.K. data from "Census of Production is used for 1968 to derive NF_i^{NUK} .

c NF_i^{EM} ; since the North of England has been shown by Fothergill and Gudgin to have a rate of new firm formation significantly below the national average, data on formation rates in the East Midlands are used to determine whether the cross section formation rates in the North are correlated with those of a region with a formation rate more typical of the UK as a whole. NF_i^{EM} takes the data supplied by Steve Fothergill and Graham Gudgin on wholly new firms in the East Midlands between 1968 and 1975 for each MLH. This is divided by the number of single plant independent firms in that industry in 1968. It must be emphasised, however, that the East Midlands data includes firms starting after 1968 but which *survived* until 1975. It does not include, unlike the Northern data, new firms starting after 1968 but which failed to survive until 1975.

d NF_i^{EMUK} ; This index takes the number of wholly new firms formed in the East Midlands in the ith industry between 1968 and 1975 and divides by the number of UK enterprises in the ith industry in 1968 according to the Census of Production.

Profitability index

The concept of expected post-entry profitability is, in unquantifiable and a suitable proxy is required. Empirical studies; have generally used ex-post profits (See Waterson, 1984). There may also be a lag between the observed opportunity for profit and an individual forming a firm to take advantage of that opportunity. The extent of this lag is likely to vary from a matter of days to years depending partly upon the individual and partly upon the industry to be entered. It seems likely that industries where initial capital requirements are high will experience a longer period between the perception of profit and actual entry than an industry where capital requirements are small. Neither we, nor other empirical studies, are able to take this into account except through the entry barriers index. Furthermore it could be argued that it is *not* the general level of profitability in industry i which affects the willingness of the individual to form his own firm since profitability in the industry as a whole may be affected by the presence of large firms. Of more relevance is the expected return which the individual could expect to obtain by forming a new firm and this will, at least initially, be more closely related to the profitability of smaller firms in the industry. The only useable data on corporate profitability is national and taken from Census of Production, so that in the model *Regional* entry rates will be compared with *National* ex-post profitability data.

$$\pi_i = \frac{(\text{Net output} - \text{Wages and Salaries})}{\text{Net output}}$$

From this general index a number of possible indices can be formed.

π^{68} = Gross Profits in 1968 in ith industry in UK
π^{70} = Gross Profits in 1970 in ith industry in UK
π^{73} = Gross Profits in 1973 in ith industry in UK
π^{76} = Gross Profits in 1976 in ith industry in UK
$^{99}\pi_i^{70}$ = Gross Profits in 1970 in UK ith industry in firms employing less than 100 workers.
$^{99}\pi_i^{73}$ = Gross Profits in 1973 in UK ith industry in firms employing less than 100 workers.
$^{99}\pi_i^{76}$ = Gross Profits in 1976 in UK ith industry in firms employing less than 100 workers.

In determining entry rates the change in the level of profit may be more important than the absolute level of profit. For example, an industry may have high entry barriers and high profits and a zero entry rate. In the event of an exogenous increase in profitability entry could be stimulated. It could also be argued that changes in the profitability of small firms, rather than the profitability of all firms in the industry, are most likely to affect expectations.

Two types of index of change in profitability have therefore been constructed:

$\Delta\Pi_i^{t,t+1}$ = Change in UK profitability in ith industry between year t and year $t + 1$.

[99] $\Delta\Pi_i^{t,t+1}$ = Change in UK profitability in ith industry between year t and year $t + 1$ in firms employing less than 100 workers.

Labour market variables

It was argued above that a factor influencing the likelihood of an individual becoming the founder of a new firm is the availability or otherwise of work locally in his/her industry.

Ceteris paribus it would be expected that those industries which were major net shedders of labour would also have the highest rates of new firm formation. However, these *net* employment changes conceal the growth in employment in some firms and the loss of employment in others. Since it is those workers in firms either *contracting* their labour forces or *closing* that are particularly "at risk", the index should express gross job losses as a proportion of total employment in industry i.

The labour market indices used are:

$L_i^{t,t+1}$ = per cent change in UK Employment in ith industry between year t and year $t + 1$, so that if $E_t > E_{t+1}$ then $L^{t,t+1} < 0$

L^N_i = Job Losses through Contractions + Closures in Northern England 1965–78 in ith industry

Total Employment in ith industry in 1965 in Northern England.

To estimate L^N_i job losses through closure are defined as employment in 1965 in establishments which had closed by 1978. Job losses through contractions are defined as job losses in establishments which although trading in both 1965 and 1978 had *less* jobs in 1978 than in 1965. Gross Job Losses are defined as the summation of closures and contractions.

Barriers to entry (X_i^L)

Scherer (1980) reviews the variety of entry barriers used in empirical studies, but the index adopted in this paper is that formulated by Lyons (1980). It estimates, for a variety of industries, the minimum efficient plant-size as a percentage of industry size (MEP/S) on the basis of a firm's decision to set up a second plant. Using the 1968 Standard Industrial Classification, Lyons provides estimates for 144 industries at MLH and sub-MLH level but he specifically excludes industries which have "miscellaneous" in their title. This is unfortunate in the present study since these industries frequently contain a large number of wholly new firms. Nevertheless, the

advantages of having entry barrier data constructed at MLH level tran-
scends these disadvantages.

The results

Difficulties arose in testing due to incomplete data for all industries and
variables. During the period there was a major change m the Standard
Industrial Classification in 1968 and a reallocation of some establishments
in 1970, both of which raise problems of comparability over the time periods. Secondly, in many instances the number of wholly new firms in an
MLH was less than five and so were excluded because of the risk of introducing "extreme" values. Finally, as noted above, the Lyons data does not
cover all industries. Given these constraints only 31 MLH's were able to
provide observations on all variables.

As noted earlier the existing empirical work has been unclear on the
functional form of a relationship between entry and profitability. It is also
unclear from a theoretical standpoint whether a linear or more complex
functional form is appropriate. For this reason Table 4.1 presents a simple
correlation matrix between the four endogenous variables (NF_i^N, NF_i^{NUK},
NF_i^{EM}, NF_i^{EMUK}), and the fifteen exogenous variables. Table 4.2 identifies
the correlation between endogenous variables. Table 4.3 presents similar
data to Table 4.1 but with all variables subjected to a logarithmic transformation. Similarly Table 4. 4 shows the correlation between the logarithmic
transformed endogenous variables. Only after these tables are regression
results presented in Tables 4.5 and 4.6.

The most striking feature of Tables 4.1 and 4. 3 is the absence of any
association between the absolute level of profit in a given year and entry
rates, however defined, in either Northern England or the East Midlands.
This statement applies to the absolute level of profit in any given year in all
enterprises within that MLH and to profitability in the smaller enterprises,
i.e. those with less than 100 employees.

The second group of variables shows the correlation between the two
entry rates for each of the two Regions and the change in profitability for a
number of time periods. A variety of different time periods was in fact
tested but only three are shown here. Again there is no evidence of any
association.

The third group of variables refer to labour shedding, the first three of
which are based on national data taken from the Census of Production
whilst the fourth identifies the gross job losses in Northern England. For
the first time in Table 4.1 the correlation coefficient for the Northern entry
rates are significant at the 5 cent level. Thus the index of gross job losses in
Northern England L_i^N is positively associated with new firm formation rates
in the Region NF_i^N. On the other hand L_i^{6876} is negatively associated with
NF_i^{NUK} which is the opposite to that predicted by the labour shedding

Table 4.1 Simple correlation matrix

	NF_i^N	NF_i^{NUK}	NF_i^{EM}	NF_i^{EMUK}
Π_i^{68}	0.0982	0.1681	0.1329	0.1405
Π_i^{70}	0.1124	0.0821	0.0753	−0.0484
Π_i^{73}	0.1049	0.1147	0.1473	0.0441
Π_i^{76}	0.0693	0.2131	0.0420	−0.0080
$^{99}\Pi_i^{70}$	−0.0091	−0.0212	−0.1003	0.0530
$^{99}\Pi_i^{73}$	0.0418	−0.0057	0.0063	0.1424
$^{99}\Pi_i^{76}$	0.1388	0.1694	0.1507	0.0071
$\Delta\Pi_i^{6876}$	0.1016	0.0391	0.0746	0.1819
$\Delta\Pi_i^{6873}$	0.0609	0.0654	−0.0145	0.1031
$^{99}\Delta\Pi_i^{7076}$	−0.1616	−0.2471	−0.2668	0.0246
L_i^{6873}	0.1101	−0.2188	0.1395	−0.0243
L_i^{6870}	0.0694	−0.2690	0.1490	−0.0717
L_i^{6876}	0.0064	−0.3429*	0.2585	0.0715
L_i^N	0.4752**	−0.1518	0.2594	−0.0803
X_i^L	−0.1158	−0.2927	−0.1542	0.2152

** Significant at 1% level.
 * Significant at 5% level.

theory. To determine whether these relationships are robust when subject to logarithmic transformations it can be seen from Table 4.3 that the significantly positive relationship between L_i^N and NF_i^N continues whereas that between NF_i^{NUK} and L_i^{6876} disappears. This suggests that labour shedding is a factor "explaining" the sectoral variations in new firm formation rates in Northern England. It is not possible to construct a similar index for the East Midlands 1968–75, but for completeness the Table shows the insignificant association between East Midlands, formation rates and L^N

Finally, the barriers to index X_i^L is shown to be significantly negatively correlated with NF_i^{NUK}, after the logarithmic transformation. This accords with the expectations from the theoretical model.

Tables 4.2 and 4.4 show the correlation between the four entry rates used in this analysis. They demonstrate the generally weak relationship between these variables, and this must be a matter of concern since it is not clear which index is the most appropriate.

Tables 4.5 and 4.6 show the "best" OLS equations, in terms of adjusted R^2, using both a linear and logarithmic form. Only about 20 per cent of the

Table 4.2 Correlation matrix

	NF_i^N	NF_i^{NUK}	NF_i^{EM}	NF_i^{EMUK}
NF_i^N	1.000			
NF_i^{NUK}	0.4833	1.0000		
NF_i^{EM}	0.1671	0.1763	1.0000	
NF_i^{EMUK}	0.0846	−0.1684	−0.0555	1.0000

Table 4.3 Correlation matrix: logarithmic transformations

	NF_i^N	NF_i^{NUK}	NF_i^{EM}	NF_i^{EMUK}
Π_i^{68}	0.1580	0.1694	0.0645	0.2316
Π_i^{70}	−0.0145	0.1916	−0.0209	0.1880
Π_i^{73}	−0.0314	0.2250	0.0434	0.2186
Π_i^{76}	0.0813	0.2518	0.0814	0.1620
$^{99}\Pi_i^{70}$	−0.0819	0.0201	−0.1054	0.1880
$^{99}\Pi_i^{73}$	0.0932	0.0564	0.0424	0.2582
$^{99}\Pi_i^{76}$	0.1230	0.1660	0.0392	0.0457
$\Delta\Pi_i^{6876}$	0.1630	0.1595	0.1463	−0.0421
$\Delta\Pi_i^{6873}$	−0.1461	−0.1774	0.1041	−0.0232
$^{99}\Delta\Pi_i^{7076}$	−0.2234	−0.0600	−0.2009	0.1271
L_i^{6876}	−0.0546	0.2791	0.0460	−0.0292
L_i^{6870}	−0.0276	0.0245	0.1855	0.3148*
L_i^{6873}	−0.0513	0.0158	−0.3308*	−0.2246
L_i^N	0.4171**	−0.1950	0.0610	−0.1439
X_i^L	−0.2062	−0.3704*	−0.1149	0.1997

** Significant at 1% level.
 * Significant at 5% level.

variation in industry formation rates is explained by the included variables, but the values of R^2 are significantly higher for NF_i^N where it is possible to identify a local index of job shedding than for other indices of formation. Of all variables included, the relationship between L_i^N and NF_i^N is the most striking. Of secondary interest is that in Table 4.5 there appears to be some support for the view that *increases* in industrial profitability in smaller

Table 4.4 Correlation matrix: logarithmic transformations

	NF_i^N	NF_i^{NUK}	NF_i^{EM}	NF_i^{EMUK}
NF_i^N	1.000			
NF_i^{NUK}	0.2632	1.0000		
NF_i^{EM}	0.4410	0.3044	1.0000	
NF_i^{EMUK}	−0.0169	−0.0945	0.2252	1.0000

Table 4.5 Best fit equations: linear form[1]

	NF_i^N	NF_i^{NUK}	NF_i^{EM}	NF_i^{EMUK}
C	2.853 (2.969)	0.0362 (5.434)	0.9167 (5.256)	−0.053 (1.26)
Π_i^{68}				0.1123 (1.91)
$^{99}\Delta\Pi_i^{7076}$	−4.575 (1.135)	−0.023 (1.191)	−1.1053 (1.5064)	
L_i^{6876}		−0.0295 (1.844)	0.8671 (1.458)	
L_i^N	469.52 (2.974)			
X_i^L		−0.003 (1.176)		0.0161 (1.67)
$\bar{R}^2$	0.2599	0.2202	0.1368	0.1331

Notes: 1. 't' values in parenthesis.

business between 1970 and 1976 are associated with higher formation rates. However none of the coefficients in the equations is statistically significant, although each has a negative sign.

Conclusions

This paper argues that a major local factor influencing the rate of new firm formation is the rate at which jobs are shed in that locality. The evidence presented shows that, at least for the Northern Region, there appears to be no association between changes in, or absolute national levels of, profitability in the *i*th industry and new firm formation, rates in that industry. On the other hand formation rates in the *i*th industry in the Northern Region are positively correlated with job shedding in the region. It is not possible to

Table 4.6 "Best" fit equations: log form[1]

	NF_i^N	NF_i^{NUK}	NF_i^{EM}	NF_i^{EMUK}
C	2.025 (2.142)	−3.653 (33.788)	−0.6916 (5.452)	−3.062 (6.553)
$^{99}\Pi_i^{73}$				1.1103 (1.741)
$^{99}\Delta\Pi_i^{7076}$	−0.3667 (1.4628)			
L_i^{6873}			−0.1143 (1.887)	
L_i^{6870}				0.1192 (1.802)
L_i^{6876}		0.0851 (1.358)		
L_i^N	0.2583 (2.582)			
X_i^L		−0.1331 (1.5665)		
$\bar{R}^2$	0.2326	0.1522	0.1094	0.2352

Notes: 1. 't' values in parenthesis.

identify an identical index of job shedding in the East Midlands where new firm formation rate data are also available, but the absence of any association between formation rates and national profitability data is again clear.

Even with stronger statistical associations, it could be argued that such an analysis is still compatible with conventional theory since the employment status of those starting the businesses is not given. However work undertaken by one of the present authors (Storey 1982) and by Binks and Jennings (1986) shows that between 25 per cent and 50 per cent of those starting new businesses claim to have been unemployed immediately prior to starting in business. Furthermore since these businesses were defined as being wholly new, i.e. not having more than 50 per cent of their share capital owned by any other enterprise, then their founders are certainly not existing asset holders buying up undervalued companies.

The evidence presented in this paper is not conclusive but it does suggest that local labour market conditions are of greater importance in influencing local rates of new firm formation than national indices of profitability.

Notes

1   We are grateful for the many helpful suggestions made by Mike Waterson and an anonymous referee. We also thank Steve Fothergill and Graham Gudgin for allowing us access to their data on establishments in the East Midlands, but the opinions expressed are those of the authors alone.Date of receipt of final manuscript: 21 April 1986

2   It is worth noting that the most appropriate measure of profitability in a profit maximisation model of limit pricing is the price-cost margin, equivalent to the profit-sales ratio.

3   This simple determinacy was criticised by Caves and Porter (1977). They argued that structural barriers to entry, seen by Bain (1956) as exogenous, are in fact subject to the endogenous behaviour of incumbent firms.

4   In developing their theory of barriers to mobility, Caves and Porter (1977) hypothesise the existence of subgroup structures within industries accompanied by group-specific entry barriers. An implication of this model is that potential entrants may also be distinguishable on the basis of the group they intend to enter. Caves and Porter define these groups primarily in terms of marketing strategies and they are therefore not strictly comparable with the distinction we propose to make between established and wholly new firms. However their approach does illustrate that much may be gained by abandoning assumptions of homogeneity.

5   "The labourer asks what he thinks the entrepreneur will be able to pay and in any case will not accept less than he can get from some other entrepreneur, or by turning entrepreneur himself. In the same way the entrepreneur offers to any labourer what he thinks he must in order to secure his services and in any case will not offer more than he thinks the labour will be worth to him, keeping in mind what he can get by turning labourer himself." (Knight, 1921)

6   In a survey, carried out in the area which is now Cleveland county, 26 per cent of new firm founders claimed to have been unemployed prior to starting their business (Storey, 1982). Other authors who have seen unemployment as a stimulus of new firm formation include Dahmen (1970), Wedervang (1965) and Oxenfeldt (1943).

7   The Cleveland survey, which covered all industries except retailing, found that 60 per cent of new firm founders had remained in the same industrial order (Storey, 1982). The comparable figure produced by Johnson and Cathcart (1979) was 50 per cent.

8   In the empirical section of this paper it is assumed that NF_i is a multiplicative function, log-linear in terms, X and L.

9   Another factor, explored by Kihlstrom and Laffont (1979) is the degree of risk aversion amongst entrepreneurs, whilst differences in wage rates in i and j could also affect the model specification.

10 The construction is described in detail in Storey, Keasey, Watson and Wynarczyk (1987).

References

Bain, J. S. (1956). *Barriers to New Competition*. Cambridge, U.S.A.: Harvard University Press.

Bayldon R., Woods, A. and Zafiris N. (1984). Inner City versus New Towns: A Comparison of Manufacturing Performance. *Oxford Bulletin of Economics and Statistics*, Vol. 46, No. 1. pp. 21–30.

Binks, M. and Jennings, A. (1986). *Small Firms as a source of Industrial Regeneration*, in J. Curran, J. Stanworth and D. Watkins (ed) "*The Survival of the Small Firm*", Aldershot, Gower.

Caves, R. E. and Porter, M. E. (1977). From Entry Barriers to Mobility Barriers: Conjectural Decisions and Contrived Deterrence to New Competition. *Quarterly Journal of Economics*, Vol. 91, pp. 241–261.

Clarke, R. (1985). *Industrial Economics*. Oxford: Basil Blackwell.

Dahmen, E. (1970). *Entrepreneurial Activity and the Development of Swedish industry* 1919–1939. Homewood, Illinois: Richard D. Irwin.

Deutsch, L. L. (1984). Entry and the extent of multiplant operations. *Journal of Industrial Economics*, Vol. 32, No. 4, June, pp. 477–487.

Fothergill, S. and Gudgin, G. (1982). *Unequal Growth*. London: Heinemann Educational Books.

Fothergill, S., Gudgin, G., Kitson, M. and Monk, S. (1984). Differences in the Profitability of the U.K. Manufacturing Sector between conurbations and other Areas. *Scottish Journal of Political Economy*, Vol. 31, No. 1. February, pp. 72–91.

Gorecki, P. K. (1975). The Determinants of Entry by New and Diversifying Enterprises in the U.K. Manufacturing Sector 1958–1963: Some Tentative Results. *Applied Economics*, Vol. 7, pp. 139–147.

Henderson, R. A. (1980). An Analysis of Closures among Scottish Manufacturing Plants between 1966 and 1975. *Scottish Journal of Political Economy*, Vol. 27, pp. 152–174.

Hymer, S. and Pashigan, P. (1962). Firm Size and Rate of Growth. *Journal of Political Economy*, Vol. 70, pp. 556–569.

Johnson, P. S. and Cathcart, D. G. (1979). New Manufacturing Firms and Regional Development: Some Evidence from the Northern Region. *Regional Studies*, Vol. 13, pp. 269–280.

Kihlstrom, R. E. and Laffont, J. (1979). A General Equilibrium Entrepreneurial Theory of Firm Formation Based on Risk Aversion. *Journal of Political Economy*, Vol. 87, pp. 719–748.

Knight, F. H. (1921). *Risk, Uncertainty and profit*. New York: Houghton Mifflin.

Lyons, B. (1980). A New Measure of Minimum Efficient Plant Size in U.K. Manufacturing Industry. *Economica*, Vol. 47, pp. 19–34.

Mansfield, E. (1962). Entry, Gibrat's Law, Innovation and the Growth of Firms. *American Economic Review*, Vol. 52, pp. 1023–1051.

Marcus, M. (1967). Firms' Exit Rates and their Determinants. *Journal of Industrial Economics*, Vol. 16, pp. 10–22

Orr, D. (1974). The Determinants of Entry: a Study of the Canadian Manufacturing Industries. *The Review of Economics and Statistics*, Vol. 56, pp. 58–65.

Oxenfeldt, A. R. (1943). *New Firms and Free Enterprise*. Washington, American Council on Public Affairs.

Sawyer, M. C. (1981). *The Economics of Industries and Firms*. London: Croom Helm.

Scherer, F. M. (1980). *Industrial Market Structure and Economic Performance*. Chicago: Rand McNally.

Storey, D. J. (1982). *Entrepreneurship and the New Firm* London: Croom Helm.

Storey, D. J. Keasey, K., Watson, R. and Wynarczyk, P. (1987). The Performance of Small Firms. London: Croom Helm.

Van Derck, G. (1984). Entry. Exit and Profitability. *Managerial and Decision Economics*, Vol. 5, No. 1, pp. 25–31.

Waterson, M. (1984). *Economic Theory of the Industry*. London: Cambridge University Press.

Wedervang, F. (1965). *Development of a Population of Industrial Firms*. Oslo: Scandinavian University Books.

5

Small Firms' Seedbed Role and the Concept of Turbulence*

M. E. Beesley and R. T. Hamilton

*Source: *Journal of Industrial Economics* 33, 4 (1984), 217–29.

Introduction

An important role of independent small firms is often asserted to be to function as the 'seedbed' for new enterprises capable of challenging established businesses. The authors bring original data to bear on this, suggesting a workable definition of what constitutes a seedbed; measuring its industrial incidence; and defining the part played by independent firms in it. The study reveals substantial variation in the level of such activity among manufacturing industries. It is shown that seedbed activity is essentially innovative (the precursor of new industries) rather than a source of increased rivalry within existing industries. Conclusions are drawn about small firms policy, in particular that government aid for small business should be aimed more at reducing death rates among small firms.

The seedbed function

The notion of a seedbed process influencing industry population over time is implicit in Marshall's analogy with "... the young trees of the forest as they struggle upwards through the benumbing shade of their older rivals" (1920, Chapter 8, p. 263). Marshall describes a continuous process of birth and death in the forest's undergrowth, with few undertakings reaching maturity and surviving, perhaps in perpetuity, as joint-stock companies. Since he was concerned at that point with aggregate industry structure, Marshall did not need to consider the variation of fertility and mortality across industries. The seedbed role was seized upon in 1971 by the Report of the Committee of Inquiry into Small Firms (the Bolton Report [1971]). This inquiry confined itself to small *independent* firms (i.e., those managed by the people who own them) and excluded from its scope the subsidiary units of large companies. To quote from the Report [1971, p. 85, para. 8.5]:

> "We believe that the health of the economy requires the birth of new enterprises in substantial number and the growth of some to a position from which they are able to challenge and supplant the existing leaders of industry... This 'seedbed' function, therefore, appears to be a vital contribution of the small firm sector to the long-run health of the economy. We cannot assume that the ordinary working of market forces will necessarily preserve a small firm sector large enough to perform this function in the future."

The Committee thus expressed its major concern that, if left unattended, the fertile undergrowth may erode to such an extent as to jeopardize the continued propagation of the seedplants. In fact, in the event, the Committee went on to judge that erosion on such a scale was not then a serious prospect but that the situation be subject to "regular monitoring" [1971, P. 90, para. 8.16]. However, the seedbed process has proved more easily grasped as a concept than measured. No doubt due in large part to the lack of relevant data, the situation has not come under close monitoring. Given the public attention and resources now being devoted to the small business sector, it is important to gain some understanding on whether the benefits which it is thought society as a whole derives from the 'seedbed' are likely to exist.

The Bolton Committee perceived the challenge of independent small firms to be on two related fronts. The first emphasised the innovative role of new ventures and the threat to established industry leaders from the emergence of entirely new industries. Second, new firms expanding within established industries would erode the market power of the dominant suppliers, that is the incumbent firm's ability to deter actual entry. The major objectives of this paper are to establish the existence of a seedbed, and to clarify the extent to which the sector's contribution is either to establish new industries or to increase rivalry within well-defined industry orders.

The 'seedbed' can be viewed as the arena in which businesses are born and, judging by the body of evidence on the infant mortality of businesses (Boswell [1971]; Churchill [1955]; Gudgin [1978]; Marcus [1967]), where most will die. It follows that to show the extent and industrial composition of seedbed activity we need data on the birth and death rates of businesses by industry. Seedbed industries will be those with high birth and death rates. In other words, introducing a term which we develop below, the firm population of such industries will be subject to high levels of 'turbulence' because of the contemporaneous impact of these flows. By measuring births and deaths as distinct flows at the industry level we can identify the more active seedbed areas and begin to assess the extent to which this process is likely to lead either to more competitive industries or to more industries.

The data

The work reported here is part of a wider study into the dynamics of industry structure. Data on births and deaths of establishments were extracted from the registers of HM Inspector of Factories (HMIF) for Scotland. Births are establishments observed to have opened in Scotland between 1 January 1977 and 31 March 1980. Deaths mean establishments which closed in Scotland between 1 January 1977 and 31 December 1979. A full account of the data collection and validation process is in Hamilton [1982]. The data's characteristic advantage was that they permitted the measurement of gross birth and death rates: almost all previous studies had had to be content with measuring the effect of differences between births or deaths over a period, i.e. the net increase or decrease in the total stock.

Unlike most official information sources, the HMIF registers extend to all sizes of establishment. This is most important in any study of new and small businesses since, at least in numerical terms, it is very small units which are likely to be predominant. However, for the purpose in hand, a measurement difficulty arises because the movement of an establishment to a new location will be recorded as both an opening and a closure. To minimize this distortion all businesses were traced which, in the relevant time period, moved location within Scotland. These businesses (eighty-two in all) were excluded from the birth and death measures. Unfortunately it proved impossible to identify those businesses observed in the act of moving to or from Scotland. Thus, whilst the data are treated as births and deaths, 'births' include establishments which moved into Scotland and 'deaths' encompass units which transferred from the country. This renders the data somewhat imprecise but available statistics[1] do confirm business movement to and from Scotland to be much less frequent than internal movement. We are therefore confident that our measures closely approximate true births and deaths.

As seen earlier, we must distinguish between independent businesses and 'dependent' operations (i.e., subsidiary or associate companies; branch plants; and franchises). This is the dichotomy intended[2] in the Bolton Report. So in a 'birth' or 'death' the distinction must be maintained. Moreover, the processes leading up to the birth (or death) of a dependent unit are likely to be essentially different from those of an independent business. To achieve this distinction between dependence and independence, elements of the database were checked through trade directories and editions of *Who Owns Whom*. Each business was presumed to be independent in the absence of contrary evidence and so a number of dependent units –

Table 5.1 Births and deaths in manufacturing industry

Employment:	Births		Deaths	
	IB	DB	ID	DD
	Period: 4½ years		Period: 3 years	
10 or less	719	163	890	175
11–49	259	88	341	102
50+	29	42	87	90
Unknown	287	104	121	50
Total	1294	397	1439	417
Rates (based on June 1973 stock of 9606 units)				
Total/Stock %	13.5	4.1	15.0	4.3

particularly the smallest – may have been misclassified as independent (rather than vice-versa).

The HMIF registers cover all of manufacturing and register entries (business premises) are classified to a Minimum List Heading (MLH) under the 1968 Standard Industrial Classification. At this stage the database was four absolute flows for each MLH industry: independent births (IB); dependent births (DB); independent deaths (ID); and dependent deaths (DD). The final step in the construction of the database involved transforming the individual flows into industry birth and death rates by dividing each flow by a count of the initial stock of establishments in that industry. The appropriate denominator for this calculation had to meet stringent requirements. Stock figures had to relate to Scotland at the MLF industry level. Enumeration must not have involved either sampling or the imposition of lower cut-off limits in terms of size (otherwise, this would have led to the exclusion of considerable numbers of small units). Finally, stock numbers were required to apply to a point in time before the start of the birth and death flows. These requirements were met by the data produced by the Annual Census of Employment (ACE) for June 1973, and this is the source of the denominators used to obtain industry birth and death rates. Table 5.1 aggregates the various flows to convey the size and structure of the database.

Upon viewing Table 5.1 the reader is reminded that the birth and death flows relate to monitoring periods of different durations. This is a consequence of HMIF rules governing the retention period of register details on businesses which have closed. What information we have on the employment size of these establishments is sufficient to emphasize the extent to which we are indeed dealing with a host of small firms, independent and dependent. The birth and death rates calculated in Table 5.1 are global mean values for manufacturing in Scotland. Despite a shorter monitoring period,[3] deaths outnumber births – a result consistent with the general decline in Scottish manufacturing over the years to which our data relate.

The concept of turbulence

The term 'turbulence' is introduced to denote the flux created in an industry's total composition by flows of births and deaths. A few authors have come close to this concept but none appears to have carried through with the analysis. Caves and Porter [1976] suggest that:

> "Firms may go through life cycles, with lifespans varying from industry to industry. If some industries experience higher rates of generational turnover, perhaps due to greater frequency as amplitude of disturbances, they will show (*ceteris paribus*) more deaths and more births than other industries.... If industries vary in their rates of turnover, the occurrence of exit should be positively related to the occurrence of entry, with entry serving as a proxy for the unknown underlying forces that speed the generalizational turnover of settlers."

Caves and Porter go on to claim to have uncovered evidence of systematic differences in industries' rates of generational turnover. This evidence is in the form of a positive though weakly significant association between dummy variables which reflect the occurrence but not the extent of both entry and exit. Gudgin [1978, p. 193] broaches our concept of turbulence thus:

> "There are thus industries characterised by high turnover in firms and establishments and others with low turnover. This situation, which is also described by Wedervang for Norwegian industries, is only part of the story since some industries with high closure rates also have low entry rates."

Gudgin does not appear to have expanded on this casual observation. Our concept of turbulence reflects the same phenomenon which has attracted the attention of these authors. At this juncture it is useful to clarify terminology. A number of industrial economists have developed narrower measures of intra-industry mobility (or turnover). This also expresses the idea of challenge to established positions, in that it considers displacement of top ranking firms in industries by others. Such movements take place over many years. Thus particular studies (see Scherer [1980, pp. 54–56]) have been confined to analyses of changes over long periods of time in the size rankings of none but the largest corporations drawn from widely defined

Table 5.2 Components of turbulence in high and low turbulence industries

Components of turbulence	High T industries	Low T industries	All manufacturing
IB + ID/Stock (mean)	0.49	0.15	0.28
DB + DD/Stock (mean)	0.11	0.06	0.09
Number of industries	10	26	123

areas (e.g. the whole of manufacturing industry or the population of all non-financial corporations.

According to Boyle and Sorenson [1971] a general weakness of such studies has been their lack of industry specificity. Our turbulence analysis is conducted within narrowly defined (MLH) industries but the time-scale is short. We cannot identify the rank size order in each industry at any point in time. Hence our analysis is not of mobility (or turnover) as these terms have come to be used. Turbulence expresses a different source of challenge – by change in the identity of separate units in particular industries over a shorter period.[4]

Extent and nature of turbulence

Drawing on the discussion of the data section, our measure of industry turbulence is:

$$T = \frac{(IB + ID) + (DB + DD)}{Stock}$$

In the manufacturing industries as a whole, the global mean value of T is 0.37. In calculating T values for individual industries we must guard against the possibility of very small industries generating extreme values. Hence our detailed analysis of turbulence is confined to those MLH industries with a stock of at least fifty establishments. This serves to reduce our sample size to fifty-seven MLH manufacturing industries (from 123).

In Figure 5.1 we have plotted birth rate against death rate for these fifty-seven industries. The quadrants arise from imposing on to this scatter diagram the global mean rates for the whole of manufacturing (see Table 5.1). The ten industries in the upper right quadrant have above average rates of birth and death. The lower left quadrant contains the twenty-six industries with below average birth and death rates. Other quadrants contain industries with either an above average birth or death rate, but not both. The small group of high birth, high death rate industries are turbulent in the fullest sense with an average T value of 0.60. This compares with a mean of 0.21 for the low birth, low death grouping. (The difference between these

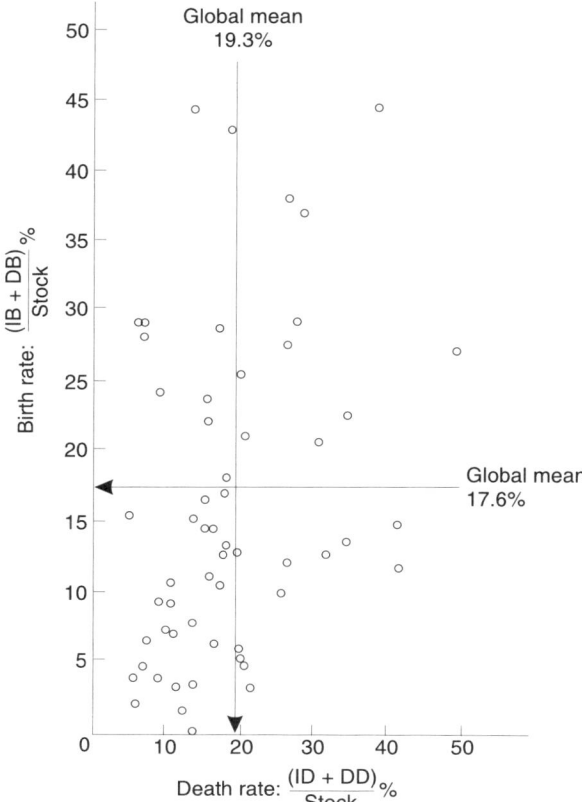

Figure 5.1 Plot of birth rate against death rate for 57 manufacturing industries.

means is highly significant on a Student's *t* test.) Remaining industries have an average *T* score of 0.39, close to the global mean (0.37) for all manufacturing.

Having revealed the extent to which turbulence varies across industries, let us now concentrate on the groups of high and low turbulence industries (upper right and lower left quadrants respectively of Figure 5.1). When the average turbulence values of these industries are decomposed into their independent and dependent components, the result is set out in Table 5.2.

It is readily apparent that turbulence is essentially a phenomenon involving independent businesses. In the group of high *T* industries, the contribution of the dependent component (mean 0.11) is not markedly different from its average over all manufacturing (0.09). It is the very large independent component which renders these industries highly turbulent. In the set of twenty-six low *T* industries, whilst both components are much lower, the bulk of the fall in total turbulence is due to the threefold reduction in the independent component. So it is correct to identify the seedbed as involving independent businesses primarily.

To take the analysis further we note that the very highest levels of turbulence occur in the following industries:

MLH 349   Other mechanical engineering not elsewhere specified ($T=0.65$)
MLH 399   Metal industries not elsewhere specified ($T = 0.66$)
MLH 479   Miscellaneous wood and cork manufacturers ($T = 0.76$)
MLH 496   Plastic products not elsewhere specified ($T = 0.83$)

These extremely turbulent industries have in common a lack of precise definition. Each is a residual category intended to capture those businesses whose products are such as to defy ready classification into more narrowly-defined MLH industries. It seemed very likely that these classifications are biased towards products which are either novel or unconventional (or both). Thus discussion of turbulence leads us to those ill-defined areas of the Standard Industrial Classification in which new industries are developed, later to become recognisable as independent industries. Turbulence indicates a process of commercial trial and error (birth and death), predominantly involving independent entrepreneurs. It is in this sense and to this extent that we might regard the 'seedbed' role of small firms as correlated with innovatory behaviour.

Influences on turbulence

The foregoing analysis has been confined to the extremes of very high and very low turbulence. To generalise, we must extend our scope to include all fifty-seven industries contained in Figure 5.1. So our concern in this section is to identify industry attributes (in addition to classification specificity) which seem to govern the variation in turbulence across industries.

We treat turbulence as the joint product of birth and death (or gross entry and exit) at the industry level. This enables us to draw on the separate birth and death (entry and exit) literature to generate hypotheses on what influences turbulence. We concentrate on five kinds of influence on births and deaths, viz. the capital cost of entry to an industry; the proportion of small units in it; industry profitability; industry growth; and concentration. Two of these are readily related to turbulence, but three are not and so we must make distinctions different from those of previous authors. This need arises because we deal with gross flows of births and deaths whereas previous studies have in the main been concerned with explaining the net effect of births and deaths, i.e., whether over a period the stock of businesses has risen or fallen. If a given influence is expected both to raise birth rates and raise death rates, there is a straightforward inference for effects on turbulence – it will be higher. The converse applies when the influence is likely to reduce both birth and death rates. But other cases are not clear. For example, if one anticipates a raised birth rate and a lower death rate, the effect on turbulence is unclear.

The higher the capital (and other) costs of entry, the more difficult it is thought to be to enter (Mansfield [1962]; Gorecki [1975]) and exit (Caves and Porter [1976]). Moreover, the greater the share of larger units (or conversely, the smaller the proportion of small units, the greater is inertia inherent in operations. Both these factors, obviously not unrelated themselves, would tend to be clearly related to turbulence – they would lower it. Higher profit is thought to encourage entry and lead to a net increase in units in an industry (Mansfield [1976]; Gorecki [1975]). But with respect to turbulence the effect is uncertain because circumstances favourably affecting profits would simultaneously increase births and decrease deaths (Marcus [1967]). So also for industry growth. Higher concentration would normally be expected to raise profit levels and so encourage entry (Duetsch [1975]). But rising concentration would also discourage births because of associations with entry barriers in general (Orr [1974]). We therefore expect the last three influences to be ambiguous for turbulence. To sum up: the level of industry turbulence (T) should be negatively related to the capital cost of entry to the industry; positively related to the proportion of very small units in the employment structure of the industry; but statistically independent of measures of industry profitability; growth; and concentration. In addition to these hypotheses, and drawing on the conclusion of the previous section, we also postulate a strong positive association between turbulence and the lack of specificity in an industry's classification. We now analyse these influences on turbulence. If and when the direction of the ambiguous effects is established, we can attempt further explanations.

Statistical analysis strongly confirms that two of the three ambiguous elements – profitability and concentration – are insignificant concomitants of total turbulence. The results of regression analysis involving the remaining explanatory variables[5] are presented in Table 5.3. In equation (I) the small firm share (SHSM) coefficient is statistically insignificant. This can be attributed in part to the degree of correlation between entry cost (KINT) and SHSM (see correlation matrix). Omitting SHSM (equation (2)) has very little effect on the explanatory power of the regression. Introducing a dummy variable (DMY) reflecting the specificity of industry classification serves (equation (3)) to substantially increase the $\bar{R}^2$ value. In this final equation all the coefficients are highly significant (with no serious multicollinearity) and we explain forty per cent of the variation in industry levels of turbulence. The KINT and DMY coefficients have the expected signs and the size of the DMY coefficient confirms our earlier observation about the nature of the most turbulent industries. However, the significant positive relationship between turbulence and growth (GTH) is contrary to expectation. The most obvious explanation for this is that growth stimulates births but, even over the short time span covered by this study, high

Table 5.3 Multiple regression analysis of turbulence

Equation	Y	Constant	KINT	SHSM	GTH	DMY	N	$\bar{R}^2$	F
(1)	T	0.26	−0.004	0.002	0.002		43	0.26	5.94
		(2.07)	(−1.75)	(1.19)	(2.77)				(3.39)
(2)	T	0.40	−0.006		0.003		43	0.25	8.12
		(12.29)	(−2.43)		(3.10)				(2.40)
(3)	T	0.37	−0.005		0.002	0.20	43	0.40	10.39
		(11.60)	(−2.41)		(2.87)	(3.30)			(3.39)

Notes: The figures in brackets are the t-values.
N represents the number of observations used.
Serial correlation absent in each estimated equation (Durbin-Watson test).

Correlation matrix

	KINT	SHSM	GTH	DMY
KINT	1.00	−0.40	−0.05	−0.10
SHSM		1.00	0.22	0.43
GTH			1.00	0.17
DMY				1.00

birth rates themselves come to be associated with high death rates. (The simple correlation coefficient between the total birth and death rates plotted in Figure 5.1 is +0.31). Death rates could thus be due to factors independent of industry types, but related to the fact that the population is young; seedlings are more vulnerable. To test this hypothesis would require data relating particular births to particular deaths.

Turbulence and industry concentration

The second aspect of small firms' seedbed challenge involves the erosion of the market power of dominant suppliers. We have just reported total turbulence (T) to be independent of the level of industry concentration. However, we can explore further the relationship between total turbulence and concentration by distinguishing the dependent and independent firm components.

The industry concentration ratios used are the percentage of 1973 industry employment in units each employing more than 500 people. Each of the fifty-seven industries was allocated to one of three groups depending on the value of the concentration ratio. Within each grouping, we calculated the mean value of total turbulence (T) and the means of the independent and dependent components. This information is contained in Table 5.4.

Table 5.4 Turbulence and industry concentration

Concentration range	0–15.9%	16.0–49.9%	50–100%
Mean concentration	*4.5%*	*30.4%*	*65.9%*
T (mean)	0.34	0.34	0.37
IB + ID/Stock	0.28	0.26	0.24
BD + DD/Stock	0.06	0.08	0.13
Number of industries	22	20	15

Table 5.5 Birth and death rates of businesses at different concentration levels

Concentration range	0–49.9%	50–100%
IB (% mean)	11.5	13.0
DB	2.9	8.1
ID	15.8	10.4
DD	4.0	4.7

The concentration ranges were chosen to ensure a reasonable spread of industry observations across the groups. Noting the mean concentration ratio for each group, we can reasonably regard the data as relating to low; medium; and high levels of concentration.

The slight increase of turbulence (to 0.37) in the most concentrated industries is not statistically significant. The independent component of T falls slightly with increased concentration but this decline is more than offset by the large (and statistically significant) increase in the dependent component when we move into the highly concentrated industries. The immediate inference to be drawn is that, whilst dependent businesses are only involved to a minor degree in the overall turbulence of the less concentrated industries, such businesses do make a major contribution to turbulence in highly concentrated industries. We can in fact refine this conclusion because the simple correlation coefficient (r) between dependent birth and death rates is insignificant at +0.02 (between independent birth and death rates, $r = +0.44$). Thus, the high dependent component of turbulence in these industries is very much more likely to be the consequence of a high rate of birth or death, but not both. Table 5.5 sets out individual birth and death rates according to the level of industry, concentration.

Of the increases and decreases reported in Table 5.5, only the increase in dependent birth rate is statistically significant (Student's t test).

To refine our original inference, the increased contribution of dependent businesses to the turbulence of highly concentrated industries reflects their much higher birth rate in these industries. But why should dependent businesses gravitate so strongly into these areas? The most likely explanation following Berry [1974], is that only large firms are able to encroach – via the setting up of dependent units – into areas already dominated by other large firms. Less likely, drawing on Brozen [1974], is that concentration is indeed a good proxy for profits and that, in this respect, established companies are more perspicacious than independent entrepreneurs. Thus, the overall level of seedbed activity is not influenced by concentration level but seedbed composition is markedly different in the most concentrated industries. Independent founders do not appear to be significantly repelled by increased concentration. However, the competitive challenge of dependent units is much more selective and directed at the areas of highest concentration. On these grounds we would argue that the more serious competitive threat to dominant suppliers is from the strategic entry moves of other large companies rather than the activities of the archetypal small entrepreneur.

Conclusions and implications for UK small firms policy

An essential function of the small business sector is alleged to be the seedbed of the new initiatives from which will emerge the successful businesses and industries of the future. This notion is intuitively plausible but we have so far lacked any measure of the extent or nature of seedbed activity. The concept of a seedbed cannot be disassociated from business trial and error (birth and death). Active seedbed industries will be in continuous flux due to contemporaneous birth and death flows. The usual measures of intra-industry mobility (or turnover) are inappropriate as indicators of this type of flux. We have developed the idea of turbulence into a direct measure of the flux created within individual industries due to the coincidence of birth and death flows.

The first point to emerge on the nature of seedbed activity is to confirm that it does involve independent much more than dependent units. The most turbulent MLH industries, we found, had the least specific definitions. It is to such open-ended industries that one would tend to classify those innovative ventures based on products sufficiently novel or unconventional as to prevent their being recorded in any narrowly-defined industry. Thus, seedbed activity is indeed associated with innovation. We intend to pursue the determinants of inter-industry variation in birth and death rates making up turbulence in subsequent work.

Further, we observed the nature of turbulence to be significantly influenced by industry concentration. Whilst independent founders do appear to be predominantly innovative, we see the major competitive challenge to dominant suppliers as coming from the diversification moves of other established companies.

From the early 1970s – provoked by the recommendations of the Bolton Committee – successive UK governments have contributed to the *ad hoc* development of a small firms policy. Towards the end of the decade the thrust of policy had become more selective in favour of new firms (rather than all small firms). Our evidence suggests that the benefits from such a policy will be in the form of innovation and new industries rather than the erosion of producer surplus in established industries. The more effective attack on this is likely to come from other established firms. In terms of the selectivity of policy instruments, we have traced high seedbed activity to a few ill-defined areas of industry. Our data reveal many, independent entrepreneurs prepared to try something out of the ordinary – and that many fail in the attempt.

Initiatives intended to stimulate new business creation must anticipate turbulence and be able to tolerate high death rates. Their lack of industrial definition will make it difficult to channel specific support into such areas. To reduce the anticipated early, failure rate of new businesses requires a method of choosing the 'best', *ex ante*, on the basis of formal plans and entrepreneurial skills. Apart from the question of the policy operators' ability to make the judgements, the method would require detailed analyses of 'industry' prospects and trends, when we have indicated that many entrepreneurs focus on ill-defined, and thus necessarily badly documented industries. Such individuals are likely to have extreme difficulty obtaining the data to support their claims. (They might have even greater difficulty accepting the need to reveal and justify their ideas on paper).

These difficulties of running a policy based on *ex ante* encouragement are as desirable as they are inevitable. The willingness to act in the face of uncertainty is just what we require of entrepreneurs. Hence we are led to suggest that if aid to seedbed activity is to be given, it should be directed more at the problem of helping established firms recognise the symptoms of incipient failure in advance, i.e. of reducing the general tendency for young firms to be especially vulnerable. This, in turn, would redirect attention to increasing management skills, opportunities for finding consultancy advice, and like activities; that is, to a policy based on adding to the skills of entrepreneurs whilst engaged in running their business. This shift to a post-entry policy is supported by our finding less variance among death rates than among birth rates when industries are compared. But in general, the instinct to support small business, which has grown remarkably irrespective of government changes since the Bolton Committee reported, has been shown to have rather more solid support in fact than the Committee was itself able to demonstrate.

Appendix

Table 5.A1 Definitions and statistical sources of the explanatory variables.

Variable	Definition	Statistical sources
Capital cost of entry (KINT) (£,000)	Net capital expenditure per employee (1975) times mid-point of modal employment size band (1975).	Scottish Abstract of Statistics (SAS) 1980, Table 12.7. Annual Census of Employment (ACE) 1975.
Share of small units (SHSM) (%)	Percentage number of units with less than 25 people in June 1974.	ACE 1974 (Scotland).
Industry profitablity:		
*NQHD (£,000 per employee)	Net output per person employed (1975).	SAS 1980, Table 12.7.
*MARG (% profit margin)	Net output less wages and salaries, as % of industry sales.	Business Monitor PA1000, Census of Production 1976 (UK data).
Industry growth (GTH) (%)	Percentage change in industry employment between 1970 and 1977.	SAS 1974, Table 118. SAS 1981, Table 12.5.
*Concentration (CONC) (%)	Percentage of 1973 industry employment in units each employing more than 500 people.	ACE 1973 (Scotland).
Industry classification specificity (DMY) (dummy variable)	Value of 1 in following MLH industries: 229, 279, 349, 369, 399, 469, 479, 489, 496, 499.	Based on the 1968 Standard Industrial Classification.

* Statistically insignificant as determinants of the level of industry turbulence.

Notes

1   See *Regional Trends* 1981, Table 10.5, page 115.
2   The Bolton Committee of Inquiry was not able to make this dichotomy in the quantitative sections of its report because official statistics are not complied on this basis.
3   To standardise for the different monitoring periods we presume the HMIF registers to operate with constant lags between birth or death and the monitoring thereof. Hence the annual rate of IB is $(13.5 \div 4.5)\% = 3.0\%$, cf. ID rate of 5.0% per annum. For DB and DD the annual rates are 0.9% and 1.4% respectively.
4   In operating at industry level our measures also avoid a problem which arises with these studies' use of rank correlation coefficients as measures of mobility over time. These coefficients are sensitive to the ranks assigned to new entrants to, and exits from, the sector over the period. This measurement problem becomes more critical if rank correlation is used to reflect mobility within a larger number of more narrowly defined industries.
5   The reader is referred to the Appendix for definitions and statistical sources of the explanatory variables used in this investigation.

References

Berry, C. H., 1974, 'Corporate Diversification and Market Structure', *The Bell Journal of Economics*, Vol 5, No 1 (Spring), pp. 196–204.

Bolton Report, 1971, Committee of Inquiry on Small Firms, Cmnd 4811, (HMSO, London).

Boswell, J., 1971, *The Rise and Decline of Small Firms*, (George Allen & Unwin, London).

Boyle, S. E. and Sorenson, R. L., 1971, 'Concentration and Mobility: Alternative Measures of Industry Structure'. *The Journal of Industrial Economics*, Vol 19, No 2 (April), pp. 118–32.

Brozen, G., 1974, 'Concentration and Profits: Does Concentration Matter?,' *Antitrust Bulletin*, Vol 19 (Summer), pp.381–99.

Caves, R. E. and Porter, M. E., 1976, 'Barriers to Exit', Chapter 3 in *Essays on Industrial Organisation in Honor of Joe S. Bain*, edited by R. T. Masson and P. D. Qualls, (Ballinger Publishing, Cambridge, Mass.).

Churchill, B. C., 1955, 'Age and Life Expectancy of Business Firms', *Survey of Current Business*, Vol 35, No 12 (December), pp. 15–19, 24.

Deutsch, L. L., 1975, 'Structure, Performance and the Net Rate of Entry into Manufacturing Industries', *The Southern Economic Journal*, Vol 41, No 3 (January), pp. 450–56.

Gorecki, P. K.,1975, 'The Determinants of Entry by New and Diversifying Enterprises in the UK Manufacturing Sector 1958–1963: Some Tentative Results', *Applied Economics*, Vol 7, No 2 (June), pp. 139–47.

Gudgin, G., 1978, *Industrial Location Processes and Regional Employment Growth*, (Saxon House, Farnborough).

Hamilton, R. T., 1982, *Measures and Determinants of Entry and Exit Rates of Businesses in Scotland*, Unpublished PhD thesis, University of London.

Mansfield, 1962, 'Entry Gibrat's Law, Innovation and the Growth of Firms, *American Economic Review*, Vol 52, No 5 (December), pp. 1023–51.

Marcus, M., 1967, 'Firms' Exit Rates and their Determinants', *The Journal of Industrial Economics*, Vol 16, No 1, (November), pp. 10–22.

Marshall, A., 1920, *Principles of Economics*, (8th edition), (Macmillan & Co Ltd, London).

Orr, D., 1974, 'The Determinants of Entry: A Study of Canadian Manufacturing Industries', *Review of Economics and Statistics*, Vol 56, No 1 (February), pp. 58–66.

Sherer, F. M., 1980, *Industrial Market Structure and Economic Performance* (2nd edition), Rand McNally, Chicago).

Part 2

Deaths

Introduction

This part contains a selection of very different styles of writing. Five of them are quantitative analyses of the factors influencing the survival of small – primarily new – enterprises. The context for these studies, however, is provided by the writing of MacDonald and Coffield – containing no tables, no numbers and certainly no equations – about the experience of young people establishing businesses in the area of England known as Teesside. This is an area where employment is dominated by large manufacturing establishments and which has experienced high levels of unemployment for several decades.

MacDonald and Coffield provide 'real life' illustrations of concepts that are used in the five quantitative papers that follow. They demonstrate that business failure can, in some instances, inflict serious mental scars upon those unfortunate enough to experience it. For example, the description by 'Lynne' of her experiences should be provided as an antidote to all those who view an 'enterprise culture' as an unmitigated benefit.

MacDonald and Coffield also valuably illustrate the huge diversity of trades and activities in which small businesses are started. Even in this restricted geographical area they identified 'two young men who specialised in watch and clock repairs, a writer of historical novels, two picture framers, a signwriter, an interpreter, a man who imported and exported silverware, a man who ran a nappy delivery service and a mountain guide'.

However, it is in the addressing of analytical issues that the paper has true value. It demonstrates that almost all the individuals running these businesses are 'plodders'. They work long hours, often for a very modest income. Their attitude is stoical and resilient, rather than entrepreneurial. So why do they persist? Some believe they have a prospect of 'winning the lottery' – although almost all know that they will not; many derive considerable job satisfaction working for themselves rather than for others; third, they know they are unlikely to obtain well-paid jobs as employees. The writing, therefore, clearly sets up the analytical 'choice' faced by individuals in deciding whether or not to start as an entrepreneur.

The article also highlights the elements incorporated within the quantitative analysis: the importance of access to finance and the role of parents in providing funding for their offspring's business. As MacDonald and Coffield say, families provided 'essential physical, financial and emotional support. Their sacrifices to the success of new businesses often goes unrecognised in practitioner guide books to starting and running businesses'.

Finally, MacDonald and Coffield also examine the choice facing those in businesses as to whether or not to continue. This is encapsulated in their quote from 'Duncan' who says: 'Well, there's no point in packing it in 'cos there's nothing there to do if you do'.

All these highly qualitative points are developed in the five quantitative papers which discuss the factors influencing small, but primarily new, firm survival in the United States, Portugal and Germany.

Some of the factors influencing small firm survival identified from the five studies are shown in Table 1. They are grouped into three categories: entrepreneurial characteristics, firm characteristics and strategy. These categorisations have previously been used by the author – Storey 1994 – as a mechanism for clustering small enterprise characteristics.

Entrepreneurial characteristics are essentially the characteristics of the entrepreneur, which are identifiable *prior* to him or her starting a business. They are the '*pre-start*' characteristics. Firm characteristics are essentially set *when* the firm starts in business. They are 'start up' characteristics.

Third, the firm is able, once it begins trading, to have a wide variety of approaches to attracting customers and running the business. These we refer to as 'strategy', since they are implemented, *after* the business begins to trade.

The Mata and Portugal study of Portuguese manufacturing illustrates the approach of industrial economists to the subject of exit. It takes little account of entrepreneur characteristics or of strategy. Instead, its prime focus is upon the characteristics of the sectors in which the businesses operate, industry growth rates, the number of new firms in the industry, the minimum efficient scale of firms in the industry and concentration levels.

The study by Carter, Williams and Reynolds, which looks at businesses that discontinue in the United States, is illustrative of research emerging from the management literature. In contrast with the Mata and Portugal study, sector influences are held constant since only firms in retailing are considered. However, a much wider range of factors influencing survival is included, such as entrepreneur characteristics, firm characteristics and strategy.

The third study, by Bates, focuses on entrepreneur and firm characteristics but takes no explicit account of strategy variables. Instead, it emphasises that access to finance – which can be an important influence upon whether or not a business survives – can be considered an endogenous, rather than an exogenous, influence. In other words, entrepreneur characteristics determine the source of finance used, which in turn influences business survival. Finance does not therefore exert an independent influence on survival/non-survival.

Table 1 Factors influencing small/new firm survival

	Mata & Portugal	Carter *et al.*	Bates	Brüderl *et al.*	Gimeno *et al.*
Entrepreneur characteristics					
Age of founder			45–54 peak		++
Ethnicity			Whites only		
Education			++	++	++
Self-employed parent			ns	ns	++
Self-employment experience		++		ns	ns
Gender		ns	Males only		
Management experience			ns	ns	ns
Sector experience		++		++	++
Firm characteristics					
Size at start	++	++		++	++
Partners		++			
Sector	+	+		+	+
Finance		ns	+	++	++
Time trading		++	++	Invested U.	++
Location		++	++	ns	++
Strategy					
Radius of sales				++	++
Price-based		ns			
Quality-based		++		ns	
Niche		ns		ns	
Numbers of observations	3,169	203	4,429	1,621	1,547
Failure rates	48% in 4 years	34% in 6 years	26% in 6 years	34% in 4 years	39% in 3 years
Types of firms	New manufacturer	Retail firms	New firms started by white males	New firms	New firms
Analytical method	Cox Proportional Hazard	Logistic Regression	Logit	Event History Analysis	Tobit and Grouped Data Regression
Country	Portugal	USA	USA	Germany	USA
Time period	1983–88	1986–92	1976–82	1985–90	1985–87

++   significant positive influence   –   significant negative influence
ns   no significant influence   +   some sectoral influence

The article by Brüderl, Preisendörfer and Zeigler is particularly valuable because it includes variables from the entrepreneur characteristics, firm characteristics and strategy clusters. It is also helpful because it analyses firms in Germany, which might be expected to have very different characteristics from the United States.

The final contribution is by Gimeno *et al.*. This is included because, for the first time, it seeks empirically to view the decision to continue in self-employment as a balance between the income generated from self-employment and the opportunities for employment elsewhere. This can be considered as operationalising the views expressed by the self-employed young people in Teesside, as reported by MacDonald and Coffield. Gimeno *et al.* formulate their analysis in the form of a threshold over which those people who do not achieve their target monetary and psychic income levels, then exit from self-employment.

Turning now to the rows in Table 1 we look firstly at entrepreneur characteristics. Eight entrepreneur characteristics, used in the five studies, are identified. This does not imply that these are the only eight characteristics used in the studies, or that these are the only possible entrepreneur characteristics that have been used in studies looking at new/small firm survival. For example, the recent work on self-employment duration by Taylor (1999) includes variables such as unemployment experience and whether individuals quit their previous job, their occupational class, and so on. Nevertheless, the selected eight variables do tell a fairly consistent story, which is that survival in self-employment is positively influenced by education – even though Gimeno *et al.* show that education also leads to higher levels of income inside both self-employment and paid employment. The table also shows that having worked in the sector prior to starting the business is also a factor positively associated with firm survival. Finally, the age of the founder is of importance, with founders starting businesses between 45 and 54 tending to have the highest survival rates. Much weaker results are found for previous self-employment experience, and having a parent in self-employment. No support is found for the hypothesis that higher managerial experience is associated with better small firm survival.

Regarding firm characteristics, it is clear that those firms which are largest when they start are more likely to survive, but it is also clear that there are significant differences in survival rates by sector. Finally, in general, those businesses that are longest established are the least likely to fail. However Brüderl *et al.* find that businesses are least likely to survive at around eighteen months but, after that time, survival increases with age.

What is more difficult, from the studies, is to isolate a clear and consistent picture of the impact of strategy on survival. In part this is because only two studies address this issue. Probably the only consistent finding is that those businesses that are heavily dependent upon the local market are most at risk.

6

Risky Business?*

R. MacDonald and F. Coffield

*Source: *Risky Business? Youth and the Enterprise Culture*, The Falmer Press: London (1991), 129–64.

In the last chapter [of the book from which this is taken; see above] we examined the process of starting up in business; in this chapter we report the experiences of the same group as they actually ran their new businesses. First, we provide basic information about the firms and examine some key issues (for example, business finance, premises, managerial style). Following this, we look more directly at the experience of entrepreneurship which will lead us to a consideration of the expectations people had and the likely future of their enterprises. The focus then switches to the experiences of those who no longer traded in the enterprise culture and looked back upon their earlier business practices often with a more critical eye. Before concluding the chapter, we offer an analysis of the success and failure of these small businesses based on a three-fold typology of the experiences of informants.

Selling and serving: types of young business

First of all, the types of business need to be described. Teresa Rees has characterized alternative work for young people in the enterprise economy as consisting, at the 'loonier fringe', of 'pet rocks, kissagrams and boot-strap enterprises' (Rees, 1986:15). A *Guardian* (6 January 1989) double-page spread on youth enterprise corroborated this picture of strange and unusual practices. It featured a pet-food supplier, a hat maker, a manufacturer of four-poster beds and a stick insect breeder. In Chapter 5, however, we hinted that much of the business conducted by this group lacked any obvious innovatory design or ideas, nor were they initiated by any real entrepreneurial zeal. These enterprises largely reflected jobs in the local economy, rather than being the weird and wonderful enterprises favoured by the media. As Curran says:

> The great majority of those who start ... a small business should not be seen as 'entrepreneurs' in any strict sense ... the term 'entrepreneur' ... might more properly be reserved for those who create a new successful enterprise based on a novel product or service and/or a novel organizational means for producing a good or providing a service and/or the novel marketing and distribution of goods and services. Most small businesses owners are simply cloning an existing, well proven form of enterprise.
>
> (Curran, 1986:17)

Moreover, the type of work carried out by individuals in new businesses did not challenge traditional gender stereotyping. This is perhaps not surprising given the difficulties in starting any business, never mind an enterprise which works against the grain of a labour market with strict gender divisions.

We decided not to group the businesses by occupation, nor by industrial division. This would tell us only that the vast majority of businesses formed by our sample involved retailing or some form of service business. Nationally the self-employed tend to be concentrated in the service, distributive and retailing sectors. Within the EAS, construction and retailing have always featured as the largest industrial categories, with approximately 65 per cent involved in service businesses (Allen and Hunn, 1985). Both our figures and those from national surveys support the view that enterprise policies may be (re)creating a nation of shop-keepers: 'with the high proportion of retail management among the occupations, the profile of the typical self-employed person is reminiscent of a certain Grantham shopkeeper' (*Labour Research*, 1986:15).

The classification below breaks the sample of those seventy-four informants, who were in co-ops or small firms at the time of the interview, into ten loose categories.[1] They are listed in declining importance of size, with, for instance, nearly twenty people in the first group and two in the last. Of course there are other ways in which these businesses could be classified, but in grouping them according to the relative frequency of particular business types, we hope to give an idea of the actual businesses owned and run by the informants:

1   the design, production and retailing of clothes
2   graphic design, illustration and art-related work
3   non-clothing related retailing – usually grocers or specialist food shops
4   beauty therapy and hairdressing
5   the servicing, retailing and programming of computers or computer-related products
6   photography or video production

7   skilled or semi-skilled manual work (cabinet maker, mechanic, welder and gardener)
8   technical services to the local music industry
9   printing and publishing
10 business and financial services

A number of people worked in areas difficult to fit into these categories. These included two young men who specialized in watch and clock repairs, a writer of historical novels, two picture framers, a signwriter, an interpreter, a man who imported and exported silverware, a man who ran a nappy delivery service and a mountain guide.

Defining the structures of the businesses is a simpler process. Well over half of the informants operated their businesses as self-employed sole traders, whilst one-quarter were in partnerships. Nine were still trading in co-operatives. One person owned a limited company and a handful of business people were preparing to 'go limited'. In this way our sample is broadly typical of EAS participants generally (Bevan *et al.*, 1989). Two-thirds of all self-employed run 'micro-businesses' or what a recent report calls 'microfirms' (Nabarro *et al.*, 1986) on their own, employing few if any workers (Hakim, 1988).

The time in business is perhaps the last piece of factual information we can provide as background information. Some (three) were very new and had only been running for a few weeks when the business owner was interviewed. Others had been in operation for several years. Ten informants had been in business for over two years, with one informant self-employed for five years. The majority fell somewhere in between. Over half were still in their first year and still drew upon the assistance of enterprise agencies and the EAS in the operation of their businesses. About one-fifth had been trading for between one and two years. Of those people who were no longer trading (eighteen) most had managed to remain in business for approximately a year at least, with the financial assistance of the EAS. This provided a £40 per week prop for new businesses, which, when withdrawn however, was often a contributory factor in businesses going bust at the twelve-month point or in the months following. Only three out of the eighteen who had closed down had managed to last beyond two years in business.

Although our method has not been longitudinal, we can still gain something of a long-term perspective on the experience of running businesses by drawing upon the accounts given by informants at these different stages of business development. In the next section we identify the key issues prioritized by informants in discussing how they ran their businesses.

Running businesses

Premises

One of the first problems for any new business is to establish a working base. Informants ran their businesses from three types of location: home, enterprise start-up units, or rented business premises (shops, offices, factory units) in the towns of Teesside. Each of these types of premises brought both advantages and disadvantages. Although working from home (usually the parental home) cut the cost of renting office or workshop space, other potential expensive overheads (telephone, heating, lighting) and time and money spent on travel, it was also reported as having a number of drawbacks. Space was often cramped, interruptions and distractions frequent and people felt isolated from the 'real world' of business.

Renting premises overcame some of these problems but brought new ones. Of course, the main cost is financial with the price of a retail outlet near the centre of Middlesbrough or Hartlepool being quite prohibitive for most informants. Those that were in any way affordable were in great demand and highly sought after. One informant had searched for nearly a year to find appropriate premises at a reasonable rent. Even when premises became available to young entrepreneurs, the majority could not afford anything but the most basic accommodation. Premises were often poorly heated, scruffy and hidden away in the back streets – all negative influences, particularly when relying upon custom coming to these business locations.

Many new enterprises were poorly located, situated some distance from central commercial areas and lacking the shop-front needed, in particular, by retail outlets. Two young women, Felicity and Vivien, complained vigorously about the location of the shop unit they finally rented. It was upstairs in a small complex of business units about one mile from the centre of Middlesbrough. The distance from town, the lack of passing trade and the invisibility of their business were perceived as the reasons behind its eventual failure. They regarded the building as jinxed and reported that several new businesses located there had folded during their tenancy.

Further problems associated with premises included difficulties in meeting legal and insurance requirements, given particular business practices. For instance, Trevor spent several hundred pounds and many weeks modifying his already expensive industrial unit to meet health and safety requirements (to allow spray painting). These changes had not been anticipated by Trevor and set his business back considerably. Shops, in particular, were often old and in poor physical repair. A number of the shop traders reported this as having made them vulnerable to the burglaries they had suffered. One young man, Carl, had his shop in Hartlepool burgled twice in six months; the second time he had been physically attacked. (When last visited he had bought a Rottweiler dog, baseball bat and starting pistol for protection.)

Despite the various dangers and difficulties experienced by those young entrepreneurs who had taken premises for their businesses, locating young enterprises in a 'real' economic environment, rather than at home, sometimes proved beneficial. If young businesses can give the appearance of being a credible, commercial organization (e.g. by having modern, smart, accessible offices), it is more likely that they will be treated positively by potential clients.[2] Location was important for one final reason. Lesley was self-employed as a beauty therapist and ran her business from a small complex of similar businesses (health foods, hairdressing and fitness centre). The location of her enterprise, in the immediate vicinity of these other related businesses, generated a lot of spin-off trade. Customers would come and use several of the services, including hers, in one visit.

Working either at home or in rented commercial premises both brought problems, albeit of different kinds. A half-way house between a home-based business and location in a more commercial setting is a starter unit provided by local enterprise agencies. These can, to some extent, overcome the isolation, the lack of credibility and the distractions associated with working from home, and they avoid the sometimes crippling rents charged in.the market place. One of the key activities of the enterprise industry has been the provision of low-cost, supervised workshop and office space. Many of the informants were contacted through local enterprise agencies and some were interviewed in these start-up units. The general message gained from this group was that working from such locations was beneficial, with only a few drawbacks.

The major advantages over working from home were that start-up units provided reasonable physical space, heating, lighting, telephone answering and reception services at a low cost. Obviously the cost of these units was cheaper than similar premises available in the market place, and they were run on subsidies to help young entrepreneurs establish themselves. Rents here varied from about £12 to £20 per week in 1989. Coupled with the advice available from counsellors, and the community support generated by working alongside other young entrepreneurs, these cheap rents provided the main attractions of start-up units.

Relatively minor complaints were received about such premises; these often boiled down to personality clashes and apparently petty squabbles between clients and the staff of the centres. The main issue seemed to be the atmosphere of the enterprise centres, particularly those specializing in advice and help for young business people. Some complained about 'being treated like kids' and that it was 'just like school, full of petty regulations and attitudes'. Access to the buildings was difficult at times with one informant having to argue long and hard for the right to come to work in her unit over a two-week period at Christmas time (when the centre's staff were on holiday). In short, a minority felt that they were not being treated as serious business people running serious businesses.

A more important planning problem in the provision of start-up units was identified. Tenancy of such premises is restricted to a time duration of usually between one and two years, the reasoning being that subsidized rents cannot be offered to all Cleveland's young entrepreneurs. So facilities are provided for a limited period of time which allows businesses to establish themselves before moving out into premises charging market rents. A fresh batch of tenants can then take the opportunities provided by start-up units.

The problem comes when they have to move out at the end of their allotted tenancy. It would be a backward step to move the business home so young entrepreneurs started to look for premises to rent in the local towns. The difference between the costs for these clean, modern, subsidized workshops and the costs for much less attractive accommodation at market prices was considerable. Two young men in a partnership run from an enterprise agency paid £8 each per week for their unit. Contrast this with one informant who was paying nearly £70 per week for his shop in Middlesbrough. The step from subsidized units to 'real' premises was made even more difficult by the timing of the move.[3] Often tenancies expired at the same time as EAS allowances ran out (i.e. after a year).[4] People who had been struggling to set up a business for a year were now faced with the problem of losing both essential financial support and premises in one fell swoop. It is no wonder that many of those who go out of business do so at this point or shortly afterwards.

Business capital and equipment

A second significant element in running a business is the amount of capital available to the new entrepreneur. This group appeared to be very undercapitalized in the business start-up stages. Unfortunately the general picture did not change once businesses were up and running.

Some individuals were successful in securing quite large bank loans or overdraft facilities (up to £25,000) and these often became crucial in the early stages of businesses. They were used to locate enterprises in suitable commercial properties, to purchase necessary equipment and stock, to advertise products or services and to employ workers. Basically, funding of this sort at an early stage enabled new businesses to develop themselves comparatively quickly, which in turn generated the necessary business to repay bank debts and, in some cases, to start to expand. As we suggested in the last chapter, funding at anywhere near this level was quite rare and was restricted to a handful of informants. A number of key factors influenced the securing of early capital investment.

Firstly, the attitude of bank managers was important. They seemed to favour applications from more educated, middle-class, older males.

Secondly, and relatedly, parents and family occasionally donated funds directly into their children's businesses. Help was also given indirectly in the form of collateral (e.g. the parental home) for their offsprings' bank loans. The third main influence on the level of early business capital was the availability of Regional Development Grants.

These three sources of help – banks, parents and government grants – amounted to considerable sums of investment in a small number of the businesses studied. One young man had offices, telephones, heating and all other business overheads paid for by his parents for his first year in business. Additionally, he lived at home and only paid £10 per week board and lodging. This level of family assistance was very rare but could provide a dramatic head start in enterprise.

Two successful informants working in a partnership had managed to invest £2,000 of personal savings, £6,000 in grants, a £3,000 bank loan (secured with their own house as collateral) and a £1,000 overdraft in their business. They had thus been able to rent a large factory unit, take on a small number of employees (some on government schemes) and advertise their products. Running their business on a reasonable financial footing from the outset had allowed them to compete successfully in the market place for business. For some businesses large scale capital investment was crucial. Necessary equipment, in a small publishing/printing firm, cost nearly £100,000. Regional Development Grants, before their demise, were particularly useful in funding the purchase of machinery and other equipment. The only problems involved the bureaucratic delays in the arrival of grants once they had been allocated, which could sometimes mean disaster for businesses on very tight budgets.

Beyond these sources there was little financial backing for young entrepreneurs. Typically, businesses were run on a shoestring with personal savings (perhaps of a few hundred pounds) and £40 per week from the EAS. The majority of young entrepreneurs had little or no money in the bank. Most of the enterprises involved very little in the way of elaborate or expensive production processes. They tended to rely on the services and labour of the informants rather than on capital or equipment. Lillian, from Stockton, ran a business as a photographer from home. The only equipment she needed was a camera which cost her £135. Others might need a sewing machine or a computer in a front room to run their businesses, which were frequently the extension of teenage hobbies and often these items were already owned.

Finding markets and managing businesses

Curran (1986) provides a neat review of research upon managerial styles in the small enterprise. Firstly, he identifies a boom in 'how to do' books, which has accompanied the rise of the enterprise movement generally:

practical guides for the new business person covering particular aspects of business practice. These manuals tend to emulate practices identified in the success of big business and pay little attention to the realities running small firms and inicro-businesses.

One of the major findings of the second, more academic part of this large body of research literature draws a causal relationship between the owner-manager's personal characteristics (for instance, his or her 'entrepreneurial personality') and ensuing managerial style. It is argued that, for instance, the desire for autonomy inhibits delegation of managerial tasks and business growth. Curran reports that many owner-managers are found to be unwilling to innovate, delegate, borrow, or lose independence. Intuitively this would seem to make some sense; however, we would suggest that a factor of equal importance in determining entrepreneurial styles and practices is the local economy. If many people display a similar managerial style, this may be because they operate in similar, severely competitive markets, not because of similar personality traits. Curran also notes that business style is often characterized by 'fire-brigading' – attempts to solve a constant stream of crises, and that growth takes second place to 'steady state', independent existence.

The ways in which businesses were run were seemingly not out of the ordinary. There was little in the way of new, dynamic, enterprising business practices here. This is not difficult to understand. The motivation to start businesses lay not in the desire to make or market new products or to develop new methods of business proprietorship, but in more mundane reasons (see Chapter 5).

Generally, businesses ran close to debt, insolvency and potential closure. They had to compete with other small firms (new and old), with established larger firms and with the informal economy. Profit margins tended to be very low and new businesses often tried to establish themselves in the market place by competing on price. In this way older businesses or last year's crop of EAS businesses were undercut and customers could be attracted. This business strategy, reported by many, continued as follows. Good service and products would then ensure that the customer base was maintained and hopefully expanded. In time young entrepreneurs would start to charge nearer the 'going rate' for their work. The support of Enterprise Allowance money and subsidized premises in part permitted this strategy. With a guaranteed £40 per week young business people could afford to cut their charges to a minimum, in some cases barely covering the costs of materials.

There were other clear problems in this type of business management. Underpricing of goods or services was occasionally reported as a bad commercial move. It apparently suggested to customers that the businesss was not serious or credible and was therefore unreliable. Helen, the fine artist, sold her pictures at shows and to galleries. She found that initial attempts to sell at very low prices met with little success, but that when she raised her charges business increased. This point reflects one we made earlier about business premises: the more commercial and real they appeared, the more credible and potentially successful the business.

Competing on cost, with the help of the EAS, also generated difficulties in the second year of business when the allowance stopped. Once informants had started trading in cheap services or products, this practice became expected by customers in the long-term. If young business people could not afford to offer such bargains in their second year, customers could simply switch to more commercial, high street shops. In this way young entrepreneurs became trapped in a business practice they could neither afford to carry on nor to give up. Terry made a similar point. When he began trading unofficially as a joiner, whilst still working for his employer, he could afford to do weekend jobs 'on the side' very cheaply. After all, this was just a lucrative supplement to his weekly wage. Once he set up in business, however, customers expected him to charge the same rates as previously, making it very difficult for him to earn a wage similar to that previously earned as an employee (especially as he was unsuccessful in gaining entry to the EAS). The displacement effect of new small firms like these has been recognized officially (National Audit Office 1988) and was of concern locally. In an interview with Training Agency staff in the area we were told:

> The Small Business Club on Teesside are not happy with EAS. They see small businesses being pushed out by the next EAS person that comes along. That's their moan. It's the crunch time just after twelve months, but there's always another EAS person to come along and take their place.

Some of the arguably more successful entrepreneurs were operating less usual businesses. They offered products, but more frequently services, which were quite specialized and drew upon uncommon skills and areas of expertise. One young man had a business offering a specialist repair and maintenance service for a very particular type of machinery. His market was national and his work was in great demand. In his first year of business he had a turnover of more than £50,000. Seemingly he had very few competitors, even within the wider, Northern region. The only problem he faced was a product of his success. Constant demand resulted in incredibly long working hours, with little room for a social life. He was not keen to take on employees and he had to ensure that he did not over-trade (i.e. take on too many customers) which would have resulted in poorer quality work, jobs being done late and dissatisfied customers.

Some businesses, though offering specialist work likely to capture a good slice of the market (e.g. two informants who learnt the watch repair business from their grandfather), were limited by that very specialism.

The work was highly skilled and of a rare sort. Hence, it was unlikely that they could employ someone with the same skills to help them without having to spend time training them. This time was not available – they had a business to run. Furthermore, the demand for specialist skills and products is probably limited on Teesside, compared with more prosperous areas. Middlesbrough does not have markets to compare with Covent Garden or Camden Lock in London, nor the same numbers of young, middle-class customers keen to buy stylish, specialist and unusual goods.

The problems of success, of over-expansion and over-trading, were not ones shared by most of the other informants. The potential for growth of these businesses was probably very limited. The vast majority employed nobody but the owner and most anticipated that this would remain the case. The majority simply could not afford to take on employees and the conditions of the local labour market ensured that growth was an unlikely prospect.

As has been reported elsewhere (Curran, 1986; Scase and Goffee, 1987), there was also an aversion to expansion. Independence, autonomy and flexibility were key positive factors influencing the move into self-employment in the first place and most preferred to keep their businesses very small. This allowed continuing personal control over the day-to-day running of the enterprise. Young entrepreneurs enjoyed being involved in all aspects and stages of their businesses. Being an employer, rather than a self-employed sole trader, was perceived as presenting unnecessary bureaucratic difficulties. Even the thought of taking on a trainee through a government scheme was daunting to most informants. The rules, regulations and relative costs and benefits were unclear and deterred sole traders. The unwillingness which in some became opposition to taking on employees, acted as a severe break to the growth of these concerns.

A minority of new businesses employed staff other than the owner. More often, though, young entrepreneurs received assistance from their family. In some cases wives became quasi-employees doing secretarial, delivery, book-keeping and other tasks for the entrepreneurial husband. This sort of help was also given by parents. The families of young business people provided essential physical, financial and emotional support. Their sacrifices and contribution to the success of new businesses often goes unrecognized in practitioners' guide books to starting and running businesses. But without their help many of the informants we studied would not have been able to set up in the first place.

The majority of business people ran firms which traded in a very local, confined market, and in a market which already offered many of the products and services they hoped to sell. As Ashton and Maguire argue 'opportunities for individuals to develop their own initiatives for creating employment are closely linked to the level of economic activity in the local labour market' (1986:45). In every sense these businesses were *small*. They had few if any employees, operated on miniscule budgets and profit margins, worked within a very restricted geographical area, and were run with low expectations and with limited entrepreneurial flair. What they lacked in size they made up for in sheer hard work and perseverance. Youth enterprise in Cleveland could be argued to be a prime case of 99 per cent perspiration, and 1 per cent inspiration.

Despite their efforts, custom was often very hard to develop. They were in competition with much more established, well-known and successful companies. They had the advantage of various types of support from the enterprise industry, but in general this only served to get them going in the early stages. As soon as they set up and began trading (advertising, buying stock, renting premises, charging for work) they were at the mercy of the market place. In becoming self-employed they did not suddenly become liberated from the demands and pressures of bosses; rather, young entrepreneurs found themselves at the command of their clients. Every (potential) customer was now the boss. Terry, the joiner, said:

> You're never your own boss. It's a fallacy that. You get your arse kicked by more people. When you're working you've only got your boss to worry about. When you're working for yourself you've got everybody else to worry about. Customers on your back. Bank manager after you. DHSS after one thing or another. Tax man chasing you. Everybody's taking their bit.

A handful of young business people managed to secure highly valuable contracts from much larger companies in the area. An informant in a video-production company earned £500 for one day's work for a local engineering firm. Contracts like these were crucial in the process of trying to establish a precarious young business. Not only did they bring in much-needed finance, they gave the chance to develop reputations and further contracts. Working for the local 'big fish' did present problems for these entrepreneurial minnows, as Jonathan, who had a company in Middlesbrough, described:

RM: Would you describe yourself as successful?
Jonathan: I could probably answer that at the end of the second year. We're successful-ish. We can pay our way … // … Something could happen next week and we could go bankrupt. There's always that chance with any small business. If our one big client pulled out we'd be totally jiggered. We've got that hanging over us all the time. And the problem is – the bigger the client, the longer it

takes them to pay up, and the longer we've got to put the money up. They know we need them. They don't need us. If we get an £8,000 job, we maybe have to pay out £4,000 to get it done. If you've got three of those sort of jobs floating about that's £12,000 you've got to find from somewhere. You've already spent up and you're waiting for the money. It causes immense cash-flow difficulties.

Jonathan's company had been successful in getting a big order which continued to bring in the bulk of money and work. The profits from each completed job were reinvested in financing the next one. Success of this sort was, however, a double-edged sword. He had become reliant on this contract which could be lost at any time. He acknowledged that his business would most likely fold if this happened. Even 'successful-ish' enterprises involved risky business. Moreover, large companies demanded up to ninety days to pay for work done, but usually gave no credit or time to pay to new, small businesses in return. Apart from presenting severe cash-flow problems, meeting big orders demanded that work be carried out to a highly professional level very quickly, equalling more hard work and longer hours for these struggling entrepreneurs. Occasionally these business people ran into problems of non-payment, resulting in considerable time and effort trying to recoup money owed. Ray ran a sign-writing business, and had had one or two 'big jobs' with local firms:

Because my work might cost them £1,000 and they might have bills of £20,000 to pay to someone else, they just forget about me. They just treat people like me like dirt. They don't think twice about not paying you. They don't think you are trying to make a living as well. I'm sick of it.

Despite these problems, which are experienced by all sorts of small businesses, not just young entrepreneurs, big money contracts were highly valuable to these informants. Getting them, and more importantly keeping them, was a vital part of building a business likely to survive in the long-term. Most operated businesses which had to rely on a wider and variable range of customers, usually individuals purchasing personal products or services.

One aspect of business practice which was interesting and quite common involved networks of trade between young entrepreneurs. Many of the informants knew, and traded with, each other. A good proportion of them had been based in local enterprise agencies at some time and perhaps shared neighbouring start-up units. A business services agency might use a graphic designer who might in turn employ a self-employed photographer.

In this way new firms run by young adults supported each other and spread work around.

Again there were some drawbacks to this style of enterprise. These informants were engaged in a form of sub-contracting. One business would gain work, which it was unable or unwilling to complete on its own, and then pass parts of it to other new business. For instance, one firm of leisure-wear manufacturers (run by young people who were not inter-viewed) provided most of the work for two small firms that we did study. Orders for these garments brought the majority of their work. Initially, however, they had set up to make specialist, original designer clothing for the fashion market. Now they had to sacrifice their independence, creative control and grander plans for these subcontracted, 'bread and butter' jobs. Some of our informants thus became cheap and reliable out-workers for other small companies.

Particular businesses were in some cases only part of the wider work in which young adults were involved. Informants, as well as running busi-nesses as self-employed sole traders, were occasionally employed else-where. One man, a self-employed hairdresser, additionally worked in a newsagents from five o'clock to nine o'clock every morning. A self-employed woman who ran a design business also taught one day a week in a local technical college. In this way extra money could be earned from jobs outside the business. This employment could provide vital financial support for the self-employed business person.

Income and hours: 'If I don't make it, I can't take it'

Whilst the enterprise industry provided help, the major reason why these new enterprises functioned at all was due to the hard work of young busi-ness people and the fact that they took very little in the way of financial rewards from their enterprises. The following extract is from an interview with Gary, who had run a graphic design business for a year in Middlesbrough. He had been unemployed for several years before attempt-ing to join the enterprise culture and was unemployed again at the time of interview. His wife Shirley was present and also contributed to the discussion.

Shirley: Nothing happened in the last quarter – he made no money at all in the last twelve weeks ... he was disillusioned – it just sickened you a bit, didn't it?

Gary: Well, it was a pleasure to go out to work. You wonder whether you are going to make any money. Tax your brains if you didn't – 'how could you make any money?'. It got a bit lonely, just sitting around. But it wasn't bad because you wonder whether you are going to make £15 during the week or whether you are going to make £20. You've got it in the back of your mind that things might pick up and you'd make £70 a week.

RM: Did you manage to take a regular wage from the business?

Gary: I never took a penny from the business apart from the odd cash job which might have been up to £5 or £6 … I was taking the £40 and that was it. I gave that to the wife. I got a rise in my pocket money from £5 to £7 per week. I had to pay for my own petrol and cigarettes.

RM: It's not a lot, is it?

Gary: It's not a lot to earn.

Gary's case is not dramatically different from many of those investigated. He was one of the lowest paid, but some reported taking less money home as a wage, and he did at least have the EAS to help support his wife and two young children.

Personal finances are a particularly difficult subject to enquire about. It is also a subject which can attract greater attention than more qualitative research findings. It may be that in some research informants may choose to exaggerate (or underestimate) the pay they receive. One or two young men in our sample seemed to be rather wild in their claims for success. However, we feel that the information we gathered about money earned through enterprise is fairly reliable. The ethnographic method allowed reasonably in-depth discussions of often sensitive issues. In a small number of cases informants were hesitant about providing financial information. After reassurances about anonymity and the purpose of the questioning, only four out of the group of seventy-four people decided not to divulge the pay they took out of their businesses. It should be added that the pay of self-employed people is doubly difficult to estimate. Informants sometimes actually took very little money which could be described as pay from their businesses. Income from the business was confused and uncertain. We have attempted to arrive at a figure which could be regarded as income after business expenses had been paid. These problems aside, we were able to estimate reasonably accurately the pay of young entrepreneurs as follows.

When considering the income figures it should be remembered that many people were still receiving £40 per week from the EAS. This amount has not been deducted from the following figures. Over half were earning £40 per week or less and seven people reported taking home less than £25 per week. Two-thirds of the informants who gave informantion were working for less than £50 per week. Overall three-quarters were earning £80 per week or less for themselves. Three people made over £100 per week, with the highest paid informant earning £250 per week himself. These figures are lower than in other surveys of EAS participation (e.g. Allen and Hunn, 1985).

Like pay, the hours spent working in enterprises every week were usually highly variable. One male informant for instance was involved in the publication of a magazine. Immediately preceding publication he would work over seventy hours per week, but the following week he might not work at all. Thus, the figures we present for both pay and hours are average estimates. The clear majority were working for forty hours per week or more, with a concentration of people working around forty-five to fifty hours per week. Nine People usually worked for over sixty hours per week, with the highest average reported being 110 hours per week (this informant was one of three mentioned above who earned over £100 per week).

Youth enterprise, then, means low pay and long hours. The average pay of individual entrepreneurs was divided by the average hours worked to arrive at an average rate per hour. Again this paints a bleak picture. Only six people reported earning more than £2 per hour. Over two-thirds were working for £1 per hour or less. It is not surprising that a majority clustered around this figure given the heavy reliance upon EAS money by businesses in this first year. What it also indicates, though, is that very few managed to increase their earnings above EAS levels in the second and later years of business. Additionally, those that were earning comparatively high amounts were working long hours in order to do so.

We should remember when considering the money earned through self-employment that our sample of informants, though young, were predominantly in their early twenties. Pay at this sort of level has been reported amongst other people in the 16–19 age group. By comparison our sample were not teenagers but young adults (with the average age of twenty-one) who might, quite understandably, expect to be earning more than this. Many of those toward the older end of the age spectrum in our sample had families to support and mortgages to pay.

The experience of entrepreneurship

If enterprise for young adults in Cleveland means long hours and little money, why do they carry on? One immediate answer is that for many, as we illustrated in the previous chapter, there is simply no alternative. For some self-employment was an answer to unemployment, and to give up their new businesses would mean a return to the dole queues. However, the answer is not as straightforward as that. The practice of entrepreneurship did have its own attractions and these provided some reward on a more social and psychological level.

The first example is a section from an interview with Joanne, from Middlesbrough, who ran a knitwear business:

RM: So it's going well?
Joanne: Very well, I can't believe it.

RM: How many hours do you put in?

Joanne: It varies. The two months after Christmas was the least which was about forty hours per week. We will be more busy from now until Christmas. It's well over forty hours. Sometimes I am knitting until ten or eleven at night, it depends how urgent it is.

RM: Do you give yourself a steady wage or does it …

Joanne: (interrupts) … No, it's just a steady wage. £40 per week. It's just literally to keep me going more than anything else.

RM: Some people might say it's an awful lot of work for little money?

Joanne: Well, that is it. I understand it's only business, just starting off. That you can't claim a big wage – I mean, literally, I'm struggling by, but it's a case of, well, waiting for the business to build up, and then I'll be able to claim a higher wage … // … money's not that important to me really, so long as I can keep my car and go out one night a week, I'm happy.

Few anticipated earning much money through enterprise, in the early days at least. A dominant theme which emerged from the interviews was this phlegmatic realism. Phrases such as 'struggling by' and 'plugging along' characterized a determined and hopeful, but also stoical attitude to the practice of enterprise. Hard work and long hours would not be rewarded by large sums of money immediately or even in the near future. One day businesses might blossom and then higher wages could be taken. In the meantime informants were happy with the minimal money earned and other less tangible rewards.

The second passage is from an interview with Fraser who had previously been self-employed as a joiner specializing in home improvements. He was asked about the advantages and disadvantages of running his own business, in comparison to being an employee:

You know that you are responsible for the money you get in the bank, whereas if you are working for somebody else, like I was before, I made so much of a product, someone else made so much and someone else painted it. So that was one [advantage] – job satisfaction. Another thing was that you didn't have someone on your back all the time. When I was at work if you stopped and blew your nose, they would crack the whip. Disadvantages? Well, when it isn't going too good you're directly responsible. Security is one of the main things. I always had the feeling that I hope the next six months go as well as this six months and you never quite know. You can see about ten feet in front of you but after that, it's a bit hazy. That's one of the disadvantages. In certain phases, yes. It does get a bit depressing because you start to think to yourself

'What am I doing? Where am I going?' and you've got nobody looking after you – it's a one-man band ... // ... it is very easy to keep flogging a dead horse. You are very enthusiastic and you can go up the wrong road and keep putting in 100 per cent plugging away and plugging away when really you should be taking a step back and thinking about what you are doing.

For Fraser, the disadvantages of being self-employed included the uncertainty of business and the (sometimes) disheartening pressure to find work. His trade was very seasonal, with plenty of work in the summer months but little in the winter. Opportunities to structure and manage his own time were positive benefits in comparison to previous employment. Relatedly, job satisfaction was higher. He became more of a craftsman involved with several stages of production, rather than only dealing with one part of a job. He finally gave up the business, a decision he should have taken earlier, because he was only just surviving and not making a decent living. At the time of interview he was employed part-time by a local firm and was being paid a similar wage to that he earned for very long hours in self-employment.

The insecurity of earnings, week by week and month by month, was reported more generally. Demand for products and services fluctuated quite markedly, with boom times before Christmas and a slump in trade afterwards. Helen, the artist, did very well in December making a record £340. In January, however, her income was £4 for the whole month. Poor budgeting compounded this insecurity, with pre-Christmas earnings being spent quickly leaving little for the leaner months. Increasing demand was, of course, welcomed but it also meant increasing working hours. Helen, to earn her bumper takings, had been getting only three or four hours sleep per night. One woman reported working for nineteen hours a day for a month to meet pre-Christmas orders for her knitwear products.

The unpredictability of work and income also meant that informants found it difficult to make social plans for the future. Holidays were particularly rare. Even if these could be scheduled, most informants reported that they could not affort to spare the time or potential earnings lost by taking two weeks off Jonathan, with the graphic design business in Middlesbrough, said:

Jonathan: It's probably the best job satisfaction you'll ever get in the world. Everything you create is for yourself ... // ... We work together more or less like a family. We look after each other. You don't get that working for someone else ... // ... I might only earn £50 but I've earned it myself and maybe I've done five or six things to get that. You're actually producing something. Half of it, most of it is the job satisfaction.

RM: What are the disadvantages?

Jonathan: It's a bit risky. With a job you know you've got so many years
and x amount of salary and you can plan things and get a
mortgage. There's not much security. In six months you might
be earning £20 per week, the next six months – £100 per week.
It might be five or six years before it's going to be secure.

Carl also identifies both positive and negative aspects of entrepreneurship.
He ran a clothes shop in Hartlepool.

RM: What are the best things about self-employment?

Carl: Freedom, money and being the owner of your business. If you
go wrong, there's only you to blame. If you want money you can
take it out of the business. It is there, if you want it.

RM: Disadvantages?

Carl: Pressure and bills. There is a hell of a lot of pressure on you. I
can't sleep some nights worrying about bills. You never get any
time for yourself. If I was working for somebody nine to five, I
could go home and forget about it. With being self-empioyed I
go when the work is finished. When I was doing the shop up I
was working from eight in the morning until two in the morning.
Now I finish at six unless there is people in the shop. Sometimes
I work 'till two in the morning making up garments. But it's
doing me more harm than good.

Freedom and ownership of a business, it will be recalled, were key elements in the positive reasoning behind starting businesses (see Chapter 5).
Carl also mentions money. Unfortunately he was one of the few who
avoided the question about his earnings. It is possible that he was already
reaping reasonable rewards for the hours he was putting into his business.
However, he had only been trading for a few months and was paying a large
rent for his shop premises. It is more probable that, like other informants
who stated that money was 'a good thing' about being self-employed, he
felt that *in the long term* enterprise would financially reward his efforts.

Johnny ran a fashion design business. He had a very mixed attitude to
self-employment and was one of the few people who would have actually
preferred to be employed by someone else:

It's difficult to say what I like. I like the studio. You feel good
actually coming to work and having your own place. You feel like
King of the Castle. And the actual recognition – that people know I
am a designer. I'm on the market now. People see your style of
work. The flexibility of working hours – you don't have to bow
down to any big boss. The challenge – to find gaps in the market

and sell your work. Disadvantages? Well, the paperwork, if you're working for somebody else, you don't have to worry about that. You don't get a steady wage. It's lonely . When I was at college I was working with maybe forty other people. Now it's just me ... //
... all I need is one big break. It is getting better, even though the work really isn't coming in. It's a very difficult life, really ... // ... I don't think it has changed my attitudes. I'm still not a cut-throat businessman. If someone paid me £100 per week to work, I'd go for that. I'd be happier.

For Johnny, working in the enterprise culture meant a 'difficult life'. He specialized in a particular kind of fashion design and had not been successful in finding employment. After nearly a year on the dole he had set up in business. Trade was very slow, money extremely limited and only compensated for by less material rewards, like a feeling of pride in the work he did, in his studio and in knowing other people now regarded him as a designer and not as one of the unemployed. Working for himself had not overcome the feelings of isolation and loneliness previously encountered in unemployment. He and others felt cut off from a normal working and social life. Like a number of informants he was pleased to be interviewed – he enjoyed the unusual chance for social contact and the opportunity to talk to someone about his business.

Pressure from bills was the main drawback for many. Not sleeping at night because of business worries was mentioned by a lot of the informants. The ability to 'switch off' and forget the business once you went home was a key quality recommended for those anticipating starting businesses. Young entrepreneurs experienced considerable and continuous stress. When and where were the next orders coming from? How were the bills and bank debts to be paid? Would the business become successful? These were the worries for a highly stressed group of young business people. We cannot agree with Hakim's recent finding that 'becoming self-employed and running a business turns out to be a great deal easier than most people expect' (Hakim, 1989:292). Gordon, who was comparatively successful in his computer-related business, had received medical attention for migraine attacks caused by overwork and stress.

A number of these young entrepreneurs, although identifying several rather negative dimensions of running a business, still referred to the experience of self-employment *overall* as a positive one. Being your own boss was very highly valued. Informants rated their job satisfaction highly (one woman described feeling 'absolutely ecstatic' when she pulled in business). Pride and self-achievement were feelings often previously denied to these young adults. One young man described himself prior to setting up as a 'lost person'. His friends and family were continually encouraging him to enrol for government schemes to help him out of his long-term unemployment. He became listless, depressed and aimless. In self-employment he had 'found his vocation'; he was happy, optimistic and hard-working. The personal psychological boost provided by owning and running a business compensated for the lack of financial rewarcs.

Some young men and women could find little to complain about in their self-employment. For them the move into the enterprise culture seemed an easy and straightforward step. We have reported the usual and typical difficulties in the passages above. Others, admittedly only a handful of people, had to rack their brains to think of 'bad things' about self-employment. They gave the impression that running their own businesses was a natural, unremarkable way of earning a living. Bob was twenty-five years old, lived in East Cleveland with his parents and had been running a one-man business as a freelance forestry worker:

RM: If someone came along and offered you £100 per week to do this as a job, but he would be the boss, would you take it?

Bob: No. There's no point working for someone else when you can do it yourself. There is a clear attraction in self-employment. Definitely. Basically I do what I want. I make all the decisions. I like running it all myself. It's all down to me anything goes wrong. I like the responsibility ... // ... on a small scale like this it is pretty straightforward. There aren't any financial risks. I've not borrowed loads of money or anything like that. If it doesn't work out I don't stand to lose anything ... // ... I like getting paid for doing what I enjoy. If I was on the dole, I would be doing it anyway. It is as simple as that.

RM: What about the insecurity of it? Is that one of the drawbacks?

Bob: No. I've never had any sort of security in my life – it's not something I'd be interested in. There's no such thing as security. I've never had a nine to five job since I left school. I don't know what security is ... // ... I don't think I'll ever be a millionaire doing this but I'm pretty sure I can make a living at it. A job for a few years at least. I'm not complaining. I'm quite happy with it and the way it's going.

Bob was an interesting informant. He seemed completely at ease in his situation as a self-employed worker and spoke contentedly of his life, despite the fact that he realized he had little security and was earning relatively little money. Two points help explain his positive attitude to running businesses. First, he actually enjoyed the work and had been doing it for many years prior to practising it as a business. As he said, he was now being paid for doing what he would be doing if unemployed.

Second, his career to date had not consisted of a series of jobs which he could compare to self-employment. He had never worked nine to five and had never known the security and material bonuses of permanent employment. The experience of growing up with a mixture of life on the dole, government training schemes or further education could be argued to prepare people for enterprise. In many ways in *practice*, rather than in theory, the experience of enterprise in an area like Teesside is not dissimilar to that of unemployment.

One informant described her prior life on the dole and in education as essential training for her new life of enterprise. She was now twenty-five years old and was adept at living a life of little money, low personal security and high stress levels ('There hasn't been anything else in my life, really'). In reading the accounts of informants, the ability to cope with this sort of life emerged as a major quality which they needed. Perhaps the key enterprise skill can be summed up in one word – resilience – rather than in the extravagant lists promoted in practitioners' and academics' publications (see Chapter 2). Coping with little money, relying on parents for financial support and accommodation, living with uncertainty and low expectations for the future, structuring and managing time and generally learning to get by in a harsh economic climate, are all skills demanded of young adults like these. It is perhaps not surprising that people who had picked up these skills informally, like Bob, should continue to display a pragmatic, coping, stoical and even sometimes optimistic attitude when they take on the mantle of the young entrepreneur. Perhaps, then, we should talk less of enterprise skills and more of the skills needed to survive unemployment.

So, for the majority of informants the disadvantages of enterprise, which started with the long hours and low pay and continued through insecurity of work, stress, isolation, lack of social life and holidays, were, in the main, just outweighed by the advantages of being self-employed. Certainly the impression given by informants was one of enthusiasm, dedication and diligence. These people were not just playing at business; they had a realistic and level-headed view of their situation and prospects. For them working in their own businesses brought self-esteem, feelings of achievement and pride, enjoyment in actually making things and giving service, excitement, flexibility, independence and control of their working days and life. Overall it provided work, which for many was a prime motivation behind their earlier decision to set up in business. Some were more successful than others and managed businesses which would probably run for some time. Others seemed to be doing less well and were involved in very risky enterprises. Shortly, we will examine the experiences of those who were no longer running businesses. Before that, however, we will turn to a discussion of the expectations informants had for their businesses.

From little acorns …

One of the main political aims of government enterprise policies is to reduce unemployment, at least temporarily, and to rejuvenate local economies in the longer term. New, small firms are seen as at least part of the answer to economic decline in areas like Cleveland (we will consider the success of these aims in detail in the final chapter). We have already demonstrated how the majority of these young entrepreneurs were providing employment for themselves only. Only a handful of new businesses had created jobs. However, it could be argued that enterprises like these may be more successful in generating new employment in the long term. Consequently, informants were asked about the future of their enterprise as they saw it.

Some informants expressed what could be described as the expected view. They had big plans and expected their hard work to be rewarded by big money in the future. Adrian had a 'crazy dream' about retiring at the age of thirty and sailing the world in a yacht. Stewart felt that his business would be running itself in a few years at which time he would have made enough money and satisfied his personal ambitions. He then intended selling the business and taking on a new challenge. Shane expected to be employing fifty people in five years' time. Others hoped to get shops in Paris, New York, London and Middlesbrough. Carl typified these ambitions for the future:

> I want to be very rich. I've got ambition. There is no way you'll get rich by working for somebody else. I'd love a job that was paying me £100 a week but there's no future in it. In ten years' time I want a 9/11 Turbo and a big massive house – that's where I want to be. This [his shop] is just a stepping stone, a start. Next I want a factory.[5]

Far more common, though, were less glorious views of the future. 'Muddling along', 'plugging away' and 'plodding along' were the usual ways of describing the prospects of new businesses. Lillian compares her likely future with popular views of entrepreneurship:

> I'm just keeping my head above water, I think. I mean, I'd love to be Richard Branson and the rest but you've got to be realistic. Unless I hit upon some brilliant money-making scheme … // … you've got to face it that you're not. You're never going to be a millionaire, like a big film star. It's easier if you come to terms with it. I just see it as keeping my head above water. Just being my own boss really.[6]

Enterprise proved to be far less glamorous than some, like Carl, sug- gested. It was not a life of flash cars, massive houses and big bucks. In short, the reality of enterprise was rather harsh and contrasted markedly with popular images of 'budding entrepreneurs'. When asked what infor- mants saw themselves doing in one or two years' time, a very frequent answer was that they would be on the dole. Despite the effort, hard work, determination and sacrifices of young adults in enterprise, inevitably many will not succeed and many do not expect to.

Between the devil and the deep blue sea

We interviewed a number of people who had gone out of business. For them the attractions and benefits of being your own boss were shortlived. The first passage we present in this section is from an interview with Duncan. He had run a business for just over a year as a freelance cartoonist from home in Middlesbrough. Previously he had been at art college for sev- eral years followed by thirteen months' unemployment.

RM: What caused you to close down? What were the main problems?

Duncan: The isolation – people not even knowing you're there. I struggled a lot. If this job hadn't come along I don't know what would have happened … it got dispiriting. You thought, well, there is no point in packing it in 'cos there's nothing there [to do] if you do. But you wonder whether it is worth carrying on with nothing [when the £40 per week finished]. You were putting a hell of a lot of hours in and getting nothing back at all. Some days I was working from eight in the morning till eleven at night. Some weeks nothing at all. Nobody expects to pay for anything and everything's supposed to be done yesterday. If I haven't been living at home, I wouldn't have survived as long as I did.

RM: How do you feel emotionally about being in business now?

Duncan: I wished I could have got a job straightaway, with good pay – something I enjoyed doing. Straightaway when I left college. It was just unfortunate. It seemed the only option at the time. I wouldn't recommend it to anyone, having done it. There's a few people said to me 'I'm thinking of starting up'. I've said: 'Really make sure you can get the work in'. I've said: 'I've struggled myself, make sure you don't end up like me'. My advice would be: don't do it.

Duncan closed down because of the insecurity of his enterprise. The pay was low and getting worse and he resented the stress and humiliation of continually scratching around for work. He had been supported by the EAS and by his parents but still he found that his time in business consisted of very negative, dispiriting and depressing experiences. Following his self-employment he was back on the dole for a further fourteen months. At the time of interview, however, he was much happier working in a job employed by a local company as a graphic designer.

Belinda had been engaged in running a small co-operative:

> I was putting everything I had into it and getting nothing at all back. I was leaving the house at 5.30 am and not getting back in 'till 5.30 pm. And all that for £40 per week which to me was peanuts. When we were doing outside work we would be working 'till the early hours of the morning as well. I would come home and just sleep. I thought as though we were just flogging our guts out for nothing at the end of the day ... // ... I didn't realize how much it can kill you. We were absolutely shattered. It was just a nightmare. I used to be seething that we were up to our eyeballs in so much debt ... I used to cry all the time. I used to say 'I'm not going back – it's awful'. I used to be like that about twice a week. Worried about how much debt we were in and what we would do if we closed down – how we would survive.

Belinda's efforts to leave the ranks of the unemployed through her own enterprise in a co-operative had met with problems similar to those experienced by Duncan: long hours, low pay, high levels of stress and worry, mental and physical exhaustion. The final crunch came when, out of the blue, they received a rent and rates demand for the premises they had been occupying. The £1,000 bill, which they thought the bank had been paying by standing order, arrived at the same time as their EAS money ran out. Bailiffs arrived to seize what little equipment and assets they had and they were forced to close their business, virtually overnight, with, in all, £7,500 in outstanding debts. Belinda did not know to whom she owed money and whether these bills had been paid off by the co-operative organization which had supported their enterprise. Her time in the enterprise culture was in a sense not yet complete. She still worried about having failed and the stress of being in debt remained with her.

The final, long extract we present to illustrate the almost wholly negative experience of closing down businesses and leaving the enterprise culture comes from an interview with Lynne. She was one of our oldest informants and looked back on her experiences of running a small business in her early to mid-twenties. She was a single mother with one young child. Since leaving school she had participated in a number of government schemes, had been employed in various part-time and temporary jobs and had had several periods of time unemployed. She had started a business as a market trader in fruit and vegetables in Stockton:

RM: Why did you go into self-employment. How do you feel about it now?

Lynne: It was something I had to try. I was getting nowhere. I couldn't see any future in what I was doing. I'd levelled off and I wanted to climb. I wanted self-esteem. Looking back it's been totally the opposite. I'd had two relationships that'd failed. My life has been a failure since leaving college to now. I needed something to succeed. As it happens, I failed in that as well. Perhaps I'm just a born failure. But at least I've had the experience. I haven't just sat back moaning on the dole. I.'ve tried to get out of the poverty trap. Fine, it didn't work but at least I've gained the experience ... // ... So now a year later I have about £10,000 debts and I can't afford to declare myself bankrupt so that amount is rising with the interest. I got taken to the High Court by a supplier for £1,300. Then I had the County Sheriff on my doorstep with a possession order. Because he was a nice chap, and he could see I had a kid, he left the furniture but he had possession of them so if I took anything out of the house or sold it, I would be charged with theft. So he owns the furniture and I'm being charged interest on that at twenty seven pence a day and fees of fifty eight pence a day and that has been going on since last year. The taxman has also caught up with me and he wanted to take the furniture, but he couldn't 'cos it belonged to the County Sheriff. I'm between the Devil and the Deep Blue Sea. I'm totally in the dark at the moment about what I owe people but I can't phone them to find out in case that reminds them about it. I'm stuck – just waiting for the axe to fall. I could have the £10,000 hanging over me for the rest of my life ... // ... I went through hell mentally with it. Straitjacket time, St Nicks' here I come ...[7]

During the interview Lynne tried to retain a detached and dispassionate perspective on her experiences and there is perhaps little we can add to her account. Prior to setting up she had been unemployed for a year and following her business failure she had returned to the dole queues for another eight months. At the time of interview she was working part-time 'on the side' as well as claiming unemployment benefit: nothing more than a survival strategy.

She appeared resilient in her defeat even though she had experienced more personal failure.[8] Like many of those in business who had gone bust, she had persevered heroically to keep her business afloat (running up bigger and bigger debts). Some may argue that she should have ceased trading earlier than she did. With little professional advice on closing businesses (see Chapter 5) and with few remaining alternatives, 'failures', like Lynne, kept on going. Their keen determination to make a success of something led them to start up in the first place and delayed them from closing businesses even when they had reached a parlous state. Rees (1986) describes the troubles and failures of young adults in the enterprise culture as 'blaming the victim, mark two': unemployment is 'caused' by the unemployed themselves (mark one); business failure is 'caused' by young business people themselves (mark two).

Though young entrepreneurs may make mistakes in running their businesses, the blame for entrepreneurial failure should not rest with them: we should not blame these young victims of business failure. Rees and Thomas studied the potential for successful small businesses amongst redundant coal miners in South Wales (a locality with economic problems similar to those of Teesside). They identified cultural and economic factors, rather than individual reasons, behind the low entrepreneurial potential of their informants:

> Not only are they ill-equipped in terms of the requisite 'resources', but also they are culturally predisposed to avoid risk-taking and indebtedness, which are necessary prerequisites to small business development. Moreover, and perhaps most fundamentally, the same local economy which so cruelly restricts their opportunities of satisfactory employment, also acts to block the potential for the development of innovation in new business enterprises. (1989:16)

We asked those who had left the enterprise culture why they had done so. The answers collected are not surprising and reflect problems identified by those still running businesses and in other research (e.g. Bevan *et al.*, 1989; Rees and Thomas, 1989; Hakim, 1989a; Smallbone, 1990). Reasons for closing most often stemmed from very basic business failure. There was general lack of capital (which was by far the most frequent response) and the market for goods and services was felt to be swamped and highly competitive. Informants identified lack of trade (and seasonal downturns in what business there was), fear of increasing debt and the threat of being entangled in legal proceedings as further, related elements of their decision-making. Advertising proved cripplingly expensive or simply unaffordable. Premises were often very poorly located and too costly. Businesses often lacked the basic finances or equipment necessary to survive (one mobile catering firm and one mobile hairdresser had no transport, for instance). Young business people struggled to keep their enterprise afloat under very difficult conditions. Business did not expand and withdrawal of support from the enterprise industry (e.g. start-up units and EAS) after a year or so proved disastrous for many who had to close down. The low pay, long hours and high risk resulting from these efforts were also given as prime reasons for closure.

As one young woman said, the reason for her business failure was 80 per cent financial and 20 per cent personal. She, like many others, used the word 'disheartening' to describe the whole experience. She found that it was 'not glamorous, not a big romantic dream'. Loneliness and the desire to work with other people rather than in isolation were given as further reasons. Physical and mental health suffered and these disheartening experiences led to declining motivation and commitment to the business. It was often when all or many of these problems came together that businesses were closed and the informants decided it was time to abandon the enterprise culture.

Our group of informants may, like other recent entrants to the ranks of the self-employed, be particularly vulnerable to business failure. Capital, or rather lack of capital, was the most pressing issue during the start-up phase, through the period of running a business and was foremost amongst causes of business failure. Rees argues that: 'the single most frequent direct cause of folding is insufficient capital – young people are at a particular disadvantage given their high risk status in the eyes of potential investors' (1986:18).

Allen and Hunn (1985) and Finn (1986) suggest that it is amongst those groups, for instance women and younger people whose participation in EAS has recently increased, that the survival rate is likely to be the lowest. Although we cannot, by the nature of our research methodology, offer any estimation of survival rates for this sample, what we can draw attention to is the quality of the experience of enterprise (as above) and a description of the location of self-employment in this sub-group's career trajectories. In our sample, eighteen people had ceased trading. Of these, thirteen had been unemployed immediately preceding start-up, with the average length of unemployment being nine months. Immediately following closure, fourteen of this small group of people returned to the dole, two went on to government schemes and two found jobs of some sort. The majority of the small group who seemed to be successfully running businesses (see the next section) had not entered self-employment from unemployment. These figures support our argument that self-employment was being pursued by many as a response to unemployment, but also that for this group it turned out to be an unsuccessful or short-lived bid to lift themselves out of the ranks of the unemployed. Those that did not enter self-employment from unemployment appear to be more successful in running businesses. Bevan *et al.* (1989) found that only 38 per cent of their lapsed self-employed sample had found full-time employment: 54 per cent were unemployed at the time of their survey.

In the same survey it was also found, however, that two-thirds of these 'failed' entrepreneurs would give self-employment another go. That finding, given the sort of evidence we present here, is perhaps rather surprising. However, some of our failed entrepreneurs (admittedly not two-thirds of them) also said they would consider re-entering the enterprise culture. What we found was that, despite the often crushing experience of presiding over the closure of a failing business, the resilience and doggedness of some of these young entrepreneurs pushed them towards thinking about new business ideas. We gained the impression that part of the reason for this was to have the chance to correct the mistakes they felt they had made. They thought that they had learnt what had gone wrong and knew the realities of entrepreneurship and, hence, they would now be better suited to running a business.

We met one young man, Trevor (who had closed his business that week), in a local enterprise centre. He was in debt to the tune of several thousand pounds and was now seeking medical assistance for the depression and stress-related ill health he had been experiencing. He was unemployed but visiting the advisory staff there to rework and develop his original business plan. It is unlikely that he would actually start up a second time (particularly as he was unlikely to receive bank credit ever again). For Trevor, this was more a matter of pride. He wanted to learn for himself what had gone wrong and put this right in written form (in the original business plan).

Against the odds, even some of those who had run disastrous new businesses saw some positive outcomes of their enterprise (see Chapter 8 for a discussion of the concept of 'positive outcomes'). This also helps explain the ambivalent attitude of young entrepreneurs to their own personal failures. Even the darkest clouds could hold a silver lining. Whilst they clearly failed to develop a successful small business, they could draw attention to some more hopeful outcomes of their activities. Typical was the comment 'Well, at least I've tried'. They could look upon their own efforts to leave the so-called dependency of unemployment as evidence of their own self-worth, and, additionally, this could be offered as evidence of commitment, self-motivation and hard work to future employers. Gary (who ran a graphic design business for less than a year) said.

> I knew where I'd gone wrong, so the *success* was finding that out. That I didn't have enough experience. I learnt lots of things: to be my own salesman, my own receptionist, my own planner, my own time-keeper. At the end of the day it was worth it because I know now where I went wrong. I know what I need to do to make a success of it in the future ... // ... I need better premises, capital behind me, the right advertising – basically that's it.

Though, for an outsider, it may be difficult to identify anything positive in the experiences of people like Duncan, Belinda and Lynne, it seems that some informants can describe at least a few positive aspects of business failure. This stands as testimony to their sheer determination, pride and resilience – characteristics which carried informants into starting businesses and were drawn upon and much needed when young enterprises collapsed.

Fallers, plodders and runners: success and failure in the enterprise culture

Though informants like Lynne, above, had apparently little difficulty in labelling themselves failures, attempting to define success and failure in enterprise more generally is a very difficult task. We had little access to definitive financial data (e.g. bank accounts) and we relied wholeheartedly upon less quantifiable data. Great care was taken in broaching this subject in interviews. To ask informants whether they considered themselves to be a success or failure, after they had, for instance, described the emotional pains of closing businesses would be insensitive in the extreme. Nevertheless, success in new small businesses lies at the heart of government enterprise policies. We feel it necessary, therefore, to try to classify the success or failure of our informants.

Success and failure in youth enterprise are particularly ambiguous terms. What are the criteria by which we judge whether a new business is successful? Official Training Agency evaluations of the EAS, for instance, generally use jobs created and 'survival' rates as indicators of success in self-employment. By the latter they mean the length of time people remain in business. Recent Department of Employment-sponsored surveys have found survival rates of 73 per cent at eighteen months and of 65 per cent still trading three years after starting in business (RBL Research International, 1987; Department of Employment, 1988b).

However, an evaluation of the scheme conducted by the National Audit Office (NAO) concluded that only 57 per cent of EAS participants were still trading two years after the scheme had finished (NAO, 1988). Part of this difference can be explained by the fact that the former reports exclude those who drop out during the first year from their calculations whereas the latter includes them. Finn (1986) found that 10 per cent of EAS participants drop out of the scheme during the first year (which was confirmed as the figure for Cleveland by local EAS staff). There are apparently no figures of local survival rates available for the county but we were told by Training Agency officers that 'there is no reason to doubt that these equate favourably with the national figure'.[9]

Even these levels of success must be weighed against what is called 'deadweight' (those who would have set up in business anyway, without the help of EAS) and 'displacement' (the amount of jobs in existing businesses which are lost through competition with EAS participants). The NAO estimates that deadweight can be estimated to be 44 per cent (i.e. nearly half would have set up in business without the EAS). It also suggests that about half of all jobs created simply displace other already existing jobs.

Even by these official criteria enterprise, through EAS, seems to have limited success. We would argue, however, that this quantitative analysis of self-employment only provides a bare, numerical sketch success and failure in youth enterprise. A fuller picture can only be gained by drawing upon a qualitative understanding of these experiences. In this chapter we have already provided much ethnographic data to suggest that simply staying in business is not the only dimension by which youth enterprises should be judged. There may be a particular *quantity* of people still trading in new enterprises but what is the *quality* of their entrepreneurial experiences? We have tried to develop a broader understanding of success and failure, drawing upon a more in-depth appreciation of what counts as success in youth enterprise. We suggest that a number of further inter-linked issues can be identified in the difficult job of trying to assess success and failure.

First, and perhaps obviously, given our stress upon ethnographic methods, attention needs to be paid to informants' own definitions of their success. Self-report data of this sort is tricky to analyze because people work with different personal criteria. Nevertheless, this sample of young entrepreneurs had apparently little difficulty in answering our questions in this respect. A few said they definitely were successful. One informant classified himself so. When asked why or how he could say he was successful, he leant back in his chair (in his modern, high-tech office) pulled up the matt-black window-blind and simply gestured to his and his partner's cars standing in the office car park. He owned a Porsche, colleague an Audi Quattro, both new and bright red.

However, it became clear from the interviews that very few of the informants would describe themselves as successful. They were weighed down by the pressures of day-to-day business survival and thought that success, if it came at all, was a long way off. 'Getting by', 'keeping their heads above water' and 'plodding along' were the images they used to describe their status as young entrepreneurs.

A second and related criterion for judging success is the likely future of young businesses. We have already shown that the majority were rather gloomy about their prospects. Their businesses were felt to run a high risk of collapse or decline in the long term. Uppermost in their mind was keeping themselves afloat, rather than business growth.

Third, we should take note of the employment potential of new businesses (an aspect of official criteria). Again few imagined actually expanding their businesses to the point where they could take on extra workers. Keeping businesses as they were was difficult enough for this sample and only a small minority had or intended to take on any employees.

A fourth related issue in judging business success is length of time in business. This criterion, used by the Training Agency, is supported by those we have described already. Our method does not allow a direct estimation of business survival rates. For this we would need a larger longer-term, longitudinal survey. What our evidence suggests, though, is that many businesses will not last beyond two or three years. It was difficult to locate young entrepreneurs in Cleveland who had traded for this long. Most of our sample were in the first year or two of business. They reported that the twelve-month point was, or was anticipated to be, a particularly testing time. Indeed, some thought it highly unlikely that they would be able to continue after a year. This is supported by the evidence from those who had already closed down businesses. Twelve of the eighteen people in this sub-sample ceased trading before the thirteen-month point. Finn (1986) has also found that two-thirds of the closures he studied happened at exactly the twelve-month point.

A fifth point in assessing success, which we have not yet mentioned, concerns dependency upon the EAS. If these new businesses are successful, they should be able to operate happily without government grant assistance. Generally, this was not the case. EAS money was crucial in supporting these firms. The withdrawal of £40 per week after twelve months was the major factor in explaining the actual or potential collapse of businesses after a year. Indeed, three of the more prosperous businesses never received this support. One of these informants actually said that EAS invited dependency amongst young entrepreneurs and that part of his own success could be explained by the fact that from the outset he had had to operate along real commercial lines.

Sixth, the money earned through enterprise, especially as it relates to the hours worked is a simple and clear indicator of success. The fact that about three-quarters of the sample were working long hours for as little as £80 per week or less must tell us that success was a long time coming.

To summarize, we can see that even official, scanty surveys tend to question the potential success of enterprises like those carried out by our informants. We have considered six more criteria for assessing youth enterprise and found that on all counts it would be difficult to characterize the majority experience as one of successful entrepreneurship. Equally, though, the experience of entrepreneurship cannot be described as complete failure. Overall the fortunes of our informants were mixed. Below we develop a three-part typology of entrepreneurial experiences based on the above criteria.

Some, as we have described, left the enterprise culture after one or two years of disheartening and wearing troubles. In terms of our sample these amounted to a minority (eighteen). However, it is likely that some of those we talked to who were trading as self-employed would join the enterprise fall-out. Cases of absolute disaster – crippling personal financial debt and severe emotional strain – were relatively rare, More common was a general feeling of failure, disappointment and dismay. Many had hoped to leave the ranks of the unemployed through their endeavours in enterprise only to find themselves back on the dole after giving all their commitment and effort to new businesses. Perhaps two in ten of our sample can be characterized in this way. These were the *'fallers'* in the enterprise sweep stakes who failed to make it over the first or second hurdles.

About one in ten seemed to be doing well in self-employment. They were the winners in the enterprise stakes. They had businesses which appeared to be commercially viable, soundly-based and managed, reasonably financed and likely to expand to some degree. These we call the *'runners'* – those who had established successful new firms.

The majority fell somewhere between these two extremes. Roughly seven out of ten of our informants were running business on a shoe-string with little intention or hope of expansion in the foreseeable future. These were the *'plodders'* who ran businesses day-by-day on hard graft; who were 'just surviving nicely'. Enterprise in the majority of cases meant risky business; failure was close at hand, and even new firms which were in their second year and employing people could go out of business over-night if a single important contract was lost. On the other hand, over a period of years, through a combination of good fortune, hard work and low pay they may be able to work themselves into a more secure, success-ful position.

This middle group of young entrepreneurs is particularly interesting. Not only are they the most significant in terms of numbers, they also inhabit a generally ignored part of the entrepreneurial world. Young people in business are usually absent from small business research anyway. Popular media accounts of young entrepreneurs usually focus on the success stories (in the 'local boy made good' vein).[10] More radical cri-tiques of government enterprise policies tend to highlight the horror sto-ries of enterprise, reporting business failures and disasters. We would suggest that neither perspective does justice to the more complicated world of youth enterprise as related by our informants. Of course, as we have shown, enterprise *can* bring glorious success or painful failure. But far more typical is a middle road of neither complete success nor com-plete failure but one of almost herculean effort determination and stress rewarded by low pay, new-found feelings of pride and achievement and other intangible personal attractions of being the boss of risky businesses. Most informants operate not in a shining, new, glamorous enterprise economy but 'just plod along' in a twilight world of casualized, peripheral, poorly paid work.

This is, of course, just one way of typifying and analyzing the experiences of youth enterprise and as such it is not meant as a hard and fast classification. We are, for instance, quite certain that there will be movement up and down the three categories. In the next chapter we will examine these three types of youth enterprise more directly by discussing several case studies. One story we present is that of Dawn, a young woman who, had she been interviewed a year earlier, would probably have been eligible for inclusion in the successful, 'runners' category. At the time of the interview, however, she was unemployed and looked back on her failed business and very mixed experiences of the enterprise culture.

Summary and conclusions

> Small business owners themselves have become the centre of much media attention and their activities are described in flattering terms by all the major political parties. The state and national economic policy have rediscovered the small enterprise and have offered it a central role in the restructuring and revival of the economy needed to take Britain into the next century. (Curran, 1986:43)

Neither the political promotion of the enterprise culture nor, indeed, the academic research on small business have at their roots any deep or clear understanding of the complex world of youth enterprise. Policies to encourage the movement of young adults into the enterprise culture through self-employment tend only to evaluate schemes and initiatives (e.g. the EAS) quantitatively. Hence, success is estimated simply by survival rates and job generation. Moreover, very few official studies focus on youth enterprise or upon particular localities. These, we would argue, are also serious omissions in the tradition of small business research.

This body of research has grown remarkably over the past decade but still tends to be dominated by national questionnaire surveys of the self-employed population as a whole. In this chapter we have attempted to illustrate that youth enterprise has a cultural meaning for the majority of informants which contrasts sharply with more popular images or political versions of enterprise. Growing up in Cleveland still means for many people a life comprised of government schemes, unemployment and lowly, impermanent jobs. This was certainly true of our sample.

Most had started in self-employment because it seemed to offer a reasonably attractive way of making a living when few jobs were available. These are exactly the people at whom government initiatives to reverse the 'dependency culture' are aimed. Even official data suggests that these efforts to create an enterprise culture are limited in their success. Most enterprises are short-lived and our own investigations have drawn attention to the critical problems faced by young business people, especially after a year or so in business when they lose various forms of enterprise assistance. Moreover, very few of these young entrepreneurs actually employed other people or planned to expand. We would agree with a recent finding of a study of local enterprise policy for the unemployed:

> Very few small firms ever get to employ significant numbers and the typical picture is of small units 'getting by'. The 'archetype' of the competent businessman [sic] spotting a new opportunity and making a success of a new venture clearly exists. It is not, however, typical in terms of the numbers involved.
>
> (Nabarro *et al.*, 1986:3)

In terms of the economic transformation of areas of high unemployment through job generation from new small firms like these, our evidence supports the growing research (e.g. Curran, 1986; Storey and Johnson, 1987a) which suggests that small firms are *not the* answer to unemployment. We will return to the broader question of the economics and politics of enterprise promotion policies in the final chapter. We conclude, here, that judging by the ethnographic accounts collected, most young entrepreneurs could not be classed as successful. The majority, however, did enjoy enterprise, and the more positive dimensions of entrepreneurship (in comparison with unemployment and working in jobs) at least partly compensated for poor pay and hard work. Few, though, were optimistic about the future. Miller says: 'The irregular economy of small enterprises with low wages, hustling, job insecurity ... is an important component of the small business sector. The individuals involved in the irregular economy largely comprise the working poor' (1986:157).

The conditions of work for self-employed people like these are very poor. They are generally not entitled to a range of benefits afforded employees (e.g. maternity leave, sick pay, paid holidays, pension schemes, Unemployment Benefit), and employment is often dependent upon the whims of local big business. The majority of these people, in choosing to run new, small, capitalist enterprises, are not taking a step up the class ladder into the *petit bourgeoisie* (the traditional home of the self-employed) but rather remain in a casualized world of insecure work founded upon lower-class, poorly paid jobs, government schemes and the constant threat of unemployment. Rees sums up well the position of entrepreneurial young adults like ours:

what we are seeing is a further segmentation of the labour market, with the ranks of those in the low paid, insecure, prospectless secondary labour market being swelled by a new breed of casual labour, the 'self-employed'. This is a far cry from the economic miracle anticipated through the rebirth of Britain's 'enterprise culture'. (1986:20)

In the next chapter [not included in the present volume] we will examine further the successes and failures of this group of newly self-employed young people. Six cases are presented more fully to illustrate the experiences of 'runners', 'fallers' and 'plodders'.

Notes

1   In other parts of the book we have disguised the identity of informants by sometimes changing the type of their business slightly (see Chapter 1). In this paragraph, however, we describe the actual businesses run by our sample.
2   The inaccessibility of many new businesses run from both home and rented premises can be confirmed by one of the authors (RM) who on several occasions spent considerable time trying to locate them.
3   Even if tenancies in enterprise centres were available over a more extended period charges could soar markedly. One young woman faced a jump in accommodation costs from £79 to £140 per month after a year in business, just as she lost her enterprise allowance.
4   During the research the interviewer (RM) found himself taking a more positive attitude to those businesses which had attractive, business-like premises.
5   Carl went out of business in the summer of 1990, about a year after he was interviewed.
6   Interestingly, Lillian refers to Richird Branson, Chairman of the Virgin Group Limited. He was the only individual ever named by informants when they discussed their self-image and status. Usually they compared themselves negatively with this self-made man, preferring more modest self-descriptions. This contrasts very sharply with a recent market research report on the views and ambitions of self-employed people in the region (see *Middlesbrough Evening Gazette*, 12 September 1990) which carried the title: 'In Branson's Footsteps – the North's whizzkids go for gold'.
7   'St Nicks' is a local mental hospital.
8   The comments of Sir Geoffrey Holland, made at the meeting of the Public Accounts Committee investigating EAS, and when placed next to the stories of people like Lynne, suggest how close the Permanent Secretary at the Department of Employment is to the practice of enterprise. He said: 'we do not think that anybody has been damaged by joining the EAS. Even of those who left quite a few go into employment with other people, having been given the confidence, after some considerable period of unemployment sometimes, to face a new future.' (House of Commons Public Accounts Committee, 1989:3)
9   We tried repeatedly to find out the official 'survival' rate for new firms on EAS in Cleveland. These were not available, but we find it hard to understand how it is that a regional figure can be published if county-wide figures (from which a regional aggregrate is calculated) are not collected. However, we were given the view of one local Training Agency official: 'the actual figures, the real figures are very encouraging. We believe that in Cleveland people tend to stick at it more, really because there is no alternative. They tend to stick at it because the only real alternative is the dole'.

10 For example, see Note 6 above. Our own press release to local newspapers, which gave a more realistic view of youth enterprise, was given a very upbeat and positive treatment and was printed under the title of 'Whizzkids Win the Survival Stakes'.

7

Life Duration of New Firms*

José Mata and Pedro Portugal[1]

*Source: *Journal of Industrial Economics* 42, 3 (1994), 227–45.

We follow firms created in Portuguese manufacturing in 1983 and study the determinants of their lifetime. One fifth of them died during the first year of their lives, and only fifty per cent survived for four years. Duration and limited-dependent variable models are employed to ascertain the relative importance of industry and firms specific variables to explain the period between firm birth and its disappearance from economic activity. New firm failure varies negatively with firm start-up size, the number of plants operated by the firm and the industry growth rate, and positively with the extent of entry in the industry.

Introduction

Entry of new competitors into markets is deemed to be an important phenomenon both in the introduction of new products and processes and in imposing competitive discipline to markets. In recent years, a small but growing empirical literature has analysed several aspects of this phenomenon, and considerable evidence is now available on the extent of entry across markets in a number of countries.[2] Previous work on this topic has generally addressed the study of the determinants of the entry and exit flows and among the stylized facts that have emerged from this recent literature, four are particularly worth noting. The first is that very large entry rates occur in most countries, the second that the entry flows are accompanied by contemporary exit movements, the third that entrants and exitors are generally small, and the fourth that, from the initial pool of entrants, only a few are able to survive and acquire market share.

The knowledge of what happens to entrants after the moment entry takes place is quite important, because the impact of entry on market performance depends not only on the number and size of entrants, at the time of entry, but also on how long they last, and how much market share they eventually obtain. Surprisingly, however, very few studies have actually observed these patterns of post-entry survival and expansion. Dunne,

Roberts and Samuelson [1989] and Phillips and Kirchhoff [1989] have followed cohorts of entrants, and explored the subject of survival and growth for the US while Mata [1994] has addressed the same topics for a European country. Audretsch [1991] has also followed a cohort of entrants during the first ten years of their lives, and studied their rate of survival. He has found that the determinants of new-firm survival are quite different, depending on the length of the period across which survival is measured, bringing into question the issue of what determines the duration of the lives of firms.

Econometric duration models are relatively new in economics. Despite the intensive use and popularity of the Proportional Hazards Model in Biometrics and the Accelerated Failure Time Model in Reliability Testing, the economists bypassed those methodologies until the late seventies. The job search and the strike literature, in particular, developed the need for such empirical strategies and, in this context, a broad spectrum of new research devices were developed.[3]

The study of firm duration is even more recent and, to our knowledge, it has only been previously addressed by Troske [1989] and by Audretsch and Mahmood [1994], both focusing on the US economy. Troske studied the firm-specific characteristics determining firm duration, finding that the probability of failure was negatively related to firm size. In addition to firm specific variables, Audretsch and Mahmood employed industry variables as explanatory variables, finding that firms last longer in fast growing industries, and in those where innovation and R&D are less important.

In this paper, we study the duration of new firms in Portuguese manufacturing. We identify firms created in 1983 and measure for how many years they stay in the market. We find that twenty per cent of new born firms died during the first year of their lives, and that only fifty per cent survived for the four years. We employ non-parametric procedures, especially designed to analyse duration phenomena, to ascertain the relative importance of industry- and firm-specific variables in explaining the time period between firm birth and its disappearance from economic activity. We find that size and ownership structure, as well as industry growth and industry turbulence are important determinants of firms' lifetimes. The next section describes the data set. In the third section, the models employed to analyse the firms' duration and the variables that are expected to influence the length of firms' lifetimes are presented. The fourth section presents and discusses the empirical results. A few concluding notes appear in the fifth and last section.

The data set

For this study we were able to use data from a yearly survey conducted by the Portuguese Ministry of Employment., which is an excellent source for the study of firm duration. There are three main reasons that make this survey a good source for this purpose. The first is its comprehensiveness.

In manufacturing, it includes virtually all firms with five or more employees, although very small firms are not so well covered.[4] Secondly, this survey is conducted on a yearly basis, and its identifying scheme allows accurate identification of firms and enables the following of firms' paths during their lives.[5] Finally, this is the only source in Portugal that allows the matching of firms with the establishments they operate. This is important because measures of economics of scale and of the importance of multiplant firms, that would be otherwise impossible to obtain, can be computed. Naturally, this source also has its own limitations. The most important one for our purposes is that, since it was primarily designed to collect data on the labour market, very little information is collected outside this particular field, and the only reliable measure for firm size is the number of people employed. This survey was first conducted in 1981 and, at the time this study was undertaken, 1988 was the latest year for which data was available.

Our purpose was to follow a cohort of firms that had started operations in the same year, during the first years of their lives. As we had direct access to raw files containing information on each one of the firms operating in manufacturing in each year from 1982–1988, we were able to identify firms created in 1983 and to ascertain for how many years they stayed in business. We identified entrants by finding, in the 1983 file, those firms whose identifying number was greater than the highest number in the 1982 file. This assures that firms classified as entrants have not been previously included in the files.[6] The treatment of firms' deaths is somewhat more delicate. A firm may be not included in the firms' file in one particular year for a number of reasons, other than permanent end of operations. It may be absent from the file because it suspended operations, because it had no paid employees in that year, or simply because it failed to fill and send the survey forms to the Department of Statistics of the Ministry in due time. We can reduce the risk of counting these firms among the deaths by classifying as exit only those firms that do not appear in the files in two consecutive years. A consequence of this procedure is that we cannot use data for the last year we have a file available, and therefore we present only data until 1987.[7]

Modelling the duration of new firms

Duration models

Conventional statistical methods, such as OLS, are ill-suited to tackle duration analysis. The main reason arises from the fact that information with respect to duration is typically incomplete, since at the time of the survey there persists a number of cases that did not fail. Those observations are called right-censored because all the analyst knows is that durations exceed a given (known) threshold. Standard estimation procedures do not account properly for this problem, producing biased and inconsistent estimates. One needs, therefore, to employ models specifically designed to take this problem into account, which leads us naturally to the hazard models.[8]

The hazard function $h(t)$, depicting the instantaneous escape rate from operation, may be written

$$h(t) = \lim_{\Delta t \to 0^+} \frac{P(t \leq T \leq t + \Delta t \setminus T \geq t)}{\Delta t} = \frac{f(t)}{S(t)} \qquad (1)$$

where T is the firm's life duration, $f(t)$ is the probability density function and $S(t)$ is the survival function.

Associated with the hazard rate is the notion of duration dependence. Positive (negative) duration dependence implies that the hazard rate increases (decreases) with time, that is, $dh(t)/dt > 0$ $(dh(t)/dt < 0)$. Duration dependence and the related issue of unobserved individual heterogeneity play an important role in the theory of firm survival (Jovanovic [1982]). Empirical estimates of either survival or hazard rates can easily be computed employing respectively the Kaplan-Meier estimator or the life-table methodology.[9] However, the focus of this analysis is not confined to the evaluation of those indicators. Of interest is the investigation of the influence of the covariates on the probability of failure. In other words, we shall implement a multivariate model of the life duration of firms. A useful parsimonious specification is the Proportional Hazards Model (Cox [1972]):

$$\ln h(t) = \ln h_0(t) + X\beta \qquad (2)$$

where $h_0(t)$ is the baseline hazard function, X is a vector of explanatory variables, and β is a vector of parameters.

Clearly, the baseline hazard function equals the hazard function for $X = 0$. Accordingly, the effect of a unit change in a covariate is to produce a constant proportional change in the hazard rate. In other words, the effect of the covariates is to act multiplicatively on $h_0(t)$. Parametric procedures require that $h_0(t)$ assumes a specific form, but an improper choice of the baseline hazard function can produce unreliable (and unstable) estimates (Heckman and Singer [1984]). Fortunately, this problem can be circumvented since the β vector can be estimated without imposing any assumptions regarding the baseline hazard via the definition of the proper partial likelihood function (Cox [1972]). A non-parametric procedure can, then, be used to compute $h_0(t)$ (Cox and Oakes [1985]; Kalbfleish and Prentice [1980]).

Parametric representations of the duration distribution, if properly specified, lead to more efficient estimators, imply less computational difficulties, and facilitate the probabilistic analysis of the duration dependence phenomenon, *vis-a-vis* their non-parametric counterparts.[10] A natural first choice is the Weibull model, where the baseline hazard function is defined as:

$$h_0(t) = \lambda\rho(\rho t)^{\lambda-1} \tag{3}$$

For this specification, $\lambda > 1$ implies monotonically increasing (positive duration dependence) and $\lambda < 1$, monotonically decreasing hazard rates (negative duration dependence). For $\lambda = 1$, an exponential hazard function (constant hazard rates) is implied.[11]

Recently, Han and Hausman [1990] proposed a flexible semi-parametric specification of the hazard function. Their procedure, which is based on a competing risk model approach, appears to serve our purposes well, given the nature of our data.[12] Han and Hausman generalize the Cox regression model along three directions: specifying a piece-wise linear function for the baseline hazard; adding a parametric function to account for the presence of unobserved individual heterogeneity; and allowing for multiple risks of failure and for an unrestricted correlation among them. The basis for their model is a multivariate ordered probit (and logit) specification, where separate parameters are (jointly) obtained for each baseline hazard function in each interval of observation. In the context of a single risk model, as in our case, the bivariate ordered logit (and probit) employed by Han and Hausman simplifies to a straightforward ordered logit (and probit) estimation procedure (Maddala [1983]). We shall also use this methodology.

Explanatory variables

We now turn to the variables to be included in the X vector, which are described in Table 7.1.

Small firms are less likely to last longer. They employ the less able managers, and will be the first to leave the market when, for example, wages grow and the opportunity cost of being an entrepreneur increases (Lucas [1978]). Lower quality managers are also likely to commit the greatest mistakes in estimating their true ability level. Larger firms should be able to survive longer because, if they find themselves to be less efficient than they had expected, they may become small before they exit, and also because, if they actually commit fewer mistakes, they would have less reason to shrink. Besides, because entry size signals the priors of entrepreneurs (larger scale entry indicates greater *a priori* expectations of success), in the case of large scale entry, more periods with bad results will be needed to eliminate the *ex ante* positive profit expectations (Frank [1988]). Lack of internal finance and imperfections in capital markets may compel prospective competitors to enter at a smaller scale than the one they would have chosen had they had the funds. In the presence of difficulties that may arise from incumbents' reactions or from unforeseen market developments, these new firms are those which will be able to sustain their positions for less time. Finally, in most cases, firms use different technologies according to their size. Small firms employ less capital intensive methods and, thus,

Table 7.1 Independent variables

Variable	Description	Min.	Max.	Mean	Std. Dev.
Start–up size	Logarithm of the employment in the firm at the time of entry	0.0000	7.1531	1.6440	1.0896
Ownership	Number of plants operated by the firm in its main industry	1.0000	5.0000	1.0148	0.1762
Growth	Industry growth rate (1982–1983)	–0.8367	1.1111	0.0065	0.0910
Entry	Logarithm of the number of new firms in the industry	0.0000	6.0331	4.2839	1.5131
Entrants' size	Logarithm of the employment in new firms in the industry	0.0000	8.7229	6.4693	1.5249
Industry size	Logarithm of the number or firms in the industry	1.0986	7.7407	6.2175	1.4091
MES	Logarithm of one half of the average size of the firms that, on average, operate 1.5 plants (see Lyons [1980])	1.7918	7.1869	4.3301	0.7132
Suboptimal scale	Proportion of industry employment in firms smaller than Minimum Efficient Scale	0.0088	0.8864	0.5685	0.1790
Concentration	Herfindahl index	0.0018	0.9038	0.0321	0.0709

variable costs represent a greater proportion of total cost.[13] If prices go down, these differences in the composition of cost implies that smaller firms would exit first.

In the large majority of the cases, new firms start with a single plant, but nevertheless a small number of them start with several plants at the same time. These are normally among the largest entrants, but it seems reasonable to admit that, even after controlling for firm size, multiplant entrants last longer because entry with several plants signals optimistic priors and reveals a less binding financial constraint. Moreover, exit of multiplant firms is less likely since it implies the simultaneous failure of all their plants. Recall that in our database all entrants are firms that did not employ paid labour before 1983. Therefore, entry with several plants is not entry by already established firms as in Storey and Jones [1987], Dunne, Roberts and Samuelson [1989], Mata [1993] or Audretsch and Mahmood [1994]. It is, of course, possible that some of the firms that we classify as entrants were already operating without paid labour prior to 1983. It is also plausible that the reasons that lead the self-employed to hire people (and thus create a firm that will report to our source) are different from the reasons that determine the wholly new firms creation as suggested, for example, by Robson [1991]. However, this distinction cannot be made with our database, since we do not have information on the previous occupational statuses of the firms' owners.

The dynamics of industry evolution is also likely to affect the duration of firms' lives. In fast growing industries it may be easier to survive, since firms may grow without inflicting market share losses to their rivals and, therefore, the likelihood of aggressive reactions is lower. On the other hand, it is during the first stages of the industry life cycle that industries grow faster, and that the conditions in the industries are more unsettled, leading to the highest turnover rates (Gort and Klepper [1982]). In this stage, firms enter essentially by introducing innovations embodied in new products or processes, and while some are successful and prosper, a large number never acquire buyers' acceptance, and quickly leave the market.

Entry represents continuously renewed challenges to incumbents, and in markets with higher entry rates we expect the firms' lifetime to be shorter.[14] In such markets, not only is each new firm subjected to more intense competition from those of its own kind, but also each generation of entrants has to face a continuously renewed challenge posed by the new waves of entrants each year. Because the effect of entry depends on the relationship between the extent of entry and market size, we also included a measure of industry size.

Entry typically occurs in a small scale and to become viable, in most cases, entrants need to expand towards the Minimum Efficient Scale (*MES*). The larger the *MES*, the greater the troubles to attain it, and the lower the prospects of new firm survival. Still, operation at the efficient level will be most required in industries where firms smaller than MES face important disadvantages *vis-a-vis* their efficient competitors, and we would expect that, in markets where firms smaller than *MES* constitute a larger proportion of industry population, newer firms have better chances of survival. Finally, we included a measure of industry concentration among the regressors because of the potential of collusion it represents, and the likelihood of aggressive behaviour by the incumbents that it threatens.

Results

We start by looking at how the survival rates vary with firm start-up size. Table 7.2 presents some preliminary analysis of this topic, showing the empirical survival rates at the different ages, computed by the Kaplan-Meier estimator for seven different classes of firm start-up sizes. The overall survival rate is about eighty per cent in the first year, but almost fifty per cent of the new born firms die before they reach the age of four.[15] These figures, however, are substantially altered if the firm's initial size is taken into account. From those firms that were born employing one or two

Table 7.2 Survival rates and size change by start-up size

	Start-up size class							Full sample
	Size (1–2)	Size (3–4)	Size (5–9)	Size (10–19)	Size (20–49)	Size (50–99)	Size (100+)	
Survival rates								
After 1 year	0.7045	0.7597	0.7944	0.8397	0.8467	0.8657	0.9545	0.7763
After 2 years	0.6100	0.6600	0.6881	0.7494	0.7663	0.8358	0.9318	0.6819
After 3 years	0.5084	0.5517	0.5986	0.6772	0.7050	0.7761	0.8162	0.5895
After 4 years	0.4400	0.4807	0.5189	0.6185	0.6551	0.7015	0.7500	0.5204
Mean duration*	5.81	6.64	7.48	10.18	11.52	14.00	17.82	7.44
N	836	803	715	443	261	67	44	3 169
Size class after four years								
Size(1–2)	0.4631	0.1398	0.0405	0.0037	0.0000	0.0000	0.0000	
Size (3–4)	0.3378	0.3964	0.0917	0.0328	0.0058	0.0212	0.0000	
Size (5–9)	0.1444	0.3265	0.4582	0.0839	0.0118	0.0212	0.0303	
Size (10–19)	0.0355	0.1088	0.2803	0.5145	0.0585	0.0000	0.0000	
Size (20–49)	0.0164	0.0260	0.1023	0.3248	0.6667	0.1277	0.0000	
Size (50–99)	0.0027	0.0025	0.0189	0.0365	0.2164	0.5319	0.1212	
Size (100+)	0.0000	0.0000	0.0081	0.0037	0.0409	0.2979	0.8485	

*Assuming an exponential distribution.

employees, thirty per cent failed within the first year, but more than ninety five per cent of the firms created with 100 or more employees survived during the identical period. Survival rates in the fourth year also exhibit sharp differences across initial size classes: three quarters of the total number of entrants in the largest size class still being in operation, while the corresponding figure for the smallest size class is less than half. This relationship between survival rates and initial firm size persists across classes, survival increasing monotonically with size, regardless as to how many years later that survival is observed. As expected, firms that entered by opening more than one establishment simultaneously are much less concentrated in the smaller size classes than single plant entrants (see Table 7.A1 in the Appendix). Moreover, their survival rates are rather higher than the corresponding figures for single plant entrants.[16]

Given the empirical survival rates computed, and assuming a particular distribution for the baseline hazard function, it is possible to obtain measures of the expected life duration of firms, at the time they are created. The corresponding estimates, computed assuming an exponential distribution, are also presented in Table 7.2 and should be regarded as crude summary measures. The figures displayed there show that firms last, on average, for about seven years and five months, and that the ratio between the average duration of firms in the most extreme size classes is greater than three.

Exit is only one of the possible events that may follow entry, although perhaps the most dramatic. The bottom portion of Table 7.2 complements the analysis of the post-entry performance of new firms by presenting a transition matrix showing the destiny of the 1993 entrants that survived until 1987. Two important results can be drawn from this matrix. The first is that among survivors the tendency is to grow rather than shrink, as the percentages below the diagonal are larger than those above. The second is that post-entry mobility seems to decrease with size, as the figures in the diagonal increase with size. In general, these findings are consistent with an interpretation of post-entry performance of firms as a process of learning and survival (Jovanovic [1982]), with the story of small firms' flexibility (Mills and Schumann [1985]), and with previous evidence on the relationship between the size and age of firms and their patterns of survival and growth (Evans [1987a, 1987b], Hall [1997]).

Survival rates widely differ across industries (see Table 7.3). Nine out of the twelve firms that entered the fish preserving industry in 1983 died before they reached the age of five. In contrast, twelve out of the fourteen entrants in the glass industry were still in business in 1987. There is an impressive concentration of the industries with the lowest failure rates in textiles, leather and footwear (two digit industry 32). Two industries included in this two-digit sector also appear among the list of the industries with lowest survival rates. However, unlike the majority of the industries included in the top survivors, these are consumer-oriented industries, and

Table 7.3 The industries with the lowest and the highest survival rates

CAE	Industry*	N	Survival rate after four years
31142	Fish preserving	12	0.250
31172	Pastry	72	0.347
32201	Made-to-measure clothing	58	0.379
32122	Household textile products	22	0.409
36102	Pottery	17	0.412
36911	Clay products for construction	19	0.421
36993	Cement products	82	0.427
39099	Manufacturing n.e.c.	18	0.444
38199	Fabricated metal products n.e.c.	43	0.467
38320	Radio and TV communication equipment	19	0.474
38249	Machinery for the industry n.e.c.	13	0.615
32310	Tanning and dressing of leather	11	0.636
37109	Iron and steel industry	14	0.643
32409	Footwear n.e.c.	26	0.654
36995	Cut stone and stone products	64	0.656
32130	Knitting industry	67	0.657
31111	Slaughtering	22	0.680
32112	Spinning, weaving and finishing of wool	13	0.769
32113	Spinning, weaving and finishing of cotton, artificial and synthetic fibres	21	0.810
36202	Glass products	14	0.857

*Industries with less than 10 entrants were excluded.

this diverse orientation of the industries included in the top and bottom lists seems to be the chief pattern revealed by Table 7.3. Also somewhat surprising is the complete absence of three two-digit industries from both lists: wood and cork (33), paper and printing (34) and chemicals, rubber and plastics (35).

Given that firm failure rates vary so extensively across industries, let's now turn our attention to the sectoral determinants of the hazard rates and inspect the regression results from the Cox Proportional Hazards Model displayed in Table 7.4. For a brief moment we will ignore the direct effect of firms' start-up size, and concentrate on the results in column I. In this column, no direct measure of the firms' initial size is included. Two contradictory effects are shown by the *Entry and Entrants' Size* coefficients: Entry attracting a minus sign, while *Entrants' Size* obtaining a positive sign. These results could be interpreted as evidence that, in industries with plenty of room for new firms, the probability of new firm failure is lower, and that in those industries characterized by high turbulence new firms face a higher risk. However, as both the number and the size of entrants in the industry enter the regression in logarithmic form, the combined effect of the two variables also reflects the effect of the entrants' average size. Our results can thus be interpreted as reflecting that the average size of entrants in the industry has an overall negative effect in the risk of failure. Note that the inclusion of the *Industry Size* variable also allows us to interpret the parameter estimate of *Entry* as the effect of the entry rate on the instantaneous failure rate. Therefore, we conclude that substantially higher hazard rates are implied whenever industries are characterized by high entry rates. The estimated coefficient of the *Growth* variable is negative. After the effect of industry turbulence is taken into account, fast growth makes new entry easier to accommodate, and increases the expected duration of new firms. Finally, we note that *Ownership* influences negatively (as expected) the hazard rate.

In column II we account for the direct effect of firms' start-up size. To allow for a possible non-linear effect, this variable is included *via* a set of dummy variables. Each one of these variables gets the value 1 if the firm's employment at the time of entry is encompassed within the interval it is referred to, and 0 otherwise. They are labelled *Size(L-H)*, in which *L* and *H* are respectively the lower and the higher bound of the respective interval. The expected influence of these variables is clearly born out in the results. The larger the firm's start-size the lower the risk of failure and, although non-linear, the estimated effect is clearly monotonic. Not surprisingly, the coefficient estimates of the other explanatory variables decrease somewhat (in absolute magnitude), especially the *Entrants' Size* parameter estimate which, moreover, is only marginally significant. The effect of the entry rate on the hazard rates persists, even after the inclusion of these variables but, given the similarity between the *Entry* and the *Industry Size* parameter estimates, the empirical evidence of an independent effect of *Industry Size* vanishes.

The third column displays our preferred specification. Here, the non-linear effect of the *Start-Up Size* variable is accounted for via the logarithmic transformation. This specification seems to be reasonable given that the value of the likelihood increases. The associated coefficient can now be interpreted as a constant elasticity and, accordingly, a one percent change on the start-up size implies, approximately, a 0.19 percent negative change

Table 7.4 The determinants of firm survival

Regression results from the Proportional Hazards Model (n = 3169)

Variables	Specification I	II	III	IV
Start–up size			−0.1898 (6.729)	−0.1904 (6.739)
Ownership	−0.6332 (2.125)	−0.4463 (1.524)	−0.4372 (1.486)	−0.4278 (1.453)
Growth	−0.6268 (2.054)	−0.5322 (1.706)	−0.5566 (1.797)	−0.5571 (1.787)
Entry	0.3229 (3.782)	0.2135 (2.458)	0.1984 (2.285)	0.2067 (2.103)
Entrant's size	−0.1775 (4.166)	−0.0642 (1.407)	−0.0546 (1.200)	−0.0531 (0.890)
Industry size	−0.1652 (2.091)	−0.1729 (2.185)	−0.1704 (2.156)	−0.1904 (2.151)
MES				0.0028 (0.062)
Suboptimal scale				0.0627 (0.290)
Concentration				−0.1612 (0.292)
Size (5–9)		−0.1439 (2.233)		
Size (10–19)		−0.4015 (4.648)		
Size (20–49)		−0.4917 (4.268)		
Size (50–99)		−0.6650 (2.881)		
Size (100+)		−0.7298 (2.329)		

continued on next page

Table 7.4 The determinants of firm survival (cont.)

Variables	I	II	III	IV
Baseline hazard rate after				
One year	0.1979	0.1952	0.1951	0.1951
Two years	0.1445	0.1430	0.1430	0.1430
Three years	0.1263	0.1258	0.1259	0.1258
Four years	0.1107	0.1107	0.1109	0.1109
Log-likelihood	−11 929.23	−11 907.57	−11 905.98	−11 905.84
Chi square	40.24	83.52	86.70	86.99

Asymptotic (t) statistics in parenthesis.

on the hazard rate. All the other estimates closely resemble the ones discussed earlier.

Finally, the last column displays the results of estimation of the complete model and illustrates the lack of statistical significance of the *MES, Suboptimal Scale*, and *Concentration* variables. Insignificance of the concentration variable was not at all unexpected, as it was previously found that fear of aggressive behaviour was not deterring entry in Portuguese manufacturing (Mata [1991]). Notwithstanding, the lack of a statistical relationship between the probability of failure and the *MES* and *Sub-optimal Scale* variables is somewhat striking, both on *a priori* grounds and given the previous empirical work by Audretsch and Mahmood [1994], who have found a positive effect of *MES* on firm failure. A possible explanation, however, lies in the results of a study on the determinants of firms' start-up size (Mata [1992]). In that study, firms' initial size was found to depend on *MES* and on *Sub-optimal Scale*, which suggests that the influence of the technological conditions on firm duration may be already taken into account *via* the firm start-up size variable.

At the bottom of the table, the estimates of baseline hazard rates, i.e. the hazard rates adjusted for the individual differences implied by the covariates, are depicted. Those figures, computed for a firm with mean characteristics (that is, using the explanatory variables in deviation form), are obtained using a non-parametric procedure in sequence of the estimation of the Cox model, and closely conform to the empirical survival rates presented above. As before, after a hazard rate of around twenty percent for the initial year of operation, the risk of failure declines. In other words, those estimates appear to suggest negative duration dependence.[17]

A formal test of duration dependence can be easily performed using the Weibull model. From the results in the first column of Table 7.5 we clearly reject the null hypothesis that the λ coefficient equals one, thereby reinforcing the previous suggestion that the hazard function exhibits negative

Table 7.5 The determinants of firm survival: regression results for different model specifications and sample definitions

Variables	Weibull	Ordered probit	Ordered logit	Cox proportional hazards		
				*I**	*II***	*III****
Start-up size	-0.2085	0.1692	0.2762	-0.1889	-0.1986	-0.2450
	(7.375)	(7.769)	(7.754)	(6.164)	(6.774)	(4.225)
Ownership	-0.4457	0.2312	0.4610	0.2215		-0.5103
	(1.514)	(1.356)	(1.416)	(0.823)		(1.575)
Growth	-0.6151	0.5248	0.8737		-0.571	-1.0855
	(1.972)	(2.103)	(2.189)		(1.796)	(2.553)
Entry	0.2157	-0.1694	-0.2943		0.1965	0.2984
	(2.473)	(2.469)	(2.657)		(2.261)	(2.375)
Entrants' size	-0.0591	0.0450	0.0764		-0.0528	0.0047
	(1.267)	(1.248)	(1.286)		(1.158)	(0.071)
Industry size	-0.1865	0.1476	0.2556		-0.1736	-0.3349
	(2.343)	(2.342)	(2.538)		(2.191)	(2.873)
Constant		-0.2216	-0.4706			
		(0.876)	(1.052)			
ρ	0.9932					
	(1.869)					

continued on next page

Table 7.5 The determinants of firm survival: regression results for different model specifications and sample definitions (cont.)

Variables	Weibull	Ordered probit	Ordered logit	Cox proportional hazards		
				*I**	*II***	*III****
λ	0.7052 (30.432)					
μ_1		0.2921 (18.197)	0.4913 (17.988)			
μ_2		0.5445 (26.606)	0.9026 (26.101)			
μ_3		0.7239 (31.981)	1.1915 (31.224)			
Log likelihood	−4082.44	−4074.29	−4073.95	−10280.65	−11848.16	−4519.23
Chi square	103.64	106.38	107.05	117.85	78.14	41.95
N	3169	3169	3169	2789	3138	1530

Asymptotic (t) statistics in parenthesis.
*The regression includes 51 industry dummies and excludes industries with less than 10 entrants.
**Excluding multi–plant firms.
***Firms with start–up size equal or greater than 5.

duration dependence, given that the parameter estimate is 0.7052. Further-more, the regression results from the Weibull specification closely mimic the ones presented earlier.

The monotonic decrease of the hazard rates that we found may evince either true duration dependence or the presence of unobserved individual heterogeneity. Bates [1990] noted that differences in the characteristics of entrepreneur's are statistically correlated with firm longevity. If unob-served firm characteristics influence the probability of failure, this implies that the sample of survivors is increasingly made up of firms with attributes associated with higher survival, thereby producing spurious negative dura-tion dependence. A first attempt to take the unobserved characteristics into account is performed by replacing the industry level variables by a set of industry dummies. The results (in the fourth column) show that the effect of firm start-up size remains not only significant, but quite stable at −0.19. Because there may also be unobserved heterogeneity at the firm level, we also attempted to perform two standard corrections for the individual heter-ogeneity based on the binomial and gamma assumptions regarding the dis-tribution of heterogeneity (Lancaster and Nickell [1980]). In both cases, however, the solutions obtained indicated that the data does not accommo-date any of these assumptions.

The robustness of our results is also confirmed by the regression results of the ordered probit and logit models, shown in Table 7.5. As the depend-ent variable is now the number of years that a firm stays in the survey (an indicator of their age), we shall expect a sign reversal in the regression parameter estimates. Moreover, since these methods assume equations for latent dependent variables which could be interpreted, for example, as indi-cators of the vitality of firms, strict comparison of the magnitude of the parameter estimates with the ones obtained from the hazard model is not straightforward. Note, however, that the signs and the statistical signifi-cance are consistent with previous results. Furthermore, the values obtained for the baseline hazard rates from these models (0.2181, 0.1218, 0.1371, 0.1194 and 0.2175, 0.1213, 0.1372, 0.1199 for the ordered probit and logit respectively) closely follow those obtained from the Cox Propor-tional Hazards model. Given that the ordered probit and logit are expected to be less sensitive to the presence of individual heterogeneity (Han and Hausman [1990]), this result seems to provide additional support to the hypothesis that our evidence of negative duration dependence is not mostly induced by unobserved individual heterogeneity.

A final note concerns the robustness of results to the exclusion of multiplant and very small firms. It might be conceivable that the determi-nants of the duration of the firms that start with several plants are different from those that start with a single establishment. Given the small number of entrants and the high degree of censoring in this sample, a separate regres-sion for these entrants is not feasible, but we ran a separate regression for the single plant entrants. These results are displayed in the fifth column and are quite similar to those obtained using the full sample. In the data section, we expressed concern with the quality of the coverage of our data set for firms smaller than five people. Consequently, we suspected that our results might have been altered for this incomplete coverage and ran the same regressions as above with only firms with five or more employees included. The results (shown in the last column) do not reveal, however, reversals in the signs or appreciable changes in statistical significance.

In summary, we would like to stress the strong effect of the *Start-Up Size* variable enabling firms to survive for a longer period of time, which is a fairly well established result, both theoretically and empirically. A previously uncovered result is the positive effect of the entry rate on the instantaneous failure rate. This presumably reflects either low entry (and, thus, exit) barriers, congestion, or both.[18] Furthermore, *Growth* consistently has a positive effect on firm duration, indicating that, after the effect of turnover is taken into account, fast growing industries offer a less hostile environment for the entering firms. Finally. our results suggest that the hazard function exhibits negative duration dependence, i.e. that the instantaneous probability of firm failure decreases with the age of firms. These findings are consistent with a view that sees entry as a process of selection and learning, as in Jovanovic [1982]. As time goes by, inefficient firms are being pushed out of the market. Survivors, based on their previous experience, believe that they are efficient and, in each period, the news that they require in order to make them abandon the market must be worse than in previous periods rendering, therefore, exit less likely.

Conclusion

Playing the competitive game, new firms challenge (and some times replace) old established firms' positions. When successful, these new firms acquire market share and become themselves established and, in this new position, are subsequently subjected to renewed challenges posed by new entrants. For each new firm that achieves success, there are many entrants that never reach maturity. The process of entry is a process of learning, in which new firms find out about the adequacy of their products to the tastes of buyers, and about their productive efficiency. In this process, firms continuously observe their performance and update their expectations of success and, with these revised expectations in hand, decide to continue the trial or to give up and leave the industry. The length of this process depends on some entrants' attributes and on the structural conditions of the industry where entry takes place.

We found that larger entrants and firms that have entered with multiple establishments are more likely to stay in the market for more periods. The industries in which the expected duration of new firms' life is likely to be greater are those that are growing fast and that can accommodate more new firms, and those in which fewer firms attempt to enter. Somewhat surprisingly, economies of scale and the extent of the presence of inefficiently scaled firms do not seem to affect the duration of firms in the market.

A novel result is the effect of the entry rates on firms' duration. This seems to be of particular importance in analysing the effect of entry on market performance. It was already known that in markets where entry occurs more intensively, the exit flows also tend to be more important. Not infrequently, this positive correlation has been interpreted as evidence of the competitive role played by entry, as new (more efficient) firms would replace old (less efficient) units. Without contradicting this interpretation, our results seem to suggest that some caution in analysing the efficiency improving effect of entry is required, since we have found that it is in those industries in which entry is more important that the entrants' lives are shorter.

We consistently found similar results, irrespective of the distribution assumptions, model specification and sample definition. Yet, a few developments emerge as natural steps from this study. The first refinement of the analysis would he to allow a proper distinction between the effects of age and of the overall economic environment. For that purpose, the researcher would benefit from having access to a longer period of follow-up and concomitantly a larger number of cohorts. A second major issue to be addressed by future research is the analysis of the relationship between the post-entry growth of firms and their survival prospects. Dunne, Roberts and Samuelson [1989, p. 689] found "no evidence of lower failure rates for plants that have expanded beyond their initial size class." Nevertheless, further investigation on the relationship between post-entry expansion and the survival patterns in the context of duration models that properly account for a time heterogeneous environment seems to be a necessary step.

Appendix

Table 7A.1 Empirical survival rates for single and multi–plant firms

Start-up size	N	Empirical survival rates after				Mean duration (in years)
		1 year	2 years	3 years	4 years	
Single plant firms						
Less than 3	836	0.7045	0.6100	0.5084	0.4400	5.81
Between 3 and 4	802	0.7606	0.6608	0.5524	0.4813	6.64
Between 5 and 9	711	0.7940	0.6878	0.5977	0.5176	7.46
Between 10 and 19	436	0.8372	0.7454	0.6720	0.6124	9.98
Between 20 and 49	252	0.8492	0.7698	0.7063	0.6548	11.53
Between 50 and 99	64	0.8750	0.8432	0.7813	0.7031	14.16
Greater than 99	37	0.9459	0.9189	0.7838	0.7297	16.20
Total	3 138	0.7757	0.6807	0.5873	0.5178	7.39
Multi–plant firms						
Between 3 and 4	1	0.0000	0.0000	0.0000	0.0000	
Between 5 and 9	4	0.7500	0.7500	0.7500	0.7500	
Between 10 and 19	7	1.0000	1.0000	1.0000	1.0000	
Between 20 and 49	9	0.7778	0.6667	0.6667	0.6667	
Between 50 and 99	3	0.6667	0.6667	0.6667	0.6667	
Greater than 99	7	1.0000	1.0000	1.0000	0.8571	
Total	31	0.8387	0.8065	0.8065	0.7742	18.71

*Assuming an exponential distribution.

Notes

1 We are grateful to Boyan Jovanovic, Manuel Mendes de Oliveira, two anonymous referees and the participants at the first Industrial Economics Meeting held in Braga for their comments. The usual disclaimer applies.

2 See Cable and Schwalbach [1991]. Geroski [1991] provides an excellent survey on the empirical literature on entry.

3 See Keifer [1988] for a survey.

4 Only firms with paid employees are legally required to report to this survey, which means that this source does not consider very small firms with only self employed people or family workers. Evaluation of its effectiveness in covering the other employment size classes is not normally possible but, as final data from the Census of Mining and Manufacturing are now available, an appraisal can be done. Comparison between these two sources reveal that even though the Ministry's survey investigates only one quarter of the total number of firms employing less than five people that were considered by the Census, it reports more firms in all the other employment classes and records a greater employment figure than the Census itself. Except for very small firms, it can thus he regarded as a highly reliable source.

5 Firms are identified by numbers which are given in sequence to firms by the time they first report

to the survey. Before a new identifying number is given to a particular firm, the Ministry staff makes sure that the firm was not included in their files in previous years. This check can be quite effective, since firms include in their statements the number given by the Firms Register when they are legally established as an autonomous legal entity.

6   Although data is available since 1981, we did not measure entry in 1982 because in 1981 the data is considered as not being very reliable by the Ministry itself. Given the way we measured entry, availability of reliable data for the year before the one we are interested in, is crucial for the accuracy of the measurement. Besides, the fact that we only count as entrants those firms that did not appear in the 1981 nor in the 1982 files increases our confidence that entrants are, in fact, new firms.

7   It is, of course, possible that a firm, which is absent from the files for more than one year, appears again later. These firms' status could have been recorded as well, but the price we would have to pay would be the corresponding decrease in the number of years available. We decided instead to exclude the 107 firms with this condition from our sample. Some other 139 firms were excluded. The majority of them are firms that could not be classified in a five digit industry, or whose main industry has changed between 1983 and 1987. A few were also deleted because the industry in which they operated had less than three firms in 1982 or 1983, or because there was no establishment in the firm's main industry that was recorded as belonging to the firm. Our final sample includes 3169 entrants.

8   See Kiefer [1988] for a detailed discussion of duration models in economics.

9   See Kalbfleish and Prentice [1980].

10 For a discussion on the distributional assumptions of duration models, see Addison and Portugal [1987].

11 The log likelihood function for the Weibull proportional hazards model is written

$$LL(\rho, \lambda, \beta) = \sum_{i:T_i \leq 1} ln\left[1 - S_i(1)\right] + \sum_{i:1 < T_i \leq 2} ln\left[S_i(1) - S_i(2)\right] + \sum_{i:2 < T_i \leq 3} ln\left[S_i(2) - S_i(3)\right]$$
$$+ \sum_{i:3 < T_i \leq 4} ln\left[S_i(3) - S_i(4)\right] + \sum_{i:T_i > 4} ln\left[S_i(4)\right]$$

12 There are four main characteristics that makes this procedure quite attractive to our case, namely: it is conceived for discrete duration data, it can accommodate a large number of tied failure times, the true parameters of the covariates are invariant to the time intervals chosen, and this methodology seems to be less sensitive to the inclusion of parametric heterogeneity.

13 This makes small firms' average cost curves flatter, and Mills and Schumann [1985] suggested that, because of this, smaller firms would more easily adapt to fluctuations in industry demand, being therefore more flexible.

14 Considerable evidence is now available suggesting that markets in which entry is more important are those in which a greater proportion of previously existing firms are displaced (Cable and Schwalbach [1991]). Some of these displaced firms are old established firms, but a large number are certainly recently born firms that fail to be accepted in the market, and the existence of a negative relationship between firm age and the probability of exit is already widely documented (Evans [1987a, 1987b], Dunne, Roberts and Samuelson [1989]).

15 Due to the limited number of years available and the high degree of censoring, an in depth analysis of the post-1983 entry cohorts is not yet feasible. Nevertheless, for the 1984 and 1985 cohorts we could confirm that the hazard rates are higher in the first year of life than in the subsequent years.

16 Note that we are conditioning on firm size. Most studies that have controlled for the ownership structure focused on plants, not firms. Our result that, for a given firm size, firms with more (and therefore smaller) plants last longer, seems to be stronger than the finding that, for a given plant size, plants owned by a multiplant (and hence larger) firm are more likely to survive.

17 This result does not confirm the ones in Audretsch and Mahmood [1994] and Troske [1989], which seem to suggest an inverse U-shaped hazard function, but are consistent with the findings of Boeri and Cramer [1993]. The results (both ours, Audretsch and Mahmood's, and Troske's) may have been affected by changes in the overall macroeconomic situation, and more work, using different cohorts of entrants, seems to be in order to properly disentangle the effects of the economic environment and age.

18 Dixit and Shapiro [1996] have shown that firms make their entry decisions simultaneously, overcrowding occurs with positive probability. If sunk costs do not catch firms in the industry, in the subsequent periods some firms will he forced to leave the market.

References

Addison, J. and Portugal, P., 1987, 'On the Distributional Shape of Unemployment Duration', *Review of Economics and Statistics*, 68(3), pp. 520–526.

Audretsch, D., 1991, 'New-Firm Survival and the Technological Regime', *Review of Economics and Statistics*, 72(3), pp. 441–450.

Audretsch, D. and Mahmood, T., 1994, 'The Rate of Hazard Confronting New Firms and Plants in US Manufacturing', *Review of Industrial Organisation*, 9(1), pp. 41–56.

Audretsch, D. and Acs. Z. 1991, 'Innovation as a Means of Entry: an Overview', in Geroski, P. and Schwalbach, J. (eds), *Entry, and Market Contestability: An International Comparison*, Oxford: Basil Blackwell.

Bates. T., 1990, 'Entrepreneur Human Capital Inputs and Small Business Longevity', *Review of Economics and Statistics*, 72(4), pp. 551–559.

Boeri, T. and Cramer, U., 1993, 'Employment Growth, Incumbents and Entrants: Evidence From Germany', *International Journal of Industrial Organization*, I0(4), pp. 545–565.

Cable, J. and Schwalbach, J, 1991, 'International Comparisons of Entry and Exit', in Geroski, P. and Schwalbach, J (eds), *Entry, and Market Contestability: An International Comparison*, Oxford: Basil Blackwell.

Cox, D. R., 1972, 'Regression Models and Life Tables', *Journal of the Royal Statistical Society, Series B*, 34(2), pp. 187–202.

Cox, D.R. and Oakes, D., 1985, *Analysis of Survival Data*, New York: Chapman and Hall.

Dixit, A. and Shapiro, C., 1986, 'Entry Dynamics with Mixed Strategies', in Lacy Glen Thomas III (ed.), *The Economics of Strategic Planning*, Lexington, Mass: Lexington Books.

Dunne, T., Roberts, M. and Samuelson, L., 1989, 'The Growth and Failure of US Manufacturing Plants', *Quarterly Journal of Economies*, 104(4), pp. 671–688.

Evans, D., 1987a, 'Tests of Alternative Theories of Firm Growth', *Journal of Political Economy*, 95(4), pp. 657–674.

Evans, D., 1987b, 'The Relationship Between Firm Growth, Size, and Age – Estimates for 100 Manufacturing Industries', *Journal of Industrial Economics*, 35(4), pp. 567–581.

Frank, M., 1988, 'An Intertemporal Model of Industrial Exit', *Quarterly Journal of Economics*, 103(2), pp. 333–344.

Geroski, P., 1991, *Market Dynamics and Entry*, Oxford: Basil Blackwell.

Geroski, P. and Jacquemin , A., 1989, 'Industrial Change, Barriers to Mobility, and European Industrial Policy', in Jacquemin, A. and Sapir, A. (eds), *The European Internal Market*, Oxford; Oxford University Press.

Gort, M. and Klepper, S., 1982, 'Time Paths in The Diffusion of Product Innovations', *Economic Journal*, 92(367), pp. 630–653.

Han, A. and Hausman, J., 1990, 'Flexible Parametric Estimation of Duration and Competing Risk Models', *Journal of Applied Econometrics*, 5(l), pp. 1–28.

Heckman, J. and Singer, B., 1984, 'A Method for Minimizing the Impact of Distributional Assumptions in Econometric Models for Duration Data', *Econometrica*, 52(2), pp. 271–320.

Jovanovic, B., 1982, 'Selection and Evolution of Industry', *Econometrica*, 50(3), pp. 649–670.

Kalbfleish, J. and Prentice, R., 1980, *The Statistical Analysis of Failure Data*, New York: Wiley.

Kiefer, N., 1988, 'Econometric Duration Data and Hazard Functions', *Journal of Economic Literature*, 26(2), pp. 646–679.

Lancaster, T. and Nickell, S., 1980,'The Analysis of Reemployment Probabilities for the Unemployed', *Journal of the Royal Statistical Society, Series A*, 143, pp. 141–165.

Lucas, R. E., 1978, 'On the Size Distribution of Business Firms', *Bell Journal of Economics*, 9(3), pp. 508–523.

Lyons, B., 1980, 'A New Measure of Minimum Efficient Plant Size in UK Manufacturing Industry', *Economica*, 17(185), pp. 19–34.

Maddala, G., 1983, *Limited-Dependent Variables in Econometrics*, Cambridge: Cambridge University Press.

Mata, J., 1991, 'Sunk Costs and Entry By Small and Large Plants', in Geroski, P.and Schwalbach, J. (eds), *Entry and Market Contestability: An International Comparison*, Oxford: Basil Blackwell.

Mata J, 1992, 'The Determinants of Firm Start-up Size', *mimeo*, Universido do Minho.

Mata, J., 1993, 'Entry and Type of Entrant: Evidence From Portugal', *International Journal of Industrial Organization*, 11(1), pp. 101–122.

Mata, J., 1994, 'Firm Growth During Infancy', *Small Business Economics*, 6(1) forthcoming.

Mills, D. and Schumann, L., 1985, 'Industry Structure with Fluctuating Demand', *American Economic Review*, 75(4), pp. 758–767.

Orr, D., 1974, 'The Determinants of Entry: A Study of the Canadian Manufacturing Industries', *Review of Economics and Statistics*, 56(l), pp. 58–66.

Phillips, B. and Kirchhoff, B., 1989, 'Formation, Growth and Survival: Small Firm Dynamics in the US Economy', *Small Business Economics*, 1(1), pp. 65–74.

Robson, M., 1991, 'Self-employment and New Firm Formation', *Scottish Journal of Political Economy* , 38(4), pp. 352–368.

Storey, D. and Jones, A., 1987, 'New Firm Formation: A Labour Market Approach to Industrial Entry', *Scottish Journal of Political Economy*, 34(1), pp. 37–51.

Troske, K., 1989, 'The Life-Cycle Behaviour of Establishments', *mimeo*, University of Chicago.

8

Discontinuance Among New Firms in Retail: The Influence of Initial Resources, Strategy, and Gender*

Nancy M. Carter[1], Mary Williams and Paul D. Reynolds

*Source: *Journal of Business Venturing* 12, 2 (1997), 125–45

Executive summary

Women-owned businesses represent one of the fastest growing segments of the US economy. Their rate has increased more than six-fold since 1970. Despite this growth rate, the number of firms owned by women still lags behind that of men, and the sales and income of women-owned firms are significantly lower than those of men-owned firms.

The discrepancy between the number of businesses owned by women and men and their economic success has been a popular theme among researchers. Some have suggested that performance differentials result from disparate structural positions women and men occupy in work and society, whereas others attribute the differences to deep rooted interpersonal orientations.

This study examines whether the performance differences can be explained by variations in initial resources and founding strategy. We test whether women have fewer start-up resources, and if they do, whether they can compensate for these deficiencies through their founding strategy. Recent work in social psychology argues that strategic choice is shaped by experiences to which individuals have been subjected, and that women and men have fundamentally different socialization experiences. We test the assumption that if the strategy that women-owners adopt exploits the unique capabilities they derive from their socialization, they can improve the performance of their firms and ward off discontinuance.

We examine the discontinuance pattern of 203 new firms in the retail industry. This industry was selected because women entrepreneurs often choose to operate in this industry, giving us a basis for comparing women-owned and men-owned firms. We classify the firms into six strategy archetypes. The archetypes range from a broad focus where founders emphasize multiple strategic foci simultaneously to narrowly targeted differentiation strategies. We assume that the experiential base of women entrepreneurs limits their successfully executing pricing strategies. We hypothesize that women-led firms decrease the odds of discontinuing by adopting one of two strategy types: (1) narrow differentiation strategies that seek to satisfy a narrow segment of the market and that do not rely on "pricing," or (2) broad "generalists" strategies that emphasize service and quality but not pricing, and take advantage of women's capability for handling multiple stakeholders simultaneously.

The results offer support for using an integrative model to explain the performance of women-owned, firms. Women-owned firms have higher odds of discontinuing than men-owned firms, and women appear to have fewer resources to start their businesses. Women owners were less likely to have instrumental experience from working in the retail industry and start their businesses on a smaller scale then men but were no less likely then their male counterparts to have access to credit from formal financial institutions, or to be disadvantaged by starting fewer other new businesses. Despite some apparent situational disadvantage, resource deficiencies do not appear to affect the odds of women-owned businesses discontinuing as much as they do men-owned initiatives

The findings indicate support for the supposition that women owners can use founding strategy to decrease the odds of discontinuing business. A broad generalists strategy that represents a multi-focused approach was found to benefit women-owned businesses most. Overall, the results suggest that men use prior business experience and human capital to affect the survival status of their businesses. Women appear to find strategic choice more beneficial.

Future research is recommended to further elaborate the integrative model. Special attention should be given to developing alternatives to measures traditionally used in gender research. Many researchers charge that those typically used reflect male derived measures. Similarly, greater attention should be given to understanding why the scale of women-owned businesses at start-up is substantially smaller than that of men, since scale has been shown to be related to subsequent growth and survival. (© 1997 Elsevier Science Inc.)

Introduction

Accumulating evidence documents the rapid rise in the portion of women-owned businesses in the US economy. Their share of all businesses grew by over 550 per cent between 1972 and 1987 (Clark and James 1992). Despite this proportionate growth, by 1987 women owned only one in three firms, and the economic scale of their businesses was substantially smaller than those owned by men (Clark and James 1992; Devine 1994).

The discrepancy between the number and economic success of women- and men-owned firms has stimulated considerable commentary among researchers and public policy makers. Some have suggested that performance differentials result from women having fewer resources or assets with which to create a firm (Cromie and Birley 1991), less access to opportunities, different managerial styles and intentions (Brush 1992; Kaplan 1988), and less beneficial social networks to assist the start-up process (Reese 1992). Others, however, have documented few differences between the needs and experiences of men and women entrepreneurs that would explain the differences in firm performance (Buttner and Rosen 1988; Kalleberg and Leicht 1991; Sexton and Bowman-Upton 1990).

Inconsistencies in the empirical findings have been attributed to inadequate research design, but varying assumptions also characterize the research efforts. Some have assumed that performance differences relate to variations in structural positions women and men occupy in work and society, whereas others attribute differences to deep rooted interpersonal orientations. Liou and Aldrich (1995) refer to these two perspectives as situational versus dispositional. Situational proponents argue that gender-based differences can be attributed to variations in the power and opportunities accorded men and women. According to this perspective, women are seen as having been denied equal access to opportunities in labor markets and organizations and thus have been hindered in acquiring the skills and capabilities necessary to compete at the same level with men. Once equal access is ensured, gender-based differences in performance seemingly disappear.

Alternatively. dispositional explanations contend that women and men have different experiential backgrounds and ways of thinking that derive from variations in their education and socialization patterns. These differences are seen as shaping the way women and men construct and interpret reality and influence the formation of their values and intentions. According to this perspective, variations in performance can be attributed to owner's motives and intentions.

Until recently, the situational and dispositional perspectives have been posed as competing models. Researchers now theorize that a collaborative or integrative approach that incorporates both perspectives offers a better explanation of gender-based differences. For example, from an extensive review of the literature, Liou and Aldrich (1995) concluded that both disposition and situation shape women's development of a relational competence. This competence, which they define as "the ability to develop and maintain long-term associations with others on the basis of mutual trust, exchange, and support," may affect the strategies women adopt and ways in which they operate their businesses (1995, p. 1). Fischer, Reuber and Dyke (1993) take the argument further and suggest that women's socialization processes may lead them to manage their firms in ways that offset sex-based discrimination or systematic bias. In other words, women may use dispositional characteristics to overcome situational barriers. The issue then is not which of the two models best explains and predicts performance, but how they contribute jointly to a more robust explanation of the phenomenon.

Theory and hypotheses

In this study we adopt an integrative model to examine performance differences between women- and men-owned businesses in the retail industry. We test whether dispositional characteristics can be used to overcome or moderate deficiencies that arise from situational differences. Recognizing that dispositional characteristics are the accumulation of influences beginning in childhood and spanning adulthood and work career, we use the implementation and execution of the firm's "founding strategy" as a surrogate measure. We believe this is one aspect of management where women's reliance on dispositional characteristics will be most obvious.

Research has established the linkage between strategy and new ventures' performance and survival (Sandberg and Hofer 1987; Romanelli 1989; Keeley and Roure 1990; McDougall and Robinson 1990: Stearns *et al.*, 1995). Implicit in these studies is the argument that an effective strategy hinges on the alignment between the organization's internal capabilities and resources and challenges offered by the external environment. For new ventures, the entrepreneur's human and financial capital are seen as major sources of the firm's internal capabilities. If the situational background of women results in them having fewer of these resources to start their businesses, the question becomes whether they exploit dispositional capabilities to compensate for the deficiencies. For example, to what extent might the relational competence identified by Liou and Aldrich (1995) be used by women to construct and implement a strategy for dealing with customers, competitors, and suppliers that effectively offsets other resource deficiencies?

We use the odds of discontinuing business as the measure of firm performance and data from new ventures in the retail industry. Businesses in retail were chosen for several reasons. First, new ventures founded by women are more prevalent in retail than in any other industry except service (Clark and James 1992; Zellner *et al.*, 1994). This provides us with a sufficient number of women-led firms to compare with those founded by men. In some industries, (e.g., manufacturing), the paucity of women-owned firms precludes meaningful comparisons. Second, the retail industry has been characterized as having attenuated career tracks and lower capital requirements than other industries (except selected services) (Clark and James 1992). Thus, the resource requirements necessary to establish businesses in this industry should be attainable by both women and men. Third, we limit our sample to one industry, because research shows that significant strategy-industry interactions exist in predicting new firm performance and survival (Keeley and Roure 1990; Sandberg and Hofer 1987; Stearns *et al.*, 1995).

Start-up resources

A key supposition in entrepreneurship research is that a firm's resources at start-up are critical determinants of success and survival. Research has focused on two sets of resources, those intangible assets individuals bring with them to the entrepreneurial process in the form of human capital, and the entrepreneur's ability to secure tangible resources from the environment (e.g., capital, partners, employees, suppliers).

Human capital

Human capital derives from investments individuals make in themselves, often through education (formal and occupational experiences) and training. Presumably, the more specific the human capital to the nature of the new firm start-up, the higher the likelihood of success. Researchers have found a positive relationship between entrepreneurs' prior experience in the industry with success of the new firm (Cooper and Bruno 1977; Van de Ven, Hudson, and Schroeder 1984).

In orthodox economic theory, the acquisition of human capital is viewed as almost entirely under the individual's control, but barriers are seen as impeding women in acquiring adequate levels of human capital. Research supporting this hypothesis finds that in comparison to men, women entrepreneurs are less likely to have experiences gained from owning prior businesses or working in private firms (Cromie and Birley 1991); are more likely to have pursued undergraduate studies in liberal arts rather than technical disciplines like business or engineering (Honing-Haftel and Martin 1986); have careers that are more frequently interrupted (Kaplan 1988); and are less likely to be part of start-up teams for high-growth new firms (Reynolds 1993). To the extent that deficiencies in human capital render new firms vulnerable, those begun by women are more likely to have higher odds of discontinuing than those started by men.

Access to resources

In addition to systemic barriers, overt discrimination has been viewed as restricting women's access to critical opportunity structures and resources in the external environment. Two sets of resources particularly critical for start-up efforts are access to financial resources and level of human resources. Access to capital markets has been regarded as among the most important resources denied women. Tigges and Green (1994) suggested three reasons why women may be disadvantaged in capital markets: (1) they tend to have less experience and equity in their businesses than men; (2) they may be discriminated against by resource lenders on the basis of outmoded gender role beliefs; and (3) their belief that they will receive differential treatment may reduce the rate of lending applications among women business owners.

Empirical studies that have tested these assumptions present mixed findings. Some researchers have found that women entrepreneurs have access to less external financing, weaker collateral positions and believe that they have been discriminated against or received unequal treatment by financing institutions or other resource providers (Goffee and Scase 1983; Hisrich and Brush 1984; Olm, Carsrud, and Alvey 1988). Others, however, have found little evidence of obvious discrimination against women (Buttner and Rosen 1988). Particularly when samples of men and women have been matched on key variables like business age, firm size, and growth rate, few differences in resource access have been identified (Riding and Swift 1990).

The number of employees and whether there are start-up partners also have been seen as critical resources. Birley (1986) demonstrated the importance of the scale of human resources in her finding that the employment size at start-up influences the extent to which businesses will survive and grow. Typically, the scale of women-owned firms has been smaller than that of men-owned firms. This difference has been attributed to the motives or intentions of women owners. Women have been viewed as focusing on goals other than growth and economic performance (Brush 1992). But if women have been limited in acquiring adequate financial resources to start their businesses either because they haven't taken on partners to increase the resource base or are denied access to formal lending, they would seem less able to take on costs associated with hiring and training employees.

H1:   High levels of human capital and access to outside resources decrease odds of businesses discontinuing.

H2:   Women-owned firms have lower levels of human resources and less access to financial resources from outside sources than men-owned businesses, increasing the odds they will discontinue.

Women's style

Over the past two decades a considerable body of research has addressed women's segregation in the workplace. Increasingly, interests concerned with determining women's "relative worth" within organizations have turned to identifying the styles of leading and managing exhibited by women, and why those styles are particularly useful at this time in history (Astin and Leland 1991). Sheppard's (1992) work on how women in management view themselves as women and as organizational members is representative of this trend. Studying a small, but purposive sample, Sheppard found that women managers and professionals view themselves as "humanistic" and "personal oriented" as opposed to "cost oriented." Their management style was described as being service oriented with an emphasis on persuasion, appeasement, and maintaining good relations. Sheppard characterized women's decision-making as having a strong "relational" component and as being embedded within a particular context.

Sheppard's findings complement those of earlier studies. Neider (1987) found that women perceive themselves as having better human relations skills, which allow them to deal effectively with employees and customers. Others have found that women have a "feminine" style of leadership which fosters participative decision-making and may translate into employee satisfaction and increased performance (Chaganti 1986; Hisrich and Brush

1984). Some have speculated that the skills women attain in running a household and the broad range of experiences they acquire as they follow spouses and raise children result in a diverse experiential base that transfers to their business management style (Scott 1986).

One area where differences resulting from variations in women's and men's socialization patterns may be most evident is in their choice and execution of the firm's competitive strategy. Recent work on information-processing theories from social psychology argue that strategic choice is limited by individual's belief structures or cognitive maps (Walsh and Fahey 1986). Belief structures are shaped by the experiences to which individuals have been subjected. If women develop distinctive styles of leadership or management as a result of their particular socialization patterns, we would expect their implementation and execution of strategy to reflect those unique competencies.

Predicting precisely how the choice and execution of strategy differs across gender requires speculation. Few empirical studies have related the competencies or managerial styles men and women derive from their socialization patterns to strategy and new firm performance. We rely on related research to formulate hypotheses.

Mapping style to strategy

Differences in the attributes that result from women's and men's socialization patterns can be mapped to the distinction between "specialist" and "generalists" strategies. Researchers have used this classification scheme to predict appropriate strategies for new ventures. The specialist perspective maintains that new businesses should seek a niche in the marketplace where they can avoid direct competition with larger, more established firms. According to this perspective, new firms lack adequate resources for effective organizational learning, and this "liability of newness" (Stinchcombe 1965) limits the firms' ability to compete on the basis of price (Deeks 1976; Stegall, Steinmetz, and Kline 1976). Advocates of this perspective caution that new ventures should become specialists by targeting narrow market segments that have been overlooked by larger firms and serve those customers through specially designed, high quality products or services (Broom and Longenecker 1971; Cohen and Lindberg 1974; Hosmer 1957).

Alternatively, other researchers have argued that broad strategies will lead to better survival chances for new ventures. Biggadike (1976) contended that entrepreneurs must adopt an aggressive posture when entering markets and match the broad appeal offered by competitors. Researchers concurring with this generalists perspective have argued that new ventures penalize themselves unless they compete head to head with the market leaders, including competing on the basis of price (Cooper, Willard, and

Woo 1986; MacMillan and Day 1987; Miller and Camp 1985). To successfully implement a pricing strategy requires the knowledge to achieve efficiencies and cost savings across the entire value chain of the firm's operation. Typically, the firm must keep its per unit costs low, minimize spending on unnecessary operating expenses, and have sufficient resources for broad-scale marketing (Porter 1985).

Predicting which of the two perspectives best prescribes strategies for women-owned businesses presents a dilemma. An essential distinction between the approaches concerns the firm's resource base. The generalists approach with its emphasis on pricing requires firms to have adequate resources to market effectively and knowledge of how to achieve cost-efficiencies in order to sustain adequate profits. The resources women bring to the start-up process appear insufficient for such an approach. Women have lower levels of instrumental skills gained from industry experience and fewer financial resources to achieve a sufficient presence in the marketplace. These deficiencies make it unlikely they can successfully execute a strategy that relies on pricing where adequate profits must be sustained by achieving cost efficiencies and marketing prowess.

Instead, their resource bases seem more amenable to a specialist strategy that relies on relational competencies. Narrow strategies that reflect a service orientation, emphasize a particular area of expertise or speciality or target a narrow segment of the market would seem more judicious. Such strategies would exploit women's "co-operative network of relationships" while embedding them in market niches where they are less likely to attract the attention of larger competitors.

But does the generalists approach necessarily require an emphasis on pricing? The diverse skills women gain from integrating their "web-like" connections among family, work, and community (Brush 1992) argue for developing effective broad-based strategy. Broad strategies that emphasize quality, service, and responsiveness to the varying needs of diverse customer bases correspond closely to the socialization patterns of women. To the extent that broad strategies can be developed that avoid emphasizing pricing, women entrepreneurs should be able to compensate for resource deficiencies and increase the likelihood of their business's success or survival.

Research by Kalleberg and Leicht (1991) illustrates the dilemma in predicting whether women-owned firms are better suited for executing generalists or specialist strategies. They found that men were more likely to build a strategy around offering a wide range of products and services. However, only women-owned businesses that adopted the generalists strategy were less likely to have discontinued. Women were more likely to emphasize quality but women who adopted this strategy were no more likely to have gone out of business than men who adopted a quality emphasis. Kalleberg and Leicht's (1991) findings may be attributable to a lack of statistical power. The discontinuance rate among the businesses in their sample was very low. They concluded that their data collection strategy resulted in successful, viable businesses being over-represented in the sample. Second, the firms Kalleberg and Leicht studied were not necessarily new ventures, our interest in the present study. The average age of the companies they studied was 13.19 years. It is unclear whether the strategy differences they detected arise from variations in the firm's initial founding strategy or strategic adaptations entrepreneurs made over time.

To investigate whether women-owned new ventures use a broad generalists strategy to compensate for resource deficiencies or adopt narrow specialist strategies, we offer competing hypotheses. We reason that strategy affects the performance and survival of new firms, and if within the same industry women-owned and men-owned businesses behave differently after variations in resources have been controlled, gender-role socialization accounts for the differences. We contend that strategies that avoid price competition will lower the odds of women-owned businesses discontinuing and allow women-owned firms to overcome resource deficiencies. But because the literature presents contradictory evidence for predicting women's strategy choice beyond its insight on price, we adopt an exploratory approach.

H3: Strategy decreases odds of businesses discontinuing.
H4: Women-owned firms that use a "specialist" strategy that seeks to satisfy a narrow segment of the market and does not rely on "pricing" have lower odds of discontinuing.
H5: Women-owned firms that use a broad "generalists" strategy that emphasizes service and quality and does not emphasize pricing have lower odds of discontinuing.
H6: Women-owned firms use strategic choice to lower odds of discontinuing and reduce resource deficiencies.

Methods

Sources of data

Data for assessing characteristics of new ventures were collected via a survey of new firms in two mid-western states in 1986 (Reynolds and Freeman 1987; Reynolds and Miller 1988). A stratified random sample ensured that all regions of the state were represented. The sample was based on firms listed in the Dun's Market Identifier files as between one to six years old just prior to the survey. Phone call verification excluded all listings that were not new, autonomous, and active; about one-half of the listings qualified. Each eligible new firm was sent a mail questionnaire three times, with a reminder postcard between the first and second mailings. Instructions included with the questionnaire asked that the survey be completed by a person that had major responsibility for starting the firm and is active in the management of the firm. Any of the founders could qualify. Phone interviews were completed with about half of those not returning the mail questionnaire. Final response rate was 69%. The data were developed on more than 2,500 new firms representing all industry sectors. We limit our analysis in the present study to the 203 retail firms in the sample.

Subsequent phone interviews were completed in 1992 to verify status of the respondents from the initial survey. Five categories of responses were noted: (1) firms that were still in operation at the time of the follow-up survey; (2) firms that we could confirm were out of business; (3) firms that were "dormant" at the time of the follow-up survey; (4) firms that had been "sold or merged"; and (5) firms, that despite multiple follow-ups using phone directories (four to six calls) and site visits, we were unable to contact. Since it is difficult to judge whether firms that are dormant or those that are sold or merged can be classified as surviving for the present analysis, we disregarded firms in these two categories from the analysis. Furthermore, our persistence in contacting the firms in the sample gave us confidence in categorizing those we were unable to contact as discontinued firms. The result of the paring was a sample where all businesses represented were founded by the current owner.

Measures

Gender composition of the founding team

New ventures may be founded by individual entrepreneurs or by teams of entrepreneurs, and a team of founders may be composed of women and men. We divided our sample into the following gender designations: (1) those in which the majority (greater than half) of the team members were men; (2) those in which the majority (greater than half) of team members were women. Using this method, women starting a new venture by themselves are classified as "women-owned" and men starting alone, "men-owned." Of the businesses designated as women-owned, thirty-four were started by one individual, twenty-five were founded by a team of entrepreneurs. Of the men-owned businesses, sixty-seven were started by one entrepreneur, seventy-seven were founded by a team. There is no statistical difference in composition of founding team by gender (chi-square = 3.42, p < 0.07). Approximately one-third of the businesses in the study were headed by women, a number slightly higher than the percentage reported by Kalleberg and Leicht (1991).

Firm age

The year in which the owner of the new firm first made a resource commitment to the firm also was included in the analysis as a control. All firms in the sample were six years or less in age when the first wave of data was collected in 1986. We assumed that firms that were one year of age may have differential probability of survival from firms that were six years of age in 1986. If our assumption is true, we would expect the age to be significant and negative (e.g., older firms in 1986 would have lower rates of discontinuance by 1992). By using firm age as a covariate, we partial out the effect of age at the time the firm enters into the risk set. Age was measured as the number of months since founding.

Resources

Two categories of resources entrepreneurs bring to the firm at the time of founding were considered: tangible and intangible. Tangible resources represent resources that can be secured by the individual and used to launch the firm. Intangible resources are properties of individuals that have accrued through experience and education.

Two types of tangible resources were considered: (1) size of the organization at the time of founding and (2) access to financial resources. Size was measured in two ways. Whether the business was started as a sole proprietorship rather than with partners (a start-up team) was seen as providing access to a smaller resource base. Responses were coded 1 if started without partners, 0 if a start-up team was present. The second measure of size was the number of full-time employees. To reduce the skewness and produce a more symmetrical distribution, we use the log of size as the variable measure. Whether or not the businesses used formal sources to provide capital for start-up was used as a proxy for access to financial resources. As noted by Tigges and Green (1994) this variable does not measure access to credit markets, because the sample only includes entrepreneurs who succeeded in establishing businesses. Those denied access to credit sources may not be in the sample. Instead, the variable measures whether or not the businesses rely on formal sources for capital as opposed to financing start-up from other sources (e.g., personal equity stakes). Responses were coded 1 if loans were obtained from banks or other formal lending institutions and 0 if these formal sources did not provide any of the capital infusion.

Two indicators of intangible resources were used to test hypotheses. Since the unit of analysis is the business, the indicators are aggregate values when the firm is founded by a group or team. The first indicator is the extent to which members of the founding team have prior experience starting new ventures. The variable was calculated as the percent of the founding team that had helped start at least one other new firm prior to the current venture. The second indicator is the extent to which team members have experience working in the same industry as that of the new venture. To create a more symmetrical distribution experience was measured as the square root of the total number of years team members had worked in the retail industry.

Strategy

The questionnaire method of data collection we used relies on key informants to indicate the focus of the firms' competitive strategy. As architects of the founding strategies the survey respondents are uniquely qualified to assess strategic intentions. Respondents to the survey questionnaire were asked to indicate on a four-point scale ranging from critical (1), to insignificant (4) the importance of thirteen attributes of competitive strategy to their firms' strategic focus. These items were chosen for their correspondence to previously identified strategy attributes and their appropriateness to new ventures.

In previous analyses (Carter *et al.*, 1994) these thirteen measures were shown to be associated with six strategic attributes: market sensitivity, technology, product distinctiveness, site appeal, service, and price. Appendix 1 displays the items from the questionnaire sorted by their factor loadings and Cronbach alpha reliability coefficients associated with each factor. Assuming that strategy consists of a composite or bundle of actions rather than an emphasis on one dimension, Carter *et al.*, (1994) subjected the strategic attributes from the factor analysis to a cluster analysis to discern strategy archetypes. These procedures are consistent with the prevailing conceptualization in the literature that strategy is a multidimensional construct. The six strategy archetypes as defined by the extent to which they emphasize the strategy attributes are described in Appendix 2.

Results from the original six-cluster solution determined by Carter *et al.*, (1994) were used to classify the retail firms in the present study into one of the six strategy archetypes. The cluster centroid means for each strategy dimension from the original analysis (see Carter *et al.*, 1994, p. 32) were used as initial starting values in an iterative partitioning analysis (SPSS Quick Cluster). This procedure sorts each retail firm in the sample according to its emphasis on the six strategy attributes and assigns the firm to the closest centroid vector of the original six-cluster solution. This approach assumes that the original structure identified by Carter et al., adequately represents the strategy archetypes used by new ventures across industries and avoids the construction of a typology unique to the retail industry. In related research, Stearns *et al.*, (1995) ranked the six strategy archetypes from broad to narrow depending on the number of strategy dimensions emphasized in each archetype. Appendix 2 presents the strategies from broadest in scope to narrowest according to the number of dimensions emphasized. In retail, few businesses adopt the technology value or equivocator strategy. Only two businesses head by women pursued these strategies, and neither of those firms discontinued during the time of the study. Because our intent is to determine the odds of businesses discontinuing, we eliminated firms that pursued equivocator and technology value strategies.

Results

Data analyses

We first use descriptive statistics and *t*-tests to compare women-owned and men-owned firms in the sample. Second, we use a series of equations in which the firm's survival status is regressed on groups of variables entered sequentially. Because the dependent variable is dichotomous, we use logistic regression analysis. We use a step-down regression approach where the control variable, organization size, is entered in the first step, followed by groups of main effects variables. This method introduces variables as "sets" and allows us to examine the relationship between the resource variables, strategy, gender, and the dependent variable as each set of explanatory variables is entered. We then include product terms representing the interaction between gender and resources, and gender and strategy, with all main effect variables controlled. This allows us to test whether women-owned business's use of strategic choice improves the fit of the model after all other variables are controlled.

Because the strategy variable is categorical, we used deviation contrasts. This approach compares each level, or factor, of the strategy variable to the pooled effect of all levels. For example, if the pooled effect of strategy is statistically significant as indicated by the Wald chi-square value, the effect of each strategy type can be evaluated in comparison with the average effect of all strategies.

Descriptive analysis

Descriptive statistics for the dependent variable and predictor variables for women-owned and men-owned firms are presented in Table 8.1. Appendix 3 presents correlation coefficients of all variables in the study. Table 8.1 shows that within the retail industry, women-owned firms have a higher rate of discontinuing than men-owned firms. More than one-third of the women-owned firms discontinued during the time frame of the study. Just over 20 per cent of the men-owned firms ceased operation.

Age of the businesses was included in the study as a control variable. It was expected that age may differentially affect the probability of survival. To the extent that this effect may exist, it does not appear to relate to gender of the founding team. On average, the firms in the sample have been operating for four years, and the length of time women-owned firms had been in business was no different than that of men-owned firms.

The resource variables indicate mixed support for the supposition that women-owned firms have fewer resources at the time of start-up than men-owned firms. As expected, men-owned businesses have significantly more employees at start-up, but they are no more likely to start with partners than women and there were no apparent differences in access to sources of

Table 8.1 Means, standard deviations, and percentage distribution of predictor variables

Variables	Women-owned			Men-owned		
	Mean	*SD*	*%*	*Mean*	*SD*	*%*
Discontinuance	0.34[a]	0.48		0.22[a]	0.41	
Firm characteristic						
Age (months)	48.98	20.61		47.06	22.17	
Resource access						
Credit from formal sources	0.51	0.50		0.51	0.50	
Number of employees	4.34	5.30		8.99	14.89	
(measured as logarithm)	0.45[b]	0.38		0.64[b]	0.49	
Start-up team	0.48	0.50		0.57	0.50	
Owner characteristics						
% prior start-up experience	30.17	44.61		32.64	43.99	
Years industry experience	4.53	6.44		7.92	9.54	
(measured as square root)	1.46[b]	1.55		2.09[b]	1.89	
Strategy						
Super achievers			32.88			43.14
Quality proponent			10.47			10.98
Price			13.17			12.41
Niche purveyor			43.48			32.88

[a] Indicates significant differences between samples (t-test $p \leq 0.01$).
[b] Indicates significant differences between samples (t-test $p \leq 0.001$).

financial credit. Women-owned firms were no less likely to rely on outside financial credit. Approximately 50 per cent of all firms in the sample rely on credit from formal financial institutions.

The expectation that women-owned firms possess a lower stock of human capital at start-up received some support. As predicted, businesses headed by women have significantly fewer years of experience working in the retail industry. However, men-owned firms are no more likely to benefit from knowledge acquired from founding other new ventures than women-owned firms. On average, 30 per cent of the founding team in women-owned firms had experience in starting previous businesses; 33 per cent of the entrepreneurs in men-owned firms had such background.

Regression analyses

Table 8.2 presents results from six logistic regression analyses. The extent to which each set of variables improves the fit of the model is evaluated by the chi-square improvement.

The results displayed in column 1 indicate that when firm age is entered in the first step it has no significant impact on the survival of new firms in the sample (Wald = 2.46; $p < 0.l2$). The findings in column 2 display the results of main effects tests. The findings provide support for hypotheses 1 and 3 (Model chi-square improvement = 20.15; $p < 0.001$). Hypothesis 1 stated that high levels of human capital and access to outside resources decrease odds of businesses discontinuing. Experience in starting other businesses (B = –0.01; $p < 0.01$), experience working in the industry (B = –0.31; $p < 0.001$), starting the business with partners (B = –0.34; $p < 0.05$), and having employees (B = –0.69; $p < 0.05$) all decrease the odds of discontinuing. Only access to formal lending sources (B = 0.01; $p < 0.92$) was not statistically significant. The results indicate that both the human capital founding teams bring to the start-up process and the scale of the business at start-up explain the odds of discontinuing.

The results also support H3, indicating that the founding strategy adopted by start-ups affects the odds of discontinuance. The findings show that broad strategies significantly affect discontinuance, but narrow strategies have no apparent effect. The two broad strategies, super achievers and quality proponents, both emphasize multi foci simultaneously. The major difference between the strategies is their emphasis on pricing. The super achiever strategy promotes seeking a flexible and responsive position in the market by emphasizing characteristics of site location, exploiting advanced technology, and emphasizing the quality of their distinctive products and services relative to the price charged. The quality proponents strategy emphasizes service and distinctiveness, and de-emphasizes price. The findings indicate that the super achievers strategy (B = –0.73; $p < 0.001$) decreases odds of discontinuing, whereas implementation of a quality proponent strategy (B = 1.12; $p < 0.001$) increases odds of discontinuing business. Evidently, the absence of a pricing emphasis renders start-ups vulnerable to competition. This finding supports earlier studies that argued new ventures must match the broad appeal offered by competitors, including competing on the basis of price.

Column 3 in Table 8.2 shows the effect of adding gender to the model. The coefficient is positive and statistically significant, indicating that women-owned businesses have a higher probability of discontinuing than men-owned businesses after resources differences are controlled. The inclusion of gender with the other main effect variables significantly improves the overall fit of the model (Model chi-square improvement = 5.17; $p < 0.02$).

Column 4 displays the results associated with testing H2 that women-owned firms have lower levels of human resources and less access to financial resources, increasing the odds they will discontinue. The inclusion of the product terms to the equation significantly improves the overall fit of the model (Model chi-square improvement = 18.75; $p < 0.002$). An

Table 8.2 Determinants of log odds of discontinuing business

Step variables	1 b	SE	2 b	SE	3 b	SE	4 b	SE	5 b	SE	6 b	SE
1. Firm age	-0.01	0.01	-0.02[e]	0.01	-0.02[e]	0.01	-0.02[e]	0.01	-0.02[e]	0.01	-0.02	0.011[d]
2. Resources												
Prior start-up experience			-0.01[e]	0.00	-0.01[e]	0.00	0.01[e]	0.00	-0.01[e]	0.01	-0.01[d]	0.00
Industry experience			-0.31[f]	0.08	-0.27[f]	0.08	-0.33[f]	0.10	-0.35[f]	0.11	-0.36[f]	0.11
Start-up team			-0.34[d]	0.15	-0.37[e]	0.15	-0.38[d]	0.16	-0.37	0.17	-0.37	0.18
Number of employees			-0.69[d]	0.33	-0.61	0.33	-0.34	0.36	-0.29	0.41	-0.30	0.41
Credit for formal sources			0.01	0.13	0.00	0.13	0.06	0.14	0.16	0.16	0.17	0.16
Strategy												
Super achievers			-0.73[f]	0.22	-0.70[e]	0.22	-0.76[f]	0.24	-1.18[f]	0.32	1.14[f]	0.32
Quality proponent			-1.12[f]	0.28	1.15[f]	0.28	1.34[f]	0.31	1.59[f]	0.37	1.56[f]	0.36
Price competitor			-0.09	0.28	-0.11	0.28	-0.12	0.31	-0.02	0.33	-0.02	0.33
Niche purveyor			-0.30	0.21	-0.33	0.21	-0.45	0.23	-0.39	0.26	-0.39	0.26
3. Gender												
Women's firms					0.32[d]	0.14	0.04	0.27	0.01	0.28	0.04	0.29
4. Resource by gender												
Prior start-up experience × women's firms							0.01[e]	0.00	0.01[f]	0.00	0.02[e]	0.01
Industry experience × women's firms							-0.05	0.10	-0.04	0.11	-0.04	0.11
Start-up team × women's firms							0.48[d]	0.16	0.40[d]	0.17	0.41	0.22
Number of employees × women's firms							0.44	0.37	0.43	0.41	0.42	0.41
Credit from formal sources × women's firms							-0.10	0.14	-0.03	0.16	-0.03	0.16

continued on next page

Table 8.2 Determinants of log odds of discontinuing business (cont.)

Step variables	1 b	SE	2 b	SE	3 b	SE	4 b	SE	5 b	SE	6 b	SE
5. Strategy by gender												
Super achievers × women's firms									-1.05^f	0.28	-1.04^f	0.32
Quality × women's firms									0.43	0.36	0.57	0.40
Price competitor × women's firms									0.39	0.33	0.31	0.35
Niche purveyor × women's firms									0.22	0.26	0.15	0.28
6. Resource by strategy by gender												
Team by SA × women's firms											-0.07	0.25
Experience by SA × women's firms											-0.01	0.01
Constant	-0.66	0.27	1.04^e	0.40	1.08^e	0.41	0.95^d	0.42	0.82	0.43	0.83	0.43
2-log likelihood	438.98		375.04^c		369.87^a		351.12^b		336.18^b		335.37	

[a] Model chi-square improvement significant at 0.05.
[b] Model chi-square improvement significant at 0.01.
[c] Model chi-square improvement significant at 0.001.
[d] $p < 0.05$.
[e] $p < 0.01$.
[f] $p < 0.001$.

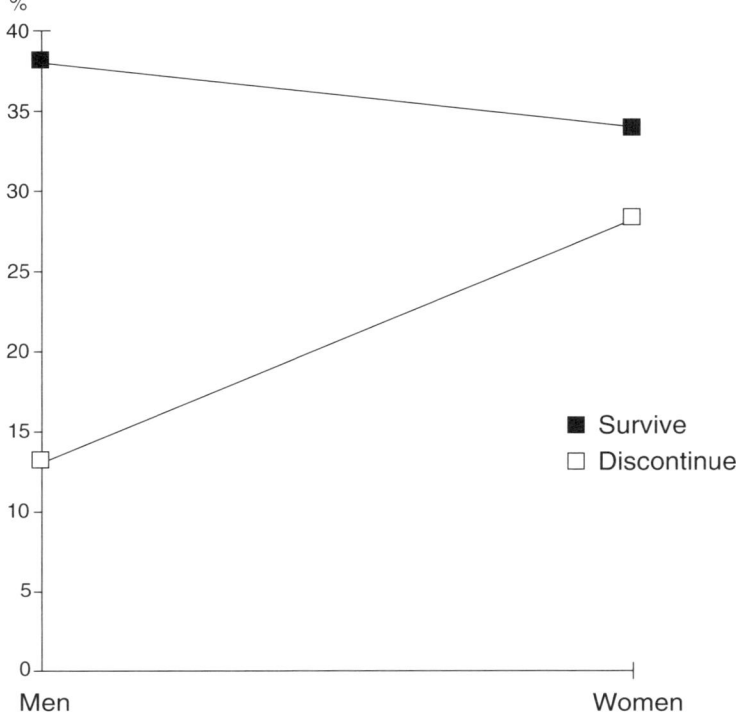

Figure 8.1 Prior start-up experience.

examination of the coefficients reveals that only two resources contribute significantly to the model improvement. Only prior start-up experience and whether the business was started by a team differentially affected the odds of women and men-owned businesses discontinuing. The means associated with the resource by gender interactions are displayed in Figures 8.1 and 8.2.

Contrary to expectations, the lack of prior start-up experience does not differentially affect the survival status of women-owned businesses. On average, almost 27 per cent of the start-up team in women-owned firms that discontinued had prior start-up experience compared with 32 per cent of the teams in surviving businesses. The probability of men-owned businesses surviving is significantly enhanced by owner's prior experience in starting new businesses. Only 13 per cent of the start-up team in men-owned businesses that discontinued had started other firms. In businesses that survived, almost 38 per cent of each team had prior start-up experience. It appears that men-owned businesses utilize experience gained in starting previous new ventures to enhance the survival chances of their businesses. Such knowledge does not appear to benefit women-owned businesses in the same way.

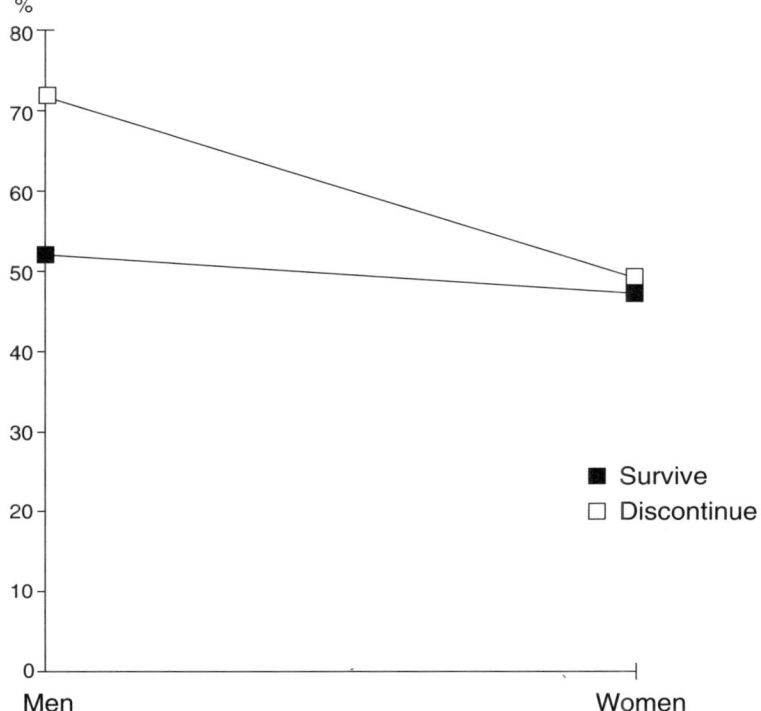

Figure 8.2 Start-up team.

The supposition that women-owned businesses would be differentially disadvantaged by starting their businesses without partners was not supported. Figure 8.2 indicates that neither form of start-up impacted odds of survival for women-owned businesses. On the other hand, men-owned businesses in retail appear disadvantaged by having start-up partners. Men-owned businesses, on average, were more likely to be founded by a team. But the higher the probability that men-owned businesses was started by partners, the higher the odds of the business discontinuing. In men-owned businesses that discontinued, 73 per cent had been started by a team.

Means tests presented earlier showed that founders of women-owned businesses had fewer years of industry experience and fewer employees than men-owned businesses. The coefficients associated with these resources indicate that these deficiencies do not differentially affect women-owned firms. Apparently, the negative impact of having inadequate numbers of employees and fewer years of industry experience is shared by women- and men-owned businesses.

The findings displayed in column 5 of Table 8.2 report the test of H5. Adding the product terms of strategy and gender to the equation

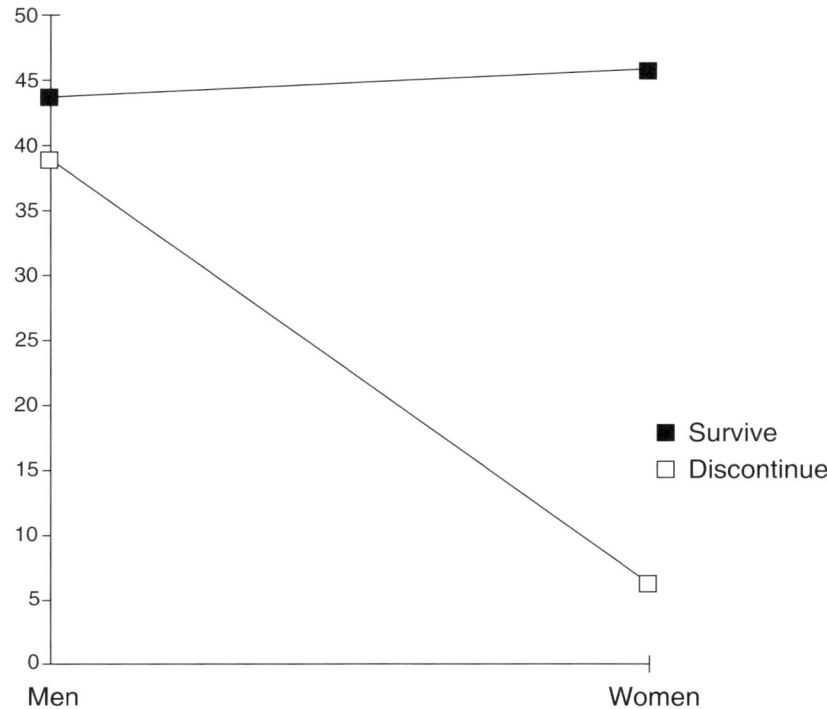

Figure 8.3 Super achievers strategy.

significantly improves the fit of the model (Model chi-square improvement = 14.93; $p < 0.002$). The supposition that a gender-strategy interaction predicts probability of retail businesses surviving beyond that explained by the business's initial resource base is supported. We predicted that women-owned firms that pursue a generalists strategy that emphasizes service and quality, but not price, would have lower odds of discontinuing. This strategy is best represented by quality proponents. The coefficient associated (B = 0.43; $p < 0.24$) with this parameter is not statistically significant. Instead, the results indicate that only the interaction between super achievers, a generalists strategy that does include a pricing emphasis, significantly contributes to the model improvement (B = –1.05; $p < 0.001$). Figure 8.3 displays the means associated with the interaction. The results reveal that the nature of the strategy-gender interaction was not as expected. Women-owned businesses that adopt a super achievers strategy have a significantly higher probability of surviving. Of the surviving women-owned firms, 46 per cent reported pursuing the super achievers strategy. Only 6 per cent of those that discontinued were pursuing the generalists strategy. For men-owned businesses, the choice of strategy made little difference in their odds of discontinuing business.

Column 6 reports the results of adding terms to represent the three-way interaction among the two significant resource by gender interactions and the super achievers strategy by gender interaction. The three-way terms were added to assess whether women can use strategic choice to compensate for resource deficiencies and reduce odds of discontinuing. The three-way interactions did not significantly contribute to improvement of the model (Model chi-square improvement = 0.82; $p < 0.66$). There was no support for H6.

Discussion

An integrative approach that incorporates both the situational and dispositional perspectives was used to examine the role that initial resources, founding strategy, and gender play in predicting new firm discontinuance. The results indicate that women-owned retail businesses have higher odds of discontinuing than those owned by their male counterparts and that the lack of human and financial resources significantly increase the odds of businesses discontinuing. Despite there being some evidence that women have fewer resources to start their businesses, the resource deficiencies do not appear to differentially affect the survival of their businesses relative to those owned by men. The founding teams of men-owned businesses were more likely to have greater experience working in the industry than the founders of women-owned businesses. Men also were more likely to start their businesses on a larger scale with more employees then women. On the other hand, women were no less likely to have access to credit from formal financial institutions, nor were they at a disadvantage from starting fewer other new businesses. Only the lack of experience starting other new ventures and having a start-up team differentially predicted discontinuance for women- and men-owned businesses.

Contrary to expectations, the lack of prior start-up experience had a much greater impact on predicting the odds of men-owned businesses discontinuing than those owned by women. Low levels of prior experience significantly increased the odds of men-owned business discontinuing. Knowledge gained from starting previous businesses did not differentiate the survival status of women-owned businesses. Similarly, men-owned businesses did not appear to derive a benefit from being started by a team. We had expected that partners would bring additional human and financial resources to the start-up process, which would affect chances of surviving and that women would have less access to such resources. Men-owned businesses were more likely to be started by a team, but these same businesses had higher odds of discontinuing. Having a start-up team does not appear to affect the survival status of women-owned businesses. Perhaps the addition of partners in men-owned businesses increases overhead costs beyond that which can be supported by the business. As partners draw on revenues for personal support, the burden on the business may be too high.

The results indicate that broad-based strategies are more effective in retail than narrow niche strategies. Previous research had suggested that by adopting a narrow specialist strategy new ventures might be able to secure a protected position in the market where they would be overlooked by larger competitors. Such strategies do not appear to effect survival status in retail. The findings also support the supposition that women-owned firms can decrease odds of discontinuance through strategic choice. Founding strategy was portrayed as representing differences in women's and men's belief structures that derived from variations in their socialization patterns. By choosing a founding strategy that fit their particular competencies, women appear to manage their businesses in ways different from men and with different outcomes. Our analyses show that strategy is more important for the success of women's businesses than for men's.

Unexpected was the finding that the most beneficial strategy for women-owned businesses in retail appears to be the super achievers strategy. It may be that the effectiveness of the super achievers strategy reflects the fact that women are particularly adept at "scrambling" to give the customers whatever they want whenever they want it. By emphasizing multiple strategy foci simultaneously and "being all things to all people," businesses headed by women may be able to ward off discontinuance. Kalleberg and Leicht (1991) refer to this approach as a thrashing process whereby organizations adapt to high environmental uncertainty by trying a variety of approaches in order to stay in business.

Alternatively, it might be argued that the effectiveness of the generalists strategy reflects women's relational orientation. Women were seen as emphasizing co-operative networks among family, society, and person. The ability to juggle expectations from many quarters may be the underpinning of effectively executing the super achievers strategy.

Conclusions

This study adds to the knowledge pool about the effects of gender on organizational performance. The use of situational and dispositional perspectives in an integrative model provides an explanation for some of the contradictions in the literature. The findings suggest that whereas men use human and financial resources to enhance the chances of their firms' survival, women find strategic choice more beneficial.

Although the findings are supportive of the integrative model, future research should respond more fully to challenges that measures traditionally used in gender research reflect male-derived measures. Greater attention should be given to the development of measures that appropriately represent both spheres of gender. Similarly, alternative measures of access to financial resources are needed to provide additional insight into the question of the existence of systematic barriers and may reveal stronger support for the theory of situational factors determining business discontinuance rates. Additionally, other forms of human capital like skills needed to interface effectively with critical stake holders such as customers and suppliers may better represent the theory.

In addition, subsequent analyses should extend to other sectors of the economy. We chose to limit this study to one industry to control for extraneous influences and to ensure an adequate sample size to test hypotheses. Because the retail industry is characterized by attenuated career tracks and lower capital requirements for starting a business, differences between genders is less likely than would be found in other industries. Thus, the findings are probably a conservative representation of gender-related situational disadvantages. Future efforts should examine the effect of strategy in overcoming situational resource deficiencies specific to other industries.

Appendix 1

Factor analysis of new firm competitive strategy associated with factor dimensions

Competitive aspects emphasized	*Descriptive*
Factor 1 alpha = 0.63	Market sensitivity
Fast response to changes in markets (0.81)	Knowledge of the market emphasized to reach and respond quickly to key customer needs.
Serve those missed by others (0.69)	
More effective marketing/advertising (0.68)	
Factor 2 *alpha* = 0.81	Technology
Develop new/advanced technology (0.92)	Emphasize process or product technology by developing or using new or advanced technology.
Utilize new/advanced technology (0.87)	
Factor 3 *alpha* = 0.61	Product distinction
More contemporary, attractive products (0.76)	Seek to distinguish the firm from others in the market place by providing unique products or services.
Distinctive goods/services (0.71)	
More choices (0.64)	
Factor 4 *alpha* = 0.71	Site appeal
Superior location/customer convenience (0.84)	Attractiveness and convenience of facilities and location emphasized.
Better, more attractive facilities (0.83)	
Factor 5 *alpha* = 0.68	Service
Better service (0.86)	Provide a higher level of service than competitors.
Quality products/services (0.81)	
Factor 6	Price
Lower prices (0.93)	Sell products or services at a lower price than competitors.

Appendix 2

Strategic archetype descriptions

1   *Super Achievers* – Firms pursuing this strategy strive to promote multiple strategic attributes simultaneously. New ventures adopting this strategy attempt to be all things to all people. They seek a flexible and responsive position in the market by emphasizing characteristics of their site location, exploiting advanced technology, and by emphasizing the quality of their distinctive products and services relative to the price charged. This strategy is broad based in its efforts to exploit a diverse set of resources.

2   *Quality Proponents* – Firms adopting this strategy also have a penchant for a broad market. Quality Proponents are much like Super Achievers except they do not emphasize price as an integral strategic foci. This strategy emphasizes service and distinctiveness.

3   *Equivocators* – Firms adopting this strategy fail to emphasize any particular strategy focus. This strategy may be analogous to Porter's (1985) description of firms "stuck in the middle." At best ambivalent, uncertainty seemingly characterizes strategy formation in these new ventures. Because a distinct strategic emphasis is absent, this strategy can be considered neither broad or narrow.

4   *Price Competitors* – This strategy reflects new ventures' attempts to rely on a combination of marketing/advertising and low price to attract customers. This strategy appears to be the most flexible since pricing and advertising can be changed quickly in response to competitor actions.

5   *Niche Purveyors* – These firms emphasize site qualities. Attractive facilities at superior, convenient locations are seen as creating customer value. By coupling convenience with exceptional or unique products at competitive prices, firms pursuing this strategy narrow their scope and attempt to secure a distinctive foothold in the competitive landscape by focusing on a narrow segment of the population.

6   *Technology Value* – Firms adopting this strategy pursue a narrow differentiation approach. They attempt to distinguish themselves by making price-competitive products through the use and/or development or new technology. This strategy is narrow based as technology products and services limit the market segment they seek to serve.

Appendix 3

Correlation matrix[a]

Variables	1	2	3	4	5	6	7	8	9	10	11
1. Out of business		-0.05	0.02	-0.05	0.02	-0.06	-0.26[b]	-0.40[b]	0.17	0.06	0.34[b]
2. Firm age	-0.12[c]		0.06	-0.11	0.23[c]	-0.16	-0.21[c]	0.09	-0.09	-0.13	0.18[c]
3. Firm size	-0.14[c]	-0.04		0.04	0.18[c]	-0.21[c]	-0.09	-0.01	-0.32[b]	0.28[b]	-0.09
4. Credit resources	0.03	-0.09	0.01		0.02	-0.09	-0.08	-0.01	-0.29[b]	0.27[b]	-0.09
5. Start-up team	0.16[b]	0.08	0.28[b]	-0.04		-0.10	-0.34[b]	-0.04	-0.12	0.08	0.07
6. Prior start-up experience	-0.23[b]	-0.18[b]	0.27[b]	-0.04	0.10		0.31[b]	0.11	0.03	-0.08	-0.08
7. Industry experience	-0.20[b]	-0.01	0.10	0.15[c]	-0.17[b]	-0.06		0.25[b]	-0.13	-0.08	-0.12
8. Super achievers	-0.04	0.01	0.07	-0.06	0.04	0.18[b]	0.10		-0.27[b]	-0.61[b]	-0.24[b]
9. Price	-0.06	-0.02	-0.04	0.03	-0.14[c]	-0.19[b]	0.03	-0.33[b]		-0.34[b]	-0.13
10. Niche	-0.05	0.02	0.02	-0.05	0.11	-0.03	-0.15[c]	-0.62[b]	-0.27[b]		-0.30[b]
11. Quality	0.21[b]	-0.03	-0.10	0.14[c]	-0.08	-0.04	0.02	-0.31[b]	-0.13[c]	-0.25[b]	

a Correlations for women's businesses are above the diagonal, those for men below the diagonal.
b p < 0.01.
c p < 0.05.

Note

1   Address correspondence to Nancy M Carter, College of Business Administration, Marquette University, Milwaukee, WI 53233.The initial data collection in Pennsylvania, completed in 1986 at the University of Pennsylvania Snider Entrepreneurial Center, was sponsored by the Appalachia Regional Commission and the Pennsylvania Department of Commerce. The initial data collection in Minnesota, completed in 1986-87 at the Univerisity of Minnesota for Urban and Regional Affairs, was sponsored by ten state, regional, and local agencies in Minnesota. The 1991-92 follow-up data collection has been a joint effort of the Marquette University Center for the Study of Entrepreneurship, University of Minnesota Carlson Entrepreneurial Center, and University of Pennsylvania Snider Entrepreneurial Center.The authors thank Howard E. Aldrich, Candida Brush, Patricia G. Greene, Margaret Gret, and A. Rebecca Rueber for insightful comments on earlier versions of the article.

References

Astin, H.S., and Leland, C. 1991. *Women of Influence, Women of Vision*. San Francisco, CA: Jossey-Bass Publishers.

Biggadike, R.E. 1976. *Corporate Diversification*: Entry, Strategy and Performance. Boston, MA: Harvard University Press.

Birley, S. 1986. The small firm-set at the start. In R. Ronstadt, J.A. Homaday, R. Peterson, and K.H. Vesper, eds.. *Frontiers of Entrepreneurship Research*. Wellesley, MA: Babson College.

Broom, H.M., and Longenecker, J.G. 1971. *Small Business Management*, 3rd ed. Cincinnati, OH: South Western.

Brush, C. 1992. Research on women business owners: Past trends, a new perspective and future directions. *Entrepreneurship Theory and Practice* 16(2):5–30.

Buttner, E.H., and Rosen, B. 1988. Bank loan officers' perceptions of the characteristics of men, women and successful entrepreneurs. *Journal of Business Venturing* 3(3):249–258.

Carter, N.M., Stearns. T.M., Reynolds, P.D., and Miller, B. 1994. New venture strategies: Theory development with an empirical base. *Strategic Management Journal* 15(1):21–41.

Chaganti, R. 1986. Management in women-owned enterprises. *Journal of Small Business Management* 24(4):18–29.

Clark, T.A., and James, F.J. 1992. Women-owned businesses: Dimensions and policy issues. *Economic Development Quarterly* 6(1):25–40.

Cohen, T., and Lindberg, R.A. 1974. *Survival and Growth: Management Strategies for the Small Firm*. New York: AMACOM.

Cooper, A.C., and Bruno, A. 1977. Success among high-technology firms. *Business Horizons* 20(2):16–23.

Cooper, A.C., Willard, G.E., and Woo, C.Y. 1986. Strategies of high performing new and small firms: A re-examination of the niche concept. *Journal of Business Venturing* 1(3):247–260.

Cromie, S., and Birley, S. 1991. Networking by female business owners in Northern Ireland. *Journal of Business Venturing* 7(3):237–251.

Deeks, J. 1976. *The Small Firm Owner-Manager.* New York: Praeger.

Devine, T.J. 1994. Characteristics of self-employed women in the United States. *Monthly Labor Review* 117(3):20–34.

Fischer. E.M., Reuber, A.R., and Dyke, L.S. 1993. A theoretical overview and extension of research on sex, gender, and entrepreneurship. *Journal of Business Venturing* 8(2):151–168.

Goffee, R., and Scase, R. 1983. Business ownership and women's subordination: A preliminary study of female proprietors. *Sociological Review* 31(4):625–648.

Hisrich, R., and Brush, C. 1984. The women entrepreneur: Management skills and business problems. *Journal of Small Business Management* 22(1):30–37.

Honing-Haftel, S., and Martin, L. 1986. Is the female entrepreneur at a disadvantage? *Thrust: The Journal for Employment and Training Professionals* 7:49–64.

Hosmer, L. 1957. Small manufacturing enterprises. *Harvard Business Review* 35(6):111–122.

Kalleberg, A., and Leicht, K. 1991. Gender and organizational performance: Determinants of small business survival and success. *Academy of Management Journal* 34(1):136–161.

Kaplan, E. 1988. Women entrepreneurs: Constructing a framework to examine venture success and business failures. In B.A. Kirchoff, W.A. Long, W.E. McMullan, K.H. Vesper, and W.E. Wetzel, Jr., eds., *Frontiers of Entrepreneurship Research*. Wellesley, MA: Babson College.

Keeley, R., and Roure, R. 1990. Management, strategy, and industry structure as influences on the success of new firms: A structural model. *Management Science* 36(10):1256–1267.

Liou, N., and Aldrich, H.E. 1995. Women entrepreneurs: Is there a gender-based relational competence? Presented at the 1995 American Sociological Association meeting, Washington, DC.

MacMillan, I.C., and Day. D.L. 1987. Corporate ventures into industrial markets: Dynamics of aggressive entry. *Journal of Business Venturing* 2(1):29–40.

McDougall, P., and Robinson, R.B., Jr. 1990. New venture strategies: An empirical identification of eight "Archetypes" of competitive strategies for entry. *Strategic Management Journal* 11(6):447–467.

Miller, A., and Camp, B. 1985. Exploring determinants of success in corporate ventures. *Journal of Business Venturing* 1(1):87–105.

Neider, L. 1987. A preliminary investigation of female entrepreneurs in Florida. *Journal of Small Business Management* 25(3):22–29.

Olm, K., Carsrud, A., and Alvey, L. 1988. The role of networks in new venture funding for the female entrepreneur: A continuing analysis. In B.A. Kirchoff, W.A. Long, W.E. McMullan, K.H. Vesper, and W.E. Wetzel, Jr., eds., *Frontiers of Entrepreneurship Research*. Wellesley, MA: Babson College.

Porter, M.E. 1985. *Competitive Advantage*. New York: The Free Press.

Reese, P. 1992. Resource acquisition: Does gender make a difference? Presented at the Second Annual Global Entrepreneurship Research Conference, London.

Reynolds, P.D., and Freeman, S. 1987. *1986 Pennsylvania New Firm Survey*. Washington, DC: Appalachia Regional Commission.

Reynolds, P.D., and Miller, B. 1988. *1987 Minnesota New Firm Survey*. Minneapolis, MN: University of Minnesota Center for Urban and Regional Affairs.

Reynolds, P.D. 1993. High performance entrepreneurship: What makes a difference? Working paper. Milwaukee, WI: Marquette University.

Riding, A., and Swift, C. 1990. Women business owners and terms of credit: Some empirical findings of the Canadian experience. *Journal of Business Venturing* 5(5):327–340.

Romanelli, E. 1989. Organization birth and population variety: A community perspective on origins. In L.L. Cummings and B.M. Staw, eds., *Research in Organizational Behavior.* Greenwich. CT: JAI Press Inc.

Sandberg, W.R., and Hofer, C.W. 1987. Improving new venture performance: The role of strategy, industry structure, and the entrepreneur. *Journal of Business Venturing* 2(1):5–28.

Scott, C. 1986. Why more women are becoming entrepreneurs. *Journal of Small Business Management* 24(4):37–44.

Sexton, D.L., and Bowman-Upton, N. 1990. Female and male entrepreneurs: Psychological characteristics and their role in gender-related discrimination. *Journal of Business Venturing* 5(1):29–36.

Sheppard, D. 1992. Women manager's perceptions of gender and organizational life. In A.J. Mills and P. Tancred, eds., *Gendering Organizational Analysis*. Newbury Park, CA: Sage Publications.

Stearns, T.M., Carter, N.M., Revnolds, P.D., and Williams, M. 1995. New firm survival: Industry, strategy and location. *Journal of Business Venturing* 10(1):23–42.

Stegall, D.P., Steinmetz, L.L., and Kline, J.B. 1976. *Managing the Small Business*. Homewood, IL: Irwin.

Stinchcombe, A. 1965. Social structure and organizations. In James G. March, ed., *Handbook of Organizations*. Chicago, IL: Rand McNally.

Tigges, L.M., and Green. G.P. 1994. Small business success among men- and women-owned firms in rural areas. *Rural Sociology* 59(2):289–310.

Van de Ven, A., Hudson, R., and Schroeder, D. 1984. Designing new business start-ups: Entrepreneurial, organizational, and ecological considerations. *Journal of Management* 10(1):87–107.

Walsh, J.P., and Fahey, L. 1986. The role of negotiated belief structures in strategy making. *Journal of Management* 12(3):325–338.

Zellner, W., King, R.W., Byrd, V.N., DeGeorge, G., and Birnbaum, J. 1994. Women entrepreneurs. *Business Week* (April 18):104–110.

9

Entrepreneur Human Capital Inputs and Small Business Longevity*

Timothy Bates[1]

*Source: *Review of Economics and Statistics* 72, 4 (1990), 551–59.

Abstract

Small business longevity is investigated, utilizing a nationwide random sample of males who entered self-employment between 1976 and 1982. Highly educated entrepreneurs are most likely to create firms that remained in operation through 1986. Owner educational background, further, is a major determinant of the financial capital structure of small business startups. Financial capital endogeneity notwithstanding, firms with the larger financial investments at start-up are consistently over-represented in the survivor column. Firm leverage, finally, is trivial for delineating active from discontinued businesses. Reliance upon debt capital to finance business start-up is clearly not associated with heightened risk of failure.

Introduction

Small business longevity is investigated in this study, utilizing a nationwide random sample of non-minority male entrepreneurs who entered self-employment between 1976 and 1982. Owner human and financial capital inputs, according to the findings, are capable of differentiating active firms from those that had discontinued operations by late 1986. Specifically, highly educated owners employing larger financial capital inputs are more likely to create viable, lasting firms than poorly educated cohorts whose financial capital inputs are less bountiful.

Entrepreneur factor inputs are directly related to firm longevity, but input levels are frequently linked to each other as well. The ability of owners to raise debt capital is related to the values of other explanatory variables: the financial capital structure of the small business at the point of start-up is therefore endogenous. Specifically, the level of owner education is a major determinant of the loan amounts that commercial banks extend to small business formations. The problem of explanatory variable inter-relatedness is handled initially by excluding financial capital variables and by assuming that there is no relationship between the viability of the firm and its financial structure. Logit models are estimated for a sample of 4,429 firms owned by non-minority males utilizing owner human capital measures and demographic traits as explanatory variables. This exercise identifies owner education level as a key determinant of firm survival: yet this same factor is a determinant of debt inputs for small business start-ups. Factors that explain debt inputs are examined in detail, and sample subsets are identified in which owner education and levels of debt are (1) strongly related, and (2) weakly related. Discriminant analysis models explaining firm survival are then estimated utilizing financial capital as well as human capital and demographic measures as explanatory variables. Financial capital input levels, irrespective of owner education, are strong determinants of small business survival prospects. The logit and discriminant models produce entirely consistent results regarding the impact of demographic and human capital variables on small business longevity. Separate analyses of sample subsets possessing differing degrees of financial capital endogeneity do not alter this conclusion.

The behavior of recent self-employment entrants

Economists to date have performed few empirical or theoretical studies of entrepreneurship: there have been numerous studies of production functions but few of entrepreneurs. Sociologists and psychologists have dominated the field pursuing studies of the characteristics of self-employed persons (Brock and Evans, 1986, pp. 39–41). On the theoretical side of economics, however, several recent articles on entrepreneurship have produced a rich crop of hypotheses about small business behavior. A straightforward model by Lucas suggested that persons having relatively more entrepreneurial ability became entrepreneurs while those possessing relatively less became workers. In the Lucas model, business formation and discontinuances involve "marginal" managers characterized solely by a known managerial ability parameter (1978, pp. 510–518).

A more realistic model developed by Jovanovic assumes that uncertainty characterizes the managerial ability factor at the point of small business start-up. Those who enter self-employment gradually learn about their managerial abilities by engaging in the actual running of a business and observing how well they do (1982, pp. 650–653). As they learn more about their abilities, firm behavior changes through time: those who revise their ability estimates upward tend to expand output while those embracing downward estimates tend to contract or to dissolve their businesses. Over time, survivors acquire through experience precise estimates of their abilities; the younger firms exhibit relatively more variable behavior because they have less precise estimates of their true abilities. Because younger

Table 9.1 Business traits: white males entering self–employment before 1975 versus those entering between 1976 and 1982

	Pre–1976 entrants	1976–1982 entrants
Discontinuance rate, 1986	$16.8%	$26.0%
1982 total sales (mean)	$198 908	$118 791
1982 total sales (std. dev./mean)	$4.26	$4.73
1982 before tax profits (mean)	$27 196	$16 066
1982 before tax profits (std. dev./mean)	$1.50	$2.13
n	$3 314	$4 429
n – for profit figures[a]	$3 118	$4 111

[a] Reported sample sizes are smaller due to deletion of firms that did not report before tax profits.

firms are commonly smaller firms, these behavior patterns are predicted to typify smaller and larger firms.

Data describing selected traits of small businesses run by white males (Table 9.1) are consistent with Jovanovic's characterizations of entrepreneurship. This nationwide sample of 7,743 small firms is split into groups of younger and older businesses: the older firms, by definition, are owned by white males who entered self-employment before 1976; the younger firms involve entry over the 1976–1982 time period. Table 9.1 reports mean values of 1982 total sales, before tax profits, measures of sales and profit variance, and finally, the percentage of the sample firms that had discontinued business operations by late 1986. Relative to the older firm group, the younger firms were (1) much more likely to discontinue operations by late 1986, (2) smaller regarding 1982 annual sales ($118,791 versus $198,908), (3) much less profitable – earning less than 60 per cent of the $27,196 mean profits reported by the older firms – and (4) more dispersed around the sales and profits mean values. The younger firms clearly exhibit the less settled behavior that is consistent with Jovanovic's hypothesis that they are in the process of learning what their entrepreneurial abilities are.

If managerial uncertainty does typify firm start-ups, then new owners may reduce this uncertainty by buying into existing firms where managerial procedures of previous owners are imbedded in the business. If this process of piggybacking upon existing expertise is successful, then buying ongoing firms should be associated with lower business discontinuance rates.

While Jovanovic captures the essence of the turmoil that typifies recently entered small businesses, other branches of the social sciences have addressed the question: who are the likely survivors of the sorting out process? Some of their findings are straightforward: entrepreneurs are relatively well educated (Douglas, 1976). Other studies emphasize less tangible elements of entrepreneurial success, such as test score patterns on psychological tests, suggesting that individuals are endowed with differing levels of business acumen (Shapiro, 1975).

This study empirically addresses the question – who are the entrepreneurs that are likely to survive the sorting process that characterizes early years of self-employment? Those who remain small business owners are expected, relative to discontinuances, to possess greater business acumen as well as conventional labor force skills and greater access to financial capital. Finally, the youngest firms are most likely to fail.

The data base

The samples of business owners analyzed throughout this study are drawn from the 1982 Characteristics of Business Owners (CBO) survey.[2] This is the first data base of national scope that describes self-employed people as individuals *as well as* describing traits of businesses these people run, such as sales, earnings, employees, capital inputs, etc.

The definition of a "small business" is by no means clear-cut. The CBO survey drew its small business universe from individuals who filed in 1982 one of the following types of federal income tax forms: (1) Schedule C, form 1040 (sole proprietorships); (2) Form 1065 (operators of partnerships); (3) Form 1120s (small business corporations). From the universe of persons filing one or more of these forms, 25,000 non-minority males were selected for further data collection. Census questionnaires covering both owner traits and business traits were sent out to these persons and over 84 per cent of the questionnaires were returned. In some instances, one owner of several firms is picked up in the sample; in other cases, multiple owners of one firm are encountered. In this study, each firm has a unique owner; financial capital variables, however, were constructed by summing the inputs of all owners in cases of multi-owner firms. Among persons filing schedule C forms, many are not small business owners according to the commonly understood meaning of the term. I identified small business owners as the subset of the sample where owners (1) had a financial capital investment in the business that was greater than zero, and (2) annual sales of a least $5,000 in 1982. Observations not meeting these criteria were dropped from further consideration. The constraint that sales total at least $5,000 forced 38.0 per cent of the otherwise eligible observations out of the sample.

The CBO survey collected data on several aspects of owner human capital, including variables measuring (1) years of education, (2) managerial experience, and (3) small business exposure within one's family. Family business background is of particular interest because this factor has been

Table 9.2 Logit model: MLE results explaining small business longevity for white males entering business in the 1976–1982 time period

	Logit coefficient	Standard error	Chi–square statistic
Constant	−1.3112[a]	1.1677	61.14
Ed2	0.1083[a]	0.0592	3.35
Ed3	0.0838[b]	0.0638	1.72
Ed4	0.2522[a]	0.0687	13.44
Ed5	0.3074[a]	0.0686	20.04
Family	0.0433	0.0365	1.41
Management	−0.0256	0.0375	0.47
Age 2	0.0274	0.0428	0.41
Age 3	0.0916[a]	0.0510	3.23
Age 4	−0.0410	0.0590	0.48
Ongoing	0.1229[a]	0.0419	8.62
Time 80	−0.3074[a]	0.0397	59.97
Time 82	−0.3990[a]	0.0482	68.63
n	4429		
Likelihood ratio	419		
Chi square	501.49	The hypothesis that the explanatory variables have no effect is rejected ($\alpha = 0.01$)	

[a] Statistically significant (5% level).
[b] Statistically significant (10% level).

repeatedly linked by social scientists to the business acumen characteristic. Family (close relative) pursuit of self-employment is expected to encourage the development of entrepreneurial values within an individual as well as increasing one's familiarity with the small business milieu. When asked, "Prior to your going into business, had any of your close relatives ever owned a business ...,"[3] 41.9 per cent of the CBO white male owner sample responded affirmatively. Shapiro found that more than 50 per cent of the entrepreneurs he studied had self-employed fathers (1975, pp. 84–85).

Variables utilized in Table 9.2, in addition to owner human capital measures, include (1) year of entry into self-employment, (2) age of owner, and (3) whether the owner created a firm de novo or entered an existing business. All of the owners analyzed in Table 9.2 were white males who entered into small business ownership between 1976 and 1982: while most were the original founders, 24.2 per cent entered businesses (largely sole proprietorships) that were already operating. The logit model dependent variable equals one if the firm is still operating in late 1986; it equals zero otherwise. Note that businesses sold to new owners are counted as continuing firms as long as they remain in operation: departure of an owner is not equated to business discontinuance. Definitions of the logit explanatory variables appear below:

Ed2:   for owners completing four years of high school, the value of $Ed2 = 1$; otherwise $Ed2 = 0$.

Ed3:   for owners completing at least one but less than four years of college, the value of $Ed3 = 1$; otherwise $Ed3 = 0$.

Ed4:   for owners completing four years of college, the value of $Ed4 = 1$; otherwise $Ed4 = 0$.

Ed5:   for owners completing five or more years of college, the value of $Ed5 = 1$; otherwise $Ed5 = 0$

Family self-employment: for owners whose close relatives (mother, father, brothers, sisters, others with whom frequent contact was maintained) either owned a business or were self-employed in professional practice, *Family* = 1, otherwise *Family* = 0.

Management experience: for owners who had worked in a managerial capacity prior to owning the business they owned in 1982, *Management* = 1; otherwise *Management* = 0.

Age2:   for owners between the ages of 35 and 44, $Age2 = 1$; otherwise $Age2 = 0$.

Age3:   for owners between the ages of 45 and 54, $Age3 = 1$; otherwise $Age3 = 0$.

Age4:   for owners 55 or older, $Age4 = 1$; otherwise $Age4 = 0$.

Method of acquiring the business – if the owner entered a business that was already in operation, *Ongoing* = 1; if the owner was the original founder of the business, then *Ongoing* = 0.

Year in which the business was started or acquired – a series of two variables reflecting the following categories:

1   *Time82*: if the business was started or ownership was acquired during 1982, then $Time82 = 1$; otherwise $Time82 = 0$;

2   *Time80*: if the business was started or ownership was acquired during 1980 or 1981, then $Time80 = 1$; otherwise $Time80 = 0$.

In Table 9.2's logit exercise, the education variable group excludes owners having less than twelve years of formal schooling and the age variable group excludes owners who were under age 35.

Empirical findings for the non-minority male sample

Small business owners, according to Jovanovic, know least about their entrepreneurial abilities at the point when they first enter self-employment. The variable *time*82 identifies the newest businesses in the white male sample: firms formed in 1982 accounted for 17.1 per cent of the total sample as well as 22.7 per cent of the 1986 discontinuances. The newest firms are most likely to fail, other factors constant, and the *time*82 variable coefficient indicates that this factor is the strongest single determinant of business survival identified in Table 9.2. Similarly, firms entered during the 1980–81 period (*time*80) were much more likely to discontinue operations by 1986 than those entered between 1976 and 1979, but they were less likely to discontinue relative to those entered in 1982. The longer the period since the owner entered into business, the more likely it is that the business will remain in operation in 1986.

Other dominant variables (Table 9.2) for delineating surviving businesses from discontinuances are education measures, particularly *ed*4 and *ed*5. Relative to owners having less than four years of high school, high school graduates (*ed*2) and those with one to three years of college (*ed*3) are more likely to see their businesses survive to 1986. The likelihood of business discontinuance falls off sharply, however, for the owner education groups having four years of college (*ed*4) and five plus years of college (*ed*5). The most conventional measure – years of education – is the strongest human capital variable for identifying business continuance.

The other human capital variables produced mixed results. The family background variable coefficient, although positive, was statistically insignificant. Past studies attributing the family business background trait to firm viability did not control for factors such as owner education or entry by purchasing an existing business; this may account for the differing findings. The insignificance of the management variable is more difficult to interpret. Alternative specifications of this variable were investigated, as were various functional forms. These different variable formulations produced unstable coefficients – due partly to correlations with two other variables, age and education.

Age of owner was expected to be related to business survival in a nonlinear fashion. A recent study of entrepreneur earnings found that "a 47 year old highly educated male has the greatest likelihood of being a high earner of self-employment income" (Bates, 1987, p. 546). Age variable coefficients in Table 9.2 are consistent with this characterization. In the *age*4 group (55 and older), age may be correlated to a lessening of owner effort that corresponds to the old age phenomenon.

Finally, Table 9.2 indicates that ongoing firms are more likely to remain in business than those started de novo. This finding is consistent with the hypothesis that purchase of an existing business may permit the new owner to benefit from established managerial practices that are embodied in the firm.

Owner inputs of financial capital

Regression analysis of debt capital

Built upon perfect market assumptions, the modern theory of finance has derived conclusions about business financing that are elegant in their simplicity. When a business investment opportunity becomes available, the owner/manager need only announce publicly the information relevant to the valuation of the project. If the project is expected to result in a positive market value (for a new company) or an increased market value for an existing company, the prices of the securities of the firm will instantly reflect this information. Life is not this simple for most small business start-ups. Often, the value of the small firm hinges upon something that cannot readily be bought and sold: the efforts of a single owner-manager. The small business owner often finds it "impossible to persuade potential suppliers of equity capital to share his subjective belief," regarding future returns from investment in the firm (Steigum, 1983, p. 637).

A recent article by Zeira demonstrates theoretically that "the exact levels of profits at larger amounts of capital can be discovered only by actually increasing the quantity of capital ..." (1987, p. 205). Zeira's model is particularly applicable to the small business start-up whose owner is unsure of his/her managerial abilities. When uncertainty typifies entrepreneurial talents, as well as the return that can be expected from investing financial capital in the enterprise, it is not surprising that capital market access is limited.

Over 98 per cent of the businesses previously analyzed (Table 9.1) received no equity capital from organized financial markets at the point of start-up, but most of them did have access to debt capital. Two dominant sources of debt – commercial bank loans were most frequent, debt from family and friends was second – accounted for 83.1 per cent of the loans received by the non-minority male sample (of 1976–1982 start-ups). Debt from former business owners ranked a distant third, accounting for 8.7 per cent of the loans received. Equity capital was supplied largely from the owner's own resources, secondarily from family and friends. Those who have access to debt capital are usually those possessing substantial equity as well as traits that are associated with small business survival, such as strong educational background.

Table 9.3 investigates the relationships between the debt capital inputs of the borrowing firms at the point of business start-up (the dependent variable) and the explanatory variables (1) owner equity capital inputs and (2) human capital and demographic traits found to possess explanatory power in Table 9.2. The debt and equity capital variables are expressed in thousands of dollars; their respective mean values for the sample of all

Table 9.3 Explaining debt capital inputs for white males entering business

	All borrowers		Commercial bank loan recipients only		Nonbank borrowers only	
	Regression coefficient	Standard error	Regression coefficient	Standard error	Regression coefficient	Standard error
Constant	1.3123	9.8612	–7.7653	12.1018	17.0179	12.6048
Ed2	6.6227	9.8712	15.9305	12.0125	–12.1199	12.7808
Ed3	7.0814	10.5940	14.0062	13.1237	–3.9546	13.3458
Ed4	12.0839	11.2144	34.5259[a]	13.9627	–10.3679	14.0047
Ed5	18.3443[a]	11.0762	22.9350[a]	13.5456	19.9373	14.2408
Equity capital	1.4406[a]	0.0346	1.8320[a]	0.0417	0.4867[a]	0.0457
Age2	7.3097	6.9869	9.9799	8.9494	5.0318	8.1236
Age3	14.8652[a]	8.0523	2.8834	10.0464	32.0620[a]	9.8499
Age4	7.0813	11.2109	10.3650	14.1287	19.7895	13.4155
Ongoing	1.7318	6.3273	13.7751[a]	8.1981	1.2975	7.2998
n	2197		1419		778	
$\overline{R}^2$	0.4501		0.5849		0.1605	
F	198.89		220.62		16.31	

[a] Statistically significant at the 0.05 level.

borrowers are $48.7 thousand (debt) and $22.1 thousand (equity). A direct relationship is hypothesized to exist between the size of debt capital inputs at the point of business start-up and (1) equity capital, as well as (2) human capital and demographic traits associated with firm survival.

Table 9.3's regression coefficients show that a highly educated middle aged white male who is investing a large sum of equity capital in his small business is going to have a maximum access to debt capital. Disaggregation of the sample into bank loan recipients and non-bank borrowers, however, indicates that a college education improves access to debt capital most directly for the commercial bank borrowers: education variables are statistically insignificant determinants of debt levels for non-bank borrowers. Table 9.3's findings indicate that equity and debt capital are complements at the point of business start-up, but dissimilar variable coefficients once again typify the bank and non-bank borrower subgroups. An extra dollar of equity capital is associated with 1.83 additional dollars of debt capital for commercial bank loan recipients, versus 0.49 additional dollars for non-bank borrowers. Explaining debt levels for the commercial bank borrower group was more precise statistically ($R^2 = 0.585$ versus 0 160 for non-bank borrowers), and more of the hypothesized determinants of debt possessed statistically significant variable coefficients. Of the variables associated with business survival in Table 9.2's logit exercise, only *Age*3 was a statistically significant determinant of debt inputs for the non-bank borrowers.

Discriminant analysis; active versus discontinued firms

Table 9.3's findings on bank borrowers call into question the validity of Table 9.2's logit model. The logit exercise indicated that certain human capital and demographic traits were capable of delineating small business survivors from discontinuances. Alternative explanations, however, are consistent with the logit findings: human capital inputs partially cause financial capital inputs, and the latter variables may be the true predictors of firm survival.

Table 9.4's discriminant analyses attempt to clarify the relationships between firm viability and owner inputs of human capital and financial capital. Causal interrelationships between human and financial capital inputs in fact typify only the bank borrower subset of the small business start-up sample. For start-ups not receiving bank loans, inputs of human and financial capital are not systematically related; factor input interrelationships, therefore, are unlikely to skew the applicable discriminant analysis variable coefficients. The entire sample of non-minority male firms started between 1976 and 1982 is examined in Table 9.4, as well as the subset of firms that excludes all bank loan recipients. As in Table 9.2, the dependent variable measures firm survival: businesses that are still operating are referred to as "active" firms; those that have closed down are "discontinued." Explanatory variables utilized in Table 9.4 include all human capital and demographic measures used in Table 9.2 and two new variables:

Table 9.4 Discriminant analysis: white males entering business in the 1976–1982 time period

Variable	Discriminant function coefficients Standardized coefficients	Group mean vectors Active firms	Discontinued firms
Entire sample			
Ed2	0.2405	0.3157	0.3371
Ed3	0.1581	0.2041	0.2363
Ed4	0.4070	0.1760	0.1477
Ed5	0.5069	0.1986	0.1460
Management	−0.0994	0.6159	0.6151
Family	0.0749	0.4253	0.3901
Age2	0.0334	0.3328	0.3197
Age3	0.1192	0.2123	0.1807
Age4	−0.0883	0.1153	0.1295
Capital	0.3772	9.4113	9.1289
Ongoing	0.1544	0.2544	0.2155
Time80	−0.6655	0.3594	0.4431
Time82	−0.7113	0.1550	0.2294
Leverage	0.0220	3.7000	3.3394
n		3278	1151

First model:

canonical correlation = 0.188
approx. standard error = 0.014
likelihood ratio = 0.964
$F = 11.61$, indicating that the group differences are statistically significant ($\alpha = 0.01$).

Sample excluding commercial bank loan recipients

Variable			
Ed2	0.0828	0.3055	0.3395
Ed3	0.0892	0.2129	0.2330
Ed4	0.2768	0.1847	0.1586
Ed5	0.2970	0.1993	0.1586
Management	−0.1165	0.6169	0.6221
Family	0.1601	0.4389	0.3879
Age2	0.1141	0.3386	0.3110
Age3	0.1507	0.2029	0.1685
Age4	−0.0158	0.1321	0.1375
Capital	0.3362	9.0477	8.7977
Ongoing	0.0854	0.2320	0.2007
Time80	−0.6925	0.3631	0.4548
Time82	−0.7867	0.1480	0.2416
Leverage	0.0185	1.6236	1.4797
n		2203	802

continued on nextpage

Table 9.4 Discriminant analysis: white males entering business in the 1976–1982
time period (cont.)

Second model:

canonical correlation   = 0.204
approx. standard error   = 0.017
likelihood ratio   = 0.958
$F = 9.327$, indicating that the group differences are statistically
significant ($\alpha = 0.01$).

---

1   *Capital*: the logarithm of the sum of debt and equity capital.
2   *Leverage*: the ratio of debt capital to equity capital.[4]

Greater quantities of both debt and equity capital inputs are expected to
improve the viability of small business start-ups. Indeed, scale economies
expected to be operative, thus reinforcing the positive relationship between
quantity of financial capital inputs and firm viability.

Theorists have produced contradictory hypotheses about the impact of
debt financing on firm viability. Clearly, borrowers suffer when incremen-
tal debt capital inputs fail to generate returns exceeding borrowing costs.
Modigliani and Miller have shown, however, that a corporate tax system
with interest payment deductibility creates a situation where the value of
the firm is an increasing function of its debt – total value ratio (1963).
Others have claimed a downside for increased use of debt financing: the
present value of the expected costs associated with potential future bankruptcy also increase (Brennan and Schwartz, 1978). The basic hypothesis –
greater financial capital inputs (whether debt or equity) ease firm viability
– is therefore qualified: higher leverage may heighten the risk of failure.

The objective of Table 9.4s discriminant analyses is to weigh and combine the explanatory variables in a fashion that forces the groups to be as
statistically distinct as possible. The exercise is successful in the sense that
the active and discontinued firms are shown to be statistically distinct.
Table 9.2's logit model, in contrast, sought to establish the statistical significance of the individual explanatory variables. Use of logit in Table 9.4
would be inappropriate because multicollinearity problems would compromise the interpretation of individual variable coefficients. Thus logit's
power to establish variable coefficient significance is sacrificed, but the
choice of the discriminant technique has produced clear-cut results without
resorting to violating the underlying assumptions that discriminant analysis is built upon.

The conclusions derived from Table 9.2's logit exercise are consistent
with those of the discriminant analyses. The *time*80, *time*82 variables possess the greatest explanatory power in all models, and the education variables are consistently strong; owners with four or more years of college are

most likely to remain in business. The financial input variables perform quite similarly in the discriminant functions of the overall sample as well as the subset of firms that excludes commercial bank loan recipients. Particularly for the latter group, the large variable coefficients for both the financial capital and the education variables indicate clearly that both factors are causally related to firm survival. Both of the Table 9.4 discriminant functions suggest that it is the highly educated owner with the larger financial capital input that is most likely to create the surviving firm. Nonetheless, the endogeneity of the financial capital variable lessens our ability to judge the relative importance of human versus financial capital inputs as determinants of survival for the entire sample of firms.

The leverage variable produced standardized coefficients of 0.0220 and 0.0185 in Table 9.4's discriminant functions. The finding that firm leverage is trivial for delineating active from discontinued businesses must be interpreted in view of the fact that the active firms (Table 9.4) are clearly more highly leveraged than the discontinued businesses. Reliance upon debt capital at the point of business start-up is clearly not associated with business weakness or heightened risk of failure. Table 9.4 shows that additional debt capital inputs increase business viability, and that the discontinued firms actually utilize debt less than the surviving businesses. This finding, however, does not clearly prove or disprove the various theories about the impact of debt on firm viability. High degrees of leverage may indeed be imprudent for some businesses; if lenders refuse, however, to supply debt to such firms, the latent inverse relationship between leverage and business viability will not appear in the econometric models.

Another highly consistent pattern in the logit and discriminant functions concerns the relationship between age of owner and firm survival. In all instances, owners 55 and over are least likely to remain in business, while those in the 45–54 grouping are most likely to endure. Finally, the family and ongoing variables emerge consistently as less important determinants of business longevity, and the applicable variable coefficients vary somewhat in magnitude across models. Further disaggregation of the data set along industry lines may reveal additional information about the impact of these factors on firm survival.

The various econometric techniques applied to the non-minority male small business sample (and subsamples) have yielded several highly consistent empirical findings. As expected, the very young firms are least likely to survive; highly educated entrepreneurs – those with four or more years of college – are most likely to create firms that remain in operation; owners 55 and older are most likely to see their firms cease to exist. Financial capital endogeneity notwithstanding, firms with the larger financial capital inputs at start-up are consistently over-represented in the survivor column. For the 32 per cent of the businesses that were launched with bank financing, having a highly educated owner is clearly associated with

investing substantial sums of capital in one's business. Leverage notwithstanding, both of these traits – human capital and financial capital – are
strongly linked to business viability, irrespective of financing source. Carv-
ing the small business sample into various subgroups does not vary these
econometric results: owner education and financial capital inputs consistently explain firm longevity.

Notes

1   Received for publication August 31, 1988. Revision accepted for publication November 17,
    1989.* New School for Social Research and American Statistical Association.Research reported
    here was supported by the National Science Foundation under grants SES84–01460 and SES87–
    13643, "On-site Research to Improve the Government-Generated Social Science Data Base." The
    research was conducted at the U.S. Bureau of the Census while I was a participant in the American
    Statistical Association/Census Bureau Research Program, which is supported by the Census
    Bureau and NSF. Any findings or conclusions expressed herein are mine and do not necessarily
    reflect the views of the Census Bureau or NSF.
2   The CBO data base is described in Bates (1990).
3   Census questionnaire item nine, CBO survey.
4   Due to the sensitivity of financial ratios to extreme values, the denominator (equity) was
    constrained to be greater than zero and the value of the overall ratio was constrained to be no larger
    than nineteen.

References

Bates, Timothy, "Self-Employed Minorities: Traits and Trends," *Social Sciences Quarterly*
    68 (Sept. 1987), 539–550.
—— "The Characteristics of Business Owners Data Base," *Journal of Human Resources* 25
    (Fall 1990).
Brennan. M., and F. Schwartz, "Corporate Income Taxes, Valuation and the Problem of Op-
    timal Capital Structure," *The Journal of Business* 51 (Jan. 1978), 103–114.
Brock, William, and David Evans, *The Economics of Small Business* (New York: Holmes
    and Meier, 1986).
Douglas, Merril, "Relating Education to Entrepreneurial Success." *Business Horizons* 19
    (Dec. 1976), 40–44.
Jovanovic, Boyan. "Selection and Evolution in Industry." *Econometrica* 50 (May 1982)
    649–670.
Lucas, Robert. "On the Size Distribution of Business Firms." *The Bell Journal of Economics*
    9 (Autumn 1978), 508–523.
Modigliani, Franco, and Merton Miller. "Corporate Income Tax and the Cost of Capital: A
    Correction," *American Economic Review* 53 (June 1963). 433–442.
Shapiro, Albert, "The Displaced Uncomfortable Entrepreneur," *Psychology Today* 9 (Nov.
    1975), 83–88.
Steigum, Erling, "A Financial Theory of Investment Behavior," *Econometrica* 51 (May
    1983), 637–646.
Zeira, Joseph, "Investment as a Process of Search" *Journal of Political Economy* 95 (Feb.
    1987), 204–210.

10

Survival Chances of Newly Founded Business Organizations*

Josef Brüderl, Peter Preisendörfer and Rolf Ziegler[1]

*Source: *American Sociological Review* 57 (1992), 227–42.

Human capital theory and organizational ecology offer a comprehensive set of factors that influence the mortality of newly formed business organizations. Human capital theory identifies individual characteristics of the founder as important prerequisites for survival. Organizational ecology emphasizes organizational characteristics and environmental conditions. We test basic hypotheses derived from both theories using retrospective data from a survey of 1,849 business founders in Germany. Organizational characteristics, especially number of employees and amount of capital invested, and organizational strategies, especially businesses aiming at a national market, are the most important determinants of business survival. The human capital characteristics of the founder, especially years of schooling and work experience and industry-specific experience, show strong direct and indirect effects as well.

After a long period of decline the number of self-employed people is increasing in many western countries and there is a tendency toward smaller units of employment (Sengenberger and Loveman 1987; Steinmetz and Wright 1989). In addition, a wave of business formation is occurring in some eastern European countries. Many hopes and expectations are connected with this development: New firms create new jobs, open up chances for upward social mobility, foster economic flexibility, contribute to competition and economic efficiency, stimulate industrial reorganization, and so on (Piore and Sabel 1984; Birch 1987; Rainnie 1989; Brown, Hamilton, and Medoff 1990). These hopes and expectations are justified only if newly founded enterprises survive. But most empirical evidence shows that a high proportion of new business organizations fails within a short time (Freeman, Carroll and Hannan 1983; Aldrich and Auster 1986; Brüderl and Schüssler 1990). Which businesses are "promising candidates," i.e., what factors determine whether a new business is likely to survive? There is a long tradition of research investigating this question (Mayer and Goldstein

1961; Boswell 1972; Cochran 1981; Klandt 1984; Carroll 1987. pp. 28–36), but the results are inconclusive. Probably the most important reason for these inconclusive results is the problematic research methods used in different studies. Most studies are based on small samples, many samples have a strong survivor bias, and inappropriate statistical tools are often used to analyze the data. A second deficiency of past research is that most studies lack a theoretical perspective guiding the selection of meaningful determinants of organizational failure. We use an explicit theoretical perspective and avoid many of the methodological shortcomings of previous studies by using data collected especially for such an analysis and employing efficient statistical tools.

Theories of organizational failure

Three groups of factors that affect the survival chances of new enterprises can be extracted from previous research: (1) individual characteristics of the founder; (2) attributes, structural characteristics, and strategies of the new business itself; and (3) conditions characterizing the environment of a new firm (Szyperski and Nathusius 1977; Klandt 1984; Aldrich and Zimmer 1986; Schüssler and Voss 1988).

Most research in the field has found that the founder is the key to organizational success. Psychologists tend to describe entrepreneurs and founders of businesses by personality traits such as a high need for achievement (McClelland 1961, chaps. 6 and 7; Atkinson and Hoselitz 1963). Economists see them as co-ordinators, risk-takers, and innovators (Barreto 1989; Hébert and Link 1989). Sociologists identify sociodemographic attributes of founders or see them as "displaced persons" (Collins and Moore 1964; Light 1979; Min 1984; Brenner 1987, chap. 2). Empirical studies of organizational failures often point to personal deficiencies of the founders like lack of experience in the field or managerial incompetence (Mayer and Goldstein 1961; Boswell 1972; Dun and Bradstreet 1981; Deutsche Ausgleichsbank 1988). Finally, the vast literature offering advice to potential founders ("How to Become a Successful Entrepreneur") emphasizes that the individual is the key to organizational success.

Several objections can be raised to this personality-based perspective (Aldrich and Zimmer 1986, pp. 14–15). Studies may be biased in favor of individual attributes by their design because it is relatively easy to observe basic attributes of founders (Fritsch 1989). The required personal resources may be different in different industries. Furthermore, there is little appreciation of the sometimes highly transitory nature of the entrepreneurial status (Carroll and Mosakowski 1987, p. 571). Finally, there is the negative evidence from so-called leadership research that – after more than three decades of study – has failed to find consistent personal attributes of "successful leaders" (Hall 1982).

Modern organizational sociology is sceptical of endeavors that associate organizational outcomes like success or survival with attributes of individuals. For example, if organizations are seen as political entities (March and Olsen 1976), then organizational activities and outcomes are determined by the dynamics of internal coalitions. Contingency theories (Thompson 1967; Lawrence and Lorsch 1967) emphasize the match of organizational structures to technologies and environmental conditions. The resource dependence school (Pfeffer and Salancik 1978) attempts to explain organizational structures and outcomes from environmental uncertainty and environmental disturbances. Ecological approaches (Aldrich 1979; Hannan and Freeman 1989) also emphasize environmental factors. Thus, modem organizational sociology accentuates the structural characteristics of organizations and environmental conditions, not the attributes of individuals.

Newly founded businesses are usually small, simple organizations. In line with most prior research, we believe, in spite of the objections above, that the characteristics of the founder do matter. To avoid all eclectic compilation of many individual variables, we use human capital theory to examine the potential effects of individuals. For organizational and environmental factors, organizational ecology provides meaningful variables for empirical analysis. Some variables that may be important to other researchers are not included in our analysis, but we believe that a theory-guided selection of variables yields more insight than a compilation of all available variables.

Human capital theory

The concept of human capital is implicit in many empirical studies of the survival chances or new businesses. These studies investigate the effects of the founder's education, career history, family, occupational background, and so on (Mayer and Goldstein 1961; Boswell 1972; Hunsdiek and May-Strobl 1986; Picot, Laub and Schneider 1989; Bates 1990a, 1990b). However, few studies make explicit their connection to the framework of human capital theory in economics (Becker 1975; Willis 1986).

Bates (1985), who focused on the effects of human capital on minority business viability, used Dun and Bradstreet data. Because these data contain no information on entrepreneurial human capital, Bates used an indirect approach. Using census data, he generated human capital measures for certain industries, which he then correlated with profit data for his firms. A positive correlation between human capital and profit showed that firms in industries that require more human capital have higher profits.

Preisendörfer and Voss (1990) explored the effects of founders' human capital for a large set of German businesses. The main problem with their analysis is that they had only crude indicators of the founder's human capital endowment, mainly the founder's age. In this study the chances of organizational survival are very low for young founders, highest for middle-aged founders, and again low for older founders. They interpreted this inverted **U**-shaped relationship as analogous to the well-known concave age-income profile in human capital research.

The basic argument that high human capital endowment of the founder improves chances for organizational survival seems plausible. Because traditional human capital theory and research have focused on earnings of employees, we have to elaborate on the mechanisms through which human capital enhances the success of self-employed persons. To begin with, we assume that the profitability of a young firm and organizational survival are directly connected (this assumption may not hold for older firms, as Levinthal [1991] argued). We then argue that greater human capital increases the *productivity* of the founder, which results in higher profits (Bates 1985). Higher productivity means that the founder is more efficient in organizing and managing the production process (human capital increases efficiency) or is able to attract more customers and new capital from investors (the environment selects on the basis of human capital). The latter may be especially important in the service sector where customers often select a firm according to personal criteria like education of the founder because the quality of the service is not readily evaluated. In addition, before granting capital, banks often resort to evaluation schemes incorporating aspects of human capital. Easily observable indicators of human capital may thus be used as screening devices by customers, investors, and other outside actors on whom the success of all enterprise depends.

However, other mechanisms may also be responsible for an observed association between human capital attributes of founders and organizational survival. These mechanisms operate prior to the founding of the new firm and are essentially *selection* effects. Based on their higher earnings as employees, people with higher human capital are in a position to set up larger and financially better-equipped businesses. They may be better able to detect profitable market niches that are not yet densely populated. Further, they may have greater knowledge of how to start a business successfully and be better able to get relevant information. In addition, such individuals usually have good employment opportunities in the general labor market and are therefore in a position to evaluate the prospects of future firms. In contrast, people with few human capital resources are often forced into self-employment. For instance, if unemployment is the incentive for setting up a business, there may not be time to look for good opportunities, make detailed plans, and seek advice. Thus, independent of productivity effects that operate after the founding, a priori selection effects improve survival chances, because well-endowed founders are in a position to select more promising projects. Of course, it is difficult to separate these two sets of mechanisms empirically.

Becker (1975) distinguishes between general and specific human capital. We use the traditional measures of *general* human capital – years of schooling and years of work experience. It is nor clear whether these conventional measures, which were developed for earnings studies, will show comparable effects in our context. Although certain components of human capital important for employees cannot be applied to the entrepreneurial role, we expect measures of general human capital to show effects similar to those for human capital earnings functions. The notion of *specific* human capital must be modified and adapted to the self-employment context. We differentiate between industry-specific human capital and entrepreneur-specific human capital (Preisendörfer and Voss 1990). The crucial role of prior experience in an industry before starting a business in that industry is a recurrent theme in past research on organizational success and survival (Mayer and Goldstein 1961; Boswell 1972; Deutsche Ausgleichsbank 1988; Picot, Laub, and Schneider 1989; Young and Francis 1991). Industry-specific experience yields knowledge about profitable niches and increases productivity.

An important indicator of entrepreneur-specific human capital is prior self-employment experience. If self-employment is a kind of "trial and error process," then knowledge gained in prior self-employment episodes, successful or not, may be the best preparation for the entrepreneurial role. Previous studies provide some empirical evidence that self-employment experience of the founder improves the survival chances of a new business. A second component of entrepreneur-specific human capital is "leadership experience," i.e., experience in managing and directing employees. If the founder of a new firm hires employees, the self-employment role becomes a "new quality" (Scase and Goffee 1982), and leadership experience should make it easier for the founder to cope with this situation. A final measure of entrepreneur-specific human capital, derived from an overview of the literature (Young 1971; Carroll and Mosakowski 1987; Bates 1990a), is parental self-employment. Laband and Lentz (1985, chap. 2) drew an explicit connection between human capital theory, parental self-employment, and business success. Children of entrepreneurs often have access to their parents' workplaces from childhood on, acquiring entrepreneurial qualifications as a by-product of everyday interactions. Self-employed parents may also serve as role models – children may learn from their parents how to manage a firm efficiently.

Organizational ecology

Organizational ecology (Hannan and Freeman 1977, 1989; Singh and Lumsden 1990) deals with evolutionary processes within or between populations of organizations observed over long periods of time. We analyze a heterogeneous set of businesses over a relatively short time period. The analysis of organizational mortality is an important topic in organizational ecology, and we believe that organizational ecology and its associated empirical research offer a background framework to derive hypotheses regarding the determinants of the survival chances of new businesses.

Businesses begin with a *"liability of newness"* (Stinchcombe 1965). Many businesses die young, and organizational ecologists have elaborated on this age-dependent pattern of organizational mortality in considerable detail (Freeman, Carroll, and Hannan 1983; Singh, Tucker, and House 1986). Young and new organizations have a higher risk of failure than older organizations. However, some recent research suggests that organizational mortality, rather than continuously declining with increasing age, actually follows an inverted U-shaped pattern (Brüderl and Schüssler 1990).

New businesses that are "followers," i.e., in which the founder enters an existing business, have a better chance of survival than firms created de novo. By "piggybacking upon existing expertise" (Bates 1990b, p. 12) "follower" businesses may benefit from previously established connections to customers or from internal routines that have proved useful (cf. Aldrich, Staber, Zimmer, and Beggs 1990). Similarly, better survival prospects are predicted for new businesses with a stable affiliation to an existing firm (e.g., a franchising system). Affiliated businesses may use the resources of their partner or parental firms, seek advice from them, build on their credit, etc. So "follower" firms and affiliated firms are new firms only in a restricted sense.

Organizational ecologists often discuss the *"liability of smallness"* in connection with the liability of newness (Aldrich and Auster 1986; Brüderl and Schüssler 1990; Audretsch and Mahmood 1991). The assumption is that large new businesses have better survival prospects than small new businesses. Initial size may be measured in terms of either the amount of financial capital or the number of people employed at the time of founding. A large pool of financial resources improves the chances of a new firm to weather the critical start-up period and to cope with random shocks from the environment. Furthermore, large organizations may have advantages in raising more capital, may face better tax conditions, and may be in a better position to recruit qualified labor. However, small enterprises have the advantage of low overhead costs and they require minimal resources for sustenance. A successful business may begin on a relatively small scale and build up step-by-step in an exploratory fashion.

A third feature of organizational ecology that is useful for our analysis is *organizational strategies*. In connection with the concept "niche," Hannan and Freeman (1977) distinguished between generalist and specialist strategies. Generalist organizations aim to occupy a broad niche, whereas specialist organizations aim for a narrow niche. In a study of California restaurants, Freeman and Hannan (1983) examined whether generalist and specialist organizations have different survival chances under different environmental circumstances. Another important distinction is between r-strategies and K-strategies (Brittain and Freeman 1980). R-strategy organizations move quickly into a niche to exploit resources as they first become available; K-strategy organizations try to compete successfully in densely settled environments. Elaborating on these distinctions, Romanelli (1989) differentiated two basic dimensions of strategy; (1) aggressiveness of a firm's approach to exploiting resources in its environment; and (2) breadth of the market addressed by a firm. Further, there is the well-known Schumpeterian distinction between innovators, who try to create new organizational forms or market new products, and imitators, who enter well-established markets (Schumpeter 1952).

Although organizational strategies are important influences on the survival chances of new businesses, there are often no clear-cut predictions regarding which organizational forms have an advantage. This may be because outcomes often depend on market conditions. For instance, generalists may fare better under high levels of environmental variability because they spread their risks, but under heavy competition, specialists might occupy "quiet" niches where they are insulated from market pressures. Innovators have no competition (at least in the early stages), but they bear all the risks of introducing new forms or products and must establish their legitimacy. Although this is not a problem for imitators, imitators may face heavy competition. Investigation of the intricate interactions between organizational strategy and environment is beyond the scope of this paper and we focus on the net effects of different organizational strategies.

Finally, the basic argument of organizational ecology is that organizational selection processes are mainly driven by *environmental* forces. Organizational ecologists have therefore worked hard to isolate important dimensions of "the environment" (Carroll 1987, chaps. 4 to 6). Carroll distinguished task environmental variables, institutional environmental variables, and effects of the political environment. Freeman and Hannan (1983) accentuated two features – environmental variability and environmental grain. Inclusion of these and other environmental factors into the set of determinants of survival chances of new businesses would advance research on business vitality rates. Again, however, there are not always clear-cut predictions on which environment is better for newly founded businesses. It is the fit between an organization's form and its environment that is decisive for its survival chances. Here, again, our interest is confined to environmental net effects.

Previous research on determinants of survival chances of new businesses has concentrated on individual characteristics of the entrepreneur. Human capital theory captures most of these individual characteristics in a theoretically meaningful way. For organizational and environmental determinants of survival chances, the organizational ecology approach promises theoretical progress. These two theories yield a rich set of testable hypotheses.

Data, variables, and methods

Data

Our data are part of the "Munich Founder Study." At the beginning of 1990, interviews were conducted with 1,849 business founders who had registered a new business with the local Chamber of Commerce in the area of Munich and Upper Bavaria (Germany) during 1985–1986. From a total of 28,646 business registrations in 1985-1986 in Munich and Upper Bavaria, we drew a stratified random sample of about 6,000 business addresses.[2] The main stratification criterion was whether the firm was still in existence in 1990. Deregistered firms were over-sampled because we expected their response rate to be lower. Because our population is confirmed to businesses administered by the Chamber of Commerce, crafts, agri-businesses, physicians, architects, and lawyers are not part of the data set.

Of the 6,000 sample addresses, 600 could not be updated. In addition, not all business registrations are "real businesses" – for nearly 20 per cent of our 5,400 updated addresses, no economic activity was observed and these "businesses" were excluded from our interviews.[3] With 1,849 interviews out of 4,320 addresses, our response rate is 43 per cent, which is relatively high compared to other studies of German business firms.[4] Of the founders interviewed, 34 per cent had given up their businesses by the date of the survey, compared to 38 per cent among the 28,646 total registrations in 1985–1986. Thus, despite our over-sampling of dead firms, we decided not to use any weighting procedure when estimating our models.

The questionnaire was broad and required an average interview time of one hour. The first part of the interview concerned start-up characteristics of the firm and its development, the second part dealt with attributes of the founder (for details on the Munich Founder Study, see Preisendörfer and Ziegler 1990).

Variables

Our crucial variable is the survival time (in months) of the businesses as reported by the respondents. A firm still alive at the time of the interview was recorded as a right-censored observation. We obtained information on survival time from 1,794 respondents.[5] Table 10.1 gives a summary and description of all independent variables.

General human capital of the founder. We use the founders' years of schooling and years of work experience up to the time of founding 1985–1986 to indicate general human capital. Schooling includes general education as well as occupational training. As is usual in German social research (e.g., Diekmann 1985), an apprenticeship, which normally takes three

Table 10.1 Description of variables: Upper Bavaria, 1990

Variable	Value
HUMAN CAPITAL RESOURCES OF FOUNDER	
General human capital	
Mean years of schooling	13.4
	(2.9)
Mean years of work experience	15.0
	(10.5)
Specific human capital	
Percent with industry specific experience	60.1
Percent with self-employment experience	33.1
Percent with leadership experience	36.3
Percent with self-employed father	36.5
Organisational characteristics	
Newness	
Age of business (months)	—
Percent follower business	24.6
Percent affiliated business	9.3
Initial size	
Mean amount of capital invested	7.84
(DM, log)	(4.77)
Mean number of employees at founding	0.53
(log)	(0.90)
Percent registered firm	31.8
Organizational strategies	
Percent specialist business	51.2
Percent innovative business	34.8
Percent national market-scope business	44.3
ENVIRONMENTAL CONDITIONS	
Location	
Percent Munich	48.2
Branch of industry	
Percent manufacturing	13.5
Percent construction	3.9
Percent wholesale/retail trade	33.6
Percent transportation	5.5
Percent restaurants	5.7
Percent computer services	7.5
Percent other services	30.4

continued on next page

Table 10.! Description of variables: Upper Bavaria, 1990 (cont.)

Variable	Value
Market conditions	
Mean intensity of competition	3.86
	(0.32)
Mean seasonality	2.73
	(0.59)
Mean clustering of business orders	2.10
	(0.48)
Number of cases	1 621

Note: Number in parentheses are standard deviations. Means are calculated for the 1 621 cases used in Table 10 3.

years, is counted half as schooling and half as work experience. We expect more schooling to improve a firm's survival chances, Compared to other studies, our measure of work experience is relatively exact – we have a complete career history of each founder, including all episodes outside the labor market that do not count its work experience (unemployment, military service, household work, etc.). Following common practice in human capital research, work experience is taken into account as a simple term and as a squared term in our multivariate analyses. We expect work experience to show a decreasing payoff.

Specific human capital of the founder. We capture potential effects of specific human capital of founders with dummy variables. Industry-specific human capital is indicated by whether the founder has prior experience in the new firm's industry. Entrepreneur-specific human capital is measured in three ways: (1) Did the founder have prior self-employment experience? (2) Did the founder have leadership experience? Because leadership experience is an advantage only if the new firm has employees, we distinguished the following two groups: founders with leadership experience and with employees at time of founding versus the remaining founders. To simplify the presentation we speak only of leadership experience. (3) Was the founder's father (up to 1985–1986) self-employed over most of his career? We expect that both industry-specific and entrepreneur-specific human capital increase survival chances.

"Newness" of the business. Business age (measured in months) enters our analyses because organizational mortality is modelled as an age-dependent process. Two additional dichotomous measures indicate the newness of a business. (1) "Newcomer" versus "follower" businesses – newcomer businesses are established by founder from scratch, i.e., the founder created firm de novo, whereas follower businesses are new in a legal sense, but

follow in the footsteps of a previously existing (more or less successful) firm, i.e., the founder enters a business that was already in operation. (2) Independent versus affiliated businesses – independent businesses have no strong link to an existing firm, whereas affiliated businesses have a strong link, i.e., they are a franchise organization or the founder directs another business that deals with similar products or services. We expect that follower businesses and affiliated businesses have better survival chances.

Initial size of the business. Size at time of founding should increase survival chances. Size is operationalized by three indicators: (1) amount of financial capital invested in the business; (2) number of employees at time of founding; and (3) legal form of the business. The amount of financial capital invested is measured in Deutsche Marks (DM, natural logarithm). One problem with this variable is that whether a given amount of capital is adequate may depend on the industry – 50,000 DM may he a solid basis for a typewriting service, but not for a manufacturing plant. Theoretically, a measure standardized on the average of each industry would be more appropriate. However, because our study covers a heterogeneous set of businesses, it is not practical to derive this average from our data. Thus we simply use the initial amount of capital. This is a reasonable proxy, given that we control for the number of employees. The number of employees at time of founding (natural logarithm) includes the founder if he or she actually worked in the firm. New businesses often engage part-time employees. Based on the usual thirty-eight-hour week in Germany, our measure takes these part-time employees into account (e.g., two employees, each working nineteen hours, are counted as one employee). Finally, the legal form of a business distinguishes between small tradesmen (Kleingewerbetreibende) and firms registered in the commercial register (Handelsregisterfirmen). Small tradesmen are mostly small businesses. If a business meets certain industry-specific size criteria for large businesses (defined by German law), it must be registered both with the local Chamber of Commerce and in the commercial register. Moreover, all limited liability commercial partnerships (GmbH) have to register. Because registered firms may have advantages independent of their capitalization and number of employees, legal form is an additional aspect of size. Legal form should have an effect after controlling for the other size variables.

Organizational strategies of the business. Founders were asked a series of questions regarding their business strategies at the time of founding. We differentiate these strategies along three dimensions: (1) Generalist organizations, which offer a wide array of products or services aiming at a broad range of customers, versus specialist organizations; (2) traditional businesses as imitators, which offer conventional products or services, versus innovative businesses, which offer new and innovative products or

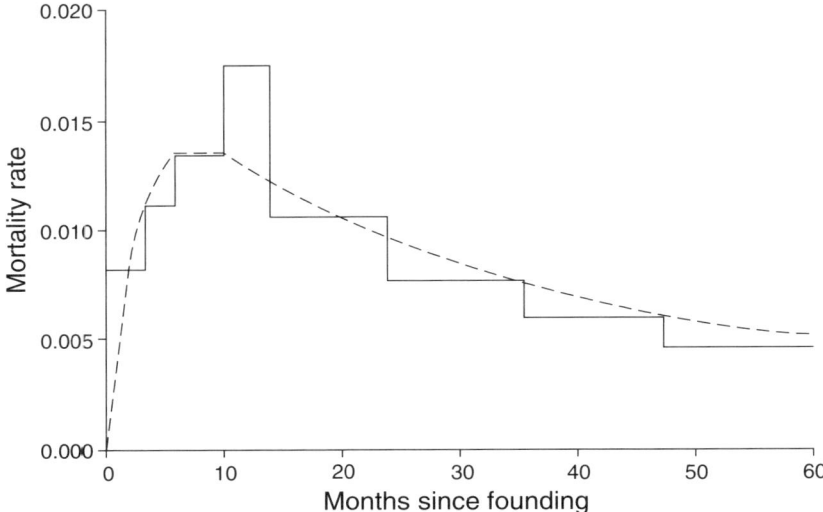

Figure 10.1 Mortality rate for newly founded business organizations: Upper
Bavaria, 1985 to 1990.

Note: The step-function is the life-table rate estimator. The dashed curve is estimated using the proportional log-logistic rate model (without covariates). The number of cases is 1,794.

services; and (3) local market-scope businesses, which confine their activities to the local market, versus national market-scope businesses, which try to reach the national (or international) market. These three strategy variables, which represent subjective assessments of the founders as to which category best described their strategy, are dichotomous. For these variables our analyses are exploratory and we have no predictions for their effects.

Environmental embeddedness and environmental conditions. In a survey it is difficult to collect comprehensive information about the environment of an organization. This is the weakest part of our analyses. We take into account the regional location of the new businesses by differentiating between businesses located in Munich and businesses outside Munich, i.e. in Upper Bavaria. The city of Munich is the economic center of the area under investigation. Upper Bavaria includes some middle-range cities (Ingolstadt, Rosenheim) and, to a large extent, it qualifies as a rural area. Competition is much heavier in Munich than in the rural areas. Therefore, we expect survival chances to be lower in Munich. The second environmental dimension is type of industry. We distinguish manufacturing, construction, wholesale/retail trade, transportation, restaurants, computer services, and other services. These dummy variables serve mainly as controls. Finally, to capture the market conditions facing new businesses, founders were asked to rate these conditions along a set of

dimensions (on a scale ranging from one to five). We attempted to eliminate subjective biases by computing the means for all founders in an
industry (for over fifty industries) and using these means as covariates.
Three dimensions of market conditions facing each new business are
examined: (1) intensity of competition. i.e., density of competing firms;
(2) seasonality, i.e., dependence of business activity on seasonal variations; and (3) clustering of business orders. A high clustering of orders
means that business is usually done by a few "big deals." The values of
these three variables represent the respective industry averages and range
from one (low) to five (high). Again, we have no clear predictions for the
effects of these three environmental conditions.

Methods

Event history analysis (Tuma and Hannan 1984; Lancaster 1990) was used
to analyze the data. We first computed nonparametric, bivariate life-table
estimates of the survivor function that show for the categories of each
covariate the percentage of firms having gone out of business two years
after founding and five years after founding.

In a second step, multivariate analyses were performed on the data using
a special parametric hazard rate model – a log-logistic model. The log-
logistic rate can model inverted U-shaped and monotonically declining
rates. The "liability of newness" paradigm proposes a monotonically
declining mortality rate, whereas Fichman and Levinthal (1991) and
Brüderl and Schüssler (1990 argued that organizational mortality follows a
"liability of adolescence": Mortality rates are low immediately after starting a business because organizations can survive on initial resources,
increase to a maximum, and decline afterwards. Only after the maximum is
reached do the usual arguments for a "liability of newness" apply (Brüderl
1991 and Levinthal 1991). In our data, the mortality process shows a "liability of adolescence" as seen in Figure 10.1. The step-function in this
figure is the plot of the life-table rate estimator. This rate reaches a maximum between nine and twelve months after the founding of all organization.[6]

Such a rate pattern can be modelled by a log-logistic function. We modified the usual function. We modified the usual function, however, and use
the following proportional log-logistic model:[7]

$$r(t) = b \frac{p(\lambda t)^{p-1}}{1 + (\lambda t)^p} \tag{1}$$

where $r(t)$ denotes the mortality rate of a firm at age t, b determines the level
of the rate, λ the time of the peak, and p the shape of the rate. If $p > 1$, the
rate follows an inverted U-shaped pattern. If $p \leq 1$, the rate shows a continuous decline. Compared to the usual log-logistic model, our model includes

(besides λ and p) a third parameter b. Covariates will be introduced into this parameter, i.e., $b = \exp(\alpha + x' \beta)$. One advantage of this model is that the third parameter gives a better fit of the model. Furthermore, because it is a proportional hazards model, the covariate effects can be interpreted as percentage effects on the rate. The good fit obtained with this model is obvious from Figure 10.1. The dashed curve is the rate estimated using the proportional log-logistic rate model.[8] It is very close to the non-parametric estimate.

Results

Bivariate life-table estimates

Table 10.2 presents the life-table estimates of the percentage of firms that have gone out of business after two and five years. Nearly one-fourth of all businesses failed within two years after founding, and 37 per cent had failed within five years after founding.[9] Most of our theoretically derived expectations are supported at the bivariate level. More years of schooling and work experience of the founder significantly improve the survival chances of a new business. Businesses whose founders had industry-specific experience, self-employment experience, leadership experience, or a self-employed father were significantly less likely to fail. Thus, our bivariate analyses confirm the hypotheses derived from human capital theory.

Among organizational characteristics, newcomer businesses have a higher failure rate than follower businesses. In contrast to our expectation, independent businesses show significantly better survival prospects than affiliated businesses. All of our three size measures – amount of capital invested, number of employees, legal form – clearly indicate that smallness is a disadvantage. We did not formulate concrete predictions for organizational strategies. The results in Table 10.2 suggest that specialist businesses, innovative organizations, and enterprises aiming at a national market have lower failure rates.

Among environmental characteristics, firms located in Munich are more likely to have failed than are firms located in Upper Bavaria. Manufacturing, construction, and computer service firms have better chances of survival than wholesale/retail businesses, transportation firms, and restaurants where more than 40 per cent of firms have left the market after five years. These industry effects agree with "everyday wisdom." Finally, using the median as a cutting point, firms in a highly competitive environment or in a highly seasonal business are significantly more likely to fail, as expected. The better survival experience of firms in industries with high clustering of business orders is more surprising.

That all group-specific differences are statistically significant in our bivariate analyses and that most differences are in the expected direction

Table 10.2 Life-table estimates of the percentage of firms that have gone out of business two years after founding and five years after founding: Upper Bavaria, 1985–1990

| Variable | Percent gone out of business | | |
	After 2 years	After 5 years	Number of cases
All businesses	23.7	37.1	1 794
HUMAN CAPITAL			
Years of schooling of founder*			
Less than 12 years	29.1	44.7	747
12 to 15 years	22.9	35.9	508
15 years or more	17.2	28.0	530
Years of work experience of founder*			
Less than 10 years	33.4	48.9	638
10 to 20 years	21.0	33.7	573
20 to 30 years	15.0	26.6	381
30 years or more	16.7	28.9	192
Industry-specific experience of founder*			
No	36.9	54.5	716
Yes	14.9	25.5	1 077
Self-employment experience of founder*			
No	27.9	42.0	1 201
Yes	15.1	27.0	593
Leadership experience of founder*			
No	30.4	45.5	805
Yes	17.8	29.7	978
Self-employed father of founder*			
No	25.6	40.1	1 101
Yes	19.5	30.7	633
ORGANIZATIONAL CHARACTERISTICS			
Newcomer vs follower business*			
Newcomer	26.3	41.7	1 352
Follower	15.7	23.3	442
Independent vs affiliated business*			
Independent	22.8	35.5	1 623
Affiliated	31.3	51.9	166
Amount of capital invested*			
Less than 20 000 DM	36.6	55.4	835
20 000–50 000 DM	25.7	38.0	233
50 000 DM or more	8.3	16.1	714

continued on next page

Table 10.2 Life-table estimates of the percentage of firms that have gone out of business two years after founding and five years after founding: Upper Bavaria, 1985–1990 (cont.)

Variable	Percent gone out of business		
	After 2 years	After 5 years	Number of cases
Number of employees at time of founding			
1 or less	35.9	54.2	785
More than 1, to 2	15.4	27.6	209
More than 2, to 3	16.2	23.3	210
More than 3	7.5	13.1	349
*Legal form**			
Small tradesman	32.0	49.1	1 220
Registered firm	5.6	11.4	568
*Generalist vs specialist business**			
Generalist	28.7	43.5	861
Specialist	18.7	31.1	903
*Traditional vs innovative business**			
Traditional	27.3	42.7	1 130
Innovative	17.8	27.3	603
*Local vs national market-scope business**			
Local market scope	30.7	47.1	990
National market scope	14.9	24.5	786
ENVIRONMENTAL CONDITIONS			
Location			
Upper Bavaria	20.8	34.3	930
Munich	26.8	40.2	864
Branch of industry			
Manufacturing	11.2	19.2	242
Construction	15.7	24.1	70
Wholesale/retail trade	28.1	42.5	602
Transportation	37.8	55.6	98
Restaurants	29.4	43.6	103
Computer services	14.2	28.4	134
Other services	24.1	38.6	545
*Intensity of competition in industry**			
Low	20.9	33.9	923
High	26.7	40.5	871
*Seasonality in industry**			
Low	20.0	31.7	915
High	27.5	42.8	879

continued on next page

Table 10.2 Life-table estimates of the percentage of firms that have gone out of business two years after founding and five years after founding: Upper Bavaria, 1985–1990 (cont.)

Variable	Percent gone out of business		
	After 2 years	After 5 years	Number of cases
Clustering of business orders in industry*			
Low	28.8	42.8	929
High	18.2	30.9	865

Difference between subgroups is significant at 0.05 level (Lee–Desu statistic. SPSSx). Some variables have missing values.

indicates that ideas from both human capital theory and organizational ecology are useful for explaining business failure rates. To control for the obvious interdependencies between covariates, however. multivariate analyses are necessary.

Multivariate analyses

In Table 10.3 we estimate a multivariate log-logistic model in which the mortality rate r(t) is the dependent variable and all independent variables are introduced simultaneously. As indicated by the χ^2 value, the explanatory power of the model is very good and the shape-parameter, ρ, is significantly greater than 1. Thus, we conclude that the risk of failure of new businesses follows an inverted U-shaped pattern corresponding to the hypothesis of a "liability of adolescence."

The effects of our *general* human capital measures are in line with the human capital theory: Increased schooling and work experience are associated with lower failure rates. However, because the squared term for work experience is positive, the overall effect of work experience is non-linear, i.e., there is a concave relationship between work experience and survival chances (the turning point is reached after twenty-five years of experience). Among *specific* human capital variables, industry-specific experience is the most important effect – starting a business without experience in the industry sharply increases the mortality rate. The importance of these three human capital variables is not the result of a selection effect because the effects remain after controlling for organizational and environmental characteristics. Schooling, work experience, and industry experience increase the productivity of a founder.

The effects of the remaining three types of specific human capital almost disappear in the multivariate model indicating that their bivariate effects mainly reflect causes of selection. The result for prior self-employment experience is especially interesting. The positive sign, though insignificant,

Table 10.3 Proportional log-logistic coefficients for business failure rate on selected independent variables: Upper Bavaria, 1985–1990

Independent variable	Coefficient	t-value
Human capital		
Years of schooling	−0.054*	3.18
Years of work experience	−0.051*	3.92
Years of work experience squared/100	0.101*	2.97
Industry specific experience	−0.332*	3.53
Self-employment experience	0.096	0.86
Leadership experience	0.190	1.39
Self-employed father	−0.105	1.09
Organisational characteristics		
Follower business	−0.446*	3.46
Affiliated business	0.278*	2.06
Amont of capital invested natural log	−0.034*	3.40
Number of employees natural log	−0.451*	5.01
Registered in commercial register	−0.793*	4.48
Specialist business	−0.189	1.94
Innovative business	−0.133	1.19
National market-scope	−0.363*	3.59
Environmental characteristics		
Location in Munich	0.131	1.49
In construction	0.522	1.38
In wholesale/retail trade	0.512*	2.74
In transportation	0.765*	3.19
Restaurant business	0.227	0.87
In computer services	0.486	1.81
In other services	0.249	1.32
Competition intensity	−0.205	1.39
Seasonality	0.132	1.45
Clustering of orders	−0.519	3.90
Constant, α	−1.088	1.35
Shape-parameter, ρ	1.552*	5.20
Scale parameter, λ	0.075	
Number of cases	1 621	
χ^2	476.2	
Degrees of freedom	25	

* $p < 0.05$

Note: The χ^2 test statistic is a likelihood–ratio test against the model without covariates. Reference groups: no industry-specific experience, no self-employment experience, no leadership experience, father not self–employed, newcomer business, independent business, small tradesman. generalist business, traditional business, local market-scope business, location in Upper Bavaria, in manufacturing. Of 1,621 cases, 65.6 percent were censored.

Table 10.4 Regression coefficients for three organizational characteristics on selected human capital variables: Upper Bavaria, 1990

Independent variable	*Dependent variable*		
	Start-up capital (log)	*Legal form (1 = in commercial register)*	*Number of employees (log)*
Years of schooling	0.178*	0.193*	0.009
	(4.46)	(8.92)	(1.25)
Years of work experience	0.153*	0.093*	0.005
	(4.28)	(4.56)	(0.78)
Years of work experience squared/100	−0.293*	−0.161*	0.011
	(3.27)	(3.29)	(0.67)
Industry specific experience	−0.772*	0.985*	0.354*
	(3.20)	(7.14)	(7.97)
Self-employment experience	1.436*	0.785*	0.143*
	(5.78)	(6.34)	(3.13)
Leadership experience	1.133	0.641*	2.87*
	(4.71)	(4.93)	(6.50)
Self-employed father	0.479*	0.439*	0.158*
	(2.10)	(3.62)	(3.77)
Constant	2.375*	−5.832*	−0.192
	(3.80)	(15.06)	(1.67)
R^2	11.5	19.3	14.2
Number of cases	1 704	1 709	1 714

* $p < 0.05$

Note: Numbers in parentheses are t-values. OLS regression estimates in columns (1) and (3), logit regression estimates in column (2). Unlike Tables 10.1–3, leadership experience is not defined as an interaction variable. Reference groups: no industry-specific experience, no self-employment experience, no leadership experience, father not self-employed.

contradicts findings from prior studies. We suspect that prior self-employment experience mainly improves the selection into starting a business and not the founders' subsequent productivity. Moreover, a certain part of this group may consist of negatively selected entrepreneurs who lack necessary qualifications and need time to realize and accept this. Only repeated failures will force them out of the self-employment sector. Finally, there may be a group of "professional gamblers" who have long histories of business registrations, often with two or more simultaneous business allowances, and who open and close enterprises frequently.

Turning to the effects of *organizational characteristics* we see that, as expected, follower firms have better survival chances than newcomer firms. Contrary to our expectation, however, affiliated businesses have lower survival chances than independent businesses. Because affiliations can take on different forms, it is not easy to explain this finding. In the course of our interviews we uncovered some qualitative hints: First of all, there are some companies in the franchise sector giving licenses with difficult or even fraudulent conditions. Founders trapped into such contracts have little chance for success. Although the founders may not know it, from the perspective of their partners or parent firms, affiliated businesses are often "experimental" or "special purpose" firms. When these experiments end or the special purposes are fulfilled, these organizations are forced out of business. The liability of smallness is clearly confirmed by our data. Failure rates are significantly higher for businesses starting with a low stock of financial capital, with few employees, or not registered in the commercial register (small tradesmen). There is no support for the intuitively plausible idea that a new business should begin on a small scale and build up step-by-step.

Concerning organizational strategies, our results indicate better survival chances for businesses aiming at the national market. There are no significant differences between specialist and generalist organizations or between conventional and innovative businesses in survival experience. The result for specialists, though not significant, is especially interesting: New businesses seem to fare better if they occupy a small niche. This need not be an empty niche, as the result for the "innovator" variable indicates. In addition, it pays if this is not only a local niche (these strategy effects are not simply size effects because we control for size). This is an interesting difference between organizational ecology and the biological framework on which it is based. Among animals, it is advantageous to settle in new, unpopulated niches. Not so, it appears, for organizations. However, these are net effects – the intricate interplay between strategies and environments is beyond the scope of this paper.

Among the *environmental variables* there was bivariate evidence that businesses located in the densely settled Munich environment had higher failure rates, but this effect is not significant in multivariate analysis. Among industries, manufacturing (the reference category) has the lowest mortality rate. However, only wholesale/retail trade and transportation have significantly higher rates. This result suggests that it is not the type of industry itself that hampers organizational survival. For instance, restaurants showed low survival chances in the bivariate analysis because their founders possess little human capital and they are small. Computer services had good survival chances in the bivariate analysis, but with controls they show higher failure rates than restaurants. This is because founders of computer firms usually possess a lot of human capital and start their businesses with much capital. Additional analyses (not reported here) reveal that start-up size differences in particular, produce these results.

Finally, we examine whether the bivariate effects found for the environmental conditions of specific industries persist with controls. The tendency for high competition to increase mortality vanishes in the multivariate analysis. Small firms often enter highly competitive environments, which lowers survival chances. However, with all other variables held constant, mortality is not higher in highly competitive industries. Highly seasonal businesses do not have significantly higher mortality. New businesses in industries with a high clustering of business orders have significantly better survival chances. Evidently, industries in which business is done in a few "big deals" and it is not necessary to have a broad array of customers offer better chances for new businesses.

Human capital effects and organizational characteristics

We have argued that founders endowed with a high stock of human capital are in a better position to identify promising business opportunities and to set up firms with high a priori survival prospects. This means that human capital should not only have direct effects on organizational survival, but indirect *selection effects* via differences in the types of businesses established by different founders. Using our set of human capital variables, Table 10.4 presents the results of three regression models estimating the effects of human capital resources on the three different start-up size measures. Results demonstrate that this expectation is broadly supported by our data.

For the amount of start-up capital, all human capital variables have significant effects in the expected direction. Founders with more years of schooling and work experience and founders with industry-specific experience, self-employment experience, leadership experience, or a self-employed father made larger capital investments. The same conclusion holds when legal form (small tradesmen versus businesses registered in the commercial register) is our indicator of size. However, when the number of employees at time of founding is the measure of size, only the industry-specific and entrepreneur-specific measures of human capital have significant effects. The decision to hire employees evidently has its own quality (especially in the highly regulated German labor market), and founders with an entrepreneurial background are better prepared to assume the social role of employer.

In sum, all human capital variables have strong selection effects: Founders with a high stock of general and specific human capital invest more, are more likely to be in the commercial register, and have more employees. Only general human capital and industry-specific experience, however, also have productivity effects (Table 10.3). Entrepreneur-specific human capital, in contrast, seems to operate primarily via selection.

Discussion

Combining human capital theory with ideas from organizational ecology, we investigated a rich set of hypotheses regarding the mortality process of newly founded business organizations. Human capital theory emphasizes the role of the founder and the founder's general and specific human capital. Education, general work experience, and industry-specific experience showed strong effects. We also found that human capital influences organizational survival via selection effects, i.e., founders with a high stock of human capital set up businesses with high a priori chances to survive.

The organizational ecology approach accentuates factors like the age of a firm, its size, strategy, and environmental conditions. Start-up size (number of employees, financial capital invested, legal form), in particular, turned out to be relevant. Bigger firms have much better survival chances. Furthermore, businesses operating in a national market have a markedly lower mortality rate. Environmental conditions also have important but less powerful effects. Overall, the effects of organizational characteristics (initial size, newness, organizational strategies) are the most crucial.

Although our study provides a relatively comprehensive analysis of the survival chances of newly founded businesses, there are still many unanswered questions. We did not examine the interplay of organizational strategies and environmental conditions. This would have required adding many interactions to our model. We might find, for example, that generalists have better survival chances in industries with high seasonality. Similarly, we could see whether the effects of individual attributes or environmental factors vary depending on the size of the business, branch of industry, etc. A finding that individual attributes of the founder are more important for small businesses, for example, would support a proposition from organizational sociology that large organizations become "political entities," with outcomes diverging from the plans and intentions of the chief executive.

In addition to human capital resources, it may be fruitful to look at the effects of so-called social resources. Are founders connected to a broad and diverse social network in a better position? Is there a positive correlation between founders' human capital and social networking resources? Can "social capital" compensate for a lack of human capital?

We should also emphasize that our dependent variable, organizational survival, is only one of many conceivable measures of organizational success. Other measures, such as growth or profit, could be used. Though these measures are strongly related to organizational survival, they. nevertheless accentuate different aspects of the founding process. Growth emphasizes the role of new firms as job-creators; profit may be important for understanding the dynamics of income distributions.

Finally, our findings lead to some practical recommendations for someone considering self-employment. First, a prospective founder should not start too small. Though smallness reduces the risk of a financial disaster,[10] it also increases the mortality rate of a business. Depending on the branch of industry, there is evidently a certain minimum start-up size, and it does not make much sense to begin a business below this level. Furthermore, our impression from interviews is that a certain financial investment seems to "speed up" people to engage in their businesses more seriously. Based on the crucial role of prior experience in the industry, we recommend that one gathers broad experience in the field. The best preparation may be as an employee in the industry, possibly in a small company in which the whole array of requirements can be seen.

Notes

Josef Brüderl is Assistant Professor of Sociology at the University of Munich, Germany. His research interests include mobility processes within organizations. A Paper on dynamic career models will appear in *Sociological Methods and Research* in 1992. His other research field is on organizational dynamics. Currently he is studying the employment dynamics of newly founded business organizations.

Peter Preisendörfer is Assistant Professor of Sociology at the University of Munich, Germany. His interests include labor market theory, organizational sociology, and sociological methods. Much of his recent research has been concerned with problems of self-employment. He and Thomas Voss recently published an article on this topic in *Organization Studies* (1990, vol. 11, pp. 107–129).

Rolf Ziegler is Professor of Sociology at the University of Munich, Germany. His interests include rational choice theory, organizational sociology, mathematical modelling in the social sciences, and network analysis. His recent article on the Kula published in Social Institutions (M. Hechter *et al.*, eds., Aldine de Gruyter, 1990) is a game-theoretical analysis of social order, barter, and ceremonial exchange. With Frans N. Stokman and John Scott he has published a comparative study on interlocking directorates in ten countries (*Networks of Corporate Power*, Polity Press, 1985). Currently he is working on newly-founded enterprises in the former GDR.

1   Direct all correspondence to Rolf Ziegler, Institute of Sociology, Konradstrasse 6. D–8000 München 40, Germany. This research was supported by the Deutsche Forschungsgemeinschaft with grant Zi 207/7-2. Helpful comments on earlier drafts were received from Howard Aldrich, Norman Braun, Glenn Carroll, Elaine Reardon, Jitendra Singh, Anand Swaminathan, anonymous reviewers, and the editor.

2   Our project had access to the official registration data of all business registrations (about 17,000) and deregistrations in Munich and Upper Bavaria between 1980 and 1989. Two prior articles (Brüderl and Schüssler 1990; Preisendörfer and Voss 1990) used the full data set of business registrations. The registration period 1985–1986 was chosen for detailed interviews as a compromise between length of observation period and reliability of founding addresses.

3   These "stillborn" businesses occur for several reasons. We believe that registrations for tax reasons constitute the majority of these businesses. Some intend to use their registration card for purchasing goods at wholesale prices. Finally, because there are few barriers to registration, some people register without any concrete idea of how to set up a business.

4   We could have obtained more interviews, but funds were limited. Moreover, several other types of business had to be excluded (minority businesses in which the founder did not speak German.

newly registered firms that did not qualify as "new" businesses, etc.).

5   About fifty founders dated the start of their business before 1985. Because these businesses (did not belong to the 1985–1986 cohort, we excluded them from the analysis. In general, There was a high degree of correspondence: between the survival times obtained from the registration data and those front the interview data

6   It may be that our finding of a liability of adolescence results from an undersampling of short-lived firms. About 20 per cent of our updated business registrations never engaged in economic activity and were excluded from the sample, and another 57 per cent did not respond to our survey. If these were short-lived businesses, their exclusion may be responsible for the observed non-monotonic hazard-rate pattern. However, we classified as stillborns only those businesses whose founders explicitly said that they never tried to do any business. Furthermore, the inverted U-shaped pattern is present in the total population of 28,646 registrations and in the sample of 6000 registrations drawn for the interviews. Thus, our finding of a liability of adolescence is not due to sampling bias.

7   This model was proposed in another context by Petersen, Spilerman, and Dahl (1989). Brüderl (1991) gave an extended discussion of this model.

8   Estimation is done by maximum-likelihood. A FORTRAN subprogram, used in connection with BMDP3R (the approach is described in Petersen 1986), is available from the authors.

9   Although "failed" firms were oversampled, the percentage of "failed" firms in our completed interviews corresponds roughly to that observed in the total registration data. Therefore, even the absolute percentages are interpretable.

10 We encountered many individual financial disasters in our study. In general, 53 per cent of founders gone out of business ended up with personal financial losses; 14 per cent of all failures entailed financial losses to others (business partners, creditors, etc.).

References

Aldrich, Howard E. 1979. *Organizations and Environments*. Englewood Cliffs. NJ: Prentice-Hall.

Aldrich, Howard E. and Ellen Auster. 1986. "Even Dwarfs Started Small: Liabilities of Size and Age and their Strategic Implications." Pp. 165–98 in *Research in Organizational Behavior*, vol. 8. edited by B. M. Shaw and L. L. Cummings. Greenwich. CT: JAI Press.

Aldrich, Howard E. Udo Staber, Cathrine Zimmer, and John J. Beggs. 1990. "Minimalism and Organizational Mortality: Patterns of Disbanding Among U.S. Trade Associations, 1900–1983." Pp. 21–52 in *Organizational Evolution*, edited by J. V. Singh. Newbury Park, CA: Sage.

Aldrich, Howard E. and Cathrine Zimmer. 1986."Entrepreneurship Through Social Networks." Pp. 13–28 in *Population Perspectives on Organizations*, edited by H. E. Aldrich. Uppsala, Sweden: Acta Universitatis Upsaliensis.

Atkinson, John W. and Bert F. Hoselitz. 1963. "Leadership in Change: Entrepreneurship and Personality." Pp. 500–507 in *Personality and Social Systems* edited by N. J. Smelser and W. T. Smelser. New York: Wiley.

Audreisch, David B. and Talat, Mahmood. 1991. "The Rate of Hazard Confronting New Firms and Plants in U.S. Manufacturing." Wissenschaftszentrum Berlin für Sozialforschung (WZB), Berlin. Unpublished Manuscript.

Barreto, Humberto. 1989. *The Entrepreneur in Microeconomic Theory*. London: Routledge.

Bates. Timothy. 1985. "Entrepreneur Human Capital Endowments and Minority Business Viability." *Journal of Human Resources* 20:540–54.

— 1990a. Entrepreneur Human Capital Inputs and Small Business Longevity." *Review of Economics and Statistics* 72:551–59.

— 1990b. "Self-Employment Trends Among Mexican Americans" (Discussion Paper No. 90–9), Center of Economic Studies, U.S. Bureau of Census: Washington, DC.

Becker, Gary S. 1975. *Human Capital*. 2d ed. Chicago: University of Chicago Press.

Birch, David L. 1987. *Job Creation in America*. New York: Free Press.

Boswell, Jonathan. 1972. *The Rise and Decline of Small Firms*. London: Allen and Unwin.

Brenner, Reuven. 1987. *Rivalry: in Business, Science Among Nations*. Cambridge, England: Cambridge University Press.

Brittain, Jack and John Freeman. 1980. "Organizational Proliferation and Density Dependent Selection." Pp. 291–338 in *The Organizational Life Cycle*, edited by J. R. Kimberly and R. H. Miles. San Francisco: Jossey-Bass.

Brown, Charles, James Hamilton, and James Medoff. 1990. *Employers Large and Small*. Cambridge: Harvard University Press.

Brüderl, Josef, 1991. "Organizational Mortality and the Liability of Adolescence." Institute of Sociology, Munich, Germany. Unpublished Manuscript.

Brüderl, Josef and Rudolf Schüssler. 1990. "Organizational Mortality: The Liabilities of Newness and Adolescence." *Administrative Science Quarterly* 35:530–47.

Carroll, Glenn R. 1987. *Publish and Perish*. Greenwich, CT: JAI Press.

Carroll, Glenn R. and Elaine Mosakowski. 1987. The Career Dynamics of Self-Employed." *Administrative Science Quarterly* 32:570–89.

Cochran, A. B. 1981. "Small business mortality rates: A Review of the Literature." *Journal of Small Business Management* Oct.:50–59.

Collins, Orvis F. and David G. Moore. 1964. *The Enterprising Man*. East Lansing, MI: Michigan State University Press.

Deutsche Ausgleichsbank. 1988. "Warum Existenzgründungen zuweilen keinen Bestand haben – Ergebnisse einer Fragebogenaktion" (Why Business Foundings Fail: Results of a Survey). Pp. 25–34 in *Jahresbericht* 1987, edited by Deutsche Ausgleichsbank. Bonn: Deutsche Ausgleichsbank.

Diekmann, Andreas. 1985. *Einkommensunterschiede zwischen Männern und Frauen* (Income Differences Between Men and Women). Vienna, Austria: Fachverlag für Wirtschaft und Technik.

Dun and Bradstreet, Inc. 1981. *The Failure Record*. New York: Dun and Bradstreet, Inc.

Fichman, Mark and Daniel A. Levinthal. 1991. "Honeymoons and the Liability of Adolescence: A New Perspective on Duration Dependence in Social and Organizational Relationships." *Academy of Management Review* 16:442–68.

Freeman, John, Glenn R. Carroll, and Michael T. Hannan. 1983. "The Liability of Newness: Age Dependence in Organizational Death Rates." *American Sociological Review* 48:69–710.

Freeman, John and Michael T. Hannan. 1993. "Niche Width and the Dynamics of Organizational Populations." *American Journal of Sociology* 88:1116–45.

Fritsch, Michael. 1989. "Einzelwirtschaftliche Analyse der Arbeitsplatzdynamik" (Microeconomic Analysis of Job Growth). Paderborn, Germany. Unpublished Manuscript.

Hall, Richard H. 1982. *Organizations: Structure and Process*. 3d ed. Englewood Cliffs, NJ: Prentice-Hall.

Hannan, Michael T. and John Freeman. 1977. "The Population Ecology of Organizations." *American Journal of Sociology* 82:929–64.

—— 1989. *Organizational Ecology*. Cambridge: Harvard University Press.

Hébert, Robert F and Albert N. Link. 1989. "In Search of the Meaning of Entrepreneurship" *Small Business Economics* 1:39–49.

Hunsdiek, Detlef and Eva May-Strobl. 1986. *Entwicklungslinien und Entwicklungrisiken neugegründeter Unternehmen* (Development of Newly Founded Businesses). Stuttgart: Poeschel.

Klandt, Heinz. 1984. *Aktivität und Erfolg des Unternehmensgründers* (Activity and Success of Business Founders). Bergisch-Gladbach: Josef Eul.

Laband, David N. and Bernard F. Lentz. 1985. *The Roots of Success: Why Children Follow in Their Parents' Footsteps*. New York: Praeger.

Lancaster, Tony. 1990. *The Econometric Analysis of Transition Data*. Cambridge, England: Cambridge University Press.

Lawrence, Paul and Jay Lorsch. 1967. *Organization and Environment*. Cambridge: Harvard University Press.

Levinthal, Daniel A. 1991."Random Walks and Organizational Mortality." *Administrative Science Quarterly* 36:397–420.

Light, Ivan. 1979. "Disadvantaged Minorities in Self-Employment." *International Journal of Comparative Sociology* 20:31–45.

March, James G. and Johan P. Olsen. 1976. *Ambiguity and Choice in Organizations*. Bergen: Universitetsforlaget.

Mayer, Kurt B. and Sidney Goldstein. 1961. *The First Two Years: Problems of Small Firms' Growth and Survival*. Washington, DC: Small Business Administration.

McClelland, David C. 1961. *The Achieving Society*. Princeton, NJ: Van Nostrand.

Min, Pyong G. 1984. "From White-Collar Occupations to Small Business: Korean Immigrants' Occupational Adjustment." *Sociological Quarterly* 15:333–52.

Petersen, Trond. 1986. "Estimating Fully Parametric Hazard Rate Models With Time-Dependent Covariates." *Sociological Methods and Research* 14:219–46.

Petersen,Trond. Seymour Spilerman. and Svenn Dahl. 1989. "The Structure of Employment Transitions Among Clerical Employees in a Large Bureaucracy." *Acta Sociologica* 32:319–38.

Pfeffer, Jeffrey and Gerald Salancik. 1978. *The Eternal Control of Organizations: A Resource Dependence Perspective*. New York: Harper and Row.

Picot, Arnold, Ulf-Dieter Laub, and Dietram Schneider. 1989. *Innovative Unternehmensgründungen* (Innovative Business Foundings). Berlin: Springer.

Piore, Michael J. and Charles F. Sabel. 1984. *The Second Industrial Divide: Possibilities for Prosperity*. New York: Basic Books.

Preisendörfer, Peter and Thomas Voss. 1990 "Organizational Mortality of Small Firms: The Effects of Entrepreneurial Age and Human Capital." *Organization Studies* 11:107–29.

Preisendörfer, Peter and Rolf Ziegler. 1990. "Adressenaktualisierung und Feldverlauf einer Studie über Gründung und Erfolg von Kleinbetrieben" (Report on a Study About Small Business Founders) ZUMA-Nachrichten 27:93–109.

Rainnie, Al. 1989. *Industrial Relations in Small Firms: Small Isn't Beautiful*. London: Routledge.

Romanelli, Elaine. 1989. "Environments and Strategies of Organization Start-up: Effects on Early Survival." *Administrative Science Quartely*. 34:369–87.

Scase, Richard and Robert Goffee. 1982. The *Entrepreneurial Middle Class*. London: Croom Helm.

Schüssler, Rudolf and Thomas Voss. 1988. "Bedingungen des Überlebens von Kleinbetrieben" (Conditions of Survival of Small Businesses). Institute of Sociology, Munich, Germany. Unpublished Manuscript.

Schumpeter, Joseph. 1952. *Theorie der wirtschaftlichen Entwicklung* (The Theory of Economic Development). 5th ed. Berlin: Duncker & Humblot.

Sengenberger, Werner and Gary Loveman. 1987. "Smaller Units of Employment" (Discussion Paper No. DP/3/1987). Geneva: International Labour Office.

Singh, Jitendra V. and Charles J. Lumsden. 1990. "Theory and Research in Organizational Ecology". Annual Review of Sociology 16:161–95.

Singh, Jitendra V., David J. Tucker, and Robert J. House. 1986. "Organizational Legitimacy and the Liability of Newness." *Administrative Science Quarterly* 31:171–93.

Steinmetz, George and Erik O. Wright. 1989. "The Fall and Rise of the Petty Bourgeoisie: Changing Patterns of Self-Employment in the Postwar United States." *American Journal of Sociology* 94:973–1018.

Stinchcombe, Arthur L. 1965. "Social Structures and Organizations." Pp. 142–93 in *Handbook of Organizations*, edited by J. G. March. Chicago: Rand McNally.

Szyperski, Norbert and Klaus Nathusius. 1977. *Probleme der Unternehmensgründung* (Problems of Foundings of New Firms). Stuttgart: Poeschel.

Thompson, James D. 1967. *Organizations in Action.*New York: McGraw-Hill.

Tuma, Nancy B. and Michael T. Hannan. 1984. *Social Dynamics*, Orlando: Academic Press.

Willis, Robert J. 1986. "Wage Determinants: A Survey and Reinterpretation of Human Capital Earnings Functions." Pp. 525–602 in *Handbook of Labor Economics*, vol. 1, edited by O. C. Ashenfelder and R. Layard. Amsterdam: North-Holland.

Young, F.W. 1971. "A Macro-Sociological Interpretation of Entrepreneurship." Pp. 139–50 in *Entrepreneurship and Economic Development*, edited by P. Kilby, New York: Free Press.

Young, Ruth and Joe Francis. 1991. "Entrepreneurship and Innovation in Small Manufacturing Firms." *Social Science Quarterly* 72:149–62.

11

Survival of the Fittest? Entrepreneurial Human Capital and the Persistence of Underperforming Firms*

Javier Gimeno, Timothy B. Folta, Arnold C. Cooper and Carolyn Y. Woo[1]

*Source: *Administrative Science Quarterly* 42 (1997), 750–83.

The model developed here explains why some firms survive while other firms with equal economic performance do not. We argue that organizational survival is not strictly a function of economic performance but also depends on a firm's own threshold of performance. We apply this threshold model to the study of new venture survival, in which the threshold is determined by the entrepreneur's human capital characteristics, such as alternative employment opportunities, psychic income from entrepreneurship, and cost of switching to other occupations. Using a sample of 1,547 entrepreneurs of new businesses in the US, we find strong support for the model. The findings suggest that firms with low thresholds may choose to continue or survive despite comparatively low performance.

It has been frequently argued that, at least in the long run, well-performing organizations survive while poorly performing ones disappear (Alchian, 1950; Friedman, 1953; Winter, 1964; Williamson, 1991). Penrose (1952: 810) summarized this theoretical view as stating that "positive profits can be treated as the criterion of natural selection – the firms that make profits are selected or 'adopted' by the environment, others are rejected and disappear." This view implies a unidimensional relationship between economic performance (defined as the economic returns to residual claimants) and survival, since the firms most likely to discontinue are those that perform the worst. From this unidimensional model, it follows that economic performance and survival should have the same determinants or predictors. Interestingly, mounting empirical evidence suggests that the determinants of performance and survival may substantially differ (Blau, 1984; Carroll and Huo, 1986; Meyer and Zucker, 1989; Kalleberg and Leicht, 1991;

Levinthal, 1991) and that factors other than performance may play a systematic role in the survival of organizations. This paper proposes a theoretical reconciliation of apparently conflicting empirical findings about the determinants of performance and survival. Our framework explains the persistence of underperforming firms and identifies predictors of such conditions.

We depart from the unidimensional model of performance and survival by arguing that organizational survival is determined by two main dimensions: (1) the organization's economic performance and (2) the organization's threshold of performance. The threshold of performance is the level of performance below which the dominant organizational constituents will act to dissolve the organization. This implies that survival is not strictly a function of economic performance, but performance relative to a firm-specific threshold. This simple elaboration, we believe, has profound consequences for theoretical and empirical research on organizational performance and survival. For example, by identifying how thresholds differ systematically across firms, we can explain why, given the same level of performance, some firms exit (discontinue operations) while others do not. We emphasize the internal attributes of the organization and, in particular, the human capital attributes of owners of new ventures, as determinants of thresholds. By considering organizational exit as a choice, our focus on organizational mortality complements existing literature in population ecology, where exit is seen as being forced by environmental conditions hostile to the firm.

Exit, performance, and the threshold of performance

Our main thesis is that organizations differ in their thresholds of performance, and exit or survival is determined by whether economic performance falls below or stays above that specific threshold. While thresholds may be shaped by the multiple voluntary participants in the organization (Barnard, 1938; Simon, 1945; Aoki, 1984), the inducements and contributions of most participants are regulated through a nexus of contracts with owners. Accordingly, it is the owners' interests, as residual claimants, that are most closely tied to the economic performance of the organization (Alchian and Demsetz, 1972; Meyer and Zucker, 1989). The willingness or ability to withstand poor performance is partly determined by the mobility of the assets and resources controlled by the organization's owners. When owners with a residual claim over these resources have alternative uses for these resources, they can liquidate the firm for a reasonable value. Consequently, they may prefer to dissolve the firm when those alternatives become more appealing (Barnard, 1938; Caves and Porter, 1976; Porter, 1976). Exit, however, would not be rational at the first sign of low performance (Brüderl and Schüssler, 1990). If there is uncertainty about future payoffs, owners may be willing to accept low levels of performance with the hope that conditions will improve (Dixit and Pindyck, 1994). A firm's ability to withstand short periods of low performance should also be partly determined by buffers of accumulated resources, such as organizational slack (Cyert and March, 1963) or initial capital endowments and established relationships (Brüderl and Schüssler, 1990; Fichman and Levinthal, 1991; Levinthal, 1991). Organizations would be able to survive at least until their original resources were depleted.

Thresholds of performance may also be influenced when owners have objectives other than, or in addition to, the maximization of economic returns to their equity. Owners may seek "amenity potential" from their businesses – gaining utility from being able to influence the type of goods produced by the firm (Demsetz and Lehn, 1985: 203). For owners of professional sports teams or media companies (newspapers, TV), winning the World Series or believing that one is systematically influencing public opinion plausibly provides utility even if profit is reduced from levels otherwise achievable. For owners of family-owned businesses, the firm may not only be a source of income but also a context for family activity and embodiment of its pride and identity (Meyer and Zucker, 1989: 78).

Low organizational performance also puts the interests of owners and other organizational constituencies (non-owners) in direct conflict (Meyer and Zucker, 1989). While owners may want to terminate the business to re-deploy assets in a more profitable arena, non-owner participants (managers, employees) who have developed firm-specific skills may stand to lose if the firm closes. With significant cost of exit, non-owners may thus exercise their voice (Hirschman, 1970) through efforts to influence the decision-making structures of the organization. Thus, the threshold level of performance would also be determined by the relative organizational influence of non-owner members. Firms in which non-owner members exercise substantial organizational influence may remain in business at low levels of economic performance despite a preference by owners to terminate the business (Meyer and Zucker, 1989). In addition to internal constituents such as employees, external constituents (debt-holders, customers, suppliers, government and community organizations) may persuade low-performing but legitimate organizations to survive (as in the bailout of Lockheed and Chrysler by the US government) or well-performing but illegitimate ones to dissolve (such as cartels, trusts, or local businesses posing environmental or social threats) by applying direct co-optation (Pfeffer and Salancik, 1978) or institutional (coercive and normative) pressures (Meyer and Rowan, 1977; DiMaggio and Powell, 1983). Thus, institutional embeddedness (Baum and Oliver, 1991), legitimacy, and co-optation by external organizations may also keep organizations alive despite low performance.

Contrast with existing views on organizational performance and mortality

Our model of thresholds of performance provides a causal link between the concepts of performance and organizational survival without assuming that they are unidimensional constructs. Clearly, higher economic performance increases the likelihood of survival, everything else remaining equal. Our point is that other things are not equal, since differences in firms' thresholds of performance should also influence mortality. Organizational survival is therefore influenced by both the determinants of performance and thresholds. Certain variables will be purely related to economic performance, while others may influence survival only through the firm's threshold. For variables that simultaneously influence performance and threshold, their survival effect is determined by their combined effects on both.

Our paper complements theories of decision making, both at the individual (Kahneman and Tversky, 1979) and the organizational level (Cyert and March, 1963; March, 1988; March and Shapira, 1992), which posit that decision-making choices are determined by comparing possible outcomes relative to some reference or aspiration level. Viewing organizational discontinuance as an individual (in the case of small ventures run by an entrepreneur) or organizational choice, one may equate reference or aspiration levels to our threshold construct. From that perspective, this is the first paper we know of that links organizational survival and exit to some reference level.

Our theoretical perspective is also complementary to a large body of management research, mainly in population ecology, that has examined the same issue we address, firm mortality (see reviews by Baum, 1996; Amburgey and Rao, 1996). Population ecology studies have not been explicit, however, in recognizing whether firm mortality is mediated by low performance or other mechanisms.[2] The popular use of the term "organizational failure" (Baum, 1996) seems to imply that discontinuance is primarily attributable to low performance, even though prominent scholars in population ecology (Hannan and Freeman, 1977: 940) and institutional theory (Meyer and Rowan, 1977: 353) have explicitly rejected a unidimensional interpretation of environmental selection based solely on organizational efficiency. Meyer and Zucker (1989: 55) suggested that these literatures view organizational performance and discontinuance as multiple indicators of an organization's isomorphism with its environment. Such an approach, unfortunately, avoids the causal link between these constructs and has hindered progress, since "researchers' understanding of dissolution, be it through merger, absorption, or outright failure, is limited by the dearth of studies that treat financial performance as a predictor of mortality" (Amburgey and Rao, 1996: 1274). Thus, our theoretical perspective complements and extends current organizational theories in that it explicitly recognizes the causal effect of firm performance on selection processes while also considering the selection effects of thresholds.

Exit, performance, and thresholds in new ventures

While the concept of threshold has broad applicability, a narrower context of study can facilitate theoretical development, empirical specification, and testing the determinants of threshold in that specific context. This paper investigates performance, thresholds, and exit in the specific context of small entrepreneurial new ventures. Entrepreneurial exit decisions occur frequently, with more than 800,000 businesses discontinued in the United States in 1992 alone (US Small Business Administration, 1994: 265). Understanding the processes that influence new venture survival has tremendous implications for the welfare of customers, suppliers, employees, and especially for entrepreneurs. Applying the concept of the threshold of performance enables us to broaden the current understanding of entrepreneurial exit by considering both economic performance and non-performance reasons for exit. Ronstadt (1986) discovered that only 31 per cent of entrepreneurs who exited did so solely because of financial difficulties, while 26 per cent indicated that financial reasons played no part in their exit decisions. Mayer and Goldstein (1961) found that 20 per cent of all new business closures were attributed to non-financial reasons, such as external job opportunities, disappointment with business ownership, or unwillingness to put up with "limited success." At least in some cases, dissolution is not forced upon the entrepreneur but involves a proactive decision to exit.

Recent studies have also found empirical evidence suggesting that factors influencing the survival of new ventures may be significantly different from those influencing performance (Carroll and Huo, 1986; Kalleberg and Leicht, 1991; Cooper, Gimeno, and Woo, 1994). Up to now, there have been few attempts to reconcile theoretically the lack of convergence on the determinants of performance and survival. We believe that considering economic performance and thresholds jointly will shed light on this important topic.

The context of entrepreneurship requires a special consideration of the determinants of performance and thresholds. In small entrepreneurial firms, the entrepreneur is likely to exert control over organizational decisions, and non-owners therefore are less influential than in larger or older firms, where there is a separation of ownership and control (Meyer and Zucker, 1989). Moreover, the organizational contributions of the owner to the venture are not limited to founding capital but also include managerial and technical work and skills. In that sense, when determining whether to continue support for the venture, the entrepreneur will evaluate the joint returns to both the financial and human resources contributed to the venture. Since the entrepreneur's skills and objectives play a dominant role in dictating the direction of newly founded businesses (Brüderl, Preisendörfer, and Ziegler, 1992), we focus here on how the entrepreneur's traits and characteristics, or human capital, influence the performance threshold.

A threshold model of entrepreneurial exit: human capital considerations

Human capital theory (Becker, 1975) uses economic logic to study individual decisions dealing with investments in productivity-enhancing skills and knowledge (schooling, training, firm-specific knowledge investment), career choices (decision to work, switching employment, labor mobility), and other work characteristics (wages, reservation wages, hours of work). It is believed that individuals choose an occupation or employment that maximizes the present value of economic and psychic benefits over their lifetimes. Human capital theorists have likened the entrepreneurial exit decision to the more general case of an individual's decision to leave current employment (Evans and Leighton, 1989; Evans and Jovanovic, 1989; Campbell, 1995; Bates, 1995). Entrepreneurs can be viewed as choosing between remaining in the current venture or obtaining alternative employment. While several studies have examined entrepreneurial exit with human capital theory (Bates, 1985, 1990; Preisendörfer and Voss, 1990; Brüderl, Preisendörfer, and Ziegler, 1992), by assuming that the factors related to poor performance will be the same as those influencing exit, they have ignored the potential for returns to the entrepreneur's human capital in alternative settings. Others have theoretically acknowledged the importance of alternative uses of human capital in entrepreneurial decision making (Evans and Jovanovic, 1989; Evans and Leighton, 1989; Bates, 1995; Campbell, 1995) but have focused on how human capital influences entry, not exit.

Expectations for ventures are generally buoyant in the early start-up stage, being generally formed under substantial uncertainty about market acceptance, competitive responses, or even the entrepreneur's actual entrepreneurial abilities and satisfaction to be obtained from the venture. As information becomes available, the entrepreneur is likely to examine the efficacy of these expectations and reconsider other options (Jovanovic, 1982). We would expect the entrepreneur to terminate the business if the expected utility of alternative employment (U_A) minus the cost inherent in switching (SC) exceeds the revised expected utility of remaining in the entrepreneurial venture U_E):

discontinue venture if: $U_E < (U_A - SC)$.　　　　　　　　(1)

U_E and U_A differ because of unequal economic performance and personal enjoyment, or psychic income Becker, 1975; Evans and Leighton, 1989), with the two options. The economic performance depends in part on the entrepreneur's previous investments in education and training, which may provide general skills or skills specific to a particular job context (Becker, 1975). The entrepreneur's economic performance (EP_E) is a function of his or her stock of general human capital, represented by the vector x_1, and of the human capital specific to the current business, represented by the vector x_2. Meanwhile, since specific skills cannot be transferred to alternative employment, the economic returns available in alternative employment opportunities (EP_A) are a function of the stock of general human capital (x_1) and of human capital specific to the alternative occupation (x_3), but not of the human capital specific to the current business (x_2). The individual's psychic income associated with either the entrepreneurial venture (PI_E) or alternative employment (PI_A) is influenced by a number of factors (respectively, x_4 and x_5), including the individual's preference for the occupation, or personal satisfaction (Evans and Leighton, 1989).

Thus, the utilities of entrepreneurship and alternative employment can be expressed as:

$$U_E = EP_E (x_1, x_2) + PI_E (x_4).$$ (2a)

$$U_A = EP_A (x_1, x_3) + PI_A (x_5).$$ (2b)

The cost inherent in switching (SC) includes those costs, usually transitory, that are a function of the expected economic cost of searching for a new alternative and the psychological cost of experiencing the uncertainty of job loss. Factors influencing the cost of switching are captured by the vector x_6. These costs should not be confounded with the potential loss of utility experienced by switching because of lower personal enjoyment in the new alternative or an inability to re-deploy skills specific to the venture, which are already captured in the relative magnitudes of psychic income and specific human capital. Substituting equations (2a) and (2b) into equation (1) and isolating EP_E on the left-hand side, leads to:
discontinue venture if:

$$EP_E (x_1, x_2) < EP_A (x_1, x_3) + PI_A (x_5) - PI_E (x_4) - SC (x_6).$$ (3)

The right-hand side of equation (3) is the threshold of economic performance required to sustain the entrepreneur's involvement in the current venture (T_E). Thus, the threshold (T_E) is determined by the expected economic returns available in other employment alternatives (EP_A), the difference in psychic income between alternative employment and self-employment ($PI_A - PI_E$), and the cost of switching to an alternative occupation (SC). The model predicts that the entrepreneur will discontinue or stay in business according to the following rule:

$$\begin{cases} \text{discontinue venture if} & EP_E (x_1, x_2) < T_E (x_1, x_3, x_4, x_5, x_6) \\ \text{stay in venture (survive) if} & EP_E (x_1, x_2) \geq T_E (x_1, x_3, x_4, x_5, x_6) \end{cases} \quad (4)$$

A critical insight that follows from the above model is that there may be situations in which entrepreneurs do not continue their business even though, in terms of economic performance, they are better off than other entrepreneurs. They may take this action because of the opportunity costs associated with staying in business – their level of education and training may warrant more attractive economic returns in alternative employment opportunities. Similarly, a poorly performing venture may continue because of the entrepreneur's lack of other attractive options, strong psychic attachment to the venture, or high costs associated with switching into new employment. As these cases illustrate, economic performance of the venture need not exclusively determine survival. Rather, it is economic performance relative to the threshold that drives the exit decision.

Hypotheses

From the threshold model illustrated in Figure 11.1, we develop hypotheses that predict how four important dimensions of the human capital of an entrepreneur – general human capital (x_1), human capital specific to the current venture (x_2), psychic income from entrepreneurship (x_4), and switching costs (x_6) – influence entrepreneurial exit by their separate effects on economic performance and threshold of performance. We do not develop hypotheses about the effects of human capital specific to alternative occupations (x_3) or psychic income from alternative occupations (x_5), since we cannot determine a priori what those alternatives are. Alternative employment opportunities are nearly infinite and may include wage-earning positions, other self-employment activities, or leisure activity. To the extent that these alternative employment opportunities cannot be fully specified ex ante, we assume a generic alternative, letting the effect of (x_3) and (x_5) be included in the error term of the threshold equation.

General human capital

The simple model presented in equation (4) generates several theoretical insights and empirical predictions, General human capital (x_1), as measured by such constructs as formal education and the prior work experience of the entrepreneur, may lead to skills that are useful across a wide range of occupational alternatives (Becker, 1975). Work experience is commonly measured as the number of years of experience but may also be signalled by achievement levels in employment, such as management or supervisory experience (Bates, 1990). While increasing levels of education and experience are likely to elevate economic performance (EP_E), they will also broaden the opportunity set of the entrepreneurs and raise their expected income from alternative employment (EP_A). Thus, while entrepreneurs with general skills may perform better in self-employment, they would also have higher performance requirements to remain in business. How general human capital influences survival will depend on its relative payoff in the venture versus alternative employment. Evans and Leighton (1989) found that business experience had about the same returns in wage work and self-employment, while education had greater returns in self-employment. A study by Fujii and Hawley (1991) revealed that self-employment had slightly lower returns associated with both experience and education than

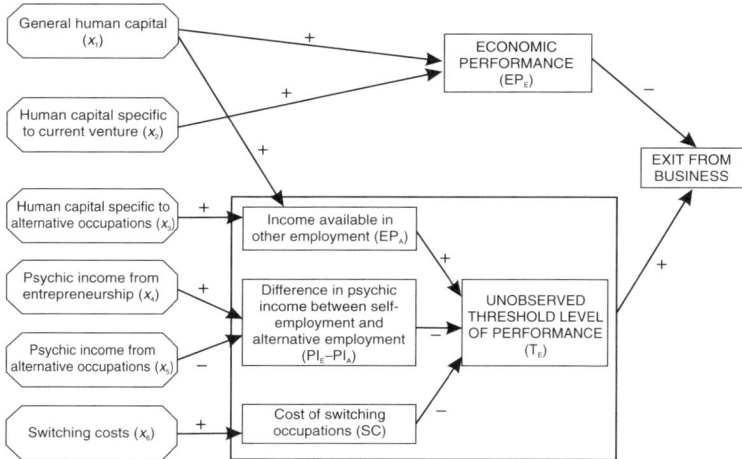

Figure 11.1 Threshold model of entrepreneurial exit: human capital considerations.

wage work, but they did not test to see if these differences were significant. Because there is a lack of consensus on the relative payoff of work experience and education, we hypothesize that the net effect of general human capital on entrepreneurial exit is indeterminate a priori:

> *Hypothesis 1 (H1)*   General human capital will be positively related to the economic performance of the venture and also to the entrepreneur's threshold level of performance. Hence, a priori, general human capital has an indeterminate effect on the likelihood of exit.

Human capital specific to the current venture

Specific human capital results from education, training, or experience that has a limited scope of applicability. Investments in specific human capital create value in a particular business context but do not have relevance in alternative occupations. Therefore, while human capital specific to the venture raises performance, it has no influence on entrepreneurs' threshold of performance. The implication is that individuals whose human capital is more specific to the venture would be less mobile (Becker, 1975). A measure of specific human capital is an entrepreneur's knowledge of customers, suppliers, products, and services within the context of the venture (x_2). This should be directly related to the degree of similarity between the new venture and the organization where the entrepreneur had previously worked. This knowledge may be critical to success, conferring a favorable asymmetry between the entrepreneurs who have been exposed to it and those who have not (Sandberg, 1986; Cooper, Gimeno, and Woo, 1994). In addition, similarity between the new venture and the prior experience may mean that the entrepreneur can build on prior relationships with relevant stakeholders and thus minimize the "liability of newness" (Stinchcombe, 1965, Aldrich and Auster, 1986). Yet such knowledge and ties largely lose their value outside of their original context.

To the extent that human capital specific to the venture raises performance (EP_E) but has no effect on performance in alternative occupations (EP_A), and therefore on the threshold (T_E), it should be negatively related to entrepreneurial exit:

> *Hypothesis 2 (H2)*   Specific human capital will be positively related to the economic performance of the venture but should have no influence on the entrepreneur's threshold level of performance. As a result, specific human capital should be negatively related to the likelihood of exit.

Hypotheses 1 and 2 assume that specific and general human capital can be measured separately. In other contexts, it may be easier to measure an individual's overall level of human capital and the degree to which such overall capital is general or specific, maybe as a ratio or a subjective evaluation. In those cases, we would expect lower thresholds for entrepreneurs with a greater ratio of specificity in their human capital, since general human capital increases thresholds while specific human capital does not. This prediction is comparable to our earlier argument that organizations (entrepreneurs) with less mobile resources (human capital) should be more willing to withstand low performance.

Psychic income from entrepreneurship

The probability of exit will also be negatively related to the psychic income, or personal satisfaction the entrepreneur derives from self-employment (x_4). Considerable research indicates that many entrepreneurs are motivated, at least in part, by non-economic goals, including satisfaction from the autonomy of self-employment or from doing the type of work they like (Smith and Miner, 1983; Lafuente and Salas, 1989). Entrepreneurs may also be personally attached to entrepreneurial activities if their parents were self-employed (Evans and Leighton, 1989; Brüiderl, Preisendörfer, and Ziegler, 1992). Since parents are seen as role models, it has been reasoned that people growing up in such families perceive entrepreneurship to be a more viable career than those without such a family background (Shapero and Giglierano, 1982). Therefore, entrepreneurs who have an intrinsic motivation for the activity or who come from entrepreneurial families are likely to obtain a higher psychic income from entrepreneurship (PI_E) than those who do not have those backgrounds and motivations. Accordingly, the threshold level of performance (T_E) is lower for such entrepreneurs, indicating that they may be willing to accept lower economic returns to gain personal satisfaction from the venture. Because a psychic attachment to the venture lowers the threshold level of performance, while having no apparent effect on the economic performance of the venture, we expect these factors to have a negative effect on the likelihood of exit:

> *Hypothesis 3 (H3)*   High psychic income from entrepreneurship should have no influence on the economic performance of the venture but should decrease the entrepreneur's threshold level of performance. As a result, higher levels of psychic income from entrepreneurship should be negatively related to the likelihood of exit.

Switching costs

Finally, the probability of entrepreneurial exit will be negatively related to the costs of switching to new employment (x_6). These costs are defined as the costs inherent in the act of switching between two alternative occupations and do not include the difference in returns in those alternative occupations. This definition reflects the efforts and expenses the individual would need to undertake in job searches and retraining, as well as the psychic costs of not knowing whether a suitable job can be found. Older people have less time to recoup the costs associated with switching jobs and thus are likely to perceive lower benefits from switching. Consistent with this view, Mincer (1974) found a tendency for investments in training to be concentrated at younger ages and to continue at a diminishing rate throughout much of a person's working life. Since employers may need to train and develop their employees, they are also more likely to prefer younger candidates, to maximize the return from their investment. Evidence suggests that older job seekers are more likely than younger ones to take more time to find a job (Shrieves, 1995) and less likely to find jobs eventually (Bortnick and Ports, 1993). For these reasons, it is expected that older entrepreneurs will be less willing to switch occupations. The existence of switching costs should decrease the threshold level of performance (T_E) and therefore decrease the likelihood of exit. This expectation was supported by the in-depth case studies of Mayer and Goldstein (1961), who found that concern about job seeking at an older age was a major reason why older entrepreneurs would continue their involvement with new businesses with marginal economic performance.

By serving as a proxy for general human capital, age may also be linked to the monetary performance of the venture (Preisendörfer and Voss, 1990). After controlling for general and specific human capital levels (hypotheses 1 and 2), however, we do not expect older entrepreneurs to perform differently from younger ones. We expect age to affect exit only through its influence on the threshold level of performance, not through economic performance:

Hypothesis 4 (H4) Factors associated with an entrepreneur's cost of switching to alternative occupations should have no influence on economic performance of the venture but should decrease the entrepreneur's threshold level of performance, As a result, higher levels of switching costs should be negatively related to the likelihood of exit.

Other influences

There are some important human capital variables that may measure a combination of general human capital, specific human capital, psychic income, or switching costs. For example, entrepreneurs with previous venture start-up or ownership experience may be endowed with human capital that is valuable in new venture situations because they have experience in the start-up process and in running their own business. This experience may not be as valuable in alternatives that include work in established firms. At the same time, owners with prior entrepreneurial experience may be psychologically attracted by the thrill of start-up and thus may decide to quit and start another venture unless current performance is high.

Another important characteristic of entrepreneurs is the number of jobs previously held. People who have been in more job settings are likely to gain general human capital that can be applied across a number of alternatives. At the same time, however, many job changes may signal that the individual was forced out of those jobs because of poor performance or low degrees of general human capital. Thus, a moderate number of jobs may be the strongest indicator of general human capital. In addition, entrepreneurs who have changed jobs frequently in the past may face lower switching costs. While job switching is associated with substantial stress (Mobley, 1977), those who have experienced it in the past may be better able to draw on "scripted behavior" that enables them to deal with the stress of job search (Lee and Mitchell, 1994). Thus, the number of jobs previously held by the entrepreneur may signal both general human capital and switching costs.

Our hypotheses are summarized in Table 11.1, which shows the expected effects of the variables included in our model.

Research design

Testing the effect of human capital on thresholds of performance in new entrepreneurial ventures requires finding a sample of new ventures in which the entrepreneurs are making substantial commitments, so that the decision to exit is not trivial. This suggests that the ventures should be primarily full-time, or with the potential to become full-time businesses, and that there should be significant investment involved, so that the decision to exit may involve a careful consideration of the income available from different alternatives and not merely a reaction to immediate pressures.

The samples used in the studies noted in the literature review are not

Table 11.1 Hypothesized impact of independent variables on performance, threshold of performance, and exit

Variable	Economic performance	Threshold of performance			Overall impact on threshold	Exit
		Impact on economic performance in alternative employment	Impact on psychic income from entrepreneurship	Impact on cost of switching		
General human capital (H1)						
Formal education	+	+	0	0	+	?
Management experience	+	+	0	0	+	?
Supervisory experience	+	+	0	0	+	?
Specific human capital (H2)						
Similar business	+	0	0	0	0	—
Psychic income (H3)						
Intrinsic motivation	0	0	+	0	—	—
Parents owned a business	0	0	+	0	—	—
Switching costs (H4)						
Age of entrepreneur	0	0	0	+	—	—

adequate for testing our theory. The 1982 Characteristics of Business Owners (CBO) sample (Bates, 1990) and the Munich Founder Study sample (Brüderl, Preisendörfer, and Ziegler, 1992) lack information about specific human capital and performance, respectively, which are critical variables in our study. The National Longitudinal Survey of Young Men (Evans and Leighton, 1989) lacks information about the business owned by the entrepreneur and provides a large enough sample size to study determinants of entrepreneurial entry, but not exit.

The sample we used includes new members of the National Federation of Independent Business (NFIB), the largest US small business trade association. NFIB members tend to have organizations with separate business addresses, full-time founders, and significant investment. For the sample, 82.2 per cent of all entrepreneurs had no part-time or full-time jobs outside of the venture, and virtually all put in more than thirty hours per week and grossed more than $25,000 in the first year. The organizations sampled at the time of the initial survey had a mean of 5.04 employees (median of three employees), and only 13.2 per cent had one full-time employee or fewer (including the entrepreneur). Their median and modal investments at the time of their first sales were between $20,000 and $50,000.

Although sampling from a trade association with voluntary membership raises concerns of self-selection and representativeness of the population, representativeness is a slippery concept when new ventures might be defined and identified in different ways (Birley, 1984; Aldrich et al., 1989). In a preliminary comparison of our sample with other probability samples (1982 CBO, Munich Founder Study data, 1985 Statistics of Income), we found no fatal biases in the distribution of revenues, employment size, industry membership, and path to ownership, although it was apparent that the NFIB sample included fewer part-time entrepreneurs than either the 1982 CBO or the Munich data. Whether the sample is representative of full-time new businesses in the United States is difficult to discern, because there are no comparable data on the population of all new full-time businesses. The fruitfulness of this study, however, does not depend on whether the sample is fully representative. The aim is not to try to determine the precise mortality rate for all new firms but, rather, to examine the effect and implications of firm thresholds on organizational survival. We view the current analysis as illustrative rather than definitive (Sutton and Staw, 1995) and encourage further replication in samples specifically collected for this purpose.

Sample

In May 1985, we sent approximately 13,000 questionnaires to members of the National Federation of Independent Business (using the NFIB address lists) who reported that they had "been in business" for eighteen months or less. We focused on entrepreneurs who had recently become owner-managers, so that relevant facts associated with start-up would still be fresh in their minds. We had previously pre-tested the survey instrument with 154 members of the NFIB and altered it to improve clarity. We received completed surveys from 4,814 entrepreneurs (37 per cent response rate), and we sent them follow-up questionnaires in May 1986 and May 1987. In the three years of the study, each survey round involved an initial mailing and two follow-up reminders. For the second and third years the response rates, calculated as a percentage of those businesses not known to have been discontinued or sold, were 47 and 39 per cent, respectively. The 4,814 firms represent a broad range of industries and all geographic areas of the United States.

Determining the status (surviving, sold, or discontinued) of a firm involved several steps. If a questionnaire was not returned in the second or third years, we sent a letter to the business with an enclosed postcard, asking the owner to indicate whether the business was still in operation, was sold, or was discontinued. If we received no response, we consulted the NFIB membership records, in which the field agents of the NFIB report whether businesses (whether they continued as NFIB members or not) had discontinued or survived. We did not use the NFIB records as our primary data source, however, because the field representatives visit each business only once each year, so that, on the average, the data are six months old. Finally, if none of the above sources indicated the status of the firm, we noted if the post office reported that the mail could not be delivered.

The responses to the first questionnaire indicated that some of the businesses were, in fact, older than the NFIB records indicated, with some having been started or acquired in 1982 or earlier. For the 4,814 respondents, we were able to determine the month in which they had become owner-managers for 1983, 1984, and 1985 (4,103 ventures), while we could not verify the exact year of founding for those organizations started in "1982 or before" (711 ventures). Because our original sample had targeted new businesses, we eliminated those older businesses that had been erroneously sampled. We also eliminated from the sample those with missing or non-valid values for the independent variables for 1985 (488 ventures). This left 3,615 firms with valid responses to the first questionnaire in the sample.

A second round of sample selection was based on the data available at the end of the third year. We maintained in the sample those firms that either had survived and responded to the third-year survey (936 observations) or were known to have discontinued by that time (611 observations). We had to eliminate those ventures that did not return the third-year survey and could not be identified as discontinued or sold (1,897 firms). We also eliminated those firms that had been sold by the third year 171 ventures). Thus, the final sample consists of 1,547 firms.

The decision to eliminate sold businesses was both theoretically grounded and supported by substantial sensitivity analysis. Sold businesses differ from discontinued businesses in that the owner may receive a premium over the liquidation value of the firm. Thus, we believe that the choice to sell may be different from discontinuing and that the two choices should not be pooled. We conducted two statistical tests based on a multinomial logit specification of the choice problem (survived, discontinued, sold) to determine whether it was appropriate either to (a) pool sold firms with those that discontinued or (b) eliminate sold firms from the sample. To examine (a), we used a log-likelihood ratio test to compare whether the vector of coefficients specific to the discontinued choice (relative to survived) were equal to the vector of coefficients specific to the sold choice (relative to survived). This test revealed that there was a statistically significant difference between the vectors of coefficients ($\chi^2 = 76.594$; d.f. $= 33$; $p < .0001$) and implied that discontinued and sold firms should not be pooled. The Small and Hsiao (1985) Independence of Irrelevant Alternatives (IIA) test showed that the coefficients specific to the discontinued and survived choices were unaffected by eliminating sold firms ($\chi^2 = 1.7748$; d.f. $= 33$; $p < .9999$). Given the results in both tests, and to preserve consistency with our theoretical model, we felt justified in eliminating sold firms from the analysis.

We examined the possibility of sample selection bias by comparing our final sample (1,547 observations) with those observations that we eliminated because they were sold or did not respond to the final survey (2,068 observations). We compared independent and control variables across these sets of firms using tests of differences of means (*t*-tests) for continuous variables and cross-tabs tests of independence (chi-squared tests) for categorical variables. The only significant differences between these groups were that entrepreneurs in the final sample had more education ($p < .001$), operated businesses of larger scope, were more likely to be in professional service industries, and were less likely to be in personal service industries. While this may indicate a slight sample selection bias, the magnitude of this problem does not seem to be great.

The period of time when the businesses in the sample were initiated (1983 to 1985) was characterized by a slightly lower index of net new business formations in the U.S. than for the whole decade of the 1980s (19.9 vs. 122.1, in an index for which 1967 = 100). Net formations hit their decade low in 1982 and were slowly on the rebound. The period of time for which we recorded the exits from these businesses (1986 and 1987) was characterized by a relatively high failure rate (per 10,000 concerns) compared with the whole decade of the 1980s (111 vs. 91), with 1986 being the peak of business failures for the decade (US Bureau of the Census, 1996: 543). Thus, the study period might be characterized as a slightly unfavorable period for entrepreneurs, which, while it may increase the baseline rate of exit in our sample, should not affect the coefficients of the independent variables in any systematic way.

Dependent variables

The theoretical model posits that the venture's economic performance and the entrepreneur's threshold jointly determine entrepreneurial exit. While threshold is not observable, it can be derived from comparisons of two observable outcomes: economic performance and venture discontinuance. When firms have equal economic performance, the incidence of exit can be attributed to differences in thresholds. Thus, economic performance and exit constitute the observed dependent variables in the empirical analysis.

$Exit_n$, a binary variable, represents the exit decision of firm n (0 if the firm continued, 1 if it was discontinued). For those firms that survived and returned the 1987 questionnaire, economic performance is represented by the amount of money (in the form of salaries, perquisites, and dividends) the entrepreneur withdrew from the venture during the third year. We lost a large number of observations as a result of nonresponse to the 1987 questionnaire, and data were not gathered on money withdrawn during either of the first two years. For firms in the final sample, however, *money taken out* represents the overall returns to the entrepreneur for both the financial and human capital invested in the venture and therefore is consistent with our theoretical focus on the economic performance for the owner. Money taken out was reported as being within a range between predetermined bounds (e.g., from $10,000 to $15,000).

Money taken out has the disadvantage of not reflecting the extent to which an entrepreneur may choose to accept lower current benefits to support greater organizational growth. In practice, distinguishing between economic returns to investment (financial and human capital) and reinvestment intensity is problematic in the study of new ventures because this distinction hinges on sophisticated accounting concepts (accounting profits, depreciation, investment versus expense, retained earnings) seldom used in small businesses, which tend to use the cash method. It may be that reinvestment intensities substantially differ by industry, in which case the industry control dummies may partial out this effect. Below, we discuss the results in light of this potential weakness and conclude that the results do not appear to be biased by it.

Independent variables

Measures for the independent variables introduced in earlier discussions are listed in Appendix A, while Table 11.2 presents descriptive statistics and correlations for the independent and control variables in the entire sample, Because we could only identify the level of education (nine

Table 11.2 Descriptive statistics and Pearson correlation coefficients*

Variable	Mean	S.D.	1	2	3	4	5	6	7	8	9
1. Formal education	0.42	0.31									
2. Management experience	0.13	0.33	0.17								
3. Supervisory experience	0.40	0.49	-0.03	-0.31							
4. Similar business	0.46	0.39	-0.03	-0.01	0.02						
5. Intrinsic motivation	0.01	0.99	0.03	-0.03	0.07	-0.05					
6. Parents owned business	0.45	0.50	0.05	-0.02	-0.02	-0.01	0.00				
7. Age of entrepreneur	36.65	9.35	-0.02	0.13	-0.14	-0.09	0.08	-0.06			
8. 1 prior job (vs. none)	0.09	0.29	0.10	0.04	0.01	0.05	-0.02	0.02	-0.16		
9. 2 prior jobs (vs. none)	0.17	0.37	0.06	0.00	-0.02	0.03	0.04	0.02	-0.08	-0.14	
10. 3 or 4 prior jobs (vs. none)	0.34	0.47	0.03	0.05	0.03	-0.02	-0.05	-0.04	-0.02	-0.23	-0.32
11. 5+ prior jobs (vs. none)	0.36	0.48	-0.15	-0.06	0.00	0.01	0.05	0.01	0.22	-0.24	-0.33
12. Entrepreneurial experience	0.25	0.44	-0.04	-0.22	-0.48	0.09	-0.07	0.07	0.16	-0.07	0.01
13. Hours worked per week	56.83	16.25	-0.07	0.04	-0.01	0.11	-0.03	0.01	-0.05	-0.07	0.00
14. Outside job	0.14	0.30	-0.08	-0.04	0.04	-0.17	0.00	0.03	0.00	0.04	-0.04
15. Initial capital (log)	10.04	1.21	0.14	0.14	-0.11	-0.03	-0.07	0.00	0.12	0.02	0.01
16. Number of employees (log)	1.16	0.85	0.11	0.18	-0.08	0.12	-0.17	-0.01	0.07	-0.03	-0.01
17. Acquired business	0.29	0.45	-0.01	0.01	-0.04	-0.11	0.01	0.03	0.05	0.00	0.01
18. Inherited business	0.02	0.13	0.03	-0.05	0.05	-0.02	-0.06	0.11	-0.08	-0.03	0.06
19. Radius of business sales	22.39	27.44	0.05	0.06	-0.03	0.11	-0.02	0.03	0.09	-0.06	0.01
20. Months in business (log)	2.55	0.56	0.05	0.05	-0.01	0.06	0.01	0.01	0.04	0.00	0.02
21. Informational ties	0.49	0.20	-0.02	0.00	0.03	0.10	-0.07	0.07	-0.09	0.00	0.03
22. Industry – construction	0.09	0.29	-0.03	0.01	0.01	0.16	-0.05	0.02	-0.03	-0.04	-0.01
23. Industry – manufacturing	0.08	0.28	0.00	0.03	0.02	0.05	-0.01	0.01	0.04	0.00	-0.02

continued on next page

Table 11.2 Descriptive statistics and Pearson correlation coefficients* (cont.)

Variable	Mean	S.D.	1	2	3	4	5	6	7	8	9
24. Industry – transportation	0.02	0.15	0.00	0.01	0.01	0.03	-0.03	0.03	0.01	0.00	-0.02
25. Industry – wholesale	0.05	0.21	0.02	0.00	-0.01	0.03	-0.05	0.00	0.04	-0.04	0.02
26. Industry – agriculture	0.02	0.15	0.11	-0.01	-0.03	0.05	-0.03	0.09	-0.04	0.11	0.01
27. Industry – financial services	0.05	0.21	0.07	0.01	-0.03	0.06	0.01	0.01	0.03	0.01	0.09
28. Industry – personal services	0.17	0.38	-0.13	-0.02	-0.03	-0.04	0.02	0.01	-0.01	-0.02	-0.01
29. Industry – professional services	0.07	0.26	0.32	0.03	0.02	0.10	0.14	-0.06	-0.04	0.04	0.01
30. Environmental dynamism	0.74	1.07	0.04	0.06	-0.01	0.05	-0.03	0.03	-0.06	-0.02	-0.03
31. Growth in GSP	0.08	0.11	-0.06	0.00	-0.02	-0.01	-0.03	-0.05	0.01	-0.02	-0.01
32. Change in competitors	0.51	0.92	0.11	0.03	0.01	0.02	0.00	0.02	0.02	-0.01	0.00

Variable	10	11	12	13	14	15	16	17	18	19	20
11. 5+ prior jobs (vs. none)	-0.54										
12. Entrepreneurial experience	-0.05	0.10									
13. Hours worked per week	-0.05	0.10	0.07								
14. Outside job	0.00	0.01	-0.04	-0.24							
15. Initial capital (log)	0.02	-0.05	0.09	0.12	-0.10						
16. Number of employees (log)	0.06	-0.03	0.14	0.17	-0.12	0.37					
17. Acquired business	-0.02	0.00	0.03	-0.01	0.00	0.22	0.04				
18. Inherited business	-0.01	-0.04	-0.03	0.00	-0.03	0.01	0.05	-0.08			
19. Radius of business sales	0.01	0.02	0.08	0.00	0.01	0.05	0.19	-0.11	0.07		
20. Months in business (log)	0.02	-0.03	-0.01	0.00	-0.02	0.00	0.14	-0.02	0.01	0.07	
21. Informational ties	0.06	-0.07	-0.03	0.01	-0.03	0.13	0.12	0.03	0.03	0.03	-0.03
22. Industry – construction	0.08	-0.05	0.04	0.00	-0.05	-0.09	0.15	-0.09	-0.01	0.04	0.07

continued on next page

Table 11.2 Descriptive statistics and Pearson correlation coefficients* (cont.)

Variable	10	11	12	13	14	15	16	17	18	19	20
23. Industry – manufacturing	-0.03	0.06	0.02	0.01	0.02	0.06	0.15	-0.03	0.01	0.21	0.01
24. Industry – transportation	-0.01	0.02	0.03	0.00	0.01	0.04	0.09	-0.02	0.05	0.11	0.01
25. Industry – wholesale	0.02	0.01	0.05	-0.01	0.01	0.06	0.04	0.00	-0.03	0.19	0.01
26. Industry – agriculture	-0.03	-0.05	0.01	0.04	-0.02	0.07	-0.02	0.02	0.11	0.01	0.02
27. Industry – financial services	-0.04	-0.02	-0.02	0.00	-0.06	-0.09	-0.01	-0.04	0.02	0.00	0.01
28. Industry – personal services	-0.04	0.04	-0.01	-0.03	0.06	-0.16	-0.11	-0.05	0.00	-0.04	-0.03
29. Industry – professional services	0.00	-0.04	-0.05	-0.12	-0.05	-0.03	-0.03	-0.07	-0.02	0.02	0.05
30. Environmental dynamism	0.02	0.02	0.03	0.13	-0.09	0.00	0.11	-0.04	-0.01	0.02	0.01
31. Growth in GSP	0.04	-0.01	0.03	0.00	0.00	-0.02	0.01	-0.05	0.04	-0.03	-0.01
32. Change in competitors	-0.03	0.03	0.01	0.01	0.02	-0.05	0.05	-0.09	-0.01	0.01	-0.01

Variable	21	22	23	24	25	26	27	28	29	30	31
22. Industry – construction	0.05										
23. Industry – manufacturing	-0.03	-0.09									
24. Industry – transportation	0.02	-0.05	-0.05								
25. Industry – wholesale	0.01	-0.07	-0.07	-0.03							
26. Industry – agriculture	-0.04	-0.05	-0.05	-0.02	-0.03						
27. Industry – financial services	-0.03	-0.07	-0.07	-0.03	-0.05	-0.04					
28. Industry – personal services	-0.09	-0.14	-0.14	-0.07	-0.10	-0.07	-0.04				
29. Industry – professional services	-0.04	-0.09	-0.09	-0.04	-0.06	-0.04	-0.10				
30. Environmental dynamism	0.11	-0.01	0.00	0.02	0.06	0.03	-0.06	-0.13			
31. Growth in GSP	-0.02	0.06	0.02	-0.01	-0.02	-0.03	0.11	-0.05	0.00	0.05	
32. Change in competitors	0.02	0.03	0.00	0.02	-0.01	-0.02	0.05	0.04	0.09	0.07	0.03

* N = 1 457; correlations greater than ± 0.07 are significant at $p < 0.01$.

categories) attained by an entrepreneur, *formal education* was measured as the percentage of people in the sample with lower levels of education than the entrepreneur in the observation. This variable ranges from 0 to 1 and is scaled based on the empirical distribution of education. While this continuous measure has been seldom used, it may be a better metric than "years of education" for several reasons. First, the productivity and earnings effects of years of education are very different for different stages of education. For instance, two years of education between high school and an associate's degree may have different effects than two years between a bachelor's degree and an MBA. Also, years of education does not take into account that earnings from education are partly determined by the empirical distribution of level of education in the labor supply.

While prior research has tended to operationalize work experience in terms of the number of years of work experience (Evans and Leighton, 1989; Brüderl, Preisendörfer, and Ziegler, 1992), such a variable was not included in our surveys. While this could be viewed as a weakness of our study, years of experience may not closely reflect skills and knowledge developed. We used alternative operationalizations, meant to capture work experience through achievement level attained by the entrepreneur. We obtained three measures of attainment from one question in the survey, asking whether the highest level of management experience achieved was "supervised managers," "supervised others," "managed own business," or "supervised no one." With "supervised no one" as the reference group, *management experience* was coded 1 if the entrepreneurs had "supervised managers," *supervisory experience* was coded 1 if the entrepreneur had "supervised others," and entrepreneurial experience was coded 1 if the entrepreneur had "managed own business." The survey also contained information about the number of prior full-time jobs held by the entrepreneur, which is likely to be somewhat correlated with years of work experience. To account for potential non-linear effects, we segmented the variable describing the *number of prior jobs* into five discrete segments (0, 1, 2, 3 or 4, or 5 or more jobs).[3]

Our measure of specific human capital is an entrepreneur's previous experience with (a) customers, (b) suppliers, and (c) products and services, each of which we measured individually on a 5-point Likert scale and then combined (Cronbach alpha = 0.8723) to create the variable *similar business* (recoded to the 0–1 range). *Intrinsic motivation* was coded 1 if the entrepreneur's most important goal in starting a new venture was "to let you do the kind of work you wanted to do" or "avoid working for others"; it was coded −1 if the entrepreneur responded "to make more money than you would have otherwise" or "to build a successful organization," and 0 if the entrepreneur's goal was "other." *Parents owned a business* is a dummy variable that takes into account the parents' history in an entrepreneurial venture. Finally, the age of the entrepreneur is the age recorded at the time of the first questionnaire. To avoid multicollinearity between age and age^2, age was operationalized as deviation from the mean (36 years) and age^2 as the square of such deviation (Aiken and West, 1991: 35).

Control variables

There are well-researched factors, unrelated to human capital, that may affect performance, threshold of performance, or entrepreneurial exit. These factors can be roughly classified as characteristics of the entrepreneur, the firm, and the environment. An important characteristic of the entrepreneur is the amount of *hours worked* in the venture. Entrepreneurs working more hours may perform better and also expect more from their ventures, while an entrepreneur's desire to readjust work hours (Mincer, 1986) to maximize the payoff to general human capital, or psychological capital, may lead to exit. Entrepreneurs who work longer hours may therefore have a higher threshold, being less willing to accept a lower level of performance. The entrepreneur's decision to maintain a full-time or part-time job outside the venture can also influence the performance and survival of the venture by drawing energy and attention from the venture and may signal the entrepreneur's lack of commitment, leading to poor performance. The effect of *outside job* on threshold is unclear. Entrepreneurs with outside employment may have lower performance thresholds because they have supplementary income to offset low performance, or they may have higher thresholds because of lower switching costs.

Controls for firm characteristics include initial capital investment, firm's size, path of ownership (whether the business was started, acquired, or inherited), breadth of geographical niche, informational ties, and age of the venture. Both firm size (defined as number of employees) and *initial capital* may improve efficiency and reduce the liability of smallness (Hannan and Freeman, 1984; Aldrich and Auster, 1986), while initial capital investment may also provide a liquidity buffer for the firm to survive under conditions of low performance (Brüderl and Schüssler, 1990; Levinthal, 1991; Fichman and Levinthal, 1991). Firms that were started by the owner are more likely to experience a higher liability than *acquired* or *inherited businesses*, since completely new roles and ties must be developed (Stinchcombe, 1965). Inherited businesses may also experience different performance and survival dynamics because the owner may have developed prior firm-specific human capital while working for the family firm and a possible psychic attachment to the firm. *Radius of business sales* reflects the breadth of the geographical market niche, a critical dimension of the firm's strategy that is likely to influence performance and survival (Carroll, 1985; Brüderl, Preisendürfer, and Ziegler, 1992). *Informational ties* of the organization, which can convey relevant knowledge and information to the owner, was measured with an index of the use and importance of seven information and advice sources (Cronbach alpha = 0.5849). *Months in business* (age of the venture) may reflect the liability of newness (Stinchcombe, 1965) as well as the extent to which the venture has experienced the effects of selection (Freeman, Carroll, and Hannan, 1983).[4] We controlled for the age of the venture to minimize the potential for left-censoring bias (Guo, 1993).

The venture's competitive environment also has important influences on economic performance and survival. Industry environments may differ in average performance (Bain, 1956), reinvestment intensity, sunk costs, and barriers to exit (Caves and Porter, 1976; Porter, 1976). We controlled for nine industry classifications using eight dummy variables (construction, manufacturing, transportation, wholesale, agriculture, financial services, personal services, and professional services), with retail as the reference group. The intensity of competition is also a function of the changes in the munificence of the environment. Markets that are growing may experience less intense competition for resources, and vice versa. We controlled for such munificence by including the *growth of gross state product* (GSP) between 1985 and 1987. We expected high growth of GSP to be associated with higher performance and survival. Because our ability to control for objective dimensions of the competitive and institutional environment was very limited, especially if compared with the industry-specific samples often used in population ecology studies, we used two perceptual variables to describe the environment: the entrepreneur's perceptions about the expected *change in* (number of) *competitors* in the next five years and how rapidly the business is changing *(environmental dynamism)*. While these perceptual measures may be quite unreliable, they help minimize the data's weaknesses in terms of omitted competitive variables.

Statistical methods

From the theoretical model formulated above, if a venture's economic performance exceeds the entrepreneur's threshold level of performance we expect the entrepreneur to continue with the venture. Conversely, if economic performance is less than the threshold level, the entrepreneur is expected to exit the venture. Thus, the decision to continue with or exit from venture *n* is endogenously determined by the economic performance of the venture and the entrepreneur's threshold level of performance, following the decision rule:

$$\text{EXIT}_n = \begin{cases} 0 & \text{i.e., venture continues,} & \text{if } EP_n *(X_n) > T_n *(X_n) \\ 1 & \text{i.e., venture is discontinued,} & \text{if } EP_n *(X_n) \leq T_n *(X_n) \end{cases} \quad (5)$$

EP_n* is a latent variable that represents economic performance as of the third year. When the venture is discontinued, economic performance (EP_n*) is completely unobservable. When the venture survives, we observe, instead, money taken out$_n$, which indicates whether EP$_n$* falls between two known bounds. T$_n$* is the latent construct of threshold performance, which is never directly observed. We seek to estimate the effect of the independent variables (X$_n$) on economic performance and threshold level of performance. This estimation presents four methodological challenges: (1) the unobservability of economic performance in the case of exit, (2) the endogenous nature of the exit decision, (3) the total unobservability of the threshold of performance, and (4) the ordinal nature of our measure for economic performance for those ventures that continued.

Our approach combines two well-known methodologies in the econometric literature involving studies of discrete and limited dependent variables (Maddala, 1983). The first methodology, censored regression (or tobit) model with unobserved stochastic thresholds (Nelson, 1977; Smith, 1980; Maddala, 1983: 174–178), is appropriate when the dependent variable is only observed when it falls above a particular level or threshold, and this threshold varies from observation to observation as a function of some independent variables. Thus, this methodology deals with the first three challenges highlighted above. This method has been used to estimate the determinants of female labor supply (Nelson, 1977) and the predictors of market transaction costs and internal organizational costs (Masten, Meehan, and Snyder, 1991). This methodology is also useful for avoiding potential problems of self-selection bias (Heckman, 1979). When the observability of a dependent variable (in our case, economic performance) is endogenously determined by a decision (exit) in, which the economic performance is itself an important factor, missing observations (on those firms that have exited) are not random. Rather, they are self-selected based on their lower economic performance, higher threshold of performance, or both, thus creating a problem of selectivity bias that could make the coefficients unreliable.

The second methodology, grouped data regression (Stewart, 1983; Greene, 1990), attends to the final challenge identified above. It is useful when the exact value of the dependent variable (in our case, economic performance, EP$_n$* is not observed but is known to be in a range between two known values. It has been applied to the analysis of income data from surveys (like ours) in which the respondent is asked whether his or her income is between some prespecified dollar amounts.

We combined both methodologies here. As in censored regression with stochastic thresholds, the decision to continue or exit is based on the comparison of the two latent constructs of economic performance and the threshold (see equation 4), which are specified as a linear function of the observable independent variables, as follows:

$$EP_n{}^* = \sum b_{1i} \cdot X_{in} + e_{1n} \tag{6a}$$

$$T_n{}^* = \sum b_{2i} \cdot X_{in} + e_{2n}, \tag{6b}$$

Table 11.3 Parameter estimates of economic performance, threshold of performance, and exit

| | Joint Maximum Likelihood Model | | | | | | Non-censored regression on economic performance (4) | |
| | Economic performance equation (1) | | Threshold of performance equation (2) | | Binomial probit on exit (3) | | | |
Variables	Coeff.	S.E.	Coeff.	S.E.	Coeff.	S.E.	Coeff.	S.E.
Formal education	6.84****#	(2.72)	0.03#	(2.79)	-0.21*	(0.13)	4.95**	(2.37)
Management experience	3.75*#	(2.75)	6.05**#	(2.97)	0.07	(0.13)	4.43*	(2.48)
Supervisory experience	5.05****#	(2.06)	1.25#	(2.19)	-0.18*	(0.09)	3.34*	(1.89)
Similar business	8.89****#	(2.12)	0.04	(2.25)	-0.38****#	(0.10)	5.21***	(1.85)
Intrinsic motivation	-0.39	(0.77)	-1.87***	(0.79)	-0.07*#	(0.04)	-1.15*	(0.69)
Parents owned business	-0.19	(1.53)	-3.20**#	(1.63)	-0.15**#	(0.07)	-2.27*	(1.34)
Age of entrepreneur	0.14	(0.10)	-0.49****#	(0.11)	-0.02****#	(0.00)	-0.10	(0.09)
Age^2	0.00	(0.01)	0.00	(0.01)	0.00	(0.00)	0.00	(0.01)
Prior job (vs.none)	5.72	(5.28)	-7.30	(5.18)	-0.55***	(0.21)	-0.17	(4.32)
2 prior jobs (vs. none)	8.59*	(4.77)	-2.42	(4.63)	-0.42**	(0.20)	4.15	(4.11)
3 or 4 prior jobs (vs.none)	6.75	(4.68)	-2.05	(4.43)	-0.30	(0.19)	3.71	(4.00)
5+ prior jobs (vs.none)	0.67	(4.69)	1.15	(4.41)	0.06	(0.19)	1.11	(4.06)
Entrepreneurial experience	4.07*	(2.36)	6.45***	(2.47)	0.07	(0.11)	5.04**	(2.14)
Houra worked	-0.01	(0.05)	-0.04	(0.05)	0.00	(0.00)	-0.05	(0.05)
Outside job	-11.68****	(2.76)	-7.34**	(2.90)	0.16	(0.12)	-10.82****	(2.63)
Initial capital (log)	2.76****	(0.71)	-1.52**	(0.77)	-0.17****	(0.03)	1.12*	(0.61)
Number of employees (log)	9.07****	(1.01)	3.52****#	(1.07)	-0.16****#	(0.05)	8.30*****#	(0.92)
Acquired business	1.06	(1.79)	-1.35	(1.88)	-0.17**	(0.08)	-1.24	(1.50)
Inherited business	2.85	(5.61)	-11.02	(7.05)	-0.63**	(0.30)	3.56	(4.51)

continued on next page

Table 11.3 Parameter estimates of economic performance, threshold of performance, and exit (cont.)

| | Joint Maximum Likelihood Model | | | | | | Non-censored regression on economic performance (4) | |
| | Economic performance equation (1) | | Threshold of performance equation (2) | | Binomial probit on exit (3) | | | |
Variables	Coeff.	S.E.	Coeff.	S.E.	Coeff.	S.E.	Coeff.	S.E.
Radius of business sales	-0.03	(0.31)	0.10***	(0.03)	0.01****	(0.00)	0.03	(0.03)
Months in business (log)	7.45****	(1.45)	-0.59	(1.39)	-0.35****	(0.06)	3.57***	(1.30)
Informational ties	1.78	(3.92)	1.54	(4.06)	-0.09	(0.18)	0.25	(3.42)
Industry-construction	12.22****	(2.70)	3.12	(2.77)	-0.32**	(0.14)	9.75****	(2.45)
Industry-manufacturing	11.11****	(2.79)	3.87	(3.11)	-0.34**	(0.14)	8.19***	(2.53)
Industry-transportation	9.17*	(4.92)	5.80	(4.91)	-0.09	(0.24)	8.88*	(4.62)
Industry-wholesale	11.62***	(3.57)	4.73	(3.91)	-0.29*	(0.18)	9.65***	(3.20)
Industry-agriculture	10.52**	(4.78)	-0.74	(6.56)	-0.55**	(0.26)	6.46	(3.96)
Industry-financial services	25.13****	(3.87)	11.66***	(4.37)	-0.71****	(0.18)	18.90****	(2.93)
Industry-personal services	6.28***	(2.24)	-0.48	(2.31)	-0.28***	(0.10)	3.96**	(2.01)
Industry-professional services	23.77****	(2.88}	6.08*	(3.18)	-0.69****	(0.16)	17.85****	(2.66)
Environmental dynamism	0.44	(0.73)	0.04	(0.77)	-0.03	(0.03)	0.09	(0.65)
Growth in GSP	34.01****	(7.23)	6.74	(7.53)	-1.20****	(0.32)	21.23****	(6.36)
Change in competitors	-0.48	(0.77)	0.24	(0.81)	0.05	(0.04)	0.08	(0.74)
Log-likelihood	-2 433.50				-890.64		-1 558.11	
N	1547.00				1547.00		936.00	

* $p < 0.10$; ** $p < 0.05$; *** $p < 0.01$; **** $p < 0.001$; two-tailed Wald test unless otherwise indicated.
a Dependent variable uses grouped data methodology.
One-tailed Wald test for hypothesized relationships.

where X_n is the vector of independent and control variables, b_1 and b_2 are vectors of regression coefficients, and e_1 and e_2 are random disturbances.

We estimated the censored regression model on economic performance and the tobit model on threshold performance simultaneously using a maximum likelihood procedure. Since there is no standard program that produces maximum likelihood estimates for this combination of models, we mathematically derived the likelihood function and maximized it using LIMDEP 7.0. Details about this maximum likelihood estimation method are provided in Appendix B.

Results

Model significance

We tested the significance of the human capital variables in the threshold model (columns 1 and 2 of Table 11.3) by examining whether the addition of these variables significantly improved the ability to explain exit through economic performance and performance threshold. We used a log-likelihood ratio test to compare the full model with two nested naive models (not shown); the first with only constants for economic performance and performance threshold, the second including only control variables. The first test produced a chi-square value of 692.85 (66 d.f.), while the second had a value of 154.09 (26 d.f.). Both tests were significant ($p < 0.0001$). The first test reflects the overall significance of the model, while the second indicates the joint significance of the independent (human capital) variables of the model.

Hypothesis testing

The results for the independent variables generally confirm the separate effects of both economic performance and threshold on the entrepreneur's likelihood of exit. The results from the full model are presented in Table 11.3. Columns 1 and 2 present the coefficients relating to economic performance and threshold, respectively. Column 3 presents the coefficients of a probit model on exit.[5] The hypotheses were tested by examining these three columns. Because we had prior expectations about the direction of hypothesized relationships, we used a one-tailed test where appropriate. Similar to column 1, column 4 presents the results from a regression on economic performance but differs in that it does not control for the self-selection problem. Although column 4 is not directly related to our hypothesis testing, we introduce it to evaluate the effect of self-selection bias in estimating performance. In general, hypothesis 1 (relationships regarding general human capital) receives partial support, while hypotheses 2 through 4 (relationships regarding specific human capital, psychic income, and switching costs) receive relatively strong support.

General human capital

Measures of general human capital should raise the economic performance of the venture and the expected returns outside the venture. Because of these offsetting factors, we cannot determine the relationship of general human capital to survival a priori; it depends on the relative payoff of human capital in the venture versus outside the venture. Hypothesis 1 received mixed support. As expected, education, management experience, and supervisory experience are positively related to the economic performance of the venture, but only management experience has the expected positive relationship with threshold. The insignificant effect of management experience on exit seems largely driven by the offsetting influence of this variable on both performance and threshold. In contrast, it appears that the negative relationship of supervisory experience and education to exit is largely driven by a greater payoff to these forms of human capital in the venture. A two-tailed Wald test shows that supervisory experience has a significantly lower payoff (one-tailed Wald test: $p < 0.10$) in other alternatives (a lower threshold) than does management experience.

While not reported here, we explored further the effect of education on performance and threshold by operationalizing education as a set of indicator variables for five different levels of educational attainment. Consistent with the linear results, entrepreneurs with higher education (with bachelor's or graduate degrees) have significantly higher performance than those with medium levels of education (high school graduates or some college), even though those without a high school diploma do not necessarily perform worse than the rest. Paradoxically, entrepreneurs with a high school diploma or with a bachelor's degree have a lower threshold than those who did not attain their high school diploma and those who went to college but did not obtain a bachelor's degree. This nonmonotonic effect may explain the nonsignificant threshold effect of the linear operationalization of education, This result may suggest that those entrepreneurs who persisted in their studies until they obtained the degree are also more likely to persist in their business.

Human capital specific to the venture

Hypothesis 2 predicted that because an entrepreneur's specific human capital will have little value outside the venture, the decision to exit will be influenced primarily by the venture's performance. Since entrepreneurs with higher degrees of specific human capital are expected to have better performing ventures, we expect them to be less likely to exit. Our measure of specific human capital, similar business, is related as expected. As depicted in column 3, the variable has a strong, negative relationship to exit (one-tailed Wald test: $p < 0.001$). That relationship is driven by the very strong and positive impact on economic performance (one-tailed Wald test: $p < 0.001$) and the insignificant effect on threshold.

Psychic income from entrepreneurship

Hypothesis 3 argued that individuals who attach high psychic income to entrepreneurship are expected to accept a lower level of performance before exiting their ventures. While they are not necessarily performing better, we expect them to be less likely to exit their business. This hypothesis received strong support. Our measures of psychic income, intrinsic motivation (one-tailed Wald test: $p < 0.01$) and parents owned a business (one-tailed Wald test: $p < 0.05$), are both negatively related to threshold, while having no statistical relationship with economic performance. This explains the negative and significant effect of both variables on exit. It seems that entrepreneurs who are more intrinsically motivated and have a family history in entrepreneurship are simply more likely to accept a lower level of economic performance to remain in business.

Switching costs

With age of the entrepreneur as a measure of switching costs, our results support hypothesis 4. The persistence of older entrepreneurs is due to their willingness to accept a lower return, i.e., their lower threshold (one-tailed Wald test: $p < 0.001$), since they do not seem to perform significantly differently than younger entrepreneurs. The main effect of age on performance is significant in a one-tailed Wald test at the $p < 0.10$ level, but not in a two-tailed test. Since we do not have initial theoretical expectations about the effects of age on performance, we believe the two-tailed test to be appropriate, but this result may indicate that age is picking up some omitted variables measuring the effect of human capital, such as years of work experience. Age^2 had no significant effects on either performance or threshold.

Other influences

Entrepreneurial experience has a positive and significant effect on economic performance (two-tailed Wald test: $p < 0.10$) and threshold (two-tailed Wald test: $p < 0.01$). It appears that the effect on threshold is greatest. Consistent with the view that too many or too few jobs may indicate low general human capital, we found that entrepreneurs with two prior jobs perform better than those with no previous work experience (two-tailed Wald test: $p < 0.10$) and than those with five or more prior jobs (two-tailed Wald test: $p < 0.001$); and entrepreneurs with three or four prior jobs perform better than those with five or more prior jobs (two-tailed Wald test: $p <$ 0.001). The same result does not hold for the threshold equation. Instead, entrepreneurs having held five or more prior jobs have higher thresholds than entrepreneurs with only one prior job (two-tailed Wald test: $p < 0.05$). This suggests that entrepreneurs who have held many jobs are less willing to tolerate low performance, perhaps because they have lower economic or psychic switching costs.

Control variables

The results in Table 11.3 also illustrate several interesting relationships for the control variables. Of the remaining variables related to the entrepreneur, hours worked was not related to any of the dependent variables. As expected, the economic returns to entrepreneurs with an outside job was significantly lower than those concentrating solely on the venture. Interestingly, outside job was also related negatively with threshold, presumably because entrepreneurs could afford to accept lower performance.

Several of the firm-level control variables had important influences on economic performance, threshold, and exit. Initial capital, number of employees, and months in business had significant positive effects (two-tailed Wald test: $p < 0.001$) on economic performance, suggesting that better capitalized, larger, and older firms were better performers. This explains the strong and significant negative effects of these variables on the probability of exit (two-tailed Wald test: $p < 0.001$). The variables, however, differed in their effect on threshold of performance. Initial capital had a significant negative effect on threshold (two-tailed Wald test: $p < 0.05$), number of employees had a significant positive effect (two-tailed Wald test: $p < 0.001$), and months in business had no significant effect on threshold. The path to ownership of the venture, whether the firm was acquired, inherited, or developed, seemed to have no significant bearing on either performance or threshold, although owners who inherited their businesses seemed to be willing to accept lower performance (two-tailed Wald test: $p < 0.12$) than those who started their firms. Both acquired businesses and inherited businesses were less likely to exit than start-up firms. While firms with a wider radius of business sales tended to exit more often, this result was due primarily to the firms' higher thresholds, because there were no significant performance differences. Information ties did not show significant effects in our analysis.

Several industry dummies also had significant effects on performance, threshold, and exit. All industries were compared against the largest industry group – retailing – and all showed higher economic performance than that group. Firms in financial and professional industries tended to perform better and exit less frequently, As expected, economic returns to the entrepreneur were greater when growth in GSP was higher. Our measures of environmental change and change in competitors had no significant influence on performance, threshold, or exit.

Effects of self-selection bias

A methodological problem of studying determinants of economic performance in businesses with high attrition rates is that the dependent variable is only available for firms that survive, yet survival is more likely for firms with high performance. This creates a self-selection problem. To highlight the effects of self-selection bias on the analysis of economic performance, we compare column 4, a simple grouped data regression model without correction for self-selection bias, with column 1, which corrects for this bias. The magnitude of the self-selection problem will differ for each predictor variable, depending on whether the variable is expected to be related to the selection function, in this case survival (Heckman, 1979). Variables that have a strong effect on survival suffer more from self-selection, which biases downward their coefficients on performance, because firms that fail are more likely to have lower values of these variables. By modelling performance effects with only surviving firms, the distributions of affected variables fall within a narrower range, creating effects that are less significant.

In some cases self-selection bias can make insignificant coefficients appear to be significant in the performance equation. This bias was reflected most visibly in our measures of psychic income: intrinsic motivation and parents owned a business. From column 4, it appears that entrepreneurs who were intrinsically motivated or whose parents owned a business have lower performance, but this conclusion reflects the potentially incorrect interpretations of biased results, Our earlier discussion suggested that these entrepreneurs were more likely to survive simply because they were willing to accept lower levels of performance to stay in business. This selection mechanism led to the spurious observation that surviving "unsuccessful" entrepreneurs were more likely to have intrinsic motivation or family ties to entrepreneurship, even though the relationship was not causally related to a lack of economic success. Another interesting observation is that the coefficient of months in business, one of the strongest effects on performance, became strongly biased downward (to less than half of its unbiased value) if the estimation of the effect was only based on surviving firms. This result suggests that the apparent lack of consistency between the effect of venture age on survival and performance – an observation that motivated Meyer and Zucker's (1989: 19) theory of permanently failing organizations – may be partly due to self-selection bias. These examples emphasize the importance of controlling for self-selection bias and are consistent with Barnett, Greve, and Park (1994), who also found that controlling for selection bias substantially influenced the statistical effects of variables on performance.

Discussion

Assumptions about the relationship between performance and survival are so entrenched in social science research that little work has investigated them empirically. In some perspectives, those with Panglossian overtones, it is assumed that the efficiency of markets will lead to the "survival of the fittest." This rhetoric implies unidimensionality between performance and survival: the lowest performing organizations are also the least likely to survive. Scholars espousing other perspectives recognize that selection does not necessarily favor the best performing organizations (Hannan and Freeman, 1977; Meyer and Rowan, 1977) but have failed to study the causal relationships between these constructs (Meyer and Zucker, 1989; Amburgey and Rao, 1996). Our theoretical model and empirical results suggest that survival is enhanced by economic performance but not uniquely determined by it. Rather, organizations have different required thresholds of performance, and survival (or exit) is determined by whether performance falls above (or below) the threshold. In small and new ventures, the threshold of performance is fundamentally influenced by the human capital characteristics of the entrepreneur, including the value of this capital in alternative uses, psychic income, and switching costs. This paper is the first, we believe, to provide empirical support for the assertion that thresholds of performance differ systematically across firms and play an important role in determining firm survival, Several of the results are worth highlighting.

First, we found that entrepreneurs with more general human capital perform better but do not necessarily survive more frequently. We had expected that entrepreneurs endowed with general human capital would have higher performance requirements for their businesses and might quit if these requirements were not met. This expectation was only partially supported by our results. We found that general management experience (having managed managers) influences an entrepreneur's threshold of performance, while neither education nor supervisory experience are related. This suggests that the value of general management experience outside the venture may be comparable to its value in entrepreneurship, while returns to education and supervisory experience may be somewhat better in self-employment, findings consistent with Evans and Leighton (1989). The apparently divergent payoffs of management experience and supervisory experience are especially intriguing. While management experience may be more generally applied, it may also be that having experience "managing managers" is more valuable in larger organizations with more formal structures.

Second, we found that entrepreneurial skills that have little use outside of the venture, such as prior experience with the venture's customers, suppliers, products, and services are related to both performance and survival. Furthermore, by demonstrating no significant relationship with threshold, our results support the expectation that human capital that is largely specific to the venture context should have little or no bearing on returns outside of the venture. Apparently, specific human capital influences survival by increasing the gap between performance and threshold (i.e., increasing performance without raising the threshold).

Third, our findings suggest that some dimensions of human capital have important effects on persistence, even when they do not influence performance. Factors such as the entrepreneur's age, family experience with entrepreneurship, or intrinsic motivation do not have any tangible effect on performance. Yet entrepreneurs with a higher level of these attributes are willing to accept a lower level of performance to survive. Entrepreneurs who have inherited businesses are also more likely to continue, apparently because of their desire to sustain the family business (lower threshold) and not because of superior performance associated with any "extra" knowledge passed on to them.

These findings provide strong support for our threshold model of entrepreneurial exit and reconcile many of the inconsistent relationships previously found in entrepreneurial performance and survival research: some human capital variables significantly influence both performance and survival (specific human capital), some influence performance more than survival (general human capital), and some influence survival but not performance (switching costs, psychic income). This evidence suggests that there are differences in determinants of performance and survival and that research agendas ignoring the entrepreneur's choice to accept a given level of performance are incomplete.

A somewhat surprising result is that entrepreneurial experience seems to have at least as much effect on threshold as it does on economic performance of the venture. If entrepreneurial experience constitutes human capital that is specific to the venture, we would expect its effect to be greater inside the venture than outside it. We interpret the higher threshold effect as suggesting that experienced entrepreneurs have reduced switching costs into alternative employment (maybe trying again with another venture), perhaps because they have developed networks or familiarity with the routine of starting businesses. Experienced entrepreneurs may also gain a certain "thrill" from the start-up process and thus experience a negative psychic income once the venture becomes stable.

As we might expect, entrepreneurs' history of previous jobs seems to reflect their general human capital. Our findings indicate that a low number of prior jobs may be associated with a lack of outside alternatives, while a high number of prior jobs may suggest an inability to perform jobs satisfactorily. Thus, both a low and high number of jobs suggest low degrees of human capital and poor performance in the venture. At the same time, we found that a large number of prior jobs increases an entrepreneur's threshold, suggesting that these entrepreneurs are less willing to tolerate low performance. This is likely due to low economic or psychic switching costs.

By incorporating the threshold construct, our analysis also provides insight into the effects of some well-studied factors bearing on organizational mortality: initial capital, size, age, and strategy of the venture. The first three variables are strongly related to performance; both initial capital and size also influence survival through their impact on threshold. The negative effect of initial capital on threshold may support the view that initial capital provides the entrepreneur a buffer to withstand poor performance and liquidity problems without having to exit the business (Brüderl and Schüssler, 1990; Levinthal, 1991; Fichman and Levinthal, 1991). It may also suggest that financial investments are largely irreversible. In contrast, the positive effect of number of employees (size) on threshold suggests that entrepreneurs of larger organizations require higher performance, perhaps because they can easily disband if they do not obtain such performance. This is assisted by a labor market that facilitates mobility. The lack of any significant relationship between age of the venture and threshold suggests that the processes underlying the "liability of newness" phenomenon tend to influence exit mainly through the performance component. Our finding that firms with broader scope exit more frequently is consistent with Brüderl, Preisendörfer, and Ziegler (1992). We found that this effect is mainly due to their higher threshold of performance.

The environmental controls show that industries differ in both their performance and threshold effects. Financial and professional services industries tend to perform better but also to have higher thresholds, while personal services and retail industries are characterized by both low performance and low thresholds. These patterns may reflect broad differences in the general human capital of entrepreneurs in those industries. Finally, environmental munificence has a positive effect on performance and exit. While it might have been expected that a good economic environment would also increase the income in alternative occupations, and thus increase threshold, the coefficient of munificence on threshold is positive but not statistically significant.

Alternative explanations and limitations

Our empirical findings may have alternative explanations. It could be that entrepreneurs differ in their decision-making speed and rationality when faced with poor performance. Entrepreneurs who simply delay the exit decision or experience a psychological escalation of commitment (Staw,

1981), perhaps because of less training, would appear in our results as having lower thresholds. It may be that formal education does not increase underlying ability but that it has value as a market signal that allows employers to segregate people of higher ability (Spence, 1974). Alternatively, an entrepreneur's high level of formal education may increase the legitimacy of a small business, facilitating access to better trading partners and leading to improved performance (Meyer and Rowan, 1977). These alternative theoretical justifications for our findings should be considered in future studies, as should factors beyond the scope of our model that are examined in prior research. Venture performance has been linked to network formation (Aldrich, Rosen, and Woodward, 1987), environments (Carroll, 1987), and strategies (McDougall, Robinson, and DeNisi, 1992), as well as interactions between environments and strategies (Romanelli, 1989; Eisenhardt and Schoonhoven, 1990). A broader array of perspectives will undoubtedly increase our insight into new venture thresholds.

There are also some empirical limitations to our research, mainly because of shortcomings in data availability and measurement. Because we chose to make the sample as broad as possible, we lacked fine-grained measures of the institutional dimensions of the environment. It would be illuminating to replicate this study in the context of a single industry or population to control more aptly for environmental dimensions. Our reliance on demographic variables (age, parents who owned a business) as proxies for psychological constructs (psychic income) or switching costs is also another limitation that could be overcome with better measures in future work. The sociological and psychological literatures may contain useful insights into how to extend our operationalization of these important constructs. Further, the lack of available information on the alternatives under consideration by entrepreneurs did not allow us to specify fully our theoretical model, which may therefore be affected by unmeasured heterogeneity. Information on liquidation values for discontinued businesses could have also helped specify the exit choice more accurately.

Another potential limitation is our measurement of economic performance as current monetary outlays. Monetary outlays to the entrepreneur may not distinguish between firms with low performance and firms with high reinvestment intensity or bright prospects. Firms with low current monetary outlays may still survive if the expected return to reinvestment activity is high, a condition that may be incorrectly reflected as a low threshold effect. Examination of our results, however, shows that lower thresholds are associated with entrepreneurs who are older, motivated by independence rather than growth or financial goals, who have little prior management or entrepreneurial experience, and who are not fully committed to the venture. This description does not fit the profile of entrepreneurs with high prospects willing to reinvest aggressively but, rather, of those with limited alternatives and positive psychic income from independence.

Implications for entrepreneurship and beyond

This research highlights the importance of considering the human capital characteristics of the entrepreneur in the survival of new ventures. Despite recent criticisms of inconsistent findings in the "trait" literature (Aldrich, 1990: 8), the multiple and critically important roles of the entrepreneur – as chief strategist and decision maker, as repository of much of the knowledge and skills that make up the intangible assets of the firm, as the person who develops the contacts and networks upon which the new venture depends – cannot be ignored. Our study suggests that the effects of these entrepreneurial characteristics on entrepreneurial thresholds are important for survival and can explain prior inconsistent findings. The implication for entrepreneurship research is that more attention is due to the outside opportunities of entrepreneurs, their psychic income, and switching costs, even if those variables do not directly influence entrepreneurial performance. Prior research has shown that entry into entrepreneurship may be more likely for those with reduced options elsewhere (Fuchs, 1982; Borjas, 1986; Brittain and Freeman, 1986; Carroll and Mosakowski, 1987). This research showed that those entrepreneurs are also more likely to survive, independent of performance, Thus, a clear appreciation of thresholds is necessary to understand the entrepreneurial process.

The concept of the threshold of performance outlined in this study can serve as an integrating construct for understanding performance and survival for all organizations, not merely new ventures. The question then becomes, "Why do organizations differ in their thresholds?" Perhaps the answer to this question must come from theoretical perspectives beyond human capital theory. Future research could focus on the role of governance structures, coalition power, and intrafirm conflict (Meyer and Zucker, 1989), which may limit the ability of owners to influence their organizations and therefore be associated with persistence under low performance. Other research could articulate thresholds as a function of slack (Cyert and March, 1963), initial resource endowments, or established relationships (Brüderl and Schüssler, 1990; Miner, Amburgey, and Stearns, 1990; Levinthal, 1991; Fichman and Levinthal, 1991) and disentangle the performance and threshold effects of these important constructs. The nature of resource commitment (whether the resources are sunk or highly mobile) would also influence both performance (Ghemawat, 1991) and exit barriers (Caves and Porter, 1976) and may constitute an interesting area for future research. These multiple theoretical lenses can be brought to bear in understanding cross-sectional and longitudinal differences in thresholds of both new and established organizations. The concept of threshold may also be applied, within the firm, to determine the minimum level of performance that a multidivisional organization requires to maintain an active division.

Proponents of the unidimensional view might argue that thresholds are simply temporary "buffers" against the inevitable success of better performing firms. While initial resources or decision-making lags may delay exit, those buffers may ultimately be depleted by continued low performance (Brüderl and Schüssler, 1990; Levinthal, 1991; Fichman and Levinthal, 1991), leaving intact the long-term, unidimensional relationship between performance and exit. Even if thresholds are temporary, however, they may be an important initial condition that has long-term implications for performance and survival by providing a buffer at a crucial stage of the organization's development (Eisenhardt and Schoonhoven, 1990; Levinthal, 1991). We believe, however, that thresholds persist over time and that they reflect a willingness to accept lower performance for the reasons highlighted in this paper. Whether a temporary buffer or an enduring quality, thresholds will influence the long-term selection processes in populations of organizations. If performance is stochastic (as in Levinthal's model of random walks), lower initial thresholds allow firms to survive during runs of bad performance until performance improves and, therefore, have a path-dependent effect on selection outcomes. Even if interim performance differences are relatively deterministic and difficult to change, organizations that are willing to remain in business at low levels of economic performance (those having low thresholds, perhaps because of low resource mobility) may increase competition and have a "crowding out" effect on better performing but more mobile firms. These arguments suggest that it is difficult to determine a priori to what extent selection outcomes in a population reflect differences in efficiency and performance or differences in thresholds. Thus, our theoretical model cautions against the use of survival as a measure of performance in empirical studies, since the "survival of the fittest," as this paper shows, cannot be assumed.

Appendix A   Variable definitions

Dependent variables	*Measure*
Exit$_n$	1 = firm discontinued; 0 = firm survived.
Money taken out$_n$	Amount (in thousand \$) of money (including salary, draw, dividends, etc.) that the entrepreneur was able to take out in the previous 12 months. The variable is ordinal with 7 values: (1) under \$10K, (2) \$10K to \$15K, (3) \$15K to \$25K, (4) \$25K to \$35K, (5) \$35K to \$50K, (6) \$50K to \$75K, and (7) over \$75K.

Independent and control variables

Attainment in work experience	Highest level of management experience achieved by owner (multinomial categorical variable). *Supervisory experience* equals 1 if "supervised others"; 0 otherwise. *Management experience* equals 1 if "supervised managers"; 0 otherwise. *Entrepreneurial experience* equals 1 if "managed own business"; 0 otherwise. Reference group is "supervised no one."

Formal education	Percentage of observations in sample with less formal education than entrepreneur.
Similar business	Index of similarity between present business and previous organization in (a) products or services, (b) customers, and (c) suppliers (1 = very similar, 0 = very different) (Cronbach alpha = 0.8734).
Intrinsic motivation	1 = the entrepreneur's most important goal in starting a new venture is to "let you do the kind of work you wanted to do" or "avoid working for others." −1 = most important goal in starting a new venture is to "make more money than you would have otherwise" or "build a successful organization." 0 = most important goal in starting a new venture is "other."
Parents owned business	1 = parents owned a business; 0 = otherwise.
Age of entrepreneur	Age of entrepreneur at the time of first questionnaire.
Number of prior jobs	Total number of full-time jobs prior to venture. Transformed to multiple binary variables measuring whether there were *1 prior job, 2 prior jobs, 3 or 4 prior jobs,* and *5 or more prior jobs.* Reference group is no prior jobs.
Hours worked	Total number of hours worked per week by the entrepreneur.
Outside job	1 = entrepreneur had a full-time job outside the venture; .5 = entrepreneur had a part-time or irregular job outside the venture; 0 = entrepreneur had no job outside the venture.
Initial capital (log)	Natural logarithm of the amount of capital (in thousand $) invested by the time of first sale (ordinal, 8 brackets).
Number of employees (log)	Natural logarithm of the number of full-time and part-time (.5) employees (including the owner) at the time of the first questionnaire.
Path to ownership	How entrepreneur became owner of present business (multinominal categorical variable). *Acquired business* equals 1 if "purchased it"; 0 otherwise. *Inherited business* equals 1 if "inherited it"; 0 otherwise. Reference group is "started it."
Radius of business sales	Radius of area in which 80% of customers are located.
Months in business (log)	Natural logarithm of the number of months since business registered its first sale at the time of the first questionnaire.
Informational ties	Composite index of use and importance of seven information sources: (a) accountant, bookkeeper, (b) friends or relatives, (c) other business owners, (d) bankers, (e) trade organizations, (f) lawyers, attorneys, and (g) franchisers or suppliers (1 = very important; 0 = not used) (Cronbach alpha = .5849).
Industry	Eight control variables for nine different industries, including *construction, manufacturing, transportation, wholesaling, agriculture, financial services, personal services, professional services.* Reference group is retail industry.

Environmental dynamism	Likert scale agreement with statement "My business is changing rapidly" (2 = strongly agree, –2 = strongly disagree).
Growth in GSP	Change in Gross State Product from 1985 to 1987 in the U.S. state where the business is located.
Change in competitors	Expected change per year over next five years in number of competitors: Increase over 20% (= 3), increase 11%–20% (= 2), increase 3%–10% (= 1), unchanged –3%–3% (= 0), decrease (= –1).

Appendix B   Maximum likelihood estimation of model

The likelihood function represents the probability that a sample was obtained from a statistical model with given parameters. By maximizing the logarithm of the likelihood function with respect to these parameters, we are able to obtain maximum likelihood estimates of the coefficients in equations (6a) and (6b).

For a given observation in the sample, we observe $exit_n$ (the binary variable representing exit), money taken out_n (the ordinal variable representing the range of economic performance, only observed if exit = 0), and X_n (the independent variables). The relevant parameters of the model are b_1, the coefficients of the independent variables on economic performance, b_2, the coefficients of the independent variables on the threshold, s_1, the standard deviation of the disturbance of the economic performance equation (e_1, which is assumed to be normally distributed, and s, the standard deviation of the difference of the disturbances of the threshold equation and the economic performance, $e_2 - e_1$. A required assumption for the full identification of the model is the assumption that e_1 and e_2 are independent (Nelson, 1977). The likelihood function, represented by $L(b_1,b_2,s_1,s \mid exit_n$, money taken $out_n, X_n)$, captures the probability that some given sample values ($exit_n$, money taken out_n, X_n) were obtained if the parameter values were b_1, b_2, s_1, and s.

For a given observation, the probability of observing exit is:

$$\text{Prob}(exit_n = 1) = \text{Prob}(EP^* \le T^*) = \text{Prob}\left(\sum b_{1i} \cdot X_i + e_2\right)$$

$$= \text{Prob}(e_1 - e_2 \le \sum (b_{2i} - b_{1i}) \cdot X_i = \Phi\left(\frac{\sum (b_{2i} - b_{1i}) \cdot X_i}{s}\right).$$

where $\Phi(z)$ represents the normal cumulative distribution function.

For a given observation, the probability of observing continuation and obtaining a value of k for money taken out,, (which means that the exact economic performance is between a known lower bound Lk and a known upper bound U_k) is:

Prob ($exit_n$ = 0 and money taken out_n = k) = Prob (T* < EP* *and* L_k < EP* <U_k)

$$= \text{Prob}(\sum b_{2i} \cdot X_i + e_2 < \sum b_{1i} \cdot X_i + e_1 \ and\ L_k < \sum b_{1i} \cdot X_i + e_1 < U_k)$$

$$= \text{Prob}(e_2 - e_1 < \sum (b_{1i} - b_{2i}) \cdot X\ and\ L_k - \sum b_{1i} \cdot X_i < e_1 < U_k - \sum b_{1i} \cdot (X_i))$$

$$= \text{Prob}(e_2 - e_1 < \sum (b_{1i} - b_{2i}) \cdot X\ and\ e_1 < U_k - \sum b_{1i} \cdot X_i)$$

$$- \text{Prob}(e_2 - e_1 < \sum (b_{1i} - b_{2i}) \cdot X\ and\ e_1 < L_k - \sum b_{1i} \cdot X_i).$$

Each of the probabilities in this equation can be represented as cumulative distribution functions of a standard bivariate normal, $\Phi_2(z_1, z_2, r)$. In this case, the first variable is $z_1 = (e_2 - e_1)/s$, and the second is $z_2 = (e_1/s_1)$, while the correlation of the variables equals $r = (-s_1/s)$ Thus, we can write Prob $(\text{exit}_n = 0$ and money taken out$_n = k)$ as

$$\Phi_2\left(\left(\frac{\sum(b_{1i} - b_{2i}) \cdot X_i}{s}\right), \left(\frac{U_k - \sum b_{1i} \cdot X_i}{s_1}\right), -\frac{s_1}{s}\right)$$

$$- \Phi_2\left(\left(\frac{\sum(b_{1i} - b_{2i}) \cdot X_i}{s}\right), \left(\frac{L_k - \sum b_{1i} \cdot X_i}{s_1}\right), -\frac{s_1}{s}\right)$$

The likelihood function aggregates these probabilities by multiplying them over all of the observations in the sample. By taking the logarithmic transformation of this likelihood function, we then obtain the log-likelihood function, which can be written as:

$$\text{InL}(b_1, b_2, s_1, s \mid \text{exit}_n, \text{money taken out}_n, X_n)$$

$$= \sum_{\text{exit}_n = 1} \ln\Phi\left(\frac{\sum(b_{2i} - b_{1i}) \cdot X_i}{s}\right)$$

$$+ \sum_{\text{exit}_n = 0} \ln\left[\Phi_2\left(\left(\frac{\sum(b_{1i} - b_{2i}) \cdot X_i}{s}\right), \left(\frac{U_k - \sum b_{1i} \cdot X_i}{s_1}\right), -\frac{s_1}{s}\right)\right]$$

$$- \Phi_2\left(\left(\frac{\sum(b_{1i} - b_{2i}) \cdot X_i}{s}\right), \left(\frac{L_k - \sum b_{1i} \cdot X_i}{s_1}\right), -\frac{s_1}{s}\right).$$

This equation is maximized for values of b_1, b_2, s_1, and s. The estimation is carried out in two steps. First, we use LIMDEP 7.0's grouped data regression with sample selection procedure to obtain performance and exit parameters, and from those we obtain initial estimates of b_1, b_2, s_1, and s following the procedure outlined by Maddala (1983: 228–230). We then use those initial estimates for the maximization of the log-likelihood function using a Davidon-Fletcher-Powell optimization algorithm (Greene, 1990), also available in LIMDEP.

Notes

1 We thank Terry Amburgey, Joel Baum, Parthiban David, William J. Dennis, John Garen, Michael Hitt, Robert Hoskisson, Mancy Johnson, David Loree, Christine Oliver, Jing Zhou, and three ASQ anonymous referees for their valuable comments on earlier drafts, and Tim Bates, Josef Brüderl, Linda Leighton and Alfred Nucci for sharing their knowledge of other data sources for entrepreneurship research. We also thank Javier Fernandez Navas and Diane Roden for their research help. We acknowledge the help and support of the National Federation of Independent Business. An earlier version of this paper received the 1992 Best Empirical Paper award from the Entrepreneurship Division of the Academy of Management.

2 There are some important exceptions to this generalization. Researchers studying the liability of adolescence and honeymoon effects (Brüderl and Schüssler, 1990; Fichman and Levinthal, 1991; Levinthal, 1991) have explicitly recognized that the initial stock of assets serves as a buffer between low performance and mortality. Institutional and interorganizational linkages can also serve as a buffer and reduce mortality for high risk organizations (Baum and Oliver, 1991; Miner, Amburgey, and Stearns, 1990)

3 We also considered a quadratic specification, but the non-symmetrical distribution of the variable, together with the fact that most observations fall in a relatively small number of cells (75 per cent of entrepreneurs had five prior jobs or fewer), led us to prefer this discrete specification. We also ran the model with a quadratic specification but preferred the discrete stepwise operationalization when we compared the results using Akaike's Information Criterion (AIC).

4 Recent ecological findings cast some doubt about the specific form of age dependence that firms experience and the liability of newness in particular These findings suggest that, after controlling for firm size, organizational age may have a negative effect on survival, or a liability of obsolescence or ageing (Ranger-Moore, 1991; Barron, West, and Hannan, 1994; Baum 1996). Given the restricted range of organizational age in our sample (the oldest firm in our sample, as of the third year, was only five years and four months old), we cannot enter this debate. To the extent that there may be unobserved heterogeneity in the sample, we expect greater mortality of younger firms during these early stages of the venture

5 This probit equation could be estimated jointly with a performance equation to increase the efficiency of the exit parameter estimates. We present the single-equation probit here because it focuses on mortality alone and is therefore comparable to prior research on mortality (no prior research that we know of has used joint estimation of exit and performance). A comparison of coefficients derived from joint estimation suggests that they are not different in any meaningful way from those derived in the single-equation probit illustrated in column 3.

References

Aiken, Leona S., and Stephen G. West, 1991. *Multiple Regression: Testing and Interpreting Interactions*. Newbury Park, CA: Sage

Alchian, Armen A., 1950. "Uncertainty, evolution and economic theory". *Journal of Political Economy*, 58: 211–222

Alchian, Armen A., and Harold Demsetz, 1972. "Production, information costs, and economic organization." *American Economic Review*. 62: 777–795

Aldrich, Howard E., 1990. "Using an ecological perspective to study organizational founding rates." *Entrepreneurship Theory and Practice*, 14:7–24

Aldridge, Howard E., and Ellen R. Auster, 1986. "Even dwarfs started small: Liabilities of age and size and their strategic implications." In B.M. Staw and L.L.Cummings (eds.), *Research in Organizational Behavior*, 8:165–198. Greenwich, CT: JAI Press.

Aldrich, Howard E., Arne Kalleberg, Peter Marsden, and James Cassell, 1989. "In pursuit of evidence: Sampling procedures for locating new businesses." *Journal of Business Venturing*, 4: 367–386

Aldrich, Howard E., H. Rosen, and W. Woodward, 1987. "The impact of social networks on business foundings and profit: A longitudinal study." In N.C. Churchill *et al.* (eds.), *Frontiers of Entrepreneurship Research*: 154–168. Wellesley, MA: Babson College.

Amburgey, Terry L., and Hayagreeva Rao, 1996. "Organizational ecology: Past, present, and future directions." *Academy of Management Journal*, 39: 1265–1286.

Aoki, Mashahiko, 1984. *The Co-operative Game Theory of the Firm*. Oxford, UK: Oxford University Press.

Bain, Joe Staten, 1956. *Barriers to New Competition*. Cambridge, MA: Harvard University Press.

Barnard, Chester I., 1938. *The Functions of the Executive*. Cambridge, MA: Harvard University Press.

Barnett, William P., Henrich R. Greve, and Douglas Y. Park, 1994. "An evolutionary model of organizational performance." *Strategic Management Journal*, 15 (Winter Special Issue): 11–28.

Barron, David N., Elizabeth West, and Michael T. Hannan, 1994. "A time to grow and a time to die: Growth and mortality of credit unions in New York City, 1914–1990." *American Journal of Sociology*, 100: 381–421.

Bates, Timothy, 1985. "Entrepreneur human capital endowments and minority business viability." *Journal of Human Resources*, 20: 540-554.

—— 1990 "Entrepreneur human capital inputs and small business longevity." *Review of Economics and Statistics*, 72: 551–559.

—— 1995, "Self-employment entry across industry groups." *Journal of Business Venturing*, 10: 143–156.

Baum, Joel A. C., 1996. "Organizational ecology." In Steward R. Clegg, Cynthia Hardy, and Walter R. Nord (eds.), *Handbook of Organization Studies*: 77–114. Thousand Oaks, CA: Sage.

Baum, Joel A. C., and Christine Oliver, 1991. "Institutional linkages and organizational mortality." *Administrative Science Quarterly*, 36: 187–218

Becker, Gary S., 1975. *Human Capital*. New York: Columbia University Press.

Birley, Sue, 1984. "Finding the new firm." *Proceedings of the Academy of Management Meetings*, 47: 64–68.

Blau, Judith R., 1984. *Architects and Firms*. Cambridge, MA: MIT Press.

Borjas, George J., 1986. "The self-employment experience of immigrants." *Journal of Human Resources*, 21: 485–506.

Bortnick Steven M., and Michelle Harrison Ports, 1993. "Job search methods of the unemployed, 1991." *Monthly Labor Review*, 115: 33.

Brittain, Jack, and John Freeman, 1986. "Births of US semiconductor firms." Paper presented at Annual Meeting of the Academy of Management, Chicago.

Brüdel, Josef, Peter Preisendörfer, and Rolf Zeigler, 1992. "Survival chances of newly founded business organizations." *American Sociological Review*, 57: 227–242.

Brüderl, Josef, and Rudolf Schüssler, 1990. "Organizational mortality: The liability of newness and adolescence." *Administrative Science Quarterly*, 35: 530–547.

Campbell, C. A., 1995. "An empirical test of a decision theory model for entrepreneurial acts." *Entrepreneurship and Regional Development*, 7: 95–103.

Carroll, Glenn R., 1985. "Concentration and Specialization: Dynamics of niche width in populations of organizations." *American Journal of Sociology*, 90: 1262–1283.

—— 1987. *Publish and Perish*. Greenwich, CT: JAI Press.

Carroll, Glenn R., and Yangchung Paul Huo, 1986. "Organizational task and institutional environments in ecological perspective: Findings from the local newspaper industry." *American Journal of Sociology*, 91: 838–873.

Carroll, Glenn R., and Elaine Mosakowski, 1987 "The career dynamics of self-employment." *Administrative Science Quarterly*, 32: 570–589.

Caves, Richard E., and Michael E. Porter, 1976. "Barriers to exit." In Rabot T, Masson and P. David Qualls (eds.), *Essays on Industrial Organization in Honor of Joe S. Bain*: 39–69. Cambridge, MA: Ballinger.

Cooper, Arnold C., F. Javier Gimeno Gascon, and Carolyn Y. Woo, 1994. "Initial human and financial capital as predictors of new venture performances." *Journal of Business Venturing*, 9: 371–395.

Cyert, Richard M., and James G. March, 1963. *A Behavioral Theory of the Firm.* Englewood Cliffs, NJ: Prentice-Hall.

Demsetz, Harold, and Kenneth Lehn, 1985. "The structure of corporate ownership: Causes and consequences." *Journal of Political Economy*, 93: 1155–1177.

DiMaggio, Paul J., and Walter W. Powell, 1983. "The iron cage revisited: Institutional isomorphism and collective rationality in organizational fields." *American Sociological Review*, 48: 147–160.

Dixit, Avinash K., and Robert S. Pindyck, 1994. *Investment Under Uncertainty.* Princeton, NJ: Princeton University Press.

Eisenhardt, Kathleen M., and Claudia Bird Schoonhoven, 1990. "Organizational growth: Linking founding team, strategy, environment, and growth among US semiconductor ventures, 1978–1988." *Administrative Science Quarterly*, 35: 504–529.

Evans, David S., and Linda S. Leighton, 1989. "Some empirical aspects of entrepreneurship." *American Economic Review*, 79: 519–535.

Evans, David S., and Boyan Jovanovic, 1989. "An estimated model of entrepreneurial choice under liquidity constraints." *Journal of Political Economy*, 97: 808–827.

Fichman, Mark, and Daniel A. Levinthal, 1991. "Honeymoons and the liability of adolescence: A new perspective on duration dependence in social and organizational relationships." *Academy of Management Review*, 16: 442–468.

Freeman, John, Glenn R. Carroll, and Michael T. Hannan, 1983. "The liability of newness: Age dependence in organizational death rates." *American Sociological Review*, 48: 692–710.

Friedman, Milton, 1953. *Essays in Positive Economics.* Chicago: University of Chicago Press.

Fuchs, Victor R., 1982. "Self-employment of labor force participation of older males." *Journal of Human Resources*, 17: 339–357.

Fujii, Edwin T., and Clifford B. Hawley, 1991. "Empirical aspects of self-employment." *Economic Letters*, 36: 323–329.

Ghemawat, Pankaj, 1991. *Commitment.* New York: Free Press.

Greene, William H., 1990. *Econometric Analysis.* New York: Macmillan.

Guo, Guang, 1993. "Event-history analysis for left-truncated data." In P. Marsden (ed.), *Sociological Methodology*, 23: 217–243. Cambridge, MA: Basil Blackwell.

Hannan, Michael T., and John Freeman, 1977. "The population ecology of organizations." *American Journal of Sociology*, 82: 929–964.

—— 1984. "Structural inertia and organizational change." *American Sociological Review*, 49: 149–164.

Heckman, James J., 1979. "Sample selection bias as a specification error." *Econometrica*, 47: 153–161.

Hirschman, Albert O., 1970. *Exit, Voice and Loyalty.* Cambridge, MA: Harvard University Press.

Kahneman, Daniel and Amos Tversky, 1979, "Prospect theory: An analysis of decision under risk." *Econometrica,* 47: 263–291.

Kalleberg, Arne L., and Kevin T. Leicht, 1991. "Gender and organizational performance: Determinants of small business survival and success." *Academy of Management Journal,* 34: 136–161.

Jovanovic, Boyan, 1982. "Selection and the evolution of industry." *Econometrica,* 50: 649–670.

Lafuente, Alberto, and Vicente Salas, 1989. "Types of entrepreneurs and firms. The case of new Spanish firms." *Strategic Management Journal,* 10: 17–30.

Lee, Thomas W., and Terence R. Mitchell, 1994. "An alternative approach: The unfolding model of voluntary employee turnover." *Academy of Management Review,* 19: 51–89.

Levinthal, Daniel A., 1991. "Random walks and organizational mortality." *Administrative Science Quarterly,* 36: 397–420.

Maddala, G. S., 1983. *Limited-Dependent and Qualitative Variables in Econometrics.* Cambridge, UK: Cambridge University Press.

March, James G., 1988. "Variable risk preferences and adaptive aspirations." *Journal of Economic Behavior and Organization,* 9: 5–24.

March, James G., and Zur Shapira, 1992. "Variable risk preferences and the focus of attention." *Psychological Review,* 99: 172–183.

Masten, Scott E., James W. Meehan, Jr., and Edward A. Snyder, 1991. "The costs of organization." *Journal of Law, Economics, and Organization,* 7: 1–25.

Mayer, Kurt B., and Sidney Goldstein, 1961. *The First Two Years: Problems of Small Firm Growth and Survival.* Washington DC: Small Business Administration.

McDougall, Patricia P., Richard B. Robinson, Jr., and Angelo S. DeNisi, 1992. "Modeling new venture performance: An analysis of new venture strategy, industry structure, and venture origin." *Journal of Business Venturing.* 7: 267–289.

Meyer, John W., and Brian Rowan, 1977. "Institutional organizations: Formal structure as myth and ceremony." *American Journal of Sociology,* 83: 340–363.

Meyer, Marshall W., and Lynne G. Zucker, 1989. *Permanently Failing Organizations.* Newbury Park, CA: Sage.

Mincer, Jacob, 1974. *Schooling, Experience, and Earnings.* New York: National Bureau of Economic Research.

———1986. "Wage changes in job changes." *Research in Labor Economics,* 8A: 171–197.

Miner, Anne S., Terry L. Amburgey, and Timothy M. Stearns, 1990. "Interorganizational linkages and population dynamics: Buffering and transformational shields." *Adminstrative Science Quarterly,* 35: 689–713.

Mobley, William H., 1977. *Employee Turnover: Causes, Consequences, and Control Reading,* MA: Addison-Wesley.

Nelson, Forrest D., 1977. "Censored regression models with unobserved stochastic censoring thresholds." *Journal of Econometrics,* 6: 309–327.

Penrose, Edith Tilton, 1952. "Biological analogies in the theory of the firm." *American Economic Review,* 42: 804–819.

Pfeffer, Jeffrey, and Gerald R. Salancik, 1978. *The External Control of Organizations.* New York: Harper and Row.

Porter, Michael E., 1976. "Please note location of nearest exit: Exit barriers and planning." *California Management Review,* 19 (Winter):21–33.

Preisendörfer, Peter, and Thomas Voss, 1990, "Organizational mortality of small firms: The effects of entrepreneurial age and human capital." *Organization Studies*, 11: 107–129.

Ranger-Moore, James, 1991. "Bigger may be better but is older wiser? Age dependence in organizational death rates." Unpublished manuscript, Department of Sociology, University of Arizona.

Romanelli, Elaine, 1989. "Environments and strategies of organization start-up: Effects on early survival." *Administrative Science Quarterly*, 34: 369–387.

Ronstadt, Robert, 1986. "Exit, stage left: Why entrepreneurs end their entrepreneurial careers before retirement." *Journal of Business Venturing*, 1: 323–338.

Sandberg, William R., 1986. *New Venture Performance: The Role of Strategy and Industry Structure*. Lexington, MA: D. C. Heath.

Shapero, Albert, and Joseph Giglierano, 1982. "Exits and entries: A study in yellow pages journalism." In Karl Vesper (ed.), *Frontiers of Entrepreneurial Research*: 113–141. Wellesley, MA: Babson College.

Shrieves, Linda, 1995. "Middle-agers need savvy resume for job hunt." *Orlando Sentinel*, July 25.

Simon, Herbert A., 1945. *Administrative Behavior*. New York: Free Press.

Small, Kenneth A., and Cheng Hsaio, 1985. "Multinomial logit specification tests." *International Economic Review*, 26: 619–627.

Smith, James P., 1980. *Female Labor Supply: Theory and Estimation*. Princeton, NJ: Princeton University Press.

Smith, Norman R., and John R. Miner, 1983. "Type of entrepreneur, type of firm, and managerial motivation: Implications for organizational life cycle theory." *Strategic Management Journal*, 4: 325–340.

Spence, A. Michael, 1974. Market Signaling. Cambridge, MA: Harvard University Press.

Straw, Barry M., 1981. "The escalation of commitment to a course of action." *Academy of Management Review*, 6: 577–587.

Steward, Mark B., 1983. "On least squares estimation when the dependent variable is grouped." *Review of Economic Studies*, 50: 737–753.

Stinchcombe, Arther L., 1965. "Organizations and social structure." In J. G. March (ed.), *Handbook of Organizations*: 142–193. Chicago: Rand-McNally.

Sutton, Robert I., and Barry M. Staw, 1995. "What theory is *not*." *Administrative Science Quarterly*, 40: 371–384.

U.S. Bureau of the Census, 1996. *Statistical Abstract of the United States*, 116 ed. Washington, DC: U.S. Government Print Office.

U.S. Small Business Administration, Office of Advocacy, 1994. *Handbook of Small Business Data*, 1994 ed. Washington, DC: U.S. Government Printing Office.

Williamson Oliver E., 1991. "Strategizing, economizing, and economic organization." *Strategic Management Journal*, 12: 75–94.

Winter, Sidney G., Jr., 1964. "Economic 'natural selection' and the theory of the firm." *Yale Economic Essays*, 4: 225–272.